To my parents

War on Crime

War on Crime

*Bandits, G-Men,
and the Politics
of Mass Culture*

Claire Bond Potter

Rutgers University Press

New Brunswick, New Jersey, and London

Library of Congress Cataloging-in-Publication Data

Potter, Claire Bond, 1958–
    War on crime : bandits, G-men, and the politics of mass culture / Claire Bond
Potter.
        p.   cm.
    Includes bibliographical references and indes.
    ISBN 0-8135-2486-5 (cloth : alk. paper). — ISBN 0-8135-2487-3 (pbk. : alk. paper)
    1. United States.   Federal Bureau of Investigation—History.   2. Hoover, J. Edgar
(John Edgar), 1895–1972.   3. Criminal investigation—United States—History—20th
century.   4. Crime—United States—History—20th century.   5. Crime—Government
policy—United States—History—20th century.   6. Criminal investigation in mass
media—United States—History—20th century.   7. Crime in mass media—United
States—History—20th century.   8. Crime in popular culture—United States—
History—20th century.   9. New Deal, 1933–1939.   I. Title.
HV8144.F43P67   1998
364.973—dc21   97-22311
                                                                                                        CIP

British Cataloging-in-Publication information available

Copyright © 1998 by Claire Bond Potter

All rights reserved

Manufactured in the United States of America

Contents

Acknowledgments

Like both lawmakers and lawbreakers, I have reaped the benefits of a network of supporters, only a few of whom can be named.

Along the way, my research and writing have been funded by assistantships and a Penfield dissertation fellowship from New York University; a Charlotte Newcombe Award from the Woodrow Wilson Foundation; and an Albert J. Beveridge Research Grant from the American Historical Association. Wesleyan's generous annual financial support permitted the additional travel, archival work, and conference participation that dissertations often require as they become books. A sabbatical leave and a term at the Center for the Humanities gave me writing time, and at a moment of cybermelt, Alex DuPuy and the Office of Academic Affairs found funds for a new computer in the budget.

The Federal Bureau of Investigation has been cooperative and generous throughout; Susan Falb helped map the way, and people whom I never was able to thank personally photocopied hundreds of pages of reports so that I could ponder them at leisure. Thanks also go to the archivists and their staffs at the National Archives, the Minnesota Historical Society, the Franklin Delano Roosevelt Library, and the Library of Congress. Chapter 4 was made possible by the Dallas, Texas, police department; Laura McGee at the Dallas Municipal Archives and Records Center; and Carol Rourke at the J. Erik Jonsson Central Library.

This book originated in a graduate seminar taught by the late Albert U. Romasco at New York University; his commitment to politically relevant scholarship has shaped my career as a teacher and a writer. Charles Tilly's generosity, seriousness, and joy in the craft of history nurtured this project, and its author, at a crucial stage. At New York Unversity, Thomas Bender, Mary Nolan, Daniel Walkowitz, and Marilyn Young provided encouragement and advice. Alan Brinkley, Paula Fass, Alice Kessler-Harris, and Sean Wilentz also offered critiques of papers that pushed the project forward. My graduate school gang—Elaine Abelson, Margaret Hunt, Marilyn Johnson, Annelise Orleck, Nancy Robertson, Suzanne Wasserman, and Renqiu Yu—went "the limit, and then some."

I could not have asked for better colleagues and students than I have had at Wesleyan University. Patricia Hill has been an intellectual mentor, friend, and invaluable critic. Readings from and conversations with Henry Abelove, Richard Buel, Christina Crosby, Ann duCille, Indira Karamcheti, Richard Ohmann, Ann-Louise Shapiro, Gary Shaw, Elizabeth Traube, Ann Wightman, and Richard Vann have made me a better historian. Susan Hirsch has been a scholar-companion and friend to the end. Pat Curley, Ben Jackson, Donna Martin, Eva Ogden, and Kay Poursine provided the daily support that makes scholarship possible.

Susan Ware, my graduate adviser and friend, is well known for her commitment to the work of younger scholars; she kept me on the right path, gave encouragement and criticism in exactly the right amounts, and made me a better writer than I knew I could be. Elizabeth Isele's humor and donated editorial talents pushed this book into the hands of an editor, and Leslie Mitchner and her staff at Rutgers University Press have made it into a real book. Beth Emery helped me learn patience, endurance, and commitment. Karen Bock's good oar, keen mind, and sense of fun transformed everything: hours of conversation about cultural studies facilitated many of the textual readings on which this book depends. Barbara Balliet has always been there for me, throughout all the stages of our friendship and careers, and I have long ceased to wonder what kind of historian I would be without her.

Finally, to Nancy Barnes, my companion of ten years, who always believed I could do this, and everything else—you are my best luck: "That is happiness; to be dissolved into something complete and great."

Author's Note

In the period under study, the Federal Bureau of Investigation had three different names. From its founding in 1908 to the spring of 1934, it was known as the Bureau of Investigation; between 1934 and the fall of 1935, it was known as the Division of Investigation; and after 1935, it was called the Federal Bureau of Investigation. For the sake of historical accuracy, if not consistency, I have used the designation appropriate to the period under discussion in each chapter.

War on Crime

Introduction

On June 17, 1933, in the Kansas City morning heat, four unknown gunmen attacked a party of three federal agents and two local officers who were transporting safe-blowing artist Frank "Jelly" Nash from Union Station to police headquarters. After the smoke cleared, two federal agents lay dying, and Nash, who had been chained to one of them, had also been killed—whether the bandits were trying to liberate Nash or "put him on the spot" was never determined. The fallen government men were special agents of the Department of Justice's Bureau of Investigation; their deaths symbolized a cultural and political crisis that catapulted Director J. Edgar Hoover into a three-year campaign against modern American bandits like John Dillinger, "Ma" Barker, and Alvin Karpis.

The subsequent "war on crime" demonstrated that, despite the failure of three Republican administrations to enforce national Prohibition, Franklin Delano Roosevelt's Democratic New Deal state could field a sophisticated and effective national police force. Although social welfare legislation and economic reform heightened dramatically the role of the federal government in citizens' daily lives, the omnibus crime bill, which was passed by Congress in May and June 1934, epitomized another type of legislation that produced a centralized state apparatus after World War I. The culmination of Hoover's eight-year effort to reform the bureau, it also positioned New Dealers as leaders of a national police professionalization movement.

This study looks beyond a political history literature that has explored a politics of social welfare and economic intervention that culminated in the New Deal, and refocuses on policing and crime control as a critical locus of twentieth-century state transformation.[1] It begins with the failures that sparked a reforming impulse within the state: political scandals that rocked the Department of Justice and the Bureau of Investigation between 1919 and 1924, highlighting, among other things, the federal government's failure to suppress the illegal markets and violent criminal organizations spawned by national Prohibition. A rash of spectacular, interstate crimes such as kidnapping and bank robbery, linked to the emergence of organized criminality, fed grassroots police reform and professionalization movements' demands for a renewed federal commitment to local law and order. The anticrime movement bridged party and regional lines, creating neutral political ground for proponents and opponents of state intervention. Thus, Roosevelt's 1932 promise of a "new deal" in the economic sphere incorporated a commitment to social order of all kinds, and the Kansas City Massacre provided a welcome opening to unveil the power of modern federal policing. Coming only a few months after the collapse and reorganization of the nation's banking system, this attack on federal officers became another dramatic opportunity to prove that national solutions could be applied to local problems.

Although economic recovery was slow and contentious, advocates for a crime war saw the potential for immediate political dividends. On the heels of Roosevelt's first hundred days, Hoover and Attorney General Homer Cummings revealed legislation that would transform the Bureau of Investigation from one of several federal police agencies to the leading surveillance and crime-fighting force in the nation. As the first six articles came to a vote in the spring of 1934, Hoover belatedly answered Indiana's call for help in the hunt for John Dillinger, and the bill passed with hardly a dissenting vote. By the end of the war on crime in 1936, J. Edgar Hoover and his "Government Men," popularly known by their underworld nickname, "G-men," had become symbols of national regeneration and a powerful state that was well organized, honest, and resolved to serve the people.

Anxieties about crime have, by the late twentieth century, become a familiar route for the creation of new government agencies and the extension of state authority. Thus, this original war on crime, and the opportunities it afforded to New Dealers and established bureaucrats like Hoover, become doubly important as scholars try to grapple with the ways states seek to assert hegemony over populations, local authority, and party politics—while they pursue material objectives such as reducing popular violence and protecting private property.

The transformation of the Bureau of Investigation from a disgraced unit of Red-baiters and blackmailers to a professional, armed, federal police force required structural reforms and cultural interventions that reflected and reinforced other types of political consolidation during the New Deal. Recasting the federal government as inherently moral and good policing as a central democratic value, Hoover's campaigns against kidnappers and bank robbers produced political narratives that articulated the benefits of an interventionist state. If, by 1954, the director could introduce a best-selling history of the FBI by stating that he and his men were "never very far from the crossroads of America, either spiritually or physically," we must conclude that crime and policing were also crucial to a revitalized nationalism before World War II.[2]

This period of professionalization between Hoover's appointment as director in 1924 and the end of the war on crime in 1936 laid structural and ideological foundations for the well-documented abuses of the postwar and civil rights eras, and critics have raised important questions about what this mythic crossroads might have looked like without Hoover.[3] Throughout his career, the director consistently, secretly, and often illegally promoted as "national security" a series of reactionary, antidemocratic, and racist agendas that mirrored his own beliefs and those of his political allies. However, few authors have explored how this powerful police agency was created in response to real demands made on the state by its publics during a moment of apparently pervasive social crisis. Furthermore, choices within the Department of Justice about what kinds of reform ideology would be brought to fruition in a national police force were made as part of the war on crime. Although secrecy and undercover operations characterize Hoover's campaigns against dissidents, public political events were equally important to the evolution of federal police power: this study traces, in particular, the failure of the Bureau of Prohibition and of the anticrime agendas associated with female moral reformers; the victory of a masculinized, military enforcement model as articulated by the police professionalization movement; and the significance of both G-men and celebrity bandits as nationalist cultural workers.

Like much of the New Deal, the war on crime was shaped by the institutionally oriented progressive politics of the early twentieth century, the state expansion of the war years, the corporatist governing philosophies of Herbert Hoover, and 1920s bureaucratic reform.[4] Made and remade in dialogue with the society it policed, federal anticrime rhetoric recast the political work that the legitimation of new spheres of authority required as a cultural struggle for the nation's soul. A study of such a process requires an engagement between the methods of political history and a more text-based analysis of the cultural transformations that contain and produce politics.[5] The relationship between a diverse anticrime movement and emerging New Deal enforcement apparatuses is particularly illuminating in this regard: reformers who sought to aid individuals and scientific managers who prioritized incarceration and punishment envisioned politically and stylistically different wars on crime. They also envisioned "the public" in radically different ways. For example, social workers tended to promote empathetic and educational programs that positioned the public as potentially moral, improvable by "weak" state interventions in families and communities; state managers, however, imagined a preexisting moral public at war with deviant others, which could be rallied for heroic "strong" state solutions to social problems.[6]

The bandits and kidnappers who were targeted by the Department of Justice between 1933 and 1936 have often been dismissed as easy targets for federal enforcement, their defeat a cheaply won grab for power by J. Edgar Hoover. Although a number of scholars, most notably Richard Gid Powers, have linked the war on crime to the postwar uses and policy directions of the Federal Bureau of Investigation, broader belief systems about crime and policing are often seen by historians as primarily cultural.[7] The figures of the policeman and the criminal were also deeply political, discursive locations for exploring the relationship between state and citizen. Here, attention to other New Deal programs is instructive. Producing a "moral state" was a political process, a series of policy choices that, simultaneously enacted in popular culture, secured citizen consent for a state in formation.[8]

During Roosevelt's first term, the confrontations between the G-man and the bandit, the Bureau of Investigation and the gang, became arenas for articulating nationalist narratives about the benefits of an interventionist state. Volumes of print, film, and other cultural texts subsequently generated by the FBI emphasize the war on depression-era bandits as a founding moment for modern criminal investigation. Most scholars have interpreted these accounts of battles against John Dillinger and the Barker-Karpis gang as falsehoods that were calculated to create a heroic aura around Hoover and his men. They are, and they did. However, given the prominence of memoirs, magazine pieces, films, books, and television shows that have given the war on crime (and the campaign against John Dillinger in particular) prominence in bureau history, this period surely represents more than a moment of public relations that interrupted Hoover's lifelong campaign against political radicals.[9] In fact, the war on crime produced lasting changes in the ways Americans would come to understand crime as a national problem, police power as socially positive, and crime control as a federal responsibility. These intellectual shifts were necessary ideological preconditions for future public opposition to the political Left, civil rights activists, homosexuals, and black-power groups, politicized enforcement agendas that came to define "domestic security" after 1945.

The force of the anticrime movement lends twentieth-century bandits a tangible political significance that has only been alluded to in accounts of the FBI or the New Deal. As public enemies and producers of a set of cultural meanings for crime, bandits also shaped the drama of state transformation and police modernization. Although variously referred to as gangsters or mobsters, bank robbers like John Dillinger and stickup artists such as Clyde Barrow were popularly known as auto bandits because they stole cars, committing crimes that were followed by fast escapes on the nation's new highway system. Newspapers in the mid- and southwestern states they frequented also employed the term "bandit" to distinguish them from the more urban, settled, and ethnic gangster. Significantly, these criminals often called themselves bandits, sometimes articulating their crimes as part of a noble criminal tradition generated by legends like Robin Hood and Jesse James.

To be a bandit in the twenties and thirties meant to be primarily an armed robber, usually a bank robber, and sometimes a kidnapper or hired killer. As Alvin Karpis put it, "My profession was robbing banks, knocking off payrolls, and kidnapping rich men. I was good at it."[10] Usually men, bandits were trained and dedicated thieves who worked as part of one or several gangs. They were almost always recidivists who began with petty theft in their teenage years and moved on to payroll heists, bank jobs, and kidnapping by joining forces with more experienced criminals they met in prison. As opposed to urban mobsters, who, by 1930, negotiated freely with legitimate businessmen and politicians, bandits and their mobile gang families understood their careers as a series of life-or-death struggles with authority.

Addressing banditry in the twentieth-century United States requires a reformulation of what has been at best a speculative debate across fields and disciplines. This literature argues that bandits, by definition, draw the attention of the state: in *Bandits* and *Primitive Rebels* Eric Hobsbawm derived a general model for the social bandit as heroic, individualistic, violent, and peculiar to pre-capitalist agricultural societies. The excitement that Hobsbawm generated with these books was an important spur to this research, but historical specificity is crucial when extending the social bandit model across time, culture, technology, and state- and class-formation processes. Not all bandits are social bandits: some are self-consciously political, and many arise in societies that have long made the transition to capitalism and industrial production.[11]

Heroic bandit identities and narratives characterize the war on crime, despite widespread public campaigns against violent criminals during the 1920s. Perversely, once bandits attained celebrity status and were declared to be "public enemies" by the Department of Justice, depression-era audiences were far more willing to understand them within Hobsbawm's "traditional" categories— as noble robbers, ignoble robbers, avengers, expropriators, and revolutionaries. Their southern and midwestern origins evoked nostalgia for frontier individualism as well. Thus, popular fascination with, and loathing of, Dillinger, Bonnie Parker and Clyde Barrow, and the Barker-Karpis gang were produced through a mythic, "traditional" American past.[12]

The Great Depression, Warren Sussman has argued, was a period obsessed with myth and symbol. The bandits of the 1930s were part of that obsession, particularly as they spoke to the individual's fateful collisions with the economy and new forms of state power.[13] Operating in a criminological context that often produced them as psychopathic, bandits engaged their audiences in a dialogue about individuality, tragedy, and history that triangulated the relationship between state and citizen. In 1934, Bonnie Parker sent a poem to a newspaper that began:

> You've heard the story of Jesse James
> Of how he lived and died;
> If you're still in need
> Of something to read
> Here's the story of Bonnie and Clyde.[14]

Connecting the oral traditions of the nineteenth century ("You've heard the story of Jesse James") to the mass media of the 1930s ("If you're still in need/Of something to read"), Bonnie reminds the historian that the gang itself is a text. Operating as her own historian, she also urged her audience not to dismiss the modern bandit's claim to a heroic past and an honorable present.

As cultural analysis is woven into a structural study of state transformation, the war on crime populates the New Deal with characters who provoke questions about the politics of myth and symbol. The emergence of heroic, elusive male bandits and their sexy, aggressive molls anticipated the creation of a new kind of cop: the scientific, hardworking, masculine G-man who became a staple of newspaper, newsreel, and pulp literature in the 1930s. During the Dillinger and Barker-Karpis campaigns in particular, Hoover erased the image of individualistic Bureau agents who employed snitches, took bribes, listened at keyholes, and looked for Reds under every bed. The modern, professional "Government Man" replaced these disgraced detectives, shaping a new rule of law and safeguarding the well-ordered families and communities promoted by the New Deal state. In terms of public relations, however, the G-man met with far more conditional success during the war on crime than historians have imagined. The principles of scientific policing did not lead to the capture of fugitives without bloody struggles and very public failures. Nor was the straight-arrow G-man image always received favorably; bandits' periodic appeals for relief from state persecution to that same public were points of particular vulnerability, opening cultural space for critiques of both the war on crime and the New Deal.

The plasticity of symbolic realms is particularly striking during the interwar years, when new forms of consumer culture and commodity distribution set nationalizing trends against local desires. As Lizabeth Cohen has argued in her study of working-class Chicago, the impact of mass culture depends not only on how it is produced and distributed but also on how it is consumed. In other words, "people's own social circumstances inspired them to view mass culture in different ways."[15] How else can we explain a steamy letter written in 1934 to Special Agent in Charge Melvin Purvis, which seems to have entirely missed the point of the G-man's clean-cut new image? "Hello Hot Shot," Ruth Dickens began. She described herself as "chesty," invited him to visit her, and teased, "Think you are pretty good, dontcha? I couldn't forget about you if I tried, with your name and pictures plastered all over the papers."[16] Dickens's provocative overtures are but one invitation to argue that G-men were not read as easily or consistently as the legendarily prudish Hoover might have wished.

The case files from the war on crime are extraordinary documents, revealing intentional and unintentional contact that occurred between state and citizen as the federal government expanded. A monument to FBI information gathering, they represent a range of investigative technologies, containing (among other things) confessions, agent interviews, reports from paid informants, recordings from listening devices in prison meeting rooms, intercepted mail, surveillance reports, memoranda, and crime-fighting advice from enthusiastic citizens, as well as internal directives on the pursuit of fugitives, inspection and progress reports, reprimands, and personal notes from the director. While these documents add to our knowledge of how the bureau evolved between 1924 and 1936, close readings also reveal the practices through which Hoover's famous files were generated: the reporting style, the eliciting of confessions, the methods of surveillance, and the accumulation and distilling of information.[17]

These files are as rich in their flaws as they are in the collections of facts they pretend to be. They describe relationships within the bureau and between bandits, as well as the connections between each group and the various publics they sought to reach. Agents' dossiers demonstrate how individuals became subject to bureau discipline and what the contours of that discipline were. Confessions also illuminate gang discipline, the ethics of criminal organization, and the circumstances under which they broke down. In addition, these documents reopen the issue of the importance of the bureau's focus on what one writer has dismissed as "the desperadoes and stumblebums of crime," revealing the crucial role of these campaigns in formulating new methods of federal surveillance, pursuit, and incarceration.[18]

Criminality and federal police reform were both produced through gendered and racialized systems of meaning, systems that are not fully recognized in the historiography of the field. For example, the unique ways that women participated in bandit crimes distinguished these criminal organizations from the urban rackets that dominate histories of American crime in the twentieth century, and often caused them to be represented as perversely gendered. The war on crime and the rhetoric with which Hoover and other state managers defined that war were also racialized, articulating criminals as ethnic or "native" whites perversely "blackened" by their pathological behaviors. These definitions were reproduced, altered, and twisted outside the sphere of the state as the bureau's powerful message was consumed and reproduced by different audiences. To the extent that the bureau could successfully articulate itself as guarding a national crossroads defined by ideologically dominant values, it relied upon the active repression of the perverted genderings and racialization that characterized these criminal identities.[19]

This book explores a formative moment for the twentieth-century United States, in which federal anticrime agendas prioritized criminalization and enforcement over social intervention. It begins in 1924, when J. Edgar Hoover's appointment as acting director began, and ends in 1936 as a reformed, national police bureau triumphed over crime and prepared to reincorporate political surveillance as one of its central functions. Chapter 1 explores the failure of national enforcement during Prohibition and the critiques of feminized anticrime efforts preceding the war on crime. Chapter 2 explores the fusion of social reform and scientific management ideologies that produced police professionalization and focuses on what new government careers in law enforcement looked like. Chapter 3 describes the emergence of "new criminals" and documents the emergence of a crime wave in the Midwest and Southwest that provoked both popular resistance and demands for federal aid against property crime. Chapter 4 argues that Bonnie Parker and Clyde Barrow's rampage across the Southwest set the terms for the war on crime: producing themselves as celebrities and committing ordinary crimes in spectacular ways, they revived popular fascination with bandits.

Bonnie and Clyde's murderous ways, particularly the killing of lawmen, also united the police community to demand federal aid; simultaneously, a rash of spectacular kidnappings highlighted the state's helplessness against an aggressive new breed of criminals. Using the ransom kidnapping of Charles Lindbergh Jr. as a cultural and political link between the Hoover and Roosevelt administrations, Chapter 5 launches the Department of Justice's war on crime, examining the crime of kidnapping as a necessary precondition to the transformation of federal enforcement into a New Deal initiative. Chapter 6 analyzes the war's first success, the campaign against John Dillinger and explores the cultural and strategic work necessary to "produce" a bandit. Chapter 7 uses the campaign against the Barker-Karpis gang, which ended the war on crime, to address the suppression of social reform initiatives at the Department of Justice by enforcement experts and the revival of surveillance as a respectable component of the scientific policing model.

The primary task of this book is to recenter and revise the history of New Deal state transformation. However, it also reconceptualizes political history—permitting cultural phenomena and the meaning of everyday lives to impinge on the state-making process and thus the political realm.[20] In some ways, the methodological inspiration of this study is contained in Woody Guthrie's "The Ballad of Pretty Boy Floyd," sung in the migrant camps of California in the 1930s: "When in this world I've traveled / I've seen lots of funny men, / Some will rob you with a six gun / And some with a fountain pen." The war on crime was fought with guns and pens, movies and legislation, radio and government hearings. All of these methods illuminate this period of state transformation, and perceptions of that emergent state, in the years of the first New Deal. The creation of both G-men and bandits as cultural heroes in this period not only explores the depression-era obsession with crime and celebrity but also lends insight on how citizens understood a nation undergoing large political and social changes. Understanding the state both as an administrative structure and as a central symbolic arena where ideologies originate, are received, and are transformed, this study moves both bandits and G-men to the crossroads of New Deal politics and culture.

One

"Crude Methods of Enforcement"

Prohibition, Crime, and Federal Policing

Captain B. C. Baldwin, of the Texas Rangers, formerly a Department of Justice agent, said that specific instructions from Washington were that the Department's men were not to take any action in regard to rum-running across the Mexican border. —*Nation*, March 26, 1924

In the spring of 1924, the Department of Justice's reputation had never been worse, and its Bureau of Investigation never more thoroughly disgraced. New accusations against Republican appointees appeared daily in the months following Warren Harding's death. Graft, political corruption, and the scandalous sale of the government's Teapot Dome oil reserve implicated congressmen, the former president, Secretary of the Treasury Andrew Mellon, Attorney General Harry Daugherty, and Bureau of Investigation director William Burns. As prosecutors uncovered illegal surveillance operations ordered by the Department of Justice, favoritism and graft were exposed once again at the highest levels of government. Daugherty and Burns were also involved in a widespread abuse of Prohibition laws that would force them out of office and implicate Republican party patronage networks.[1]

As former vice president Calvin Coolidge asked for resignations and prepared for the fall election, revelations about the Department of the Treasury's Bureau of Prohibition and the Department of Justice raised difficult questions as to whether the state could enforce the Eighteenth Amendment, or Volstead Act, against the will of politicians. Republican prosecutor Mabel Walker Willebrandt, the first woman assistant attorney general, appointed to run the Bureau of Prohibition and to give the federal government credibility among the mostly female temperance constituency, had grave doubts. "I'm tired," she wrote to her parents on the eve of testifying against her colleagues. "I'm very disgusted, that many people who profess to be for prohibition are for politics first. . . . How the president hastens to stop an investigation *when* it touches the pocketbook nerve of his election plans—Mellon!"[2]

Willebrandt's frustration is a lens on the uneven development of the postwar state, when what Ellis Hawley has called "the search for a modern order" often foundered on the shoals of machine-style partisan politics.[3] The Bureau of Prohibition's failure to suppress bootlegging was equaled by the Department of Justice's inability either to secure Volstead convictions or to halt corruption among federal and state officials. By 1924 reformers, the press, and many civic leaders—wet and dry—understood Prohibition as a moral and managerial failure that had produced a cynical, crime-ridden public, a network of powerful gangsters, and hypocrisy in government.[4]

A feminized Progressive agenda had produced federal Prohibition; party politics had placed a woman in charge of enforcing it. The failure of Prohibition thus became a crucial site from which reformers, state managers, journalists, and citizens reformulated ideas of federal policing around an enforcement model that they imagined as more properly masculine. Calvin Coolidge's choice of New Yorker Harlan Fiske Stone as Daugherty's replacement was an attempt to respond to this issue by restoring at least the appearance of manly good government. A Republican, Stone was known as an independent, honest jurist. His Wall Street partnership and upper-class origins also distinguished him from the party hacks of the former president's dissolute Ohio Gang. As Stone's older brother advised that spring, "I hope you will lay down a rule for yourself in undertaking a public career to always do what your judgement tells you is the right thing. . . . The public man who acts in accordance with his judgement rather than the thing which makes for his political success is a rarity. I think, however, such a man will meet with great approval today."[5] This opposition between politics and the public good reflected a pervasive belief in reform circles that the machinations of party interests, not the principle of federal enforcement, was the problem that needed correction in the coming years.[6]

Mabel Walker Willebrandt's hope that politics could be severed from the workings of a reform state was revived with Stone's appointment: he was "*not* a politician," she wrote to an ally in the Women's Christian Temperance Union in 1925. In one corruption case against a Republican state director of Prohibition, Willebrandt reported, "No less than 17 powerful and influential appeals have been made to me to quash the case or at least omit certain defendants." Furthermore, her subordinate in the district had refused to prosecute. This time, however,

Willebrandt called the disobedient attorney to Washington and disciplined him, "the new AG Stone standing by splendidly." Despite renewed interference from Mellon (whose nephew warned Willebrandt that she would be responsible for "another Teapot Dome"), Stone ordered her to proceed. "I *do* feel the work is worthwhile," she concluded, "when you can show the politicians they *can't* control—forever—the meting out of punishment to the guilty."[7]

Stone raised reform hopes again when, in his search for an acting director for the Bureau of Investigation, he ignored patronage and hired instead a trained bureaucrat who knew the job. Twenty-five-year-old lawyer and career civil servant John Edgar Hoover was already serving as an assistant director and, as a lifetime resident of the District of Columbia, had never voted or joined a political party. Publicity photos from 1924 show a thin, youthful version of the bulldog grimace that would become the face of federal policing for the next fifty years. Newspaper stories figured Hoover as professional, modern, and free from political obligation. The *Washington Star* reported on December 29, "Young Mr. Hoover of the new school of crime detection has no entangling alliances. Among his friends he is known to be clean as a hound's tooth. He looks at detective work from a new angle. He sees the evidence side. Instead of merely 'getting the goods,' he is concerned with making the 'goods' stick in a court of law."[8] Appointed as a caretaker, Hoover carried out reforms so swift and impressive that Stone confirmed the appointment by the end of the year.

If Hoover's reputation as a scientific manager endeared him to a range of reformers, his recent past as a Red-baiter did not necessarily damage him: the impulse that produced Prohibition was also anti-immigrant and antiradical. Using a professionalization model advocated by municipal reformers for several decades, the young director reorganized his staff of special agents as a scientifically trained national police force. The disaster of Prohibition enforcement was thus a "stimulus for institutional development," in part because continual public critiques of Volstead agents, high arrest rates, and violent confrontations between bootleggers and police created a sense that new kinds of crime were raging out of control in the United States.[9]

The national conversation about the failure of Prohibition enforcement also shaped exchanges between reformers and bureaucrats about the role police ought to play in a national community.[10] As the idea of federal policing was reshaped during the Volstead years, government agents began to embody the state in society. If it accomplished nothing else, Prohibition made the federal policeman a commonly understood cultural and political figure. By 1930, the crime commissions and police professional organizations did not ask whether the state would police the nation but how it ought to be done and in relation to what crimes.[11]

Well before the New Deal, the shape of a national police force came to reflect the nature and intentions of the state itself, as well as its capacity for shaping national life.

Thus, the failure of the Bureau of Prohibition was critical not only to the success of the Bureau of Investigation but also to the creation of a national discourse that articulated good policing as a central characteristic of a modern state. Although the federal government's policing efforts were attacked throughout three successive Republican administrations, there was no suggestion that the state cease policing. Rather, critics of the Bureau of Prohibition rested on rhetorical and ideological distinctions between "the state" (which was not political or necessarily corrupt) and "the government" (which was). As John Dewey observed in *The Public and Its Problems* (1927),

> Conceptions of "The State" as something per se, something intrinsically manifesting a general will and reason, lend themselves to illusions. They make such a sharp distinction between *the* state and *a* government that, from the standpoint of the theories, a government may be corrupt and injurious and yet The State by the same idea retains its dignity and nobility. Officials may be mean, obstinate, proud and stupid and yet the nature of the state they serve remains essentially unimpaired.[12]

Dewey himself believed that this distinction was false, but the notion of state and government as separable was a crucial intellectual move that undergirded justifications for national policing. It permitted reformers to critique interventionist government and also to demand changes that would result in an even more powerful and centralized federal branch.

Prohibition Enforcement and the Authority of the State

On October 28, 1919, Congress passed the National Prohibition Enforcement Act over President Woodrow Wilson's veto. Also known as the Volstead Act, the legislation defined "intoxicating liquor" as any beverage that contained more than 0.5 percent of alcohol, and it established the Bureau of Prohibition as a subdivision of the Bureau of Internal Revenue.[13] Temperance advocates saw surveillance and regulation as only part of what would make Prohibition work, however. Citizens recognizing their duty to the state would be the primary guarantee of a moral, liquor-free society. "Law always follows in the wake of civilization but never leads," wrote Prohibition commissioner Roy Haynes in 1923. "The purpose and the object of law are to regulate and control the relations of men to each other and the relations of men to the state."[14]

An initial 1,550 agents commissioned in eighteen administrative districts were detailed to police relations between citizen and state. A formidable force, almost as large as the Bureau of Investigation at the peak of its wartime and postwar capability, it was theoretically supported by more than 3,000 customs agents and special agents from several other government departments, as well as state police forces, highway patrols, and local officers. However, most of these lawmen had duties other than enforcing Prohibition, and the territory that each Volstead agent patrolled was often immense. As one historian has pointed out, if the force "had been relieved of all other duties and placed along the borders and seacoast, each agent would have had twelve miles to cover."[15]

Although the Volstead Act had shut down the primary target of temperance advocates, the saloon, illegal and secret sites of distribution proliferated. Breweries, permitted to produce legal near beer with most of the alcohol removed, made deals with gangsters who produced and sold the "real stuff" to speakeasies. Industrial alcohol turned near beer into spiked "needle beer"; with flavors and color added, the frequently poisonous chemical was also sold as "bonded" liquor. Loopholes also remained for distribution of legally imported intoxicants. By July 1920, more than fifteen thousand physicians and fifty-seven thousand druggists and apothecaries had applied for the necessary federal license to sell these by prescription.[16]

Perhaps the worst problem, and one that would most thoroughly vex the relationship between state and citizen, was the still. Stills had always been indigenous to rural counties, as a way for farmers to convert staple crops into much-needed cash. But when the alcohol market boomed after 1920, stills sprang up everywhere. A commercial still repaid its five-hundred-dollar cost in only three or four days; liquor produced at an average cost of fifty cents per gallon sold for between three and four dollars. A portable, one-gallon still cost around seven dollars, and "to make an evil-tasting alcohol" all the amateur brewer needed was "a tea kettle, a quart of corn meal and an ordinary bath towel."[17] Gangsters organized thousands of slum residences into microbreweries: investigators reported that a walk down many poor, urban blocks would treat the tourist to air suffused with the yeasty fog of cooking mash.

The paradox of Prohibition was that this new challenge for federal enforcement was undertaken by a newly feminized state. The professionalization of reform, temperance, and the success of the woman suffrage movement brought women and progressives into government positions and federal elective office in significant numbers. Candidates for office at all levels were often best known for being "wet" or dry," designations that often also carried nativist, racial, and religious implications. New constituencies of white, female voters threw the strength of many male legislators behind maternalist agendas such as temperance, protective legislation for mothers and children, labor reforms, and international peace initiatives.[18]

Ambitious young professional women soon made their way into Republican party ranks. Mabel Walker Willebrandt was chosen to supervise Prohibition prosecutions at the Department of Justice in 1922, and for seven years she drew on the strong support of these new constituencies, although subsequent employment as general counsel for the California Grape Growers Association eventually put her dry credentials in doubt. Before coming to Justice she had been married briefly, had served as a public defender, and had worked on the Harding campaign in California. Willebrandt was typical of one kind of educated, middle-class woman who turned away from explicitly feminist causes in the 1920s and toward state-centered reform and a newly feminized electoral politics. Choosing a professional career, she remained unmarried much of her life and sustained her personal life with a circle of close female friends.[19] As she wrote to her father after her divorce was finalized, marriage was incompatible with ambition and "so cruel to a woman" if she had any pride. "It will only be after a terrific mental struggle, if at all that I could bring myself to trust—not the man, *that* would be easy—but the social status of marriage. Seems like I feel about it like an escaped convict must when he looks at a prison wall." Respectability, and temperance politics, required that she keep her married name, but as she explained to her father, "At least *underneath* I'm free."[20]

Willebrandt's stance on marriage reflected some of the contradictions of her position as a female Volstead prosecutor: state spheres were marked as male, regardless of how crucial white women were to implementing and legitimating reform agendas.[21] In a note to Willebrandt's mother, her secretary confided that Daugherty and the other attorneys thought that Mabel "was not only an extremely smart woman but a charming one." She added, "Besides being so capable she has not lost her femininity. Some women seem to." Willebrandt's femininity was an asset to the party: in addition to supervising cases around the nation, she had to be available as a female Republican to reassure the stream of temperance women who came to Washington to bolster the government's nerve. Gracious in public, Willebrandt grumbled privately about "the 'girlie girlie' stuff" that undermined her image as a prosecutor; "why the devil they can't when they ask me [to] do something professional, treat me like a professional man, I don't know," she complained.[22]

In the years before Teapot Dome, Willebrandt was also torn between her professional duty to federal enforcement and the inevitability of political scandals, some reaching into the White House. In the first months of her appointment, her staff uncovered a conspiracy to sell liquor permits out of the Treasury Department in exchange for "donations" to a Republican campaign fund. A diary entry notes enigmatically that "the AG . . . said he was up against it concerning the NY liquor situation." There was no prosecution. A second entry records a meeting with Harding a few months before his death in which "the pres. opened the subject of liquor being delivered at the White House *after* [an associate] had challenged the whole Republican party on the rumors of bootlegging in high places."[23]

Corruption, however, was only part of the problem; Willebrandt's resources were also inadequate to the task. In a period of budget cutting, a Republican Congress continually refused to support Prohibition enforcement with the salaries or training that a professional police force required. The starting salary for a Volstead agent was twelve hundred dollars in 1920 and only twenty-three hundred by 1930. Occasionally, the bureau's budget ran out while Congress squabbled over other matters; as funding riders languished on the Speaker's desk, agents were fired for indeterminate periods.[24] There were no standard qualifications for the service, and the high percentage of political appointments made the agent's badge seem like a bridge between the state and organized crime.

State managers attempted to recuperate the public image of Volstead agents by casting them as the manly heroes familiar to consumers of detective fiction and Wild West tales. In a 1923 account, *Prohibition Inside Out,* commissioner Roy Haynes described agents who were "straight as a string," dead-shots who commanded respect, not with guns, but with their honesty and seriousness of purpose. They were, he wrote, "for the most part" fearless.

> Many have looked, at various times, down both ends of a revolver. Bravery is counted among prime requisites in selecting men for these difficult and dangerous posts. Dignity is another one of the essentials; the man who fills the office must be neither braggart nor bully. . . .
>
> How far will these picked men go in performance of their duty? To the place where there is no farther way to go.

Neutralizing the feminized politics of temperance, these agents of the state "worked like men at a task for men," in deliberate contrast to unheroic criminals "who [did] not hesitate to murder."[25]

However, the reality of Prohibition enforcement was unheroic. The corps of agents was ill disciplined, highly corrupt, and disorganized, its personnel and methods sadly inferior to the standards of most urban police forces. Individuals went into the field with a badge, a gun, a few weeks of optional training, and a naive sense of their own authority. They were young to middle-aged white men, who worked out of central field offices around the country in conjunction with local and state police officers. Some were trained investigators; most were not. For the first seven years of its existence, the Bureau of Prohibition had no basic service requirements and little agent supervision. Even agents in charge had no idea how a district could be effectively patrolled. In 1930, the Kansas office reported that a single deputy commissioner and twelve field agents were responsible for 105 counties, and some of the western counties were "nearly as large as Rhode Island."[26] A 1927 attempt to rationalize the bureau by making its employees subject to the federal civil service exam unraveled it completely, when a total of 91 supervisors were demoted, dismissed, and transferred.[27]

As crime escalated, the state's capacity to suppress it diminished. Agents complained about sloppy prosecutions, while Willebrandt's staff blamed fouled evidence and agents who had no credibility on the witness stand. Rampant bribery meant that even after a conviction, felons were not jailed. "I have succeeded in getting behind bars two bootleggers of Savannah, Georgia," Willebrandt wrote her parents. "For eight months after their case was lost in the Supreme Court of the United States they kept out of jail simply through political chicanery and pull and other things. They are extremely wealthy. . . . The oldest brother on his way to jail made the remark that they had everyone in Washington fixed but one man and that 'damned woman.' "[28] Keeping an eye on both the defendants and those who might be bribed was a tedious and expensive task and depleted Willebrandt's resources even further. In another trial, she noted, she had "just dispatched 58 agents to watch and round up witnesses and keep an eye on the grand and petit juries."[29]

Federal agents also had difficulty penetrating long-standing arrangements between criminals and local police and often complained that local officers were reluctant to uncover and break up liquor rings. As an Oklahoma prosecutor had commented in 1908, even enforcing a single liquor law across a state was nearly impossible "because local sentiment largely [controlled] the enforcement of law in the community," and in some districts it was difficult to persuade "citizens of influence to uphold the officers." Sheriffs and chiefs of police were often publicly committed to upholding the law but in practice ignored unpopular laws. In Arkansas, sheriffs claimed to support the Volstead Act. But many of them, an investigator wrote, "hop[ped] up on the fence after the election," only joining raids planned by federal agents. "[As] long as the alibi 'Uncle Sam did it' is available, most of such officers, with political fences to keep intact, will cooperate."[30]

The periodic discovery of so-called county rings involving sheriffs, politicians, and bootleggers reinforced federal assertions that local corruption was the greatest impediment to enforcement. In 1926, J. Edgar Hoover reported the apprehension and prosecution of a Chicago sheriff who had been in charge of "a number of wealthy bootleggers." Surveillance revealed that the prisoners were doing business from the jail, and one man "visited his dentist an unusually large number of times" during a period of several weeks. Exposing local corruption could backfire, however: a piqued chief of police in Fort Worth, Texas, withdrew his cooperation entirely after a government prosecutor charged that his department was a "cesspool of vice and corruption."[31]

Local prosecutors and police retaliated with charges that Volstead agents enforced the law violently and illegally. Such conflicts between local authorities and federal agents were routinely taken to court, as civil rights cases, jurisdictional disputes, and felony charges for assault and murder. These incidents were used by critics of Prohibition to publicize the dangers of unregulated federal policing; cases in which innocent civilians were injured or killed made a particularly good impact.[32] In 1927,

> at 12:55 [in] the morning . . . , continuing these investigations, Agent Hudson, accompanied by three marines, [Agent] Farley, who was driving the car, and a Mrs. McAggister, riding on the seat with Farley, had a slight collision with a Ford coupe. . . . A tire on the Ford coupe blew out, attracting some attention, and immediately after the government car started it struck a Dodge touring car in which were a Mr. E. P. Ingmire and wife of San Pedro, California. Mr. Ingmire was killed and his wife seriously injured.

A county prosecutor took the case before a grand jury, obtaining first-degree murder charges against the agents. Willebrandt employed defense attorneys whose chief legal maneuver was to seek changes of venue from hostile local courtrooms and elected judges to federal courtrooms. After such a maneuver, Farley served a brief term on a reduced charge, and Hudson's case was discharged.[33]

The shift to a federal courtroom countered demands by local prosecutors and the citizens who sat on coroner's juries that federal agents be accountable to them. Federal authorities knew that acknowledging agent incompetence jeopardized their own legitimacy, and they avoided public hearings of any kind. As a Bureau of Prohibition bureaucrat argued in regard to an agent indicted for murder, "There is more at stake than his life. In fact, the very authority and sincerity of the government is involved." Exceptions to the desire for silence are revealing. When an agent killed an unarmed Oklahoma bootlegger, he was jailed, released three weeks later by the United States district court, and then returned to county court, where the case was discharged as justifiable homicide. The incident report suggests reasons for this compromise: before he ran, the agent warned the suspect, "Boy, don't do that!" The victim in this case was almost surely black, as white men rarely referred to each other that way; and no southern jury would convict a white person for the murder of a black man.[34]

The Bureau of Prohibition offered little in return for the cooperation it so desperately wanted; furthermore, federal agents complicated the social and political contract between small-town lawmen and their communities. The daily work of enforcement depended on cooperative relationships, and in a crisis, sheriffs recruited volunteer manpower by deputizing willing citizens. Even large towns had few policemen by the 1920s; officers deployed authority through the force of reputation.[35] For example, Beaumont, Texas, employed a total of 54 men and women to police a population of 57,483. Some of these were clerical and janitorial employees, but even when they are included, the number of working officers comes to less than 0.8 per thousand population.[36]

Since the Prohibition agenda failed to recruit municipal and county officials to national law enforcement, federal agents labeled their colleagues as corrupt and backward. This was occasionally made more graphic by the tendency of locals to abandon agents who stirred up more trouble than they could handle. In Kentucky, a combined posse was "battering down the door" of a cabin when "the door opened and a volley of shots was fired from within causing the immediate death of Agent Duff." The local men who fled, and returned later to find Duff stripped of his valuables, pistol, rifle, and commission, later claimed that there were no suspects.[37]

Since only local police had the power of arrest, it was often unclear who was in charge of joint operations. Misunderstandings erupted into violence, as in a Tennessee case when a "shooting resulted from [an] order given Fuller by Scruggs to the effect that Fuller should not drink any of the seized whiskey and that he should put up a gun which he had in his lap. . . . Fuller became enraged and shot Scruggs, whereupon Scruggs fired back, killing Fuller instantly." Agent Scruggs died on the operating table. In this incident, enforcement practices and the authority they conferred were at issue. Fuller saw no professional contradiction between busting a local moonshiner and then having a drink; the federal agent perceived that evidence was being destroyed and that the law was being broken in his presence.[38]

Wets pointed to such scandals to demonstrate that Prohibition produced criminal lawmen, but drys maintained that Prohibition agents merely needed skills and training. In response to charges that agents had padded expense accounts by bribing the supervisors who authorized them, the general counsel for the Anti-Saloon League protested congressional demands that a sparer budget would end such scams. "We have worked hard to eliminate the inefficient and corrupt," he wrote to Thomas J. Walsh, chair of the Senate Judiciary Committee. "It is not the part of wisdom however to cripple law enforcement because some officers fail to do their duty."[39]

In an attempt to bolster the Bureau of Prohibition by linking it to its citizen base, Commissioner Haynes met with prominent reformer and religious leader Fred Smith in July 1923 to create the Citizenship Conference. In October, Haynes, Willebrandt, and Smith hosted a second meeting of prominent reformers intended to "arouse common sentiment to supplement the work being done by State and Federal officers."[40] Good public relations were perpetually disrupted, however, by wet assertions that Prohibition was undermining basic principles of fairness and democracy. The poor were most frequently arrested and jailed for bootlegging, opponents charged, whereas middle- and upper-class people (not to mention top gangsters like Al Capone and Arnold Rothstein) bought and drank behind the protection of country clubs, political connections, and homes they owned. A constituent wrote to his senator in 1926, "The prohibition law is enforced against the poor and weak, while the rich and powerful are not molested."[41]

This indignation against class bias was ironic, voiced as it was by many who were rich and powerful themselves, but it effectively stole temperance arguments that liquor's most deleterious effects were visited on the poor. Wet lobbyists turned the rhetoric of Prohibition back on itself with increasing success toward the end of the decade, a shift that is evident in the profusion of pamphlets and book-length studies produced by drys and state managers desperate to be understood. The stock market crash of 1929, coinciding, as it did, with several federal reviews of national Prohibition and crime policy, sparked a particular flurry of publication on both sides.[42] Federal pamphlets appealed to middle-class solidarity, asking civic leaders, businessmen, and property owners to help suppress crime and disorder by respecting Prohibition. A Treasury Department monograph proposed that "the individual citizen, having at heart the interest of home, family and community welfare, has a primary concern in furthering any proposal that advances the cause of good government." Another explained new federal interventions as "cooperation" with the states that required citizen watchdogs over state and county court systems to ensure that "justice would be done swiftly and surely."[43]

While wets represented a range of views, drys agreed on two things: that the state was a reflection of society, and that only temperance could guarantee a moral state, and this was worth the loss of some liberties. One constituent who signed himself "An Overseas War Veteran" suggested to Walsh that "the rebellious element" could be defeated "if the army could be used to enforce the Volstead law for about a year." A Presbyterian minister wrote to Mabel Walker Willebrandt to suggest that a female temperance advocate in the White House might ensure social and political morality. "From the U.S. Attorney's office to the White House is not a far step. . . . There are women governors, and why not?"[44]

However, in a period in which professional policing was understood as men's work, highlighting Prohibition's political base in feminized reform further undermined federal authority. Willebrandt spent increasing amounts of time trying to win dry constituencies to an anticrime agenda by 1927. After one such meeting, Ella A. Boole of the Woman's Christian Temperance Union (WCTU) wrote to the young lawyer, "[You should] feel assured that you have [in] back of you the prayers and good wishes of the women who belong to the Women's Christian Temperance Union and you have only to ask for what is needed and we will be ready to help." To women's clubs, Willebrandt lectured on the importance of motherhood to law observance.[45] But the dwindling membership of such groups had little influence, as policymakers increasingly advocated masculinized models of enforcement and scientific investigation.

That the state could be understood as thoroughly feminized in its ineffectiveness against bootleggers is evident in the champions it attracted. Willebrandt was periodically contacted by the Ku Klux Klan, which saw temperance as part of a mission of manly honor that included sexual regulation and the defense of white womanhood.[46] An undated letter recorded a dinner conversation with a "perfectly fine young man"; she wrote:

> I knew he was connected with the Ku Klux Klan, but I didn't realize the extent of his connection until he talked quite frankly with me concerning the political situation in the South. . . .
>
> I have always shied from having any connection with the Ku Klux Klan, as they well know. A high official of the Klan once made a trip to my office, offering to serve me in certain states where I was having a good deal of trouble on liquor cases; but I refused his tender of help, telling him quite frankly that I did not think, as a government official, I should deal with a secret organization.[47]

Although charges of class warfare never moved Willebrandt enough for her to relay them in correspondence, contacts with the right wing of the temperance movement graphically underlined the fragility of Prohibition's political alliances.

Wets pointed to Klan violence and, more important, the violence perpetrated by Volstead agents to argue that the state provoked general lawlessness by criminalizing liquor. The Association Against the Prohibition Amendment (AAPA), an upper-class libertarian organization that reorganized as the isolationist America First in the 1930s, made it its business to monitor constitutional violations and the Bureau of Prohibition's destruction of lives and property. In the first ten years of Prohibition, the AAPA noted, 144 civilians, 57 Prohibition agents, and 3 narcotics agents were killed. More than 200 incidents in the course of nine years resulted in death—11 per year, or nearly 1 per month. Urban police and political machines may have provided a restraining influence on the agents: only 4 officers, and no civilians, were killed in cities.[48]

Many AAPA members were prominent Republicans, and internal struggles over temperance provided the subtext of Herbert Hoover's inaugural speech in March 1929. While it featured integrity in government, good business practices, and restraint of party as its prominent themes, it was strangely silent on the future of Volsteadism. Shortly after he took office, although he continued to support Prohibition publicly, Hoover also obtained Mabel Walker Willebrandt's resignation. Several accounts agree that a campaign speech Willebrandt had given in Ohio linking Al Smith's Irish Catholic background with his wet politics had dogged Hoover throughout the campaign, and that Hoover's theme of a "New Day" implied departure from old reform agendas.[49] Most of all, as one historian asserts, Willebrandt was associated with enforcement practices that were increasingly understood as unethical: Hoover "disliked her dramatic methods of entrapping liquor law violators, which included sending female spies into houses of prostitution and other espionage agents into prisons to check on administrators."[50] He probably also disliked the recurrent scandals featuring high-ranking Republicans: Hoover soon appointed a commission chaired by former attorney general George Wickersham to study the continuation of Prohibition enforcement and the precipitous rise in violent crimes.

J. C. Burnham has charged in his revisioning of this period that most politicians of the 1920s were "indifferent to Prohibition *except as it affected politics*" (emphasis mine), but Prohibition enforcement and politics were inextricable.[51] The failure of Volstead enforcement, the old-style patronage politics it revealed, and the charges of hypocrisy at the highest levels it produced played a formative role in political struggles that laid the ideological foundation for J. Edgar Hoover's reforms in the Bureau of Investigation. "Good government" became synonymous with a vigorous policing, and, stirred by a vast literature on the "new" crimes associated with prohibition, poor law enforcement was articulated as the "cause" of proliferating criminal behaviors and state corruption. The first ten years of Prohibition enforcement produced demands on the federal government, and the Department of Justice in particular, to cleanse itself and provide greater aid to state and local police, who were fighting a new, and unequal, war with crime.

Rethinking Federal Enforcement

In February and March 1930, the Committee on the Judiciary in the House of Representatives held hearings on a bill to void the Prohibition amendment; inevitably, this became an arena for reimagining federal enforcement practices. A single theme frames the hundreds of pages of testimony: that the state had lost its moral authority by its failure to enforce the law. As journalist Walter Liggett testified, investigations in Detroit revealed "that not only [did] this act [result] in wholesale crime, more drunkenness, more debauchery, disorder of every sort, but it [was] directly responsible, everywhere . . . , for the corruption of high officials, for the hypocrisy of high officials." Liggett described "a wild party given at a road house" where the liquor was donated by a gangster. Guests included the governor, several chiefs of police, local politicians, socialites, and

> gamblers, criminals, bootleggers, all there fraternizing in the spirit of the most perfect equality, under the god Bacchus, and . . . there were four judges of the circuit court of Michigan at that drunken revel, at which naked hoochy-koochy dancers appeared later in the evening, and . . . these officials . . . attended that drunken debauch and the next day they said that they would enforce the law and that they believed in the dry law.[52]

The Woman's Christian Temperance Union and the formerly powerful Anti-Saloon League contended that legal alcohol would precipitate even swifter social disintegration, but many witnesses countered with anecdotes that featured the corruption of government by bootleggers and criminal profiteers.

Testimony before the committee highlights a cultural and political struggle over what caused the behaviors that threatened national order and government morality. Wets argued that the real rise in violence and outlawry associated with the new criminal organizations demonstrated that Prohibition itself had destroyed public order. In this context, the state had eroded its own authority by ceasing to distinguish between actual criminals and ordinary people who just wished to enjoy a drink in their own homes. They reclaimed familiar political symbols from reformers; formerly objects of respect and now criminalized by the Volstead Act and the 1929 Jones amendment were the little old granny making elderberry wine, the mother dosing her croupy child with whiskey, and the honest workingman relaxing with a beer.[53] In vain, white temperance advocates testified to the helplessness of women and children before uncontrolled male drunkenness; witnesses argued that the evils of alcohol could not be contained by good will. "It is as easy to abolish the liquor traffic as to regulate it," one reformer protested.[54]

However, the maternalist politics that had carried the Volstead Act to victory ten years earlier, along with mothers' pensions, protective labor legislation, and the 1921 Sheppard-Towner Infancy and Maternity Protection Act, were no longer effective. Republican politics had changed; party and state had already backed away from such interventions in private life by 1930. If old guard elite reformers like Mrs. Frank C. Porter of the New Haven, Connecticut, Mother's Club reminded the committee, "We . . . remember the saloons which used to control both our State and city governments," critics like Walter Liggett reversed the equation. Lurid images of rampant sexuality ("naked hoochy-koochy dancers") and unnatural leveling (public servants, socialites, and gangsters "fraternizing in the spirit of most perfect equality") alerted his audience to Porter's naive disregard of a state infected by hypocrisy: one nation "under the God Bacchus."[55]

The most powerful wet organization, the AAPA, reclaimed another tactic of progressive reformers: the assembling of facts to persuade the public. It conducted surveys that asked citizens, "Does harm result from the abuse of drink under Prohibition?" (the answer was an overwhelming "yes"), and conducted research, in the form of clipping files, that proved that enforcement did not work. Pamphlets issued by the AAPA were polemics against government violence as well. *Scandals of Prohibition Enforcement* (1929) and *Reforming America with a Shotgun: A Study of Prohibition Killings* (1930), both cribbed from federal reports, made familiar arguments: that Prohibition created organized crime and vast, untaxed wealth; that enforcement only criminalized innocent citizens exercising their constitutional right to a drink in their own homes; and that Prohibition agents were hooligans and grafters who undermined the state's ability to command the respect of its citizens.[56]

The AAPA became a publicity mill that arranged newspaper and magazine interviews of its socially prominent members, many of whom also seized the gendered language of temperance advocacy and turned it back on the "Great Experiment." In interviews with friendly publications such as Walter Liggett's *Plain Talk* (which featured the failures of Prohibition in monthly, in-depth studies of individual cities and states), younger socialites and established matrons testified to national and, by implication, racial decline. Failures of discipline and moral order caused by Prohibition had jeopardized a generation of elite young men— and the women who would bear future leaders. Mrs. Charles Sabin, a former member of the Republican National Committee, had been moved to the politics of repeal at the annual Harvard-Yale football game. Disgust at ruined youth, she said, inspired her "sense of patriotism," her "national pride." Her subsequent examination of federal Prohibition policies inspired activism. "It was the hypocrisy of the whole thing that got under my skin," she explained.[57] Congressional testimony from AAPA members also highlighted drunken college boys and degraded debutantes. "We view with increasing alarm the greatest menace to our country," warned Mrs. Robert Lovett of Boston, "the drunken girl of 14 to 18."[58]

As the above quotes suggest, white fears of racial decline, long the province of temperance advocates, were redeployed to depict a nation befouled and "good" citizens degraded by a state run amok. Not surprisingly, southern Democratic repeal organizations also testified to soiled white women and the awakening of latent criminality in black men.[59] A Mississippi member of the Women's Organization for National Prohibition Reform complained, "Revenue men have approached 'our' colored men and boys, asking them if they couldn't get liquor for them." She argued that this was a particularly unfair method of entrapment, since "this attitude of respect for white folks' commands [was] typical of all Southern Negroes." She continued, "[Women] have been insulted in their own homes . . . officers presenting warrants to search their homes, brushing the woman aside, and ruthlessly going through her most cherished belongings. Where is there an insult to American womanhood to equal that?" Figuring the state as a rapist and a disrupter of appropriate social relations between blacks and whites, this writer also invoked paternalist social "ownership" of blacks by whites, hinting at political anxieties about the possible uses of federal intervention in Jim Crow states.[60]

By 1929, the Association Against the Prohibition Amendment and organizations like it were dominating the Republican party, while reformers still struggled to fund and professionalize the Bureau of Prohibition. Thus, Mabel Walker Willebrandt's resignation was a blow, signaling the Hoover administration's move toward a political center that retained Prohibition itself while marginalizing what many perceived to be "fanatical" elements of the Republican party like the WCTU. The president also appointed a national crime commission to evaluate enforcement and organized bootlegging, thus moving discussions about the state away from morality and toward questions of police professionalization and crime.

In this case, as in other policy matters concerning crime, the federal government followed practices pioneered at the state level. The commission route was a common progressive solution to investigating social problems, using evidence similar to that generated by the AAPA: questionnaires, testimony by experts, collected comparative statistics, and research in public records and publications. In the postwar period, commissions had already been appointed to study crime waves in Missouri and Illinois, as well as in Chicago, where the identities of the "Secret Six" were hidden to prevent reprisal from the powerful Capone organization. Commissions were often appointed when the government's authority was under attack: because of that, the commissioners themselves had to be perceived as being citizens of the utmost integrity. The president appointed George Wickersham, a retired federal jurist, as chairman of the new national crime commission. A former attorney general, Wickersham had also played a role in reversing government antiradical convictions after World War I.[61] The commission completed its work in 1930, and the three-volume report was published in January 1931, at the same time that Hoover's unwillingness to take more active steps against the depression was escalating demands for state intervention in the economy.

The commissioners concluded that, as a police force, the Bureau of Prohibition had failed. The trade in alcohol had not been stopped; in fact, it was growing, and testimony from within the bureau argued that more resources would not reverse that. General Lincoln C. Andrews, a retired army officer and the bureau's director, testified that liquor came from numerous and diverse sources:

diverted industrial alcohol, "smuggling, the diversion of medicinal spirits, . . . and in the south and middle west moonshine liquor." Borders, the general argued, were not the main problem. It was Americans' willingness to purchase domestically produced rotgut liquor.[62]

The commission's research also argued that corruption among Prohibition agents was immune to all known reforms. In response to growing publicity about the ineptitude of the service, Congress had passed the Bureau of Prohibition Act in 1927, legislation that proposed that the worst Prohibition agents be weeded out by making them subject to the civil service laws. From mid-1927 to the end of 1929 the entire corps of agents systematically took the standard civil service test required of all other government employees. The resulting scores gutted the bureau. Only 41 percent of the force passed; the rest of the agents failed and were discharged.[63]

However, as the report noted, the loss of large numbers of men had been routine since 1920, as agents had quit or been fired at an alarming annual rate. After 1920, 20 percent of the field agents or more left the service every year. In 1921 a staggering 96 percent were fired or resigned; in 1922, 50 percent; in 1926, 49 percent; and in 1927, 38 percent. In 1921 and 1927, large numbers of supervisors were also discharged. Lack of skill and discipline was partly responsible for attrition: the act of 1927 provided the service's first training course, but that was only two weeks long. In 1930, this had been supplemented with "a correspondence course for instruction in the duties of the office, the elements of criminal investigation, constitutional law, etc." [64] Thus, new agents began their work as investigators with neither training nor a staff of experienced agents and supervisors who could train them in the field. Rapid turnover of personnel also made it nearly impossible for agents to establish the personal relationships that were valued in police work and that might have led to greater support from sheriffs and civilians alike. In fact, because administrators viewed local officers as undependable and dishonest, they actively discouraged cooperation and believed that agents should be insulated from local power brokers.

Despite these precautions, patronage and bribery were endemic at the Bureau of Prohibition. New agents were often appointed within their congressional districts, and a federal badge often reinforced other forms of unscrupulous behavior. Between 1921 and 1928, nearly a tenth of the service was dismissed "for cause," the grounds for which included "bribery, extortion, theft, violation of the National Prohibition Act, falsification of records, conspiracy, forgery, perjury," and other lesser crimes. But these were only the crimes that were uncovered. "What proportion of the total they really represent it is impossible to say," the report admitted. "Bribery and similar offenses are from their nature extremely difficult of discovery and proof."[65]

The violence and conflict that were characteristic of Volstead enforcement made federal policing the enemy, rather than the guardian, of democratic values. "Sources of resentment grow out of incidents of enforcement," the commissioners asserted. "Moreover, searches of homes, especially under state laws, have necessarily seemed to bear more upon people of moderate means than upon those of wealth or influence." In particular, it was the apparent randomness and unprofessional character of federal policing that aroused popular anger. "Resentment at crude methods of enforcement," the report noted, "unavoidable with the class of persons employed in the past and still often employed in state enforcement, disgust with informers, snoopers, and undercover men unavoidably made use of . . . add to the burden under which enforcement must be conducted."[66]

The commissioners believed that national Prohibition enforcement exacerbated fears of centralized government power that were inevitably sparked when the state took on new tasks.[67] Efforts to work with state and local governments were hampered, not just by apathy, but by "adverse public opinion . . . and by irritation in communities which feel that the ideas of conduct and modes of life of other communities are being forced upon them." The report emphasized that the good will of individual communities was crucial to achieving cooperation in any future federal police intervention.[68]

One lesson of national Prohibition was that news ought to be managed, whenever possible, to reinforce federal authority. Since World War I, bureaucrats had been aware of the impact of publicity on government and commercial agendas (the many publications produced on all sides of the Prohibition issue demonstrate this.)[69] In this case, the Wickersham commission believed that bad press had helped to poison public confidence in the government. One investigator reported that both Wichita, Kansas, newspapers had actively commented on Prohibition: the *Evening Eagle* supported local police wholeheartedly in their efforts and disparaged the government, while the *Beacon* argued that the federal government was impeded by local corruption. This kind of press debate had "a very serious and far-reaching effect on liquor law enforcement in the city," the report warned. "It creates suspicion in the minds of its readers and hinders the effective enforcement of law by the officials."[70]

In a portion of the report titled "The Bad Start and Its Results," the commissioners argued that Prohibition agents' failure to adhere to an ethical code of conduct made it impossible for federal judges to hold lower courts accountable for upholding the law and made the state's preparation of its own cases impossible. "Too often during the early years of prohibition were arrests made and prosecutions instituted without sufficient evidence to justify them," the commissioners noted.

In very many instances, unwarranted searches and seizures were made, which resulted in the refusal by Commissioners to issue warrants of arrest, or in the dismissal of the prosecution by the courts. In many of the instances, the character and appearance of the prohibition agents were such that the United States attorney had no confidence in the case and juries paid little attention to the witnesses. . . . The prohibition agents were more concerned to secure a large number of arrests or seizures than to bring to the District Attorneys carefully prepared cases of actual importance. It is safe to say that the first seven years' experience in enforcing the law resulted in distrust of the prohibition forces by many of the United States attorneys and judges.

In addition, "the federal field force as it was at first, was largely unfit by training, experience, or character to deal with so delicate a subject" as guaranteeing liberty and sanctity of the home.[71]

The country's first national police force had been a disaster, and yet the principle of federal policing survived. Ironically, by their failures, Volstead agents created a political climate that raised professional policing as a matter that ought to concern the federal branch. Significantly, James J. Britt, chief counsel of the Bureau of Prohibition, recommended to Congress a better-organized bureaucracy, enhanced professionalism and education, advanced training, and improved relations with state and municipal authority. This proposal mirrored reforms already implemented at J. Edgar Hoover's Bureau of Investigation. In fact, Britt hinted at growing support of a national enforcement effort centered in the Department of Justice. "Whatever form the administrative establishment shall take, and in whatever department it may be placed," he declared, "it should have the very best of administrative personnel, attorneys, experts, and enforcement officers that can be obtained." Enforcement must occur

strictly within the law, and in such a manner as to show the highest regard for public safety and private right, particularly for the protection of homes and the safety of individuals. To this end both the central service and the field service should, at all times in legal matters, be under the advice of experienced, well-trained and outstanding lawyers. . . . The character and dignity of its officers, the orderly and efficient manner in which they discharge their duties, with the outflowing results of law enforcement, are the best advertisements of the merits of Prohibition.

A dignified, professional force would be crucial to federal policing and would encourage states and municipalities "to perform their rightful share of enforcement." Local authorities had to be given the tools to investigate petty violators while the state took over cases "of an important character, such as conspiracies and other aggravated cases."[72]

New ideas about policing were developing more generally in the federal branch; if they were not inspired by the Prohibition disaster, they were often articulated through it. When the Bureau of Prohibition was transferred to the Department of Justice in 1930 as a preliminary step to disbanding it, J. Edgar Hoover fought attempts to place politically connected agents with the Bureau of Investigation because of their reputation for corruption and ineptitude. Arguing that this would reverse "all the work we had done to make the Bureau honest, sound and efficient," the director quarantined the disreputable agents in a special Alcoholic Beverages Unit until their collective discharge in 1933. Louis Ruppel, the deputy commissioner of narcotics (also in the Treasury Department), felt it would be best to be rid of these embarrassing agents. He admitted to Louis M. Howe, secretary to President Roosevelt, "[I have] been undiplomatic enough to tell some people that the Narcotic Bureau, if I could help it, would not become the dumping ground for all the Prohibition agents who now find themselves out of jobs or scheduled to be out of them very shortly. Even if we had jobs to give, I would take a lot of good looks at their records and then ask for more than an endorsement."[73]

However, if critiques of federal intervention were powerful enough to make these agents political poison, how had a discredited agency like the Bureau of Investigation retained enough credibility to be reformed? The answer lies in its initial purpose when it was established in 1907: to ferret out corruption in government. Teapot Dome, political scandals, and the desperate failure of the Bureau of Prohibition revealed an increased need for such an agency. Revelations of criminal activities within and outside the state inevitably produced a desire to suppress corruption and eliminate hypocrisy—or at least appear to be doing so. The Bureau of Investigation, whose Volstead responsibilities were limited to policing other police, was not only insulated from the corruption associated with Prohibition enforcement but became identified with a state free of politics rather than with patronage-style government.

This heightened desire for policing of government joined with other phenomena to produce a more efficient, and potentially more powerful, police apparatus in the Bureau of Investigation. The association of politicians, in particular, with the ineffective Prohibition experiment encouraged the separation of federal policing from politics—and created a potentially independent power base for Hoover. In addition, men and women who entered government after 1900 were increasingly a product of the civil service system and other kinds of professionalization processes. Although government bureaucrats were not homogeneous, they were subject to systematic training, evaluations, and examinations that were framed by a middle-class valorization of expertise. These ideas were also consistent in many respects with beliefs about good government voiced by the Bureau of Prohibition's critics and with the recommendations for improved federal enforcement made by the Wickersham commission.

How federal goals would be formulated in the Roosevelt administration was at least partially dependent on a preexisting national debate over crime and policing that had wedded the moral commitments of the reform movement to the need for a masculinized enforcement apparatus. As Mabel Walker Willebrandt knew, party politics and the urge to perfect society did not mix well, but the urge to perfect bureaucracy might have a chance at success. J. Edgar Hoover would make that successful link between the moral and the efficient state. In doing so, he would form close alliances between his reformed Bureau of Investigation and an emerging constituency alienated by the feminized temperance agenda: local officials, national police professional organizations, journalists, and citizens organizing against crime.

Two

"Trained and Intelligent Men of Good Character"

Scientific Policing, Masculinity, and Bureau Reform

There is a burning desire to serve in the Federal Bureau of Investigation. . . . Special agents (for the time being at least) are popular subjects of hero worship. The straight-out factual drama of the government's war on crime, together with highly-seasoned motion picture romanticization, have excited adventure seekers. —Melvin Purvis, *American Agent* (1936)

"For the sake of this book it would be pleasant to say that some valorous impulse catapulted me into the ranks of the special agents," veteran G-man Melvin Purvis wrote in his 1936 memoir; "unfortunately, this isn't true." Purvis, who had by then become a national celebrity for killing John Dillinger, began his career in his hometown. Like many other professional men and women after World War I, however, he soon aspired to a government job. "There is nothing like a small law office to make a young man hunger for adventure," he recalled about the decision to leave Timmonsville, South Carolina, for Washington, D.C. Advised that he would be more suited to the Bureau of Investigation than to his other chosen vocation—the diplomatic service—Purvis applied to the Department of Justice on December 18, 1926.[1]

The bureau that Purvis and other white, male professionals joined after 1924 was a fraction of the size of the Bureau of Prohibition and was in a period of stringent reform. J. Edgar Hoover brought fierce energy to this work, forcing changes in administrative procedure, dress, hiring practices, and work habits that brought to the federal branch a professional police model pioneered at the local level. As one historian put it, Hoover's personality was "grafted onto

31

the Bureau" in the 1920s; flurries of daily memorandums document his style and vision.[2]

Other influences converging on the Department of Justice were important as well.[3] Hoover's vision drew on a version of progressive activism that sought to modernize government service by distinguishing administrative agendas from the interests of political parties. In this context, policing became a target for good-government campaigns even before Prohibition launched a widespread demand for professional solutions to the graft and favoritism associated with federal enforcement. Hoover and other management proponents of scientific techniques pressed legislators to enact reforms that conferred prestige on state-centered professionalism and eliminated purely "political" advancement. This new class of ambitious career administrators, many promoted rapidly because of the personnel shortages of World War I, strove to eliminate patronage practices that reduced efficiency. As a group they were convinced that an administrative apparatus "tied together by the procedures of spoils appointment had to be reoriented around the procedures of merit appointment."[4]

Few reformers understood the need to create ideological change within a government organization as well as Hoover did. Merit appointment signaled a profound alteration in the terms of state rule (by 1920, almost 70 percent of the federal branch was appointed through civil service), but it made corrupt employees even more difficult to fire. Hoover, unlike most of his contemporaries, incorporated the principles of civil service in bureau reorganization while resisting incorporation into the system itself; the ability to hire and fire at his own discretion became the basis for tremendous internal power.[5] The bureau's role in Teapot Dome also provided Hoover with an opportunity to make a break with patronage practices. This permitted him to limit recruitment to men who were ideologically compatible with his philosophies; schooled in the disciplines and values of a college-educated, professional managerial class; and free of other loyalties. Before 1924, applicants to the Bureau of Investigation had been hired at the "suggestion" of powerful congressional allies: "Make out an appointment for Colonel George R. Shanton," Director William Burns wrote to Assistant Director Hoover in 1922. "This is the man that Mr. Ensted has been after us to put on—Mr. Ensted of the Appropriations Committee."[6]

In contrast to these political deals, new practices of formal application, testing, training, and acceptance signaled a decisive shift toward the real requirements of a surveillance state. By 1926, Melvin Purvis's congressional sponsor received a courteous but undeferential reply that reminded him of the director's political autonomy. "I beg to acknowledge receipt of your communication of the 20th instant in behalf of Mr. Melvin H. Purvis," Hoover wrote; "if his qualifications so warrant, he will be placed on our eligible list for consideration when any vacancies occur."[7] Such a letter ended the congressman's participation in the appointment, establishing a balance of power between state and party that was tipped toward the bureaucrats.

Although portrayed by the Department of Justice as an innovator, the director established his enforcement credentials through management techniques and orthodox ideas, not through original solutions to policing problems. Hoover himself had no police training, but he had experience for what had created efficiency and authority among local and state police forces, replicating practices he undoubtedly observed in urban Red squads during and after the war. If sheriffs and police chiefs saw floundering Prohibition policies as a sign of federal interference and hypocrisy, Hoover's small agency offered ideas that reflected their professional priorities about politicized enforcement agendas and the rise in crimes against property.[8] Hoover also understood, six years before the Wickersham commission, that police officers embodied state power. What they appeared to be had particular importance at an explosive moment in national mass culture. Like other police reformers, he understood officers as cultural workers, mediating relations between state and citizen: thus, the daily work of patrol, investigation, and apprehension offered opportunities for inspiring civic virtue.[9]

Scholars have variously interpreted the bureau's public image as an illusion that came to shape reality or as a deception that concealed the true nature of federal policing from Congress and the public. However, by the time of Hoover's appointment in 1924, distinctive and professional police officers were understood as necessary to the preservation of democracy and the promotion of the modern state. Hoover's new, professional cadres of special agents projected these values, claiming a generation of enforcement professionals and their admirers as a political constituency. Simultaneously, G-men came to understand themselves as superior to their state and local brethren. Most important, the Bureau of Investigation came to represent a positive, masculinized "federal" approach to crime: special agents, as they negotiated urban squad rooms, popular magazines, newspapers, and interstate investigations, articulated the state as modern; nationalizing practices as beneficial; and federal authority as legitimate and just.[10]

Reforming the Bureau of Investigation

Reversing the public attacks on federal enforcement, and the Department of Justice in particular, was both a challenge and an opportunity when Hoover was appointed as acting director of the Bureau of Investigation in May 1924. His status as a professional and his avowed dislike for politics figured prominently in the initial news reports, framing the appointment as a clean break with the past. "I read in the papers that the new head of the Department of Justice is cutting out the old detective tricks," one columnist wrote. "It's about time."

In a clear reference to the previous director, founder of a national detective agency, the writer noted that the bureau would no longer serve crooked politicians or elite interests.[11]

The disgraced Burns also became the symbol of an amateur past that was being replaced by professionalism. During Teapot Dome, he was widely lampooned as arrogant, old-fashioned, and a servant to powerful men. One cartoon of the fallen director showed him in an old-fashioned checked suit, nineteenth-century high-button shoes, and a bowler hat. Stories that spoke of magnifying glasses and "clews" invoked foreign British detective fiction; other critics attacked the techniques of detective agencies, particularly the use of informers against labor radicals, as un-American and unprofessional.[12]

Hidden in this story was Hoover's greatest professional accomplishment, his own antiradical work. Born the son of a civil servant and the brother of another, Hoover had entered government service at sixteen, attending college and law school at night while he worked first at the Library of Congress and then as a mail room clerk at the Department of Justice. After several failed attempts to join the Bureau of Investigation as a special agent, in 1917 he was finally appointed to a new division set up by Attorney General A. Mitchell Palmer to investigate peace activists, labor organizers, socialists, and communists. There, his energetic work habits and prodigious memory bore fruit. He soon became the division's chief administrator, largely on the strength of a cross-referenced filing system that permitted his clerks to sort surveillance information obtained by paid informants; his résumé also featured several well-publicized deportations, Alexander Berkman and Emma Goldman among them.[13]

Hoover's first celebrity career as a Red hunter came to a crashing halt in 1921 when many of the deportation cases were reversed on appeal and the methods of the Palmer raids condemned as illegal. Although Palmer resigned in disgrace, Hoover was permitted to remain, possibly because his administrative skills were already famous among Washington bureaucrats. This episode, which was subsequently repeated on an even more damaging scale after the war on crime, was suppressed entirely as he took over from Burns. Upon his permanent appointment in January 1925, Hoover obscured his lack of police experience by emphasizing his professional and managerial credentials and his commitment to building a corps of agents that reflected his bootstrap self-image.[14] One interview began, "Sheer merit has won over political pull." Depicting Hoover as having risen through the ranks of government, the story emphasized his legal education and executive skills. New agents would also be cut from an executive mold: "square-jawed, square headed" and "third-degree" detectives were a thing of the past: agents, Hoover confided, would be "men of common sense and good character."[15]

Hoover had survived the Palmer scandals and the purge of Burns's men, successfully navigated the candidacies of experienced police chiefs, and parried two congressional inquiries; his permanent appointment as director was a monument to his professional self-fashioning. As the story was later rewritten under Hoover's direction,

> Attorney General Stone had rejected the arguments that he was too young for the job. Far more important, he knew that Stone did not hold him responsible for the policies, mistakes and corrupt actions of those who had directed the Department of Justice and the Bureau of Investigation in the past.
> Finally Hoover said, "I'll take the job, Mr. Stone, on certain conditions."
> "What are they?"
> "The Bureau must be divorced from politics and not be a catch-all for political hacks. Appointments must be based on merit. Second, promotions will be made on proved ability and the Bureau will be responsible only to the Attorney General."
> The Attorney General scowled and said, "I wouldn't give it to you under any other conditions. That's all. Good day."[16]

Hoover's triumph is not personal: it is a victory for all self-made government professionals. Stone, an upper-class political appointment, satisfies conditions set by Hoover, a middle-class professional bureaucrat. Party scandals are prehistory for this young man, who sets terms for his elders, including a demand to report to other government men, not to "political hacks."

Bourgeois values of merit, education, and hard work appealed to dominant notions about the legitimate grounds for material success in a democracy. Hoover's ideas about character also hint at the gender, class, and racial boundaries delimiting who might be an agent. In fact, for decades recruitment was limited to white men, the vast majority of whom had college and postgraduate degrees and many of whom had served in the military. "I want the public to look upon the Bureau of Investigation of the Department of Justice as a group of gentlemen," Hoover said, "and if the men here engaged can't conduct themselves in office as such, I will dismiss them."[17]

Between 1924 and 1932, Hoover initiated reforms at the Bureau of Investigation that determined its shape for the next fifty years. They included rigorous training, dress regulations, internal inspections, a strict code of conduct, heavy reliance on the acquisition and sorting of information, and a system of uniform investigative procedures. The new dress code made federal agents recognizable as professionals in any group of law officers, signaling visually the beginning of a new era in federal enforcement. Agents were rotated in and out of Washington on a regular basis, and no agent was left in any one post long enough to create alliances or affiliations outside the bureau. Initially, the creation of systematic order at the bureau permitted it to "[fall] into benign obscurity, a merciful relief from its earlier notoriety." But during this period, Hoover built an entirely new organization that, with modest budget increases and a smaller staff, claimed jurisdiction over twenty felony crimes by 1931.[18] The shrewdest move of these initial years was completely unpublicized; he demanded, and received, discretion over his own budget, perhaps the most significant form of internal power a modern state offers. Such a reform made the bureau internally different from the Bureau of Prohibition, while the new director strove to convince congressmen, policemen, and the public that federal enforcement could work.[19]

Hoover's refusal to make bureau agents part of the civil service appointments system also increased their professional status. By 1920 the commission itself had "suffered an ignominious fall from its lofty status as the premier symbol of integrity in the new American state" as the wartime scramble for government jobs overwhelmed its administrative capabilities. The Bureau of Prohibition's collapse under civil service rules in 1927 may have also tainted the commission in police circles. Furthermore, in 1918, a year in which 137,620 women took the civil service exam (an increase of 441 percent over the previous year), the commissioners ruled that all departments subject to their requirements must hire women.[20] Gaining exemption from these requirements gave the bureau the homosocial status of other professional, elite institutions: Ivy League universities, urban businessmen's clubs, fraternal organizations, and the clergy.

Hoover's redefinition of the bureau's mission attracted a constituency ill served by federal Prohibition: police chiefs and their advocacy group, the International Association of Chiefs of Police (IACP). Incorporated in 1893, the IACP was founded to promote scientific techniques and the sharing of information across departments. Its most influential president was Berkeley, California, police chief August Vollmer, who, after the 1919 Boston police strike, successfully promoted a professionalization agenda that included employment stability, education, and training.[21] In 1925, at the IACP annual convention, Hoover identified armed robbery as the worst problem facing rural and small-town police and committed the federal government to administrative reforms that would address it. Already he had reorganized record keeping and procedures, creating a cross-referenced filing system that permitted an agent to take a single piece of information—a fingerprint, a physical description, a modus operandi—and trace it back to a whole criminal. The bureau began to rebuild its reputation around this issue, and in particular, auto theft, a crime that had accelerated in the postwar period because of more widespread automobile ownership; in addition, stolen cars were used by bootleggers and bank robbers. In 1925, when the Dyer Act, a law making interstate transportation of automobiles a federal crime, was upheld by the Supreme Court, the bureau began to publish national auto theft records and statistics on "crimes of greater magnitude against persons or property." As a result, experts compiled data on the "names and identities of known outlaw organizations," particularly in the Midwest and South.[22]

By 1932, national publications made some of this data accessible to the police community on a monthly basis, along with new scientific techniques adopted by the bureau. *Fugitives Wanted By Police* listed "the names, aliases, descriptions and fingerprint classifications of fugitives wanted for the commission of major crimes," and the quarterly *Uniform Crime Reports* collated crime statistics reported by participating police departments around the country. Because bureau administrators decided what statistics to collect and how to classify them, they also created crime trends and put Hoover and his IACP allies in a position to argue convincingly for particular policies that emphasized the need for larger police forces and better enforcement.

But could modern science be an effective weapon against violent lawbreakers? To answer this question, the "Government Man," or "G-man," was born, produced within a masculinized narrative that imagined him as a frontier hero in a suit. In 1926 Hoover asserted that "above everything a man must have common sense and integrity" and courage: "What we usually do is to send a new man to Oklahoma, where things are still in the raw. If he's got any yellow about him, it will come out and we get rid of him. But if he's got the courage and determination and isn't afraid to work hard, he won't have to stay there long." The route to a government career was through the frontier, where mere men became "Americans"; here, Hoover played to popular historical models that wedded democracy to masculinity and nationalism. Nine months later, another journalist reported, "Judged by the size of the Bureau of Investigation's personnel in that particular region," he wrote, "Oklahoma is the most lawless section of the country. Hoover maintains a bigger staff of sleuths in Oklahoma City than in even New York or Chicago."[23]

Rebuilding the government's reputation demanded that the director emphasize how similar he was, not only to powerful police chiefs, but to all officers who patrolled a beat. It has not been sufficiently stressed that Hoover's past as a successful Red-baiter would have been a positive qualification among these men, consistent with a law-and-order agenda he, and they, supported. These allies also enlarge a sense of how the political sphere was reconstituted in the years in which party structures lost some of their authority. By mobilizing police as a constituency, Hoover could cite local needs as a basis for enlarging state power and nationalizing trends as a renewal of local authority. In his first speech as director, Hoover told the IACP that policing was central to a moral society and that the bureau was a democratic development that would muster "all of the wisdom and power of the guardians of civilization, the protectors of Society."[24]

Many policemen began to see Hoover as their representative in Washington and themselves as an important influence on the state. The IACP and its individual members stepped forward at important moments to support Hoover's appointment, particularly after presidential elections when speculations about replacing him were always raised. At the IACP convention in June 1929, the organization affirmed that "unjust, unwarranted and unmerited attacks" had been made on Hoover and that the association deplored "unwarranted attacks on capable and efficient officials."[25]

J. Edgar Hoover's associational politics were characteristic of the postwar Progressive movement that culminated in Herbert Hoover's presidency. However, his supporters seemed to be far more numerous than they were, since they operated from at least two, if not more, professional locations, a department and one or more police organizations. Significantly, they were a constituency no other federal branch had organized or even wanted. Their enthusiasm for the bureau's apparent concern for their issues became a powerful political weapon at annual budget reviews and reappointment hearings. Hoover's personal file contains many cordial communications from these men noting his presence at professional meetings; a typical testimonial from one midwestern police chief and IACP officer asserted that the Bureau had "improved fully 100% during [Hoover's] regime."[26]

Hoover moved between federal and local worlds in his first decade, absorbing ideas from state and local reformers and cycling them back through his publications as federal anticrime proposals.[27] Connections between individual departments and the bureau were also cemented as special agents became attractive candidates for municipal policing posts, district attorneys' staffs, and private sector employment. They, too, became new sources for information and future political support. "It is with considerable regret that I tender my resignation," one agent who had been offered work in a Nashville law firm wrote to Hoover. "You are performing a great service to your country. . . . If at any time I am able to assist the Bureau, or any of its members, I shall be more than glad to be of service."[28] Service became Hoover's byword in these years, as he rebuilt relationships damaged during the Palmer and Daugherty administrations.[29] Some services consisted of simply performing jobs well. Accustomed to slipshod work from her own agents, Mabel Walker Willebrandt became one of the young director's most vocal supporters as complex investigations began to yield indictments and convictions. "I have never seen a finer or higher class group of men associated than from your Bureau," Willebrandt wrote him; "not only for the way they handled assignments but for the splendid and uncomplaining team work." A memo from the War Department thanked him for "the many excellent reports received through [his] office concerning conditions in Mexico . . . exactly the class of material most useful to the Military Intelligence Division." And days after Franklin Roosevelt's inauguration, Hoover thanked one congressman for his "expressions of confidence": "Please be assured that I shall be glad to be of any service possible in connection with any matter of mutual interest."[30]

Service, rather than graft, would be Hoover's currency and information his capital. In this, Hoover was a visionary: the gathering and sorting of information would not just be the basis of police power in the coming decades but of state power as a whole. Furthermore, the wise bureaucrat was still a dealer in gestures and favors. If a task requested by a politician or a colleague fell within his jurisdiction, he could choose to grant it—thus banking good will and gratitude. Similarly, information withheld could have political—or career—consequences.[31]

The new image of efficiency that the bureau projected placed a premium on information and the truths experts could uncover in the random and mysterious information collected as evidence. Identification, Hoover told the *Washington Post,* was "indispensable in combating crime." Although, as Melvin Purvis protested, "a crystal ball is not part of a special agent's equipment," bureau publicity from 1925 implied an almost magical crime-solving ability that stemmed from a combination of evidence collection, scientific analysis, and the proper organization of facts. Fingerprint records, the only physical characteristic unique to each human being before the discovery of DNA, made all other forms of evidence useful by linking them to the physical presence of a known felon. By 1909, the Department of Justice maintained fingerprint cards, records that were centralized at the bureau in 1923. Hoover's connections with the IACP brought its vast collection to Washington; and by 1931, virtually all government agencies were contributing fingerprints taken for any reason.[32]

Practices that were institutionalized to fight crime were often identical to methods of political surveillance and operated under similar assumptions: that every subject who could be added to the files was a potential criminal.[33] By generating information and refining the methods for using it, the bureau linked its interests to those of state and local police in a federally coordinated information network. Full cooperation on all levels, Hoover boasted to Chicago police, would make any previously convicted felon or active fugitive identifiable through the bureau's criminal laboratories. Through "coordination and cooperation," the nation had achieved "a working, practical, effective national police force," Hoover noted. "No laws have been necessary for the organic development of this condition. It has been a natural, inevitable development, based on mutual interests and mutual needs."[34]

Hoover's emphasis on inevitability and mutuality forestalled the inevitable dilemma that national policing was bound to produce: could government surveillance be compatible with a democratic political culture and a moral state? Private detectives used as union infiltrators, government "spies" operating as provocateurs during the Palmer years, and Volstead agents posing as both bootleggers and buyers had all contributed to a widespread belief that the police violated the public trust by enticing citizens into criminal acts. Journalist Walter Liggett, who himself had gone undercover to write a series of articles about corrupt enforcement, charged in his 1930 congressional testimony that federal agents were "every one of them . . . an ex-bootlegger or an ex-convict." He himself had gathered his information by stealth, but he declared vehemently, "I want to say in this connection that I am not a snooper or an informer or a spy." The audience burst into wild applause, and Liggett was asked to stop grandstanding by one representative, who nevertheless hastened to support his sentiment.[35]

Hoover's new agents confronted contradictory expectations: that they eliminate dangerous criminals by any means necessary but that they pursue fugitives in a way that reflected the "American" principle of fair play. Hoover's rhetoric of partnership between federal and local police replaced a vision of state repression with euphemisms about the exchange of information, drawing on a broader rhetoric of civic-state partnership that characterized public discourse in the 1920s. It also obscured the fact that certain kinds of information were only going in one direction. As special agents roamed federal and municipal offices, "cooperating" with other branches of government and local authorities, they collected political rumors. "Mr. Hanson of New York City telephoned," one memo to Washington read, "and stated that while at police headquarters yesterday afternoon, Special Agent Jim Amos was informed by Harry Butts, ballistics expert, that it is freely rumored around the New York City Police Department, that Mr. Hoover is going out of office as Director and that Commissioner Valentine is to succeed him; that H.E. Burckman is to take Valentine's place."[36] While others benefited from the increased capacity of the Bureau of Investigation to collect, sort, and distribute information, they, too, had became objects of surveillance.

Although Hoover's ambitions and personality are critical to understanding this new balance of power, it is perhaps more useful to view his new vision of federal policing as compatible with an ideology of professionalization that drew on, negotiated, and produced new ideas about federal responsibility in the decade after World War I. The re-creation and expansion of the Bureau of Investigation can then be seen as a corrective, not to centralization itself, but to the blunt tactics of state/class domination that had characterized the Palmer raids, labor conflict, and Prohibition enforcement. In the words of Sidney Harring, Hoover's reforms might be then understood as "part of a broader development of capitalist social institutions" and "the rationalization of social relations."[37]

A complex range of state interests were served by bureau reforms. The moral authority of the Department of Justice, and that of the Republican administrations it served, were also rehabilitated to some degree as Hoover's accomplishments were publicly linked with broader federal agendas. As early as Hoover's first sixty days in office, a Pittsburgh editorial criticizing Volstead agents for fouling evidence asserted (less than a year after the Teapot Dome revelations!) that the Department of Justice would have successfully jailed the suspect. Putting Hoover in charge of all law enforcement was "the one thing necessary to a clean-up" in Washington, the editors wrote. Praising his "capacity for work" and his "dynamic force," the editors described this new enforcement model in masculinized terms: "No one would take this human dynamo for a detective and that's in his favor. But if ever John Hoover takes hold, pity the bootlegger or briber who is under fire. He's a real D.J. man!"[38]

This editorial implied that the recent scandals were the work of political interlopers: that there was a "real" state and a "real" Department of Justice that had been hamstrung by corruption. Mabel Walker Willebrandt made a similar observation. In 1926 she praised Hoover's appointment as a step toward departmental integrity, sending her parents "an example of the fine work done by the Bureau of Investigation" of the Department of Justice. "I have sent you these reports from time to time, and . . . you see how they dovetail into all parts of the United States, and you realize why I have so often said that it is possible to enforce the prohibition laws the same as other laws if the enforcement work were done by trained men organized for investigators and not for publicity artists." Willebrandt's pleasure suggests that Hoover's ambitions for the bureau were not his alone but were part of a broader departmental vision. Investigation was now understood as a highly skilled occupation, and special agents were thus relieved of time-consuming and "unskilled" duties, which were then delegated to the United States Marshals Service. In fact, by 1930, the bureau's increasing prestige as a "scientific" service led to the reconceptualization of marshals as "professional" warrant servers.[39]

Thus, a clean-cut breed of newly scrubbed, masculinized federal police led by a director of apparently impeccable morals was deployed against the spectacle of institutionalized corruption. When the director promised delegates at the 1925 IACP convention that the bureau would "expand until the remotest village in the country, in the event of a serious crime, [could] have the service of all sorts of scientific experts at its command," he pointed to a bright, new future in which the federal government protected citizens across state and municipal boundaries, linking their interests to those of a homogeneous national polity.[40]

By 1932 Hoover had created new points of actual and ideological contact through which diverse and unevenly trained police forces around the nation might see themselves as a network of enforcement professionals. By affirming the Department of Justice's commitment to a national police force outside politics, he linked a new breed of federal police to the notion of a state purged of party interests. Making the state available to reformers who sought federal aid to control new crime problems, he also acquired influential political allies without doing "politics."[41] In addition, since advanced criminal science techniques and identification files were often completely unavailable to the understaffed, undertrained police forces outside metropolitan areas, through his publications and services Hoover extended the prestige of professionalism to small and rural forces. In short, Hoover placed his bureau—and the state itself—at the center of the police professionalization movement.

Masculinity and Police Professionalization

In February 1933, days before the inauguration of Franklin D. Roosevelt, a comic strip debuted in the *New York World-Telegram*. Featuring the adventures of "Special Agent J-8," the strip detailed the exploits of Director Hoover's best men and claimed to pick its cases straight from bureau files. This cartoon detective reflected not only Hoover's new forays into popular culture but also a general shift in public perceptions about police work.[42] In an essay contest five years earlier, contestants had responded to the question "Shall we enforce and obey the law and the Constitution?" by stressing the importance of professionalism and the use of publicity to promote lawful conduct. Many writers and the editor of the volume that was later published also praised the Bureau of Investigation as an innovator in the field of reform, suggesting that federalized enforcement would generally improve the nation's police forces.[43]

In fact, preexisting ideas at the state and municipal level about what constituted good police work and how it could be achieved had provided the ideological basis for federal reform measures.[44] As Arthur Woods, a former New York City police commissioner, argued in 1919:

> The policeman as he is few people see and know. This is partly his own fault, for he is apt to be none too frank about what he is doing, and isn't likely to open wide the door to those who come to inform themselves as to what manner of man he is. It is also the fault of the public, for they have been content to leave him as he is, without bothering to find out whether the failings they see in him are inherent, or are curable and theirs to cure.[45]

Policeman and public are gendered male and female, occupying the separate spheres that characterize much of prewar bourgeois social thought.[46] In a crude but classic masculine pose, the policeman is "none too frank" and not likely to reveal himself; only a caring public, in a feminized reform posture, can persevere to "cure" his "failings." Woods's critique is expressed through the failure of these ideal gendered roles: the public is unfeminine in its indifference and the policeman unmanly in his isolation.

Woods, like Hoover, believed that an orderly society was produced by the complementarity of state and public that this heterosocial reference suggests. Honest administration, adequate pay, good training, and proper organization provided a home for the professional police officer. The public, through its moral authority, had the right to expect in turn that policemen be providers of social order, projecting the spirit of good government into society. He would be "a teacher of cleanliness, an educator of good habits"; instead of dominating he would be "charged with the duty of radiating good nature, of trying to maintain an atmosphere of quiet and calm."[47]

If, in Woods's view, a person projected a set of values, to Berkeley police chief and IACP founder August Vollmer, professionalism "signified a person more than a concept." The good policeman should be a superior physical type, but his character and work could only be assured by the appointment of competent administrators, who would nurture innate strengths through strict training and scrutiny and cultivate good work habits through scientific management and honest example. Most symptoms of departmental demoralization were immediately "traceable to the low standard of entrance requirements, inadequate preliminary training and absence of training for sergeants, detectives and commanding officers," he wrote in 1928, as well as "the constant changing of department policies in regard to law enforcement." Well chosen and well trained, the professional policeman then stabilized the civic sphere: "Trained and intelligent policemen of good character give courage to law-abiding citizens and furnish a nucleus around which they may rally to control a lawless element."[48]

Bruce Smith, an expert in statewide policing and highway patrol, pointed to the lack of coherence in the duties, and consequently the person, of the sheriff as an ancillary cause of disorder among rural populations. "The sheriff has been saddled with a highly miscellaneous group of functions," Smith wrote in 1929; "it is easy to see how his attention might become divided and diffused." Like Hoover, Smith believed that "an established reputation for good moral character [was] probably the most important element in the preliminary qualification of a policeman." This could be established, not just by inquiring into the applicant's character, but also by investigating "the standing and reliability of the persons who have vouched for him."[49]

There was another danger to the health of the force, however: women. As Smith warned,

> The conditions under which a state policeman performs his duties, the very moderate cash salary he receives, the heavy demands upon his time, the requirement that he live in police barracks, the frequent transfers from point to point throughout the state, all operate to make the service unsatisfactory to one who is bound by family ties. . . . Some forces even go so far as to discourage, within certain limits, marriage by members of the force whose income as policemen would not permit them to maintain a separate domestic establishment.

Pennsylvania, New York, Michigan, West Virginia, and the Royal Canadian Mounted Police all limited marriage.[50]

Before Prohibition, advocates of professionalization also fought antivice legislation because of the temptations to dishonesty it offered. Hoover continued to do this at the federal level until repeal and was himself nearly unseated in 1924 because of an alleged bureau cover-up of a missing warehouse of liquor. Such charges, true or false, were the inevitable outcome of policing the underworld trade in pleasurable commodities; Woods believed that protection of lives and property, not morals, was the only legitimate function of policemen, since vice "nourished the roots of police graft." In fact, some urban support for a national Prohibition law may well have reflected the increasing pressure that local dry laws were placing on police forces before 1919 and a widespread desire to transfer these burdensome and politically delicate duties out of local departments.[51]

Campaigns against property crime were understood by the professionalization movement as the best way of utilizing expert knowledge and standardized investigation techniques. Urban officers who now envisioned policing as a career path rather than a form of wage labor were less interested in enriching themselves through graft and more interested in promotions. The best route to status was breaking major cases—mainly bank robberies, fraud, and confidence rackets; vice beats, on the other hand, consisted of dangerous and endless patrol work. Investigating crimes against property also conferred status, reflecting advanced knowledge of techniques for collecting, understanding, and analyzing evidence and a detailed knowledge of the criminal underworld.[52]

Moving the local emphasis on property crime and newly "professionalized" criminals onto the national agenda, publicity about the Bureau of Investigation wooed high-status urban policemen and inspired those who wished to possess these elite skills. The perceived need for police expertise became visibly more dramatic after 1919, as violence and theft escalated and all of these crimes exploded into formerly middle-class neighborhoods and business districts. Although Hoover recalled this decade as a period in which "the public, generally, was apathetic about crime," popular novels, films, and magazines were full of nothing but—producing additional outrage that representations of crime glamorized the underworld and undercut the authority of respectable people.[53]

Hoover's emphasis on science and technology spoke to a new generation of urban police whose work was changing quickly. One excellent example of this is the sphygmomanometer, or lie detector, which was available in most large departments after World War I. Reformers had, for several decades, criticized methods of obtaining confessions commonly known as "the third-degree," a crude technique of sleep deprivation, terror, and beatings that assumed both that a suspect would confess if he was punished sufficiently and that any confession would do. Lie detectors required two intellectual shifts, one of which was that the point of detection was to jail the actual culprit. More important, through the machine, the policeman conducted a scientific experiment, asking questions that played on the belief that a criminal's body spoke louder than his mind. A rubber tube around the chest recorded vital signs: "when a man lies, increased breathing and more rapid heart beat betray him."[54]

Expertise reshaped the look and structure of most police forces, as they grew in response to larger populations, new inventions, and higher crime rates. For example, in Tulsa, Oklahoma, from 1900 on, the police department adopted military-style discipline; a navy blue tunic, breeches, and boots; and physical training programs. Specialized tasks emerged by World War I: officers were assigned to detective, criminal identification, traffic, and juvenile divisions and bicycle, motorcycle, and car patrols. By the 1920s, a squad of female police matrons was hired, and a Police Relief Association managed pensions and a widows' and orphans' fund. By 1928, patrol officers had to know how to operate a car or a motorcycle, and they had to memorize a series of call signs that permitted them to operate car radios and police call boxes. However, even in a modern department officers were ill paid and overworked. As late as 1935, officers worked twelve-hour shifts, seven days a week, for a starting salary of $150 a month.[55]

Neither the maleness nor the whiteness of the bureau made it different from other police forces; in fact, compared with the most exclusive state police forces that did not permit marriage, the bureau might have been understood as moderate to progressive on the issue of gender. Hoover's speeches of the period explicitly linked the G-man's loyalty, patriotism, and service to the public to the support of wives and mothers; and he frequently spoke of the "sacrifices" bureau wives made so that their special-agent husbands could protect the country. "I cannot begin to talk about the magnificent bravery of G-Men's wives," Hoover told one audience in the midst of the war on crime, "and the philosophy of calm courage that is always evident no matter what happens." Excluded from the bureau's public labors, women and their children were a critical institutional lever for funding a federal professionalization agenda. Hoover wheedled pensions and pay increases out of a reluctant Congress by insisting that men needed to provide for dependents. Hoover framed such support not as charity but rather as a reward for service: "Many of these wives would go out with their men and share their risks if we could allow it," Hoover told Congress.[56]

Hoover's portrayal of these invisible federal employees was undoubtedly shared by these wives, as they moved families from city to city, responding to frequent changes in assignments and rank, or raised their children alone while the bureau claimed their husbands. Wives may have been occasionally used as unpaid staff as well. Undercover stakeouts presented a special problem for this male organization when a lengthy investigation in a residential neighborhood required that agents blend in with their surroundings. As C. W. Stein, special agent in charge (SAC) of the St. Paul office, explained to Hoover in 1936, it was "highly unusual for two men to rent an unfurnished house. It was believed that in the best interests of the investigation that the place . . . should be made to resemble as closely as possible an ordinary residence inhabited by ordinary occupants. . . . Whenever it is possible to maintain a surveillance without the wives of special agents it will be done."[57] The appearance of homosexuality was a greater infringement of the bureau's masculine ideal than endangering civilian women.

The increased role of women in government during and after World War I made Hoover's failure to hire them as agents more visible and a target of comment among journalists. However, female patrol officers outside the juvenile or vice divisions were virtually unheard of in any Western country before World War II. Furthermore, as a militarized model began to characterize police reform efforts and scientific criminal investigation displaced vice control as the primary vehicle for professionalization on urban police forces, femaleness became increasingly incompatible with a professional identity.[58]

Consequently, the value system at the center of bureau reform was heavily masculinized as well, making it appealing to those in the Department of Justice seeking to distance themselves from Prohibition enforcement. When Hoover responded to the "woman question," he explained that the unevenness and unpredictability of the female temperament precluded women from becoming agents. In one interview, Hoover said that when he was authorized for two thousand agents, he would consider hiring women (by 1935, the government employed just over six hundred). Although a woman "probably could learn to fire a gun," he granted, he could not imagine "a woman shooting it out with gangsters." In fact, women were too valuable as office staff to permit them to go into the field: "A man's secretary makes him or breaks him," the director said.[59]

If special agents were the most visible sign of Hoover's masculinized reform model, they nevertheless relied on vast numbers of unseen female laborers. Chief among them was the director's executive secretary, Helen Gandy, a pillar of support throughout his professional life. A single woman who came to Washington, D.C., during World War I from southern New Jersey, where (as one reporter wrote) "small towns are strung like beads on a ribbon," Gandy began as a messenger and was assigned to Hoover as a secretary during the Palmer years. As the most senior, and most influential, woman at the bureau, Gandy agreed that women would be bad agents. They could probably be trained not to gossip and tell secrets, she conceded, but women were physically unsuitable and "couldn't do the work."[60]

Ironically, the successful agent's masculinity was compromised daily by internal bureau demands for submission to authority. As one reporter noted acidly in 1933, "A common practice with a much-publicized bureau in a much-publicized but weak and ineffective department is firing employees as 'insurrectionists' or for typographical or other minor errors because they have resented the petty tsarism of the director and his staff of 'boot lickers.' "[61] Learning the importance of feminine subordination to supervisory staff was important to an agent's training. When Melvin Purvis protested a reprimand for lateness because the office clock was fast, an inspector responded, "This man's attitude is not exactly right and he should receive close supervision until such time as it is determined whether or not he is breaking other rules of the department which he does not believe are fair rules." Agents showed good discipline by mastering housekeeping tasks that would ordinarily be undertaken by women; others were reprimanded for "desks . . . littered with papers," "some useless articles in the drawers of the desk," and "a pair of shoes and a pair of rubbers in one of the clothing cabinets."[62]

Feminine subordination provided the basis for an authority structure that one historian has labeled patriarchal. One agent nearly lost his job for challenging the absolute nature of this authority. "The Bureau feels that you are subject to specific censure," Hoover wrote,

> for at least the poor judgement exhibited by you, which enabled the impression to be gained that you were belligerent and argumentative. Under no circumstances will the Bureau tolerate any attitude of insubordination or anything connected therewith in the dealings of an Agent with his official superior. Instructions . . . should be obeyed by the Bureau's agents without question and immediately.[63]

As veterans of the bureau have pointed out, such shaming tactics often led to the appearance of good discipline and a reluctance "to ask questions, possibly through fear of displaying lack of knowledge."[64]

An effective publicity apparatus extended the director's masculinity to his agents and mitigated internal rebellions against authority. For example, in 1932 bureau labor practices came under scrutiny: the Washington scandal sheet *Brevities* aired anonymous charges of administrative backstabbing and overwork at head-quarters. Clericals, the anonymous writer revealed, had rebelled against work-ing with the windows open, a practice instituted by the director because he believed they would work faster if they were cold. In what appears to be a direct response to these publicized abuses of authority, in 1933 Hoover launched the *Investiga-tor,* a house organ with news, gossip, and cartoons; he also announced an intra-mural sports program for female employees.[65]

The seduction of influential audiences outside Washington was also crucial to Hoover's bid for a national reputation. Through the Washington press corps, many of whom were nationally syndicated, Hoover promoted himself as an expert in manly good government and professional policing. Political columnists, who specialized in floating rumors, were crucial to the creation of favorable innu-endo; hence, a steady stream of articles appeared in Boston, New York, and other major urban newspapers as early as 1920 that identified Hoover as the "foremost Federal expert in the investigation of radical activities" and as someone who was "regarded as one of the ablest men in Washington."[66]

The new Bureau of Investigation was built not just on image but on the train-ing and retraining of police experts in a masculinized, professional model, a process that is amply revealed in the personnel files of several agents who were closest to Hoover during and after the war on crime. The process of making an appli-cant pool of diversely talented men into agents of uniform quality was meticu-lous. However, agents did not experience it the same way, nor did bureau disciplines produce agents who were particularly similar except in their appar-ent devotion to duty and the director and, most important, an almost exclusive dedication to building a career as a federal officer.

Building a Career as a Government Man

In 1930, Hoover was designated as one of the nation's "most eligible bach-elors," reflecting not only his own unmarried status but the image of the bureau itself as a bachelor society of dedicated career men. In July 1931, his third year of employment with the Bureau of Investigation, Clyde Tolson dictated his per-sonal information to a secretary, in an annual memorandum that would go to Direc-tor Hoover, in accordance with Section 33 of the Manual of Rules and Regulations. Tolson was a member of the Masonic Order, the Sigma Nu Social Fraternity, the Phi Delta Phi Legal Fraternity, and the District of Columbia's University Club. He was an officer in the Army Reserve and had taken his bachelor's and law degrees at George Washington University. Dependents? "None," Tolson responded in answer to item F. Marital status? "Single." There is a vertical double slash to the left of this last item, a margin notation Hoover used when he was amused or wished to emphasize a particular piece of information.[67]

Biographers agree that even as early as 1930, Hoover preferred to appoint to supervisory positions men who had institutional, and particularly fraternal, affiliations similar to his, eventually creating around him a close group of bureau administrators with whom he shared a variety of ritualized and distinctively male social ties. By the early 1930s, men at the upper levels of the bureau would have made annual reports similar to Tolson's: Kappa Alpha, Sigma Nu, the Masons. Youth organizations that promoted masculine value systems, such as cadet corps and the Boy Scouts, also counted in an applicant's favor. These patterns project Hoover's belief not only in the correctness of his own career path but also that virtuous men were not born but made as they adopted institutional values and disciplines.

Questions about Hoover's private life and the role of favoritism at the bureau have obscured an equally significant pattern of career similarities among those who succeeded at their jobs in these early years. The director sought out and promoted able men who replicated his own institutional history, virtually none of whom had any background in police work. Tolson exemplified a career path almost identical to Hoover's, having elected to climb the bureaucratic ladder at the War Department while attending law school at night. Melvin Purvis was, like Hoover, southern, solidly middle class, and unmarried and took a five-year law course instead of going to college. Like Hoover, Purvis was captain of his high school cadet company, and at the University of South Carolina he joined Kappa Alpha. Edward Tamm's application also suggests that a certain career path was becoming known to bureau aspirants. A member of Sigma Nu, he had altered his undergraduate program to take advantage of Georgetown's LL.B. in 1930 and explained to his interviewer that he had done it to become "a Special Agent in this service, and that if given the position he [had] no intention to practice law."[68]

Hoover's recruitment policies were purposeful. Although the status of "special agent" was an institutionally produced identity, as agents willingly subordinated themselves to the bureau's values, they brought to the Department of Justice a sense of virtuous, masculine enterprise. One of these virtues was the sacrifice of a lucrative, private career. Posted to the Atlanta office on January 24, 1927, Melvin Purvis's starting salary was twenty-seven hundred dollars per year, plus four dollars per diem expenses. This starting wage rose little over time: in 1930, Edward Tamm was appointed at twenty-nine hundred dollars. Not surprisingly, candidates were closely investigated for their feelings about money. Purvis was described by a former employer as being "not hard-boiled enough when it came to getting the utmost dollar for the Insurance Company in a settlement." The director also marked with a double slash another opinion that Purvis would not be a successful attorney "as he was not aggressive enough in going after the dollars. Not that he was not industrious and ambitious, but he . . . he was [not] cut out for a money maker." Clyde Tolson was praised by a former supervisor for having "no particular interest in women" and therefore no need for money. If Tolson had been "of a mercenary temperament," the report continued, "he could have derived a great number of benefits" from his position, but having been "tried . . . in a discreet manner," he was "found to be above reproach." The investigation of applicant Tamm noted that he had never earned more than eighteen hundred dollars a year.[69]

If an initial meeting with an applicant was successful, the candidate was fully investigated. Gentlemanly demeanor and professional middle-class values dominated the inquiry, particularly in the preponderance of questions about the prospective agent's character, comportment, moral rectitude, and manners. A former mentor commented that Tolson met people "exceptionally well" and was "very diplomatic in handling callers" that came into that office. "[He] is very courteous, absolutely trustworthy and is an exceptionally bright, clean cut young man." Another supervisor was asked "whether or not [Tolson] drank, and . . . stated that the applicant was not a drinking man." At least as important to judging Tolson's skills as a gentleman, however, were the times he *did* drink. On a trip, Tolson's superiors

> had things very much their own way [and] there was considerable drinking en route. Mr. Martyn stated that he saw the applicant taking a few drinks during this trip but was very gratified to see how applicant carried himself and refrained from any excessive drinking and only did so upon occasions when, due to the nature of the trip, it would have been a social error on applicant's part to have refused.

Another referee agreed that Tolson was "likeable and efficient," had "an exceptional faculty of meeting people well," and handled office matters "with an exacting precision."[70]

Other investigative reports reflect a contemporary emphasis on physical appearance, background, and demeanor—in other words, a belief that the body could be read, categorized, and measured to reveal character and personality. The investigative report on Melvin Purvis noted that he came "from one of the best families of the state," that his "reputation and character were of the highest[, and] . . . that everyone who came in contact with him liked him." The investigator concluded from these interviews, and from meeting the applicant, that Purvis was "a young man of excellent character, good intelligence and manner and that he [could] be developed into a good agent." By 1930, when Ed Tamm applied, examiners used a form that detailed many categories for evaluation, including "Personal Appearance," "Conduct during Interview," and

"General Intelligence." Subcategories such as "Dress" gave the interviewer a choice between "neat," "flashy," "poor," and "untidy"; the section marked "Features" offered "refined," "ordinary," "coarse," and "dissipated" (Tamm was neat and refined). The interviewer had to evaluate personality, poise, speech, assurance ("overconfident" was one possibility), nervousness, foreign accent, and tact ("tactful," "average," and the dismal "lacking" were the choices). Like that of Purvis, Tamm's investigation was a success, revealing him as a "gentleman" and the son of "very high class people."[71]

A successful investigation, personal interview, and dictation test put a candidate on an "eligible" list from which Hoover filled vacant positions. If the investigation focused on intelligence, character, and class, the period of training, probation, and appointment to full special-agent rank was dominated by the surveillance, critiques, inspections, and reprimands that constituted ongoing training in the field. Like a military recruit, the new agent turned his life and decisions over to the federal government without reciprocity: bureau rules mandated that an agent who was dismissed in his probationary period of two months would not even get a train ticket home. "You should so arrange your personal matters before taking oath of office that you will be able to accept assignment to any part of the country where your services may be needed," Hoover instructed Tamm.[72]

During the probationary period, senior agents, supervisors, and inspectors scrutinized the candidate, noting those qualities that should be cultivated. Tamm's interviewers and the training supervisor remarked on a "latent executive ability" that would "develop with experience." The "discovery" of this ability may have coincided with Tamm's early interest in administration. In March 1931, he wrote a memo to Hoover containing suggestions for improving the courtroom admissibility of signed statements by a standardized form he had devised; a second memo in 1932 suggested changes in the bureau's identification system; and later that year he volunteered for a correspondence course in bookkeeping and accounting.[73]

Assigned to the New York office as an administrator in 1932, Tamm was unfavorably reviewed after one of the director's characteristic pop inspections, and the critique reveals Hoover's belief that good administration was the key to professionalism. Low morale and poor loyalty among the investigative staff were caused by administrators who assumed "a snobbish or an unapproachable attitude ... at all times." One was "devoid of personality. ... His crudeness and 'hardboiled' attitude towards the Agents [were] shown by the incident at the so-called 'pep' talk when he made the statement that he felt like clipping one of the men on the chin." Tamm assumed "a very snobbish or superior attitude towards the Agents." Further, "His only accomplishment is that of being able to 'wise crack' or indulge in insignificant criticism. His ability as an investigator is not known but he does not know the proper attitude to assume towards men who are seeking sound advice in carrying out their duties." Only two agents had the proper "attitude": one was "fairly impressive," and another had "a pleasant, tactful, yet firm, manner."[74]

Agents coped not only with official inspections but also with a more pervasive and informal system of peer surveillance. Tamm's deficiencies in the New York office did not hinder him, but eighteen months later, appointed acting special agent in charge of the Pittsburgh office, he faced a more serious charge stemming from a casual exchange with the outgoing supervisor, E. J. Connelley. Tamm had boasted of curing a cold with three fingers of "the old-fashioned with some lemon," and Connelley reprimanded him. The next day, Tamm had mentioned having a drink again. Connelley reminded him,

> As Special Agents in Charge we should lean over backwards in supporting any rule that is for the stability of the service; that we . . . can best support [the director] by living up rigidly to all the rules which promote the interest of the service and the interest of the Director . . . that [Tamm] had placed me in an embarrassing position in this due to his action in supposedly telling me this in confidence but that . . . there could be no such confidence; that where it was a matter of friendship and the best interest of the service and the Director, friendship ceased. . . . I wanted him to fully realize my position and what would be the best example for those under him.

Reprimanded by Hoover, Tamm responded angrily that Connelley's memory was "absolutely false." The explanation must have been accepted, for he was still in charge of the Pittsburgh office in the spring of 1933 when Hoover wrote him a friendly, social note beginning "Dear Ed."[75]

Whereas Tamm was on a fast track to an administrative career—one that culminated in a promotion to assistant director by 1936 and an appointment as a federal judge in 1948—Purvis's route to the rank of special agent in charge at the Chicago office was investigative. First assigned to the Minneapolis office, Purvis was supervised by an experienced agent who gave him responsibility slowly. He was put in charge of routine interviews, and his progress was initially "satisfactory"; Special Agent Perry Watzman reported to Hoover that he was "coaching [Purvis] to be persistent and thorough," qualities that Watzman believed to be "of prime importance." Watzman suggested that, although Purvis was competent to "handle certain [tasks] alone, though under supervision," he be supervised by different agents, since "no two . . . have the same line of approach and the same ideas therein." He continued, "It occurs to me that wherever possible the new Agent should have the benefit of working with several experienced ones, so as to avoid the possibility of getting too narrow a conception."[76] While uniformity was one goal of professionalism, the intellectual work of policing required the discovery and cultivation of individual talents.

Hoover's personal interest in these three agents displays both the severity and the obligations of patriarchal power. Whereas the director scrutinized Purvis's fifteen-minute absence on November 2, 1927, his explanation for it, and an inspector's judgement "that he was inclined to believe it," we also find Purvis thanking Hoover for his "kind note of sympathy" when Purvis's mother died. Several pages later in the Purvis file there is yet another dispute over lateness brought to Hoover's attention: "I asked to see his watch and compared the same with mine which I had set by Western Union before coming to the office," his exasperated supervisor wrote. Later, while chief clerk in the Washington office, Purvis made numerous supervisory errors that he was required to explain directly to Hoover: apologies for typographical errors in documents sent to Washington, which identified the clerical worker responsible and noted his own failure to catch the error; conflicting orders sent to an agent; and agents sent on the wrong assignments. "This is the kind of thing which makes us look ridiculous," Hoover fumed about one of Purvis's mistakes.[77]

Purvis's bungling of this job may have convinced Hoover that he had no administrative talent, but the transfer was handled carefully to preserve Purvis's confidence in his abilities. "There has been some question raised as to the advisability of having an Agent with legal training assigned to the Chief Clerk's position," the director wrote kindly in May 1929; "and, consequently, I have reached the decision . . . to assign you to field duty." Transferred to the Columbus, Ohio, office, Purvis immediately apprehended two fugitives; and in the fall he was given the opportunity to supervise the office in preparation for taking over as special agent in charge. His supervisor, L. C. Schilder, reported to Hoover that Purvis had "naturally made a number of the errors of a novice on the desk." However, Schilder approved a promotion on the grounds that he was "very capable," would "improve with experience," and possessed the capacity for "at least an average Agent In Charge or #1 man": "[I] feel that under any circumstances he would be absolutely loyal, dependable, and give the best of his services." Again, attitude and character were at least as important as performance. Purvis's efficiency rating, which gained him yet another promotion, scored him in the high 80s and low 90s (out of 100) in all categories but a dismal 80 for "executive capacity." However, in "Attitude toward Work," which included "attention to duty; loyalty to the service; amenability to discipline; dependability," Purvis scored 100.[78]

This evaluation, added to other commentary on Purvis's first few years in the bureau, suggests a number of different institutional values balanced against each other in a fast-moving career from trainee in late 1926 to assistant SAC of the

Chicago office, a post that Purvis would assume in the spring of 1930. Although Purvis was not willing, or able, to pay attention to the detail that would make for an administrative career, both Hoover and several of Purvis's supervisors recognized that investigative ability required a different set of talents that could be harnessed and cultivated but not necessarily replicated. In fact, Purvis's attempts at stern leadership were invariably misplaced and badly timed, causing agents to appeal his decisions. One dispute was "petty in the extreme," wrote a disgusted Harold Nathan. "Both individuals should develop considerable maturity. . . . It is too small a matter for the Bureau to dignify by any form of ruling." In another case, SAC E. J. Connelley admitted to the director, "I don't think [the agent] would have gone so far with me."[79]

In 1931, Purvis was transferred to the Cincinnati, and then to the Washington, field offices as special agent in charge. In this latter post, he was directly under Hoover's eye again, and his file once more reveals the director's personal interest in Purvis's development—which often resulted in even more exacting criticisms. After a nasty exchange between Purvis and a reporter from the United Press (in which the reporter may have been trying to use bureau connections to evade an overdue bill from the *Encyclopedia Britannica*), Hoover upbraided his agent: "[Name deleted] cites that your attitude was brusque; that you were discourteous to him, and that you made the remark that if he paid his bills promptly he would not have any trouble. Such a remark, of course, if made, was most indiscreet. It is my desire that all Bureau employees be courteous at all times in dealing with representatives of the press." Such outbursts of temper were often followed by kindness. "Better speak to Purvis about this personally when he returns," Hoover noted in the margin the same day.[80]

Hoover's early management techniques included an intense interest in the individual; this could end an agent's career quickly or, as in the case of Purvis, Tolson, and Tamm, ensure a quick rise to the top. "I was somewhat concerned when I learned of your illness," one typical note to Purvis read. "It would be far better for you to put in only a few hours a day until you have fully recovered from the effects of the flu." Whether Hoover's interest was fatherly, brotherly, or erotic is hardly important; what is crucial is that Purvis had passed through a series of trials and tests that had resulted in his elevation to a select brotherhood of men whose most significant relationships were first to Hoover and then to each other. In January, Purvis was made acting agent in charge, and an inspection report detailed his full maturity as a "Government Man." Inspector Hugh Clegg informed Hoover,

> [Purvis] immediately impresses one with his outstanding qualities and good judgement. . . . He is a strict disciplinarian. As soon as he senses a situation

he is immediately right on top of it and has the situation well in hand; in fact his strictness in this regard may be carried slightly too far in some instances, when he would be prone to consider an unintentional remark or action on the part of a subordinate employee a little too seriously. Mr. Purvis's loyalty is intense. He has a feeling that as a part of the Bureau it is his organization, and he is willing to go the limit for the organization and for anyone connected with it, from administrative officials down to the lowest salaried clerical employee; yet, if an employee gets off the reservation he is equally alert to protect the Bureau's interests as he interprets them.

Clegg also reported that Purvis had built excellent relations with other Department of Justice officials in the area, as well as with the Chicago police.[81]

Certainly Purvis had built excellent relations with Hoover. If the director could be endlessly critical in his desire to train the perfect agents and administrators, his watchful eye also saw that, in the summer of 1933, his organization was beginning to respond to the crime wave as a professional, national police should. Looking forward, perhaps, to expanded responsibilities in a new administration, Hoover wrote to Purvis:

> I wanted to express to you, and through you to the Chicago office . . . my appreciation of the loyal and whole-hearted response given to the many heavy demands which have been recently made upon that office. I have been fully cognizant of the long hours which the personnel has been devoting to its work and it has meant much to me that the attitude of the personnel of the Chicago office has been of such a high degree of loyalty.

Indeed, Hoover's mood was so light that a stenographic error that summer drew no criticism whatsoever. "My attention has been called to my letter to you dated July 1, 1933, specifically to Section 'A' thereon indicating my personal status at the time," Purvis apologized. "I regret to inform you that I did not get married."[82]

"Ha! Ha!" Hoover noted gleefully at the bottom of the letter.

By 1933, Hoover's reformed bureau epitomized the principles of police professionalization that were articulated at local and state levels. As Franklin Delano Roosevelt rolled to a victory in November and Prohibition repeal seemed certain, the Democrats began to look at crime as one area of social policy that could be addressed by a new administration. Rumors surfaced after the inauguration that the government would indeed take action against a new breed of criminals, auto bandits and kidnappers, who seemed to have been spawned by Prohibition and nurtured by thirteen years of growing criminal influence over major cities. Journalists speculated as police professionalization experts like August

Vollmer and Raymond Moley were mentioned as possible candidates to combine all thirty-two hundred federal special agents into a Democratic "super–Scotland Yard" for a possible war on crime.[83]

Would Hoover's reforms lay the groundwork for another policeman's career? If Hoover was retained after serving in three Republican administrations, one newspaper editor predicted in early July, "wise guessers lose."[84] Bureau staff clipped hundreds of newspaper column inches and sent them up to the director's office, where he matched the latest Washington rumors about his future to information picked up in urban squad rooms and federal hallways. Keeping an eye on other candidates and lobbying his political networks furiously, Hoover seemed serene, giving interviews about the bureau's work and refusing to answer questions about the future. In the increasingly urgent anticrime climate, he had as yet no legislative mandate that permitted him to move against spectacular crimes. Indeed, Special Agent J-8 was probably better prepared to fight banditry and kidnapping than his real-life G-man pals, still carrying pens in antitrust and bankruptcy cases and, although trained to shoot, not permitted to arm themselves for a routine investigation.

Three

"People No Longer Respect Respectability"

The Making of a Crime Wave

Do not fix laxity of law enforcement upon the police agencies. It is the fault of the public. People no longer respect respectability. It is not disrespect for law. Our problem today is whether the forces of government or outlawry must dominate. You must be either with or against government. There is no middle ground. We must have the support of the public. Citizens of this country must become enemies of crime.

— J. Edgar Hoover, *The National Police Officer* (July 1931)

Starting in with the decay of morals and religion, with the breaking of homes and with untoward economic conditions, the youth is further handicapped by an intense and growing contempt for the law.

—Arthur B. Reeve, "The Vicious Circle" (1934)

J. Edgar Hoover's modernization of the Bureau of Investigation helped it survive and flourish during the political crisis that precipitated the collapse of the Bureau of Prohibition. In addition, the director's most persistent theme in these years, the emergence of new criminals and the decay of public morals, kept him at the forefront of popular debates over the decline of respectability. The language of morality found a particularly receptive audience among police and politicians at the local level, increasingly preoccupied by a rise in violent crimes against property. The apparent demise of respectable citizenship was often understood as the outcome of new consumer pleasures, producing a crime wave perpetrated by young criminals of an entirely new type. Thus, the reconfiguration of the criminal subject as a psychopathic public enemy, which fused

57

older sociopathic and hereditary models with a postwar emphasis on moral decline among adolescents and young adults, drove demands for stringent police repression that survived the anti-Volstead backlash.[1]

This decline in public respectability was firmly embedded in the notion that promiscuous opportunities for consumption entrapped the unwary, luring otherwise "respectable" young men and women to criminal habits. Contemporary assertions that such crimes represented an increased and vital threat to social stability set the terms for local police policy in the twentieth-century United States more generally, and like other police ideologies, they quickly filtered up to the Bureau of Investigation.[2]

Popular crime literature pointed to the particular vulnerability of middle-class worlds, as the sumptuous pleasures of the postwar years transformed the character of leisure time. Journalists reported the decline of formerly respectable communities like St. Paul, Minnesota, now a honky-tonk gangster hangout; other districts long famous for disorderly pleasures were now openly patronized by respectable consumers. Twentieth-century social scientists confirmed these dismaying new habits, characterizing modern life as hopelessly confused. "A citizen has one foot on the solid ground of established institutional habits and the other fast to an escalator erratically moving in several directions at a bewildering variety of speeds," wrote Robert and Helen Lynd in a metaphor that linked life choices to a technology closely associated with the department store.[3]

Respectability was under siege from an expanded leisure market that, as William Leach has argued, enticed Americans "into consumer pleasure rather than into work as the road to happiness." Movie stars, athletes, and the denizens of New York's café society came to represent this alternative set of pleasure-oriented values, as did the urban, ethnic celebrity criminal. Speakeasies, in particular, enticed straight citizens to mingle with wise guys and floozies and to flirt with criminal language. In turn, gangsters entered the realm of the respectable public through the legitimate market in pulp fiction, films, and magazines.[4] As Prohibition ended, these literal and imaginative cultural realms permitted middle-class consumers to delight in reversed authority and believe simultaneously that they were insulated from the dangers of violent crime. For example, Cornelius Vanderbilt Jr.'s 1931 article for *Liberty* magazine, "How Al Capone Would Run This Country," portrayed the immigrant liquor king as a conscientious citizen, who had opened soup kitchens in Chicago when city government failed to respond to mass unemployment. As Capone confided to his blue-blooded interviewer, "Us fellas has gotta stick together. . . . I think we both speak the same language; and I think we're both patriots."[5]

The respectable gangster became a paradoxical and powerful site for antistatist consumer pleasure in the pre–New Deal years. As Fred Allen noted, any anticrime effort would have to confront the problem of "tabloid readers, poring over the stories of gangster killings, [finding] in them adventure, splendor and romance."[6] Literary characterizations of celebrity criminals offered, as John Fiske has proposed, "the offensive pleasure of resisting the structures of domination" without becoming tangled in the consequences of crime; thus, the popularity of citizen Capone signals a turn in twentieth-century bourgeois sensibilities. The Vanderbilt article entices the reader by its scorn for the state and its mockery of law, while simultaneously asserting that there is an essential nation to which Capone and the reader both belong. And, as sensational radio journalist Arthur Reeve pointed out, governments elected by those readers were "the greatest racket of all."[7]

Ironically, the normalization of urban mobsters made bandit gangs of young kidnappers and armed robbers seem abnormal by comparison; prominent among the new psychopathic criminals, they provoked renewed pleas for federal enforcement even as the Bureau of Prohibition apparatus was being dismantled in 1930–31. Popular accounts often sought to explain bandits' savage behavior through their apparent youthfulness and theories about failed parenting. But they were also often understood as potentially respectable youths who had been harmed irreparably by the contradictory moral worlds of the Prohibition years. As the Michigan State Prison Board asserted, federal policies had created a new breed of violent repeat offenders who would otherwise have been "leading respectable lives": "After six months to a year of idleness, associating with more vicious criminals, their character is changed and they have started on a criminal career."[8]

Modern Pleasures and Contradictory Moral Worlds

Aimlessness, self-gratification, incoherent identity, and ruptured ties with one's traditions all define the sociopathology of criminality as it was understood by university-trained experts after World War I. As sociologist Paul Cressey argued in his famous 1932 study of urban dance halls, such semicriminal commercial spheres were but symptoms of the "contradictory moral worlds" generated by modern life, places where identities were invented, class and race were blurred, and convention reimagined to suit modern ambitions and desires. Such critiques were not infrequently framed through nostalgia for a vigorous, expansionist (and equally invented) national past. As Edward Burgess wrote in an introduction to Cressey's study:

> The desire for stimulation and adventure normally found wholesome expression in the varied program of events of village life, or in pioneering the settlement of the West. But with the passing of the frontier, the bright-light areas or "the

jungles" of the city became the locus of new experience. Family and neighborhood recreation have declined in direct proportion to the growth of city-
wide enterprises intent upon commercializing the human interest in stimulation.
The result has been to make the pursuit of thrills and excitement a segmented
interest detached from the other interests of the person.

For Burgess, such purposeless and culturally unanchored bodies were inevitably
transformed by the sensations and pleasures offered by modern leisure.[9]

Thus, the commercial sphere became a nexus for understanding the loss of
tradition, the incoherence of modern values, and the reimagining of respectability across class lines. Socially detached and reinvented selves, evading and
remaking the rules of respectability, were also the subject of postwar literary commentary. In Sinclair Lewis's *Babbitt* (1922), a respectable midwestern businessman is nearly torn apart as he is "born on a current of desire." Babbitt's
dissipated behavior was reflected in syndicated gossip columns, as well as scandal sheets such as *Broadway Brevities, Town Topics,* and *Photoplay.* Such vehicles of mass culture invited readers into a world of invented identities where the
notorious antics of old-money heirs and the newly rich advertised a new contempt
for respectability.[10]

During Prohibition, modern consumer pleasure was inextricably bound up
with the rackets that lured victims out of the home and into dangerous, sexu-
alized territory. White youth, as Arthur Reeve warned, was at particular risk:
"Our modern conditions," he wrote,

> have created a strange and unhealthy, little-understood world which lies far out-
> side the ken of decent, ordinary citizens. It is the world of the gyp-joints, the
> villainously ventilated, crowded, glaringly lighted dance halls, with the "Frankie
> and Johnnie" music, the world of petting parties by the roadside in the sub-
> urban counties and in the parks in cities . . . the world of girls and boys who
> stay out all night, often for many nights at a time, and return sullen and
> uncommunicative.[11]

African American middle-class reformers also feared the criminal consequences
of newly urbanized southern black women living outside conventional family
arrangements; clearly, leisure styles in this period were characterized by both
the refusal of conventional respectability and the transformation of failed
respectability into new recreational conventions.[12]

By the late 1920s, the courts were increasingly filled with young shoplifters,
car thieves, and stickup artists whose desire to flaunt respectability seemed com-
pulsive and too often lethal. The psychopathic criminal begins to emerge from
records of petty property crime as a person who was overcome by the unquench-

able desire for unearned luxuries and thrills. Indeed, the more general transformation of consumer desires into necessities in these years made these uncontrollable young adults a particular focus of moral panic following the market crash of 1929, when households economized "in those areas that had become in the last decade so important to the new adolescent styles of life: recreation, automobiles and clothing."[13]

If the psychopathic model shifted blame from society onto the individual, it also, as many cases drawn from the 1930 criminal court session in St. Paul demonstrate, became a useful defense for young, white thieves who claimed to be in the grip of an uncontrollable need for comfort and style. The lawyer for a twenty-year-old female shoplifter explained that she had been forced to falsify a charge account because she "was invited out and felt she was not presentable, so she obtained this clothing." A young man explained that he stole a car because "his feet were so blistered from walking." A maid who lifted dresses, lingerie, stockings, and a string of pearls from her employer told her parole officer that, in retrospect, "she shouldn't have taken so many." A mother told the judge in despair that she knew about her son's burglaries but felt she should not alert the police because he did not "seem to want to live just the way [the rest of the family did]"; further, "When he is not supplied with the things he wants he leaves home."[14]

Different hypotheses, one emphasizing the failure of self-discipline and the other the failure of authority, competed to explain these criminal acts. The first viewed criminality as an inherent tendency, like feeble-mindedness or viciousness, which was provoked by the lure of consumer goods. In this view, crime could be controlled through confinement but not prevented, since these criminals had no ability to moderate or alter their behavior. The other, consistent with postwar individualism, argued that criminals were made and could be unmade through swift and just punishment. These social scientists argued vigorously against simple biological explanations for criminality; instead, they pointed to fundamental institutional failures that needed to be rectified by the state: poor parenting, inefficient policing, and loss of values.[15]

Neither hypothesis could consistently explain the many personalities and delinquent behaviors that constituted property crime, and most criminologists drew on both models to explain the criminal's moral world. In 1926 psychologist Carl Murchison ran tests on a group of felons and on a group of soldiers, discovering that "normal" men (the soldiers) displayed the same range of intelligence as the "enemies of organized society." While the soldiers were of "average" intelligence, the tests demonstrated that criminals were often more intelligent. Great social harm had been done "by the propaganda which creates the impression that the criminal is feeble-minded, and an individual to be fawned over and petted. It would be of greater service if the thinking element in society could have their minds directed to the idiotic expressions on statute books, and the imbecilic attempts to execute such idiotic expressions." If they were not feebleminded, then criminals committed these acts with the full knowledge that they were wrong, a contradiction of intelligence and behavior that could only be punished, not treated: "How frequently we hear the plea that a young criminal has never had a chance, that he has been a victim of circumstances, that his behavior has been determined by his environment! . . . If it has been determined by circumstances that an individual commit crime, let it also be determined by circumstances that a social community will strike back with sure and swift punishment."[16] The category of psychopathic criminality became a way for experts to understand intelligent but incorrigible young felons in the postwar years: "Between 1919 and 1926," Estelle Freedman writes, "the percentage of inmates classified as psychopaths at one men's reformatory in New York rose from 11.6 to 50.8, while diagnoses of mental defect declined sharply."[17]

The diagnosis of psychopathology reconciled the lack of reason attributed to young felons with their obvious ability to plan and execute daring crimes that required strategy, skill, and technical sophistication. The postwar era offered criminals new resources: automatic weapons, fast cars with reinforced steel sides, bulletproof vests, paved highways, hand grenades, and tear gas were a few of the tools that bandits in particular adopted to assault the modern bank. These weapons were adopted at more or less the same moment by the police, vigilance committees, and financial institutions, although the early use of war matériel by urban bootleggers probably put army surplus equipment and military technology into circulation in the underworld first.[18] Automobiles, in particular, marked these criminals as modern, sophisticated, and—a crucial postwar attribute—fast. "Seventy-five percent of all crimes now are perpetrated with the aid of the automobile," crime writer George C. Henderson estimated in 1924. He further asserted, "Automobiles and good roads have done much to increase certain kinds of banditry. We now have a definitely established type called an automobile bandit who operates exclusively in motor vehicles, whether it is to perpetrate a holdup on a bank or merely to stick up pedestrians and rob homes."[19]

Like the criminologists cited above, Henderson wrestled with contradictory notions of how crime was produced and what a criminal intelligence was. This was a particularly difficult problem for the journalist or popular writer, who had to entice a respectable reading audience with an intricate knowledge of a thriving underworld, obtained by a man who was intimate with criminals but not protected by the respectability of a university degree. Establishing his expertise through stolen insider knowledge, he thus needed to reassert his credentials by assuring his audience that crime did not pay and that criminals would always be defeated. While the crime writer purportedly satisfied the public's desire for knowledge about the underworld, he also produced new and intriguing questions: Were criminals more intelligent than law-abiding folk or less? Were they unreasoning psychopaths or worthy subjects of study for Henderson and his fellow experts?

Like the criminologists, Henderson affirmed all possible answers to these questions in a narrative move that typified much of the popular writing about banditry in this period. In explaining how a group of working men who seemed to be good citizens turned out to be vicious bank bandits, Henderson explained:

> If we look deeper into this . . . we find the true cause for these workmen turning criminal. The leader came from a low family, his home life during boyhood had been vicious, he had no education nor other wholesome interest, his associates for years had been of the worst kind and a number of his family were even then in the penitentiary. He had escaped a career of crime this long only by accident. The other two men were psychopathic inferiors or "dumb bells" who could be persuaded into anything by a man with a glib tongue. The little man especially was deficient and weak and had insane ancestry.

In the case of another gang, "the leader was a 'border-line' case, being neither feeble-minded nor completely normal. The others were typical subnormals."[20]

Henderson's argument that the relative normality of criminals could be discerned by their position in the gang was a popular, although muddled, idea drawn from professional sociological theory. It explained criminal successes by suggesting that the underworld paralleled the legitimate world in its organization and logic: bandit gangs were made up of leaders and followers. Leaders were individuals who might otherwise been normal, had they not suffered severe and irreversible psychological damage. Followers—or the majority of criminals— were hereditarily damaged and thus susceptible to the perverse influence of a criminal elite. In a conclusion that summarized the causes of crime, Henderson foregrounded the idea that every criminal group exhibited hierarchies of pathology and intelligence. "In some penal institutions as high as 75 per cent of the inmates are morons or deficients of one classification or another," he wrote.[21] Thus, it might be clear to the intelligent reader that at least one-quarter of those imprisoned (a criminal elite corresponding numerically perhaps to any institutional elite) were indistinguishable from respectable people.

Moreover, this elite was made up of intelligent, reasoning young men whose physical power rested on their ability to manipulate other men (and, presumably, women) and whose behaviors were governed by the desire for thrills and endless, unearned wealth.[22] Bank robbers, stickup artists, and killers who became the focus of anticrime efforts by the early years of the depression were not understood as new and dangerous by respectable citizens because they were more violent than other dangerous populations, although in many cases they were. Rather, new models of deviance were articulated in this period that identified pervasive criminality as part of a larger cultural tendency toward the production of incoherent, ungoverned (and ungovernable) selves.

Armed Robbery and "New" Criminals

Because the war on crime is often viewed only as "a highly political publicity campaign" in which J. Edgar Hoover's desire for power coincided neatly with New Deal ideologies, the persistent belief among many police departments, banks, and citizen groups that vicious, new criminals posed a drastic threat to community well-being in these years has been easily obscured.[23] However, after 1925, the idea of a crime wave was convincing enough to spawn desperate editorials and demands for national police coordination and state highway patrols across the nation, particularly in the mid- and southwestern states.

It is tempting to link, as some historians have, the rash of bandit crimes that began after 1925 and continued into the early years of the Great Depression to a corresponding rise in unemployment and farm failures in these states. Evictions and mass unemployment drastically altered the fabric of social life in this region: families often broke up for a time, churches closed, people migrated in search of work, and strangers unattached to families became commonplace in communities of all sizes. As institutional life appeared to weaken, young, white men became prominent among the ramblers, hoboes, and day workers crowding cities, towns, and county seats. By 1930, census figures for Arkansas, Oklahoma, Kansas, Missouri, and Indiana showed two to three times as many Caucasian men between the ages of fifteen and twenty-nine as in all other adult male groups combined.[24]

This excess of transient young white men contributed to a growing unease about the consequences of the boom economy, which intensified when the stock market crash in 1929 added industrial workers to the ranks of the unemployed. White and black resistance to economic subordination coalesced into activism during these early depression years, and such challenges to the authority of the state by formerly respectable and relatively silent rural people alarmed policymakers and middle-class urban dwellers further. Violent and nonviolent demonstrators sought accountability from institutions: banks, railroads, insurance companies, chain stores, and the officers of the law who protected them. Moreover, the unemployed and impoverished called for justice in the language and rituals of Populist and patriotic movements, defending their own respectability and branding capitalists as criminal.[25]

This politicized atmosphere heightened the significance of bandit criminals, whose terroristic and murderous crimes targeted the same institutions. By 1926, the Bureau of Investigation's Oklahoma City office recognized the increase in well-organized bandit gangs in the region, opening one file on the Kimes-Inman gang, a mob that included Herman and Lloyd Barker, the eldest sons of future federal public enemy "Ma" Barker. Oklahoma, as I argued earlier, was a symbolic site for such conflicts; it was also the geographical linchpin of several contiguous mid- and southwestern states stretching from Minnesota to Texas that were well known for high rates of auto theft, bank robbery, stickups, and kidnapping. In the midst of this "crime corridor," as J. Edgar Hoover would call it in the 1930s, were three states whose borders formed a "tristate area"—Kansas, Missouri and Oklahoma—where gangs of armed robbers struck quickly and then eluded pursuit by crossing a state line.

The following story offers evidence about this new type of criminal youth and suggests how the psychopathic model became a powerful explanation for failed middle-class respectability and the descent into working-class viciousness. On July 8, 1930, Jimmie Lee and Thurlow Wilhite entered the R. P. Ritchie grocery store in Wichita, Kansas, and demanded that the clerk empty his cash drawer. Lee, the triggerman, was sixteen, and Wilhite was fifteen. Paul Walker, also sixteen, working in the store so that he could attend college in the fall, fought back and was shot. Grabbing $14.25 from the register, the boys fled to a stolen car; Walker staggered into the street calling for help and died. Arrested in Emporia while attempting to board a Kansas City–bound bus, Lee confessed that the grocery store was one of several planned holdups. When asked why he killed Walker, Lee answered, "I shot him because he made me mad when he swung at me." Jimmy Lee's youth made his case a sensational one, as did the life sentence he received as part of a plea bargain.[26]

The contrast between Walker, a tragic and "respectable" victim, and Lee, a vicious bandit at the same age, was an irresistible story for the *Tulsa Daily World,* which featured the case on its crime page on the day it occurred and when it went to trial. Lee, whose career demonstrated the intelligence, ungovernable desire, and violence that defined the psychopathic criminal personality, was a crime wave in microcosm. He did his first three-day jail sentence at fourteen, followed several weeks later by a seven-day stretch for auto theft and eighteen days for purse snatching. Before he had reached the juvenile age limit of sixteen, he had been arrested thirteen times for petty theft and had been sentenced to reform school as a habitual offender. Lee escaped from there several months later and went on another crime spree. He was picked up and released on burglary charges and was finally jailed for stealing an overcoat. He escaped again and "was captured a few weeks later in still another burglary attempt."[27]

As this story illustrates, the apparent inefficiency and ineffectiveness of local law enforcement contributed to anxieties that a crime wave was sweeping through middle-class communities. Communication between and within systems of justice was so poor that Lee was rarely prosecuted and confined. When he was, he convinced new confederates to help him crash out of old, insecure facilities. After one arrest, he "led three other boys, all fifteen years old, in a jail break. The youths used a tin spoon to scrape away the plaster and remove the first brick, near the floor of the ward. Then they wrapped the brick in a blanket to muffle the sound" and knocked a hole in the wall.[28]

Lee's ability to assume authority easily over weaker boys is an important theme, but the key to his psychopathology was, as the reporter framed it, an ineffective and foolish mother.[29] The parents of the other two fugitives returned them to jail, but not Mrs. Lee, who claimed that her son had "never so much as phoned," even though she had visited him regularly. Asked to explain his crimes, she replied:

> Jimmie's my baby. . . . We must have spoiled him. Since we went broke six years ago in Frederick, he's been hard to handle. Before, we always had plenty of money and we all loved him so much we'd give him what he wanted. Then, it seemed as though he had to have things, no matter how he got them. His father and I often wondered whether there might be something wrong with his mind. Even when he was a tiny baby, he was so nervous that our doctor often warned us about it.[30]

Excessive love, as well as attempts to satiate uncontrollable desires, explained the loss of innocence of this "tiny baby."

Thus, the psychopathic model described Jimmy's vicious character and permitted his mother to evade charges of poor parenting; she protected family respectability by deploying a narrative that encompassed a contradictory moral world easily. It described a son who was, as a doctor had warned, biologically abnormal. It also implied a developmental explanation, suggesting that Jimmy's descent into criminality was symptomatic of a larger social tragedy and the family's fall from comfort. Jimmy's senseless crimes were made comprehensible by evoking a paradoxical, incoherent self that could accommodate otherwise incompatible explanations. Possessing a body at war with itself, he was physically a man with adult desires but emotionally a baby, whose parents had failed to educate him to respectability and honest pleasure. His danger to society was accented, finally, by a crime of sentiment, the rejection of his mother's love.

Abnormal, perhaps, as a person, Jimmy was an utterly normal bandit. A survey of the *Tulsa Daily News* for the year 1930 that focuses on armed robberies, bank jobs, and stickups shows that although he was slightly younger than the average, Lee was part of a population of criminals distinguished by youth. The oldest bandit was forty-one and the youngest fifteen, but on average they were a little over twenty-four (in 1925, Carl Murchison showed that 47 percent of all violent criminals were under the age of twenty-five).[31] Out of 115 incidents, 111 were committed by men of European descent under the age of twenty-five working in teams of two or more. Only one was a woman, described by the press as a "bobbed-haired bandit," but several women were listed as accomplices, getaway drivers, or lookouts. Only three bandits were nonwhite: one team of men was Mexican, and another was black.[32]

At least one bank raid occurred every week in the tristate area in 1930. They almost always provoked a police chase, often joined by state troopers, vigilantes, or deputized citizens. A combination of new, paved highways and intricate back roads made it a land of opportunity for daring criminals who drove fast and knew the country well enough to elude pursuers. State lines were a short drive in any direction, and several cities provided a full array of criminal services: money and securities brokers, hideouts, and underground medical care. Kansas City, Missouri, banks and small-town banks along the Ohio-Indiana border even received national attention for their vulnerability to bandits.[33]

Small businesses in this area were also raided constantly, but bank robbery provided the big payoff. Out of fifty-seven bank robberies reported in the *Daily News* that year, only ten netted less than $100, and the average split for a two- to four-person gang was $5,217. The criteria for a successful bank job are difficult to establish, but in 54 percent, all of the bandits made a clean getaway initially, and in 26 percent, some gang members escaped with all or part of the loot. Stickups of grocery stores, filling stations, and private citizens had a slightly higher success rate, but the profits were much lower. With the exception of a hotel safe heist that netted a pair of bandits $10,000, the majority of stickups were for less than $200 and an average take of $353.[34]

The success rate and methods of these new criminals produced dread and fascination among those who believed that crime was accelerating. Bank robbery was a profitable profession in a time when the average working income in the tristate area was less than five hundred dollars per year. These profits often required extreme violence, and newspapers fed their audience's desire for the spectacular by reporting exchanges of gunfire and hideous injuries sustained on all sides. Through these stories, such as the *Daily News* report on a Lincoln, Nebraska, bank robbery, readers learned that "rod men" forced bystanders and clerks to lie on the floor, that confederates would dump cash drawers in bags, and that failure to obey orders could result in a pistol-whipping.[35]

Victims and bandits described crimes that parallel the psychopathic model emerging in scientific and popular discourse, their stories evoking terror, disjointed memories, and emotional confusion. Bandits recalled uncontrollable jitters, time moving slowly or with lightning speed, and a sense of watching themselves perform the heist. Given their youth and the risks involved, many bandits were undoubtedly frightened and fortified with alcohol; inexperience and adrenaline would account for the rage and sudden aggression witnesses reported. Veteran bank robber Ernest Booth described himself as anxious and apprehensive before a robbery but emotionless while it occurred, "an observing spectator": "The action was flat, commonplace; there was nothing dramatic about it. It seemed to me that everyone connected with it was unnecessarily serious and concerned. . . . If they—those grotesquely frozen figures—could have known the intense turmoil raging within me a few seconds ago!"[36]

Statistically, bandits may have been young because they were soon caught and imprisoned or were killed. Many, as Bureau of Investigation files compiled in the 1930s show, also made contacts with urban syndicates and moved into sedentary occupations like money laundering, pimping, and protection. One bandit who later joined the Barker-Karpis gang, Charles "Big Fitz" Fitzgerald, worked for more than thirty years as a specialist who planned bank robberies and kidnappings, receiving a hefty fee when they were completed.[37]

The psychopathic model also helps redefine the idea of the crime wave: although there were not more crimes in the tristate area than in the rest of the country, their character was changing. Measured by imprisonments, crime actually declined between 1923 and 1934, both in the tristate area and in the "crime corridor" as a whole; significantly, Prohibition enforcement also slowed and then ended during these years. These rural states also had a higher rate of imprisonment than the rest of the country: as the authors of *The Missouri Crime Survey* observed in 1926, urban courts were more likely to dismiss felony cases, suspend sentences, and assign probation.[38]

As total convictions slowed, however, crimes against property rose dramatically, particularly in the Midwest. Rising personal and business losses were documented in detail by insurance companies and were regularly conveyed to the public through crime commissions, attorney generals, and any other government official who held public hearings. Representatives of the Travelers Insurance Company testifying before George Wickersham's national crime commission supported federal policing and pointed out that the crime corridor was leading a national rise in robberies, stickups, and personal property theft. Between 1920 and 1929 the Dallas office reported a jump from 17 claims a year to 965; Gary, Indiana, from 30 to 300; and Saginaw, Michigan, from 9 to 836.[39]

Publicity given to new criminals and new crimes are two important ways to understand the crime wave as a credible concept that justified renewed calls for federal police intervention. However, confrontations between bandits and the communities they attacked are important as well, particularly if we are to understand the dimensions of the violence that came to characterize campaigns against the most spectacular of these criminals, the public enemy. What were the other forms of acceptable or deviant violence that occurred in these communities? And how were individual acts of resistance to bandit aggression part of a repertoire of rural and small-town behaviors that combined to preserve respectability?

Resisting the Crime Wave

Those who experienced bandit attacks firsthand and relayed them to a syndicated national press prepared the cultural ground for the celebrity criminals who appeared after 1930. Paradoxically, the myth of the hero bank robber was produced for a national audience in a section of the country that seems to have been virulently anticrime. Citizens despised and fought bandits; contrary to the Populist romances bandits and sensational journalists recounted, poor and working-class people not only defended themselves against robberies and stick-ups but aided besieged banks.

Although the *Tulsa Daily World* reported citizen resistance extensively, these brutal crimes were often repackaged for urban papers and true crime magazines, producing a crime wave for the rest of the nation. Throughout the 1920s, readers consumed these crimes as modern-day Wild West stories: daring shoot-outs, frightened hostages, and high-speed chases were syndicated and published around the nation. Between 1920 and 1930, the *New York Times* published feature stories on forty-three major bank robberies in the states of Oklahoma, Kansas, Arkansas, Missouri, and Indiana alone, as well as editorials calling for federal action against crime-corridor bandits. Citizens across the country who had never seen a violent crime could imagine that they might, as the physical signs of a literal war against criminals appeared in local businesses. Insurance companies urged banks to adopt armored guards, trucks, and the most modern security: bulletproof glass, steel tellers' cages, tear gas (in 1925, one company offered a 25 percent discount to banks that installed gas devices), and machine gun emplacements.[40]

Expensive fortifications in urban banks put less affluent, small-town banks, and small-town police forces, on the front lines of the crime wave. These banks and police forces called on local vigilance committees and lobbied state and federal officials for harsher sentences and parole reform. Bankers' associations that also represented large, urban institutions supported both strategies. In 1927, the Michigan House of Representatives passed a bill, which was later defeated in the state Senate, reinstituting the whipping post as a penalty for bank robbery, a punishment that one reporter noted had recently been applied in

Winnipeg, Manitoba. In July 1925 the Cook County (Illinois) Bankers' Association offered a reward of twenty-five hundred dollars for every bank bandit killed; a similar organization called the Milwaukee Clearing House offered twenty-five hundred dollars for every dead gang member and only a thousand for the capture of live criminals.[41]

"Perhaps the best indication of the inadequacy of rural police agencies," wrote the authors of *The Illinois Crime Survey* in 1929, "is to be found in the rise and growth of citizens protective associations." Bounties probably encouraged the formation of some vigilance committees, but the high prevalence of lynching and Klan activity in crime-corridor states suggests that these existing organizations found a new mission. Some professional organizations, like the Cook County Bankers' Association, recruited and armed their own vigilance or "bank guards" committees. "Smaller associations for protection against horse thieves and chicken thieves have also appeared," the crime survey noted, illustrating a lack of faith in formal justice and "the current necessity for citizen participation in police work." The Bankers' Association armed more than thirty-two hundred deputies with sawed-off shotguns and rifles, claiming that they reduced bandit attacks from seventy-three in 1924 to fifteen in 1927.[42]

Carl Degler's suggestion that historians "talk about personal violence and not simply crime" suggests a broader cultural context for the rise in vigilance as a solution for the crime problem. Gun ownership was pervasive in the white community reported on by the *Daily World;* in 1930, deliberate and accidental shootings in Oklahoma, Texas, Missouri, and Kansas were a major feature of the daily news. A large number of domestic shootings, in particular, suggest that apparently noncriminal men of all ages were accustomed to treating guns quite casually, using them to fight and brag with. A Kansas man trying to impress his fiancée with a few "cowboy stunts" from the movies accidentally shot her through the head. A young boy was wounded by a small-bore rifle a friend was demonstrating as they waited for a Tulsa street car. Guns were mixed in with other household items: a six-year-old "bandit" held police and neighbors at bay for hours with a loaded automatic he had found on the living room table.[43]

Clearly, widespread gun ownership had an impact on the number of domestic disputes that ended in death by shooting. Almost all of the shootings reported in the *Daily World* for 1930 were committed by men: fewer than 0.5 percent named a woman shooter, consistent with national murder statistics. But stories about women who killed and were killed also reveal the extent of community restraint in policing male violence: all of them contained statements from neighbors attesting to beatings and other forms of abuse. Only the most public and flagrant violations of propriety seemed to persuade local police officers or neighbors to intervene against a male head of household if the violence remained private. For example, Dick Fallis was seen by a police officer "publicly beating" his wife, Minnie, who was "already badly bruised about the face." The officer did nothing until a group of citizens chased and lynched Fallis.[44]

In contrast to family violence documented in early-twentieth-century urban industrial populations, in the crime corridor, gun ownership provided a means for family members to reinforce or subvert hierarchy. Where beatings and threats failed, men shot women; in Texas, where shooting an adulterous wife or her lover was justifiable homicide, such practices were written into law. One deserted Tulsa husband bought a shotgun, having "decided to protect [his] home at any cost." His wife returned to get her clothes, and he told her that she owned nothing in the house. "She knocked on the front door," he told the police, "then she went to the back and started kicking. I hollered at her to stop and she didn't so I shot through the door."[45]

It seems likely that vigilante defenses against bandits, articulated by bankers' associations as a policing strategy for the crime corridor, were an obvious solution, given widespread gun ownership and a high tolerance for individualistic, violent solutions to conflict. Was the crime corridor more violent than other areas of the United States? Perhaps. Sheldon Hackney has calculated that between 1920 and 1924 the rate of homicide in southern or South-influenced communities like the tristate area was 2.5 times as great as the rest of the country. But did this translate into a failure of respectability? No. Violence should be understood in its own cultural and historical context, and unjust or deviant violence was that which exceeded normal community standards.[46]

Banditry, however, not only represented a failure of respectability on the part of the thief; it threatened the victims' respectability as well. Not just theft, bank robbery depended on other violent acts in which the bodies of bystanders, male and female, were shamed and violated. Bank robbers and stickup artists did not hesitate to beat, shoot, and kidnap people at the scene to complete a job successfully. They often terrorized otherwise masculine individuals into inaction, tied them up, and made white men watch helplessly while acts of violence and disrespect were committed against white women. Tristate-area bandit attacks during 1930 show that citizens and law officers were twice as likely to be killed by a bank bandit than by an ordinary stickup man; a total of seven policemen and five bystanders were reported killed in bank robberies that year. Three law officers were wounded by gunfire, and at least thirty-eight bystanders or employees were beaten. In 1930, a bank customer or employee caught in a bank robbery or a stickup had an almost 40 percent chance of being killed, wounded, beaten, tied up, or taken hostage. In other words, bandit crime was an act of public violence, committed by outsiders to the community who violated public and personal respectability, and sparked a repertoire of spontaneous and planned defenses. In 64 out of 114 incidents in 1930, citizens either fought bandits physically, alerted law officers, or, most frequently, participated in posse-style pursuit of gangs.

By 1930, both citizens and bank employees were armed and prepared to defend themselves, a sure sign that they believed they were in the midst of a crime wave. One hot August day in Kansas City, Kansas, a bandit walked up to a teller and ordered him to place one hand on his head and put money up on the counter with the other. The teller fired a gas gun kept in the cash drawer; subsequently, a bank vice president charged out of his office firing a pistol; and finally, the bandit and his gang were chased out of town by passing motorists, some of whom fired out their windows at the getaway car. A similarly violent defense against a stickup artist was mounted by a woman filling station attendant in Joplin, Missouri. When asked for her day's receipts by two bandits, she sprayed the triggerman with gasoline and shot him. The outlaw burst into flames and fled.[47]

Communities assisted each other informally, passing on information and intelligence so that welcoming committees of deputized gunmen could be alerted to roving gangs. A Ponca City, Oklahoma, police informer overheard two men in their rooming house planning an impending job. The police reported this information to bank officials; as the two men entered the bank, a cashier tripped a silent alarm, causing a posse of seven law officers and a reporter for the *Ponca City News* to assemble around the bank. As the Tulsa paper described it later, "A grim reception committee of officers awaited [the] two young outlaws . . . as they emerged . . . with $2000 they had just taken from the safe and when the roar of revolvers had subsided, one robber lay dead, the other wounded by four bullets."[48]

Although no armed citizens described by the *Daily World* were identified, it is clear that many were, and some were organized by banks. In several robberies, depositors or clerks escaped from the bank and notified police, who immediately arrived with armed citizens. In Hardy, Iowa, enraged depositors at the People's Savings Bank jumped into their cars without alerting law officers and pursued three masked bandits, firing at them with rifles and shotguns. At Lincoln, Nebraska, a woman snuck out of the bank on her stomach after being forced to lie on the floor; she contacted a group of vigilantes, who stormed the building too late to catch the six bandits or save two tellers from being badly beaten.[49]

As the high rate of fatalities and injuries illustrates, anyone who disobeyed a bandit did so at the risk of death or serious injury. Therefore, defenses of bank or company money by unarmed citizens (calling for help, refusing to open a safe, or turning on an alarm) were acts of particular courage and conviction. At the People's National Bank of Westville, Oklahoma, a salesman came to make a deposit in his company's account and found two bandits emptying the cash drawers. He waited with his hands up until one gang member approached to take his money and then wrestled him down. The bank president then drew his gun and shot both bandits, killing one. During a grocery store stickup, two Tulsa women began to scream hysterically while a pair of bandits alternately threatened and begged them to desist. Unwilling to kill them in cold blood, or simply too rattled to continue, the thieves fled with only fifty dollars they grabbed from an open till on the way out.[50]

More experienced bandits developed strategies to avoid dangerous confrontations, locking employees and customers in the vault or forcing employees and customers to lie face down on the floor. The watchfulness of small communities often meant, however, that a local person might notice that two well-dressed bank customers were strangers; a neighborly wave might be returned with a stiff grimace; or perhaps the absence of a friendly clerk would create suspicion. An Arkansas mailman was driving by the Bank of Lowell when he saw a robbery in progress; pulling a shotgun from his truck, he shot the lone bandit in the chest. Indignation at theft, murder, and assault was a bond among respectable citizens: in addition to bank employees and depositors, a high school janitor, unemployed workers, and clerks valiantly defended banks and each other.[51]

As we have seen, crime commissions often attributed the crime wave to police inefficiency or corruption, but in small towns and rural areas police appealed to the federal government because they were isolated and outnumbered. The *Daily World* consistently featured sheriffs and police officers responding to bandit attacks with tenacity and courage. A Tulsa motorcycle officer named McGuire saw two stickup men emerge from a drug store and drive away. He "started after the men, calling them to stop, and attempting to force them into a curbing. One man, who was sitting beside the driver, started firing at McGuire and the motorcycle man returned his fire." The chase continued for several blocks, the two vehicles running neck and neck, until one of McGuire's bullets struck the driver. At that point "the companion of the man pulled the driver to one side, and slid beneath the steering wheel," still firing at the policeman. McGuire was shot and his bike overturned.[52]

This newspaper report also suggests how this battle, when it occurred between policemen and dangerous bandits, could produce each as a celebrity figure inextricably linked to the other. Although Officer McGuire was the legitimate hero of the story, the bandits emerged as heroes as well because of their valiant ability to elude him. Crime was an opportunity for men, and sometimes women, to demonstrate bravery, skill, and intelligence in a culture that produced few such opportunities for poor people. As some bandits beat the increasingly determined local police and state troopers, newspaper reporters began to follow them closely. Similarly, police who captured bandits emerged as powerful symbols of the triumph of respectability. But it was bandits who acquired nicknames and national reputations. A pair of Texans became known by their first names only, Bonnie and Clyde. Oklahoma bandit Charles Arthur Floyd was dubbed "Pretty Boy" by a creative newspaperman, and a freelance killer named Lester Gillis became known as "Baby Face" Nelson. As the depression deepened, the naming of bandits became the first step in a process that brought a very few of these men and women to the attention of the Bureau of Investigation.

Four

"It's Death for Bonnie and Clyde"

Romance, Bandit Identity, and the Rise of Celebrity Bandits

The average robber is a ruthless, vicious, depraved enemy of society. There is nothing romantic about him.
—George C. Henderson, *Keys to Crookdom* (1924)

Between March 21 and June 11, 1932, Bonnie Parker wrote a poem while she was being held in the Kaufman County, Texas, jail. Her lover, Clyde Barrow, had escaped a bungled robbery, leaving Bonnie in an abandoned church while he replaced the car that had been shot to pieces by the Kaufman posse. After a miserable day spent among cobwebs, mice, and bats, twenty-two-year-old Bonnie ventured out onto the highway to hitch a ride back to Dallas. The petite, yellow-haired young woman was instantly recognized by police officers and jailed for the only time in her life. Called to bail her daughter out, a distraught Emma Parker was soothed by the jailer's wife, who urged her not to post bond: "Time to think matters over might make all the difference in the world to the child in the future," she advised.[1]

Heartbroken, Emma Parker admitted she had no money for bail. This shame was compounded by Bonnie's imprisonment "in a cell next door to a crazy Negro woman"; for a poor white woman from Texas, an unsegregated public facility was the last line of respectability crossed. While Clyde committed daring robberies in and around Dallas, Bonnie reimagined herself as a romantic gangster's moll in a ballad, "The Story of Suicide Sal." "I fell for 'the line' of a 'henchman,'" she wrote; "A 'professional killer' from 'Chi;' / I couldn't help loving him madly; / For him even now I would die." Years later, Emma would comment sadly that

75

Bonnie's use of bandit slang signified "a strange and terrifying change taking place in the mind of my child."[2]

That passion could persuade a woman to abandon a stable and legal life was regrettable but persuasive to depression-era audiences in the United States. Emma Parker remained bitter about Clyde's influence on her daughter, explaining Bonnie's loyalty to him as the "feminine logic of a woman in love" that had "nothing whatever to do with law and order. Bonnie had become an outlaw at heart because she wanted to be with Clyde."[3] The transformation from innocence to outlawry occurred through the mingling of hearts and the eventual dominance of one "self" over another. Thus, romance and the production of a criminal self were inextricably entwined for those who followed Bonnie's criminal career.

Explaining the bandit career of a man like Clyde Barrow and representing him as a romantic character despite his murderous violence was a trickier proposition. As *Time* magazine reported in 1934 after the lovers were killed in a police ambush,

> Clyde Barrow's youth in Dallas was devoted to stealing automobiles. In 1930 he was sent to prison, paroled in February 1932. Thereafter he still stuck to petty thievery, never got more than $3,500 at one haul, but he did begin to find sport in shooting down, without provocation, people who got in his way— filling station men, constables, plain citizens. In two years he, Bonnie Parker & gang were credited with twelve murders. . . . An awe-struck Press magnified him into one of the "worst killers of the Southwest."

And yet, for Clyde's sister Nell, who collaborated with Emma Parker on *The True Story of Bonnie and Clyde,* these facts did not explain her brother. Clyde and Bonnie were tragic figures "who through circumstances became involved in a life from which there was no going back; on a road that knew no turning; as human beings who, strange as it may seem, had their own code of morals, loyalties and loves, and who lived and died by this code—I am almost tempted to say they died because of it."[4]

This chapter explores the making of two celebrity bandits and argues that the campaign against Bonnie and Clyde was a critical turning point for establishing the politics and narratives that made a federal war on bandit crime possible. For Barrow, and later, John Dillinger, a violent trajectory toward destruction was frequently framed as a fateful collision between a star-crossed individual and an unforgiving state. An early clash with authorities made such a man bitter toward the law, and police harassment turned him to a life of crime. Families often protested that persecution was compounded by official fabrications that fueled public rage. In the summer of 1934 Cumie Barrow, Clyde's mother, was arrested in a Dallas movie theater after footage of her son's mutilated corpse appeared. Screaming, "You can't do that to my boy!" she was dragged away by police but later sued the film company for defamation.[5]

Parents of celebrity bandits also had a personal stake in producing alternative explanations for psychopathic criminal behavior. Cumie Barrow's rage highlights a more generally tenuous grasp on respectability among the poor and marginally middle class as economic decline and the proletarianization of white labor led to "an increasingly precarious existence" after World War I.[6] Relatives of bandits were themselves criminalized in the course of a manhunt, both by the fact of surveillance and by expert discourses that blamed them for raising criminal children. Criminologists Sheldon and Eleanor Glueck pointed to "unwholesome or under-privileged" homes, in which discipline was "unsound." Virtually all of their subjects were judged to have some form of insanity, mental defect, or "peculiarities" in the immediate family, and a majority were nurtured in homes with "low" moral standards. A host of nasty habits preceded serious crime: stammering, nail-biting, bed-wetting, somnambulism, lying, smoking, heterosexual and/or homosexual activity (as well as "sex habits of an undetermined nature").[7] Therefore, in composing alternative explanations for their children's crimes, parents resisted dominant explanations of who *they* were.

But how did petty criminals like Bonnie and Clyde become celebrity bandits—and why was the cultural atmosphere of the New Deal suited to the production of this new identity? If the failure of respectability defines one set of terms for criminal subjectivity, the fragility, and dangers, of pleasure in a modern economy and the satisfaction of social yearnings through consumer pleasure define another.[8] In particular, consuming the news was a new form of modern leisure, one that wove intimate knowledge about exotic strangers into a national vernacular. Because concrete information about them was so rare, bandits were particularly suited to aesthetic and consumer play in a period that was characterized by the explosion of information technologies, particularly newsreels, radio, and syndicated news services.[9] Bonnie and Clyde's crimes were unusual, in part because they were accompanied by brutal murders, often of policemen. In addition, although their crimes netted little wealth, they committed an astonishing number of them, showing an almost superhuman ability to escape from desperate situations and then disappear. As their crime spree drew to a close, more people competed to tell what they knew about these elusive celebrities.

Grabbing at fame and profit, family members, confederates, and bystanders told intimate stories that produced a modern bandit romance. Eventually Bonnie herself became one of these narrators, driven to speak for herself and Clyde so that the "real" or "true" story about them might be told. The eagerness with which producers of the news sought fresh details about criminal personalities became a driving force behind the emergence of a bandit self that could

successfully engage an audience. As one study noted, those who relayed information about bandits became a crucial connection to them and as such were
"performers or informants" who maintained their own celebrity status by
"pleasing the audience, explaining archaic passages, filling in gaps, and rework-
ing and improving the artistic merit" of the story.[10]

Stories about poor people stealing from the prosperous could not help but be
saturated with insinuations about class, justice, and state power. As an author,
Bonnie consciously drew on ideas about liberty and honor to explain Clyde's violence as consistent with the (often masculinist) values of white southwestern-
ers. By the 1930s, antistatist conservative elites framed ideas about property rights
in terms of liberty; conversely, poor and middle-class people often understood
their failure to win or retain property as imposed by outside forces that included
the state. Furthermore, by 1932, the murder of police officers was probably
received ambivalently by the urban poor, since these were the men who enforced
evictions, arrested the jobless and homeless, and sent loved ones off to long prison
terms for petty crimes.[11]

Clyde Barrow and Bonnie Parker did not fight the state in any purposeful or
direct sense, but one could imagine that they did as they survived each violent
conflict with authority. Furthermore, their resistance became necessary because
of the capital crimes with which they had been charged. The inevitability of killing
policemen to save themselves implicitly raised the question of whether their right
to live peacefully had been stolen by the state at a particular moment and
whether state aggression had caused the crime spree. Texans' right to kill in self-
defense was upheld by the Supreme Court in *Brown v. United States* in 1921, and
in the crime corridor, it was not only a mark of courage and manly distinction
but was articulated by courts as "a sacred right of human liberty." In fact, as
Richard Maxwell Brown has argued, the no-duty-to-retreat doctrine was known
"generically as 'the Texas rule.'"[12]

In a short fugitive career that spun romance out of love, money, and impending death at the hands of the state, Bonnie Parker, Clyde Barrow, and others set
the terms for the production of a modern bandit self that commanded fear at the
local level but respect and awe from a national audience as that self reworked
abstract notions of justice and state power through a romantic folk idiom.[13] As
a few successful bandits rose to national prominence between 1930 and 1934, news
reports about their activities offered the possibility for political rescripting,
uncertain resolution, and cultural play on the part of actors and audience. Headline stories that had formerly only reported the "facts" of crimes were supplemented by information acquired from bandits themselves, by their families, and
by witnesses. Experienced at first hand, the bandit was a terrifying and uncivi-
lized menace. Encountered at the level of popular culture, bandits and molls

reworked notions of justice as a powerful counterpoint to the rule of law: figures of romance and ideological longing, they overcame the might of the state with automatic weapons and fast cars.[14]

The True Story of Bonnie and Clyde

Bonnie Parker was born in 1910 in Rowena, Texas, a small plains town near the Kansas line, to bricklayer Henry Parker and his wife, Emma. One of three children, she was left fatherless and suddenly poor when Henry died in 1914. Emma moved her children to her mother's home in Cement City, near Dallas; as one biographer writes, it was "one of the toughest parts of the city and a haunt of criminals." Emma got a job, relying on female kin to care for the younger children until they started school. According to Nell Cowan, Bonnie was a good student, raised "in [a home] of middle class culture and refinement, with ideals, morals and conventions drilled into [her] from birth."[15]

Emma Parker's memories also highlight discipline and order, emphasizing Bonnie's fierce independence and the measures taken to tame it. "My mother had to use hair brushes on Bonnie," she remembered. Despite spanking and watchfulness, however, Bonnie left high school to marry her first sweetheart, Roy Thornton. "Naturally I didn't want Bonnie getting married when she was only sixteen," Emma remembered, perhaps concealing her own sorrow at her daughter's lost opportunity to secure respectability through education; "but she and Roy seemed so determined that I gave my consent." Bonnie's theatricality had been expressed through high-spirited pranks, performances, and emotional outbursts, and now it was redirected to heterosexual passion. Roy was Bonnie's first obsession: at fifteen, she had his name tattooed on her thigh. "When Bonnie loved, she loved with all her heart," a cousin recalled, "and that was the way she loved Roy."[16]

The newlyweds rented a small house down the street from the Parker household, where their love affair quickly soured. "Roy would just walk off and leave her for a month or so, and then come strolling back some afternoon," Emma recounted, causing the heartbroken Bonnie to return home. A diary reprinted in *The True Story of Bonnie and Clyde* shows that by January 1928, Bonnie alternated between having "the blues" for her "roaming husband" and dating other men. Roy was often physically close, taunting his teenaged wife with a series of affairs and flirtations. "I hunted up Reba Griffin today," Bonnie wrote jealously, "just to know that she is not with him." Through with him in early 1929, although they never divorced, in 1930 Bonnie met Clyde Barrow through a mutual friend in West Dallas.[17]

Clyde Chestnut Barrow was born in 1909, the fifth child of eight, to an illiterate tenant farmer outside Teleco, Texas, who may have parceled his children out to relatives to keep them fed and clothed. "The older children are a little hazy in my mind during that period," Nell wrote, "because they were so much older, and Clyde and I had very little companionship with the younger ones because we went away early in life to visit relatives." Socially a cut below the Parkers, the Barrows were caught in a grinding cycle of farm tenancy until they took their chances in Dallas's slums. As Nell recalled, her family "rarely ever had enough to eat, scanty clothes and very few pleasures." She continued, "My father, rather a silent man . . . worked hard in the fields all day, coming in at night worn and weary. He had a single-track mind and plodded wearily from year to year, never getting anywhere. My mother, with so many babies on hand, had little time for anything else but housework. I suppose we weren't a very happy family." The word "happy" may be code here for not having the leisure and small material privileges that, after their move to West Dallas in 1922, Nell saw respectably poor families enjoy. The Barrows also had little energy for governing their children. Nell did not "remember ever getting any spankings": "I don't remember the boys got spanked either, though we certainly all needed it. . . . Maybe spankings would have been the thing Clyde and Buck needed; I don't know."[18]

Poor in fact but not in spirit, the Barrow children were "stormy" but "loyal . . . presenting a solid front to the world, and ready to whip anybody no matter how many or how big." The family had no religious affiliation, and although Nell described herself and Clyde as deliberate truants, it is also likely that frequent moves and the demands of farmwork kept them out of church and school. Resolutely happy memories thinly veil the hardships of tenancy: "We lived in a small frame building of about three or four rooms, I don't recall the exact size, except that many of us slept on the floor. We had to work in the fields, chopping cotton, hoeing corn, doing whatever was necessary, as soon as we were able. I don't recall that we minded it so much because we didn't know any better." Clyde did mind it, however, as did his elder brother. Buck "didn't like to work" and made extra money by stealing roosters and organizing cock fights. Clyde resisted the family labor system with angry outbursts: "When he cooled down he was always exceedingly sorry he'd been so bad, and would try to do anything in his power to redeem himself and get us to laughing again."[19]

When the Barrow family migrated to West Dallas in 1922, Clyde was barely literate, and at sixteen he left school for a series of unskilled jobs. Like Cement City, West Dallas was, according to one description, "a squalid semi-suburb most of whose residents were . . . poor white ex-farmers from the neighboring counties," a crime-ridden, "half-rural slum." The family's first home was a tent under the viaduct; shortly after, Nell married, and Henry Barrow rented a filling station and grocery store. Clyde, who went to live with his sister, soon slipped into the petty thefts and rackets of the Dallas underworld economy.[20]

Both Clyde and Buck belonged to the Root Square gang, specializing in burglary, armed robbery, and auto theft, for which Buck was sentenced to five years at Huntsville Prison Farm in 1926. Clyde was also well known to the police. A Fort Worth identification order, forwarded to the Dallas Bureau of Identification, lists his arrest on February 28, 1928, on the charge "Investigation—General Principles." The file included fingerprints, an alias ("Jack Hale"), and mug shots of an angry, jug-eared white boy with freckles and neatly parted hair.[21]

In the Dallas–Fort Worth area, poor, unemployed, or otherwise "suspicious" characters were routinely rounded up, a surveillance system that provided a regular pool of suspects for ongoing criminal investigations. Most of the arrest reports for the 1920s are missing, but the surviving sample shows that an overwhelming majority of male arrests were made on the grounds of "suspicion" (see first two columns of table 1).[22]

_____ *Table 1* _____
City of Dallas Arrests for Sample Months of 1926 and 1931

Date	White Men	Black Men	Felonies[†]
May 18 – June 26, 1926	361	203	40
July 19 – Aug. 1, 1931	213*	110	28
Aug. 2 – Aug. 31, 1931	571	192	42
Sept. 1 – Oct 3, 1931	615	210	43

____
Source: Figures compiled from the arrest and jail log records for the city of Dallas, the Taxas and Dallas History Collection.
[†] Includes only violent crimes against persons or property.
* Includes Bonnie's husband, Roy Thornton.

The chief method of criminal investigation in Dallas during these years was to round up men and check their alibis. A conviction made a man a permanent suspect. "Please accept my apologies for inadvertently omitting this list heretofore," the warden wrote to the chief of the Dallas Bureau of Identification in May 1932, enclosing records of recent parolees, including Clyde; "especially, as you state, it is causing you a great handicap by not being furnished with these lists forthwith."[23]

When Bonnie first met Clyde, she might have been easily persuaded that he was being persecuted by the police. Certainly he was handsome and, unlike her young husband, experienced with women. The young bandit was about 5'7" with wavy brown hair, a navy insignia tattooed on his right arm, and "a girl's bust" tattooed on the left.[24] Emma watched unhappily as Bonnie lost her heart to another attractive, unreliable man who knew the ugly side of Dallas; Nell hoped that love would turn Clyde around. All in all, Bonnie Parker was the answer to a sister's prayer: "I hoped, when she found out about it, she'd overlook Clyde's police record, make a good boy out of him and stick to him," she wrote. Shortly after they began dating, however, Clyde came over to the Parkers' house one evening and spent the night on the couch. The next morning, he was arrested and jailed on six charges of armed robbery. While Emma admitted that Clyde looked respectable—"more like a young law student or doctor than a bandit"—she disliked this new suitor. As she remembered dryly, "He had what they call charm, I think."[25]

Clyde was taken to Denton, Texas, with confederates Frank Clause and Raymond Hamilton, where prosecutors failed to make a case against him. Authorities in nearby Waco then claimed the gang, and Clyde confessed to two burglaries and five car thefts (probably a plea bargain, since he was sentenced to two years in Huntsville and a fourteen-year suspended sentence.) Bonnie visited her sweetheart frequently, moved to be near him before the prison transfer, and wrote him gushy, romantic letters. Addressing him as "little Darling," "baby," "Sugar," and "Honey," Bonnie told Clyde that her old boyfriends were coming around but she hated them. One brought candy, and she "felt like throwing [it] in his face." Other than the blues, Bonnie's most persistent theme was that they should never be parted again:

> I'm so lonesome for you, dearest. Don't you wish we could be together? Sugar, I never really knew I cared for you until you got in jail. And honey, if you get out o.k., please don't ever do anything to get locked up again. If you ever do, I'll get me a railroad ticket fifty miles long and let them tear off an inch every thousand miles, because I never did want to love you and I didn't even try. You just made me. Now I don't know what to do.

Signed "your baby" and "your lonesome baby," Bonnie's letters tugged at her bandit lover in language learned from movies, radio, and magazines. She used lines from popular songs to emphasize her love ("when you get out I will be happy and 'never cry no mo', no mo'' "); as she wrote, Gene Austin songs on the radio made her miss him even more. After jail visits, Bonnie wrote, her heartbroken tears sent "maybelline streaming down my face."[26]

These overwhelming expressions of love may have been a symptom of Bonnie's fear of losing yet another man. Clyde's devotion to his gang was clearly a source of anxiety, and the prison letters suggest that crime signified the freedom of a wandering life among men, as opposed to restricted, but honest, domesticity with her. Bonnie's chatter about love and their future escalated as Clyde made plans to break out of jail: "Frank [Clause] says you are going far away. I'm sure you wouldn't leave me for him, would you? Of course, he says if you care to have me go along, it'll be o.k. with him, but he says it in a rather disinterested manner. . . . I want you to be a man, honey, and not a thug." Perhaps because of this concern that Clyde would desert her, Bonnie proved her loyalty by stealing a gun and slipping it to him during a visit. Clyde escaped on March 11, 1930; three weeks later, he was recaptured in Middleton, Ohio, while breaking into a railroad office. Identified through the new national fingerprint identification system at the Bureau of Investigation, he was extradited to Texas by the Ohio authorities, to serve his two years and the fourteen-year suspended sentence.[27]

"The Walls," as Clyde called it in a letter to Bonnie, was the harshest prison in a Texas system famous for its brutality. When he arrived, there was one fewer than the almost five thousand inmates Huntsville contained for much of 1930: Buck had escaped a few days earlier. Taken to Eastham, one of eleven farms attached to the Walls, Clyde labored daily chopping cotton, a grueling return to his childhood. Prisoners ran to and from work, guarded by a mounted officer armed with a pistol, a shotgun, and a "bat"—a wide leather strap used for punishment—and "shoot to kill" orders from the warden. Prisoners brutalized each other for small privileges; bribed guards; stole from and raped weaker men. Self-mutilation was a path out of the fields: in 1932, Clyde had a fellow prisoner amputate two toes.[28]

Convict labor systems were designed to extract profit from prisoners, not rehabilitate them. Exposés of southern prisons in the early 1930s, often personal testimony from those who endured them, contextualize contemporary narratives about young men who went into prison for a small offense and came out "hardened" against the law. When interviewed later, a fellow prisoner and Barrow gang member, Ralph Fults, claimed that Barrow acquired "a deep resentment of authority and a bitter hatred of law officers" because of his experiences at Huntsville. Nell remembered that after his parole, negotiated by Cumie Barrow in 1932, she told a sibling that there was "a new air" about him: "a funny sort of something I can't put my finger on—but Clyde's changed. I'm afraid he's not going to go straight, Sis." In contrast, Buck Barrow did resolve to "go straight." On December 27, 1931, persuaded by his new wife, Blanche, Buck returned to Huntsville to serve the remainder of a reduced sentence.[29]

Back in Dallas, Clyde rejoined old confederates, including the recently paroled Raymond Hamilton, and began to plan new robberies. Bonnie, perhaps believing he would leave her forever, did not force him to choose between her and the boys. As Emma Parker remembered their reunion, "Bonnie was hanging around his neck, perfectly radiant, like a fire had been turned on inside her." Clyde kissed her and said he didn't think "a decent girl" would want to see him;

Bonnie, shamelessly consumed by love, "just kissed him back and giggled." On March 20, 1932, she left home, claiming that she was going to a job in Houston, but the next Emma heard from her, she was in the Kaufman jail.[30]

A Life of Crime: Perspectives on United States Bandits

Ironically, Bonnie and Clyde's career as auto bandits was made possible by the state: three hundred thousand miles of hard-topped interstate highways were financed through the Federal Highway Act after World War I. As the Pennsylvania state police explained in 1928, the national rise in armed robbery was due to changes in "the condition of human life. . . . Good highways, motor cars and other means of rapid transit [had] opened up the rural districts to the sudden attack and quick getaway of the criminals of the cities." The Illinois Association for Criminal Justice also blamed the crime wave on the "rapid extension of hard surfaced roads," which brought "many of the characteristics of urban civilization into rural districts which until recent years [had been] remote and relatively inaccessible." Rand McNally published the first national road atlas in 1924, making it possible to plan an escape across several unfamiliar states, particularly in the South and the upper Midwest, where the majority of new highways were built.[31]

It is no surprise that bandits who emerged in the United States during this period were overwhelmingly white and native-born, raised among working people whose migrations between rural and urban areas intensified with better transportation and a worsening economy. Although intermittently employed by urban criminal syndicates, they did not have the kin connections to rise to greater power in those organizations; conversely, since they were ethnically and racially unmarked, they were not bound to the more proletarian tasks of a settled criminal life. As others have noted, these bandits operated in regions of the United States that had been characterized by the bloody political and economic struggles of nineteenth-century western expansion. The tristate area had been bandit territory since the 1840s, as well as the site of Native American massacres and sectional violence. Confederate guerrillas and Union regulars terrorized the region during the Civil War, and during Reconstruction, one band reorganized as the James-Younger gang. Among other characters who figured in the bandit history of the tristate area were the Doolin-Dalton gang, who ranged over northwestern Oklahoma in the 1890s, and Henry Starr, killed robbing a bank in 1921 when he was over sixty years old.[32]

Drawing on the language and history of this folk model, Bonnie and Clyde also emerged at a moment in which state rule and the mechanisms of capitalism were being reorganized. Comparative national accounts of criminals who act in defense of tradition suggest that the elevation of bandits to a politicized folk status can be linked to the history of industrialization: state centralization, capital concentration, and the proletarianization of labor wrench the powerless away from a past that appears in retrospect to be more desirable. Precisely because they articulate a prenational past, bandits are also attractive because they reject modern, state-centered political solutions; Eric Hobsbawm's insistence on the centrality of outcast status argues that acts of banditry are

> abstracted from social and political reality: these, therefore, distinguish the traditional social bandit from his latter-day imitators or equivalents. Most people . . . did not *choose* outlawry (except, where banditry was an established way of earning a living, as a professional career). They were forced into it by what neither they nor their society regarded as a criminal act, and the rest followed.

Social banditry is virtually a counterpolitics, acted out by politicized selves produced through an audience at particular moments of expanding state authority and/or nation building.[33]

In the case of Bonnie and Clyde, this counterpolitics was coupled with a sensibility that spoke directly to modern desires. In fact, their success argues more generally that, where state expansion succeeds, as it did in the United States, new generations of bandits must regard modern life with some optimism in order to discover and take advantage of new opportunities. This had both practical and cultural implications for the crime wave by the time Bonnie left home in 1932. The structure of and crisis in the banking system, the affordability and interchangeable look of cars, the ease of anonymous travel, and expanded media technologies created the possibilities for a new bandit style, while the widespread poverty, community disruptions, and failures of authority provoked by the Great Depression provided an interpretive framework that produced bandit behaviors for a national audience.[34]

Compared with the urban underworld, bandits set an alternative standard for criminal respectability, in that they did not work for wages and gangsters did. Bandit gangs worked when they chose and divided profits horizontally (shares divided relative to work performed). Syndicates funneled money upward, a pyramid scheme in which workers cut superiors in on every job in return for permission to go on working. Individuals in the lower ranks of an organization retained a wage that was a percentage of their own labor; bosses collected the surplus value as a fee. Banditry was perhaps the sole remaining criminal activity that was not fully "transacted through a 'marketplace.'" In this context, the representation of bandits as traditionalists should be understood in relation to sophisticated forms of criminal organization that imitated the modern marketplace.[35]

However, the criminal world Bonnie entered in 1932 was partially regulated by the police and by syndicates who, in turn, regulated each other. No criminal entrepreneur could operate completely outside this web, since bandits depended on illegal goods and services. Purchasing untraceable weapons (often stolen from police or U.S. Army arsenals); exchanging "hot" money and securities; and obtaining shelter and medical services from prostitutes, abortionists, and crooked pharmacists all required the sanction of powerful criminals. The expansion of these criminal services during the Prohibition years created an institutional support system that, in turn, supported hijackers, bank robbers, and kidnappers.[36]

The organizational differences between bandit and syndicate crimes became more pronounced by the early 1930s as racketeers foresaw an end to Prohibition, invested their capital in legal enterprises, and understood public violence as less profitable. While terror and mayhem were the methods of attaining wealth for bandit gangs, violence emerged as an exception to syndicate norms in the 1930s. Gang wars drew public criticism, and organization leaders agreed to repress territorial conflicts whenever possible. In addition, as syndicate criminals increasingly understood themselves as businessmen, violent behavior became secret and disciplined.[37]

Bandits, although they lived by separate rules, could not evade syndicate work norms. They paid protection to the local mob or the police, or both. As the Bureau of Investigation office in Oklahoma City reported in 1927, the Barker brothers "in all probability . . . made an arrangement with certain County officers in this state [that] whenever these parties [were] arrested for any offense, these County officers, or some of them, appear[ed] on the scene with a fake warrant, by means of which they obtain[ed] custody of these outlaws, ostensibly to return them to Ottawa County, Oklahoma, but in reality to liberate them."[38] The crime corridor was defined by its "open" cities. In St. Paul, "Chickie" and David Berman (formerly of the Capone mob and Detroit's Purple gang) offered a "layover deal" similar to those available in Hot Springs, Arkansas, and Kansas City, Missouri. In return for a "political contribution" and an agreement not to work within fifty miles of the city limits, any bandit could stay in St. Paul as the Bermans' guest. Labor could also be demanded by one's host, and itinerant bandits were specialists in delicate tasks such as killing a close associate or collecting debts.[39]

Whereas racketeers were becoming deliberately anonymous in the 1930s, bandits were acquiring a more human face through theatrical news coverage of their crimes and the nostalgia for an invented rural past that it evoked for urban audiences. For example, the death of Ford Bradshaw near Arkoma, Oklahoma, on March 4, 1934, as reported by the *Tulsa Daily News* contained elements of drama, romance, tragedy, and heroism. Bradshaw, a fugitive bandit native to the Cookson hills region (also the home of "Pretty Boy" Floyd) was drinking heavily in a roadhouse, accompanied by his moll, "Boots" Moody. Bradshaw became abusive, sent Boots out to the car to get him a gun and a bulletproof vest, and threatened the other patrons and the owner. When Bradshaw yelled, "I feel like killing someone," the owner's sister summoned a deputy sheriff, who demanded Bradshaw's surrender. Instead, the bandit ran to his car and was mortally wounded. Newspaper readers learned that Boots "screamed and threw herself across the bandit's blood-soaked body. 'My daddy,' she wept. 'He's all I had in the world.'" As she was arrested, she swore vengeance on Deputy Harper, saying that she would "see to it that [he] got [his]" when she was released.[40]

Passion and romance dominated the taking of Bradshaw's life, and the aftermath of this incident almost excluded the state from this tragic story. Bradshaw's relatives soon arrived from Sallisaw to identify the body: through them, the reader encountered a rural sensibility of negotiated justice between families and the authorities, through which further violence was forestalled by a sensible use of the law. The Arkoma sheriff jailed his deputy pending a manslaughter investigation on March 5, perhaps to protect his life. However, on March 9, satisfied that the bandit's death occurred under reasonable circumstances, a lawyer representing the Bradshaw family asked that the officer be released. Mrs. Bradshaw, the attorney explained, still believed that her son's death was wrongful, but she did not wish the Harper family to suffer the pain she suffered.[41] By choosing this path, Mrs. Bradshaw also avoided a public hearing that would air her son's long and violent criminal history, thus preserving her own respectability.

What Bradshaw was doing in a roadhouse where people knew him raises important questions about community tolerance for bandits. Did they enjoy relative freedom in their home counties? And did they acquire status through personal generosity, permitting the rural poor to see them as allies against the law and corporate interests? Bradshaw's death suggests that—if either of these things were ever true—there was a limit to what a community would permit even from a bandit it tolerated.

Acts of charity that were supposed to have inspired popular followings are documented only in sources generated by bandits, although severe harboring statutes passed in 1934 made it improbable that anyone would come forward as a beneficiary of stolen wealth during the war on crime. In his autobiography, Alvin Karpis described one "starving" Oklahoma family who hid him; in thanks, he bought them "a brand-new crank-up victrola and fifty records." Karpis recalled,

> It was the only time I saw any smiles. . . . People poured in from all over the county to look at the victrola and listen to records. Word spread fast, and on the very night the victrola arrived, the family threw a big dance. They spread

cornmeal across the rough wood floor. It was just as smooth as the floor of a
ballroom after the cornmeal hit it, and people danced all night long. They
whooped it up like it was New Year's Eve.[42]

The attraction of this story is in its romanticization of rural life, the combination
of modern pleasure and traditional community solidarity catalyzed by Karpis himself. Similarly, bandits charged Euro-American folklore with modern meaning
when they publicly associated themselves with frontier gun fighters, historical
figures, and commercial western heroes. Adam Richetti, held by Missouri
police in late 1934, told a reporter that Charles Floyd "change[d] big money so
he could pass out dough to his friends. In the underworld they called him
Robin Hood and not 'Pretty Boy.'" Nell Cowan also wrote that in their childhood
games Clyde always insisted on playing "Jesse James, or Cole Younger, or Buffalo Bill, or William S. Hart."[43]

Poor people did accept money to hide bandits, a practice that was pervasive
enough in Oklahoma to cause the *Tulsa Daily World* to speak out against it. In
March 1934, Glen Roy Wright, a Sapulpa associate of the Barker family, surrendered after being trapped in a Cook County farmhouse he and his gang were
using as a hideout. In a raid led by N. E. Hollis of the Bureau of Investigation,
federal officers and a local posse surrounded a house leased by tenant farmer
Ira Brackett. The bandits came out with their hands up, as did two molls, one
of whom had two small children. Brackett, who had rented rooms to the gang,
also emerged with his wife and two daughters and was hustled off to jail. When
asked at his arraignment why he had broken the law, Brackett answered sensibly that the gang "helped pay the grocery bill."[44]

Claiming ignorance of their guests' true identities, the Bracketts quickly
became local media stars. The farmer's wife explained to reporters that she
had not known they were bandits, and, although it had been incautious,
poverty had led her to rent to this admittedly odd group. She did say that she
had been suspicious because of the lavishness of her guests' spending. She had
charged them ten dollars a week for their rooms, and they had purchased food
for everyone and had bought the Bracket children toy guns and dolls. "Times
have been hard for us during the last year," she explained, "and when that kind
of people drop in with the money to pay," she would have been foolish to turn
them away.[45]

Asserting that ignorance was no excuse, an editorial declared that the
"sheltering of outlaws [had] long been a black spot upon Oklahoma's name,
and the . . . punishment of harborers [was] necessary." What is also important
is that the bandits were discovered because other townspeople turned the Brack-

etts in. One tenant farmer had reported to police that an unusual amount of target shooting was going on at the Brackett place; another, that the farmer had been buying expensive food and luxuries at the local store. In fact, the Bracketts' attempt to redress their poverty betrayed them. As the reporter commented, describing the litter of consumer goods in the tenant shack, "In the toys was a story of easy money. Some expensive, some cheap and all out of place in a house of its type."[46]

Bandits were generally feared—as outsiders and as psychopathic killers who easily became violent. Bandits who paid liberally may have been able to persuade their hosts that they meant well: James "Blackie" Audett described riding openly through Shawnee, Oklahoma (the town that "Pretty Boy" Floyd had served as sheriff), with fugitive Wilbur Underhill, who stopped to greet several townspeople. Audett himself felt that rural people did not, in general, dislike bank robbers as long as they behaved respectfully.[47] However, showing respect meant paying one's way, an aspect of these stories that bandit claims to charitable spirit never fully obscures. After one bank job, Blackie and several companions stopped at a farm where they were given a big meal. "Of course, we paid her for it and paid her well," he wrote. As the couple became comfortable with their guests, they admitted great financial distress: their farm had just been foreclosed on. After conferring among themselves, the gang left five thousand dollars out of the thirty-seven thousand they had taken from the bank. "It wasn't nothing anyways," Audett concluded. "I've had to pay a crooked cop that much, more than once—for him just to throw around later on broads and booze." Tellingly, the decision to leave money established the bandit's humanity and sense of justice in contrast to the abuse of power by the law.[48]

Although there is no evidence that any bandit reversed a foreclosure, delivered groceries, threw a country dance, or paid medical bills, there is proof that bandits were reported by citizens, as Ford Bradshaw and Glenn Wright were, particularly when they became aggressive. A Cookson Hills gang consisting of three men and one woman, fresh from a bank job in Kansas, commandeered the farm home of G. V. Jenks in 1934. The gang demanded food and shelter and then proceeded to drink, quarrel, and brawl. During one of these fights, Mrs. Jenks slipped out the back door and ran to a neighboring farm, where she telephoned the police. The gang, disoriented by booze and bad temper, was captured without a fight.[49]

The scene at the Jenks's farm was at least as likely as one characterized by generosity and fun, probably more so. In fact, readers familiar with the popular expert literature on crime would expect bandits to be violent, unpredictable psychopaths. As one explained, bandits lived a "pitiable, unhappy, diseased exis-tence"; successful ones were murderers. "They cannot operate for long with-out having to shoot to escape. Some are so vicious naturally that they shoot down their victims in cold blood." They were also usually drug abusers:

> Veteran police officers estimate that two thirds of all the professional robbers are "chippy" users, that is, they "play with the white stuff." . . . When "hopped up" on coke, even an honest person plans all kinds of wild acts. Imagine what the situation is with a bunch of ex-cons. Feverishly they plan a big robbery and while still under the influence of the narcotic they steal an automobile, drive to the place which they had probably spotted a good many times, and commit the crime.

After the robbery, the bandit spent his money "at once . . . by engaging in a wild orgy of celebration or by going into a long session of gambling."[50]

The stereotypical bandit was crazed, ungovernable, unpredictable, and dan-gerous; few people ever encountered a bandit, personally or in print, who would contradict this description. In fact, the inflated reputation of a celebrity like "Pretty Boy" Floyd led to even more contempt for the ordinary bandit. In the crime corridor, a number of hoods pretended to be Floyd but were quickly uncovered by individuals who felt they would know the real thing. One attempted to hold up a bank outside Vicksburg, Mississippi, but the teller did not believe he was Floyd because he was too old and "poorly dressed." She rang the alarm and had him arrested. Another unromantic imposter approached the Rudell sis-ters outside their Tulsa home and demanded their new car. The two women, in their early twenties, knocked him down and pinned him while their nine-year-old brother ran for the police. A reporter asked how they had summoned such courage, and one replied that she knew this was not "Pretty Boy." He had been rude and rough, and she knew from the newspapers that Floyd was "very polite to women."[51]

The key to understanding the celebrity of a few bandits like Floyd or Bon-nie and Clyde may be that their audiences expected them to be rare: an elite few whom an audience might be assured they would never meet. The closer inter-war bandits are scrutinized, the more deeply embedded in mass culture mod-ern bandit stories appear to be. As one group of scholars suggested, "outlaw stories . . . reveal much about social relations, values and beliefs."[52] The ban-dit's body was a cultural location for pleasure and danger; and the bandit leg-end articulated political conflicts over personal independence, social justice, and state power. As we shall see, these were issues that Bonnie Parker and Clyde Barrow, in particular, claimed for themselves.

1. J. Edgar Hoover, in his high school cadet captain uniform, 1912. Around this time, urban police forces also adopted uniforms as a sign of middle-class professionalization. *(Courtesy Federal Bureau of Investigation)*

2. William J. Burns, director of the Bureau of Investigation, 1922–1924. Disgraced during the Teapot Dome scandal in 1924, Burns represented a corrupt past, which Hoover reformed through professionalization. *(Courtesy Federal Bureau of Investigation)*

3. Director Hoover at his desk. Typical of the many publicity shots issued during the war on crime, this one figures Hoover as an executive. Note the framed photograph to the far right, suggesting a female love interest for 1930's "Bachelor of the Year." *(Courtesy Federal Bureau of Investigation)*

4. Werner Hanni, special agent in charge, St. Paul, organized the Hamm investigation, 1933–1934. Agents were uniformed in dark suits, making them recognizable as G-men in any police setting. *(Courtesy Federal Bureau of Investigation)*

5. Melvin Purvis, "The Man Who Got Dillinger." Hired in 1928, Purvis resigned from the Division of Investigation in 1935, amid internal charges that he had used his federal career to court celebrity status.
(Courtesy Federal Bureau of Investigation)

6. Miss Helen Gandy, the division's top female employee during the war on crime, receiving a 35th anniversary pin from her boss in 1951. "A man's secretary makes him or breaks him," Hoover asserted in 1935.
(Courtesy Federal Bureau of Investigation)

7. The war on crime was part of a larger attempt to rehabilitate the reputation of the Department of Justice. Dedication of a new building on October 25, 1934, revealed the department's importance to the New Deal.
(Courtesy Federal Bureau of Investigation)

8. Fingerprinting campaigns became a popular way for middle-class audiences to participate in the war on crime. Here, an unidentified fraternal organization member prints the director himself; note the "traditionally American" log cabin setting.
(Courtesy Federal Bureau of Investigation)

9. Bandits inspired fear in many police because they were so well armed. Here, police display for reporters stolen license plates, rifles, shotguns (one with a shoulder sling to hide it under a coat), ammunition, and hand grenades.
(From the collection of the Texas/Dallas History and Archives Division, Dallas Public Library)

10. One of the photographs found in the Joplin, Missouri, hideout depicting Clyde Barrow and Bonnie Parker in a lovers' pose. By the time this picture was published in April 1934, the gang was famous for shooting its way out of tight spots.
(From the collection of the Texas/Dallas History and Archives Division, Dallas Public Library)

11. Bonnie Parker as the saucy gun moll, "Suicide Sal," April 1934.
(From the collection of the Texas/Dallas History and Archives Division, Dallas Public Library)

12. Posse members posing with items taken from a car abandoned by the Barrow gang. Note blankets on far right, used for camping out; and on the left, maps, a telegram, license plates from several states, and a detective magazine the gang had enjoyed.
(From the collection of the Texas/Dallas History and Archives Division, Dallas Public Library)

13. When the division was renamed the Federal Bureau of Investigation in July 1935, the occasion was marked by a new building, which became a popular tourist attraction.
(Courtesy Federal Bureau of Investigation)

IDENTIFICATION ORDER NO. 1221
April 6, 1934.

DIVISION OF INVESTIGATION
U. S. DEPARTMENT OF JUSTICE
WASHINGTON, D. C.

Fingerprint Classification
24 27 W I 18+
4 W 00 15+

WANTED

MARY EVELYN FRECHETTE, with aliases,
ANN MARTIN, EVELYN SPARK, EVELYN FASCHETTI, EVELYN FRISBETTE,
GRACE EDWARDS, MRS. JOHN DILLINGER, "BILLIE".

OBSTRUCTION OF JUSTICE.

DESCRIPTION
Age, 26 years (1934)
Height, 5 feet, 3 inches
Weight, 130 pounds
Build, plump
Hair, black - wavy
Eyes, brown
Complexion, fair
Scars and marks, mole on right
cheek, pit scars on face
Remarks: full round face. Hair
say be dyed light red.

RELATIVES:
Mrs. Mary Frechette Sprague, mother,
Neopit, Wisconsin.
Mrs. Anna Boiden, sister,
Neopit, Wisconsin.
Mrs. Frances Frechette Schultz, sister,
3512 North Halsted Street,
Chicago, Illinois.

Ann Martin

CRIMINAL RECORD
As Ann Martin, #2376, arrested
Police Department, Tucson, Arizona,
January 25, 1934, charge, fugitive
from justice; disposition, released
January 30, 1934.

Evelyn Frechette is wanted at St. Paul, Minnesota, for harboring a fugitive and obstructing justice.
Law enforcement agencies kindly transmit any additional information or criminal record to the nearest office of the Division
of Investigation, U. S. Department of Justice.
If apprehended, please notify the Director, Division of Investigation, U. S. Department of Justice, Washington, D. C., or the
Special Agent in Charge of the office of the Division of Investigation listed on the back hereof which is nearest your city.

(over)   Issued by: J. EDGAR HOOVER, DIRECTOR.

14. Uniform identification orders were an important device for federalizing the crime war. This one depicts Evelyn Frechette, John Dillinger's moll, her signature, fingerprints, aliases, and photograph. It also lists her physical characteristics and relatives who might shield her.
(Courtesy Federal Bureau of Investigation)

WANTED

JOHN HERBERT DILLINGER

On June 23, 1934, HOMER S. CUMMINGS, Attorney General of the United States, under the authority vested in him by an Act of Congress approved June 6, 1934, offered a reward of

$10,000.00

for the capture of John Herbert Dillinger or a reward of

$5,000.00

for information leading to the arrest of John Herbert Dillinger.

DESCRIPTION

Age, 32 years; Height, 5 feet 7-1/8 inches; Weight, 153 pounds; Build, medium; Hair, medium chestnut; Eyes, grey; Complexion, medium; Occupation, machinist; Marks and scars, 1/2 inch scar back left hand, scar middle upper lip, brown mole between eyebrows.

All claims to any of the aforesaid rewards and all questions and disputes that may arise as among claimants to the foregoing rewards shall be passed upon by the Attorney General and his decisions shall be final and conclusive. The right is reserved to divide and allocate portions of any of said rewards as between several claimants. No part of the aforesaid rewards shall be paid to any official or employee of the Department of Justice.

If you are in possession of any information concerning the whereabouts of John Herbert Dillinger, communicate immediately by telephone or telegraph collect to the nearest office of the Division of Investigation, United States Department of Justice, the local addresses of which are set forth on the reverse side of this notice.

JOHN EDGAR HOOVER, DIRECTOR,
DIVISION OF INVESTIGATION,
UNITED STATES DEPARTMENT OF JUSTICE,
WASHINGTON, D. C.

June 25, 1934

15. Hoover adapted the traditional wanted poster, which publicized reward money rather than identifying information, to federal uses. The fine print lists restrictions on who can claim the money. *(Courtesy Federal Bureau of Investigation)*

16. Dillinger gang member Lester Gillis, also known as "Baby Face Nelson," in a photo probably taken in prison. *(Courtesy Federal Bureau of Investigation)*

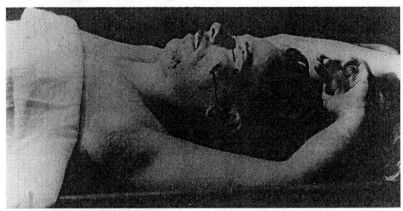

17. John Dillinger, lying in the Chicago city morgue, July 1934: bandit corpses were objects of great fascination, and a vaudeville promoter attempted to purchase Dillinger's from the family. *(Courtesy Federal Bureau of Investigation)*

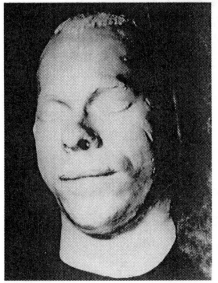

18. An enthusiastic mortician fashioned this Dillinger death mask, and presented it to Hoover as a souvenir of the division's victory over the bandit. Hoover displayed it as part of the public tour, where it remained for decades. *(Courtesy Federal Bureau of Investigation)*

19. One of the most effective weapons in the war on crime was the harboring trial, a device pioneered at the state level and included in the federal omnibus crime bill of 1934. Here, female relatives of Barrow gang members radiate defiance as they enter the courthouse in Dallas.
(From the collection of the Texas/Dallas History and Archives Division, Dallas Public Library)

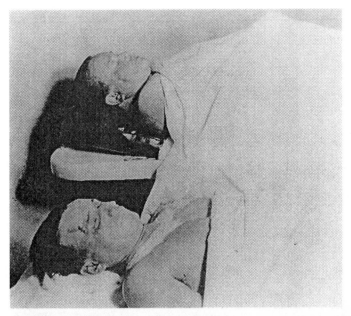

20. This morgue shot intentionally conveys the unnaturalness of Barker family relationships, as Kate (top) lies naked next to her son Fred. Fred's body has also been mended, hiding the fact that he was shot many times over. *(Courtesy Federal Bureau of Investigation)*

21. By 1935, federal agents had also adopted publicity tactics pioneered at the state and local level. Here, the display of bandit weapons and bulletproof vests outside the Barker hideout in Ocala, Florida, demonstrates why the pair could not be captured alive. *(Courtesy Federal Bureau of Investigation)*

22. The end of the war on crime: Alvin Karpis, center, is arrested in New Orleans, Louisiana, by J. Edgar Hoover, bottom left. Karpis is probably saying, "No comment."
(Courtesy Federal Bureau of Investigation)

The True Story of Bonnie and Clyde (Continued)

Bonnie's stay in the Kaufman jail—or more accurately, the decision to join Clyde in a crime—marked her transition between lawfulness and outlawry, from an ordinary existence to a life of passion increasingly punctuated by loneliness and fear. After her release on June 17, Emma recalled, she was "soberer, more quiet, and a great deal older than the Bonnie who had left home three months before." Bonnie may have wondered whether she—like "Suicide Sal"—had been deserted by Clyde, who had since been charged in a fatal shooting. What her mother read at the time as a silence born of shattered dreams may have been grief that Clyde had chosen life on the road with the boys instead of with her.[53]

But Clyde did make contact with Bonnie shortly after her release, probably driving by on a commercial street, a method the two later used to see loved ones and evade the police. Toward the end of June Bonnie disappeared, leaving word that she had a new job in Wichita Falls. "It seemed queer that Bonnie had left me without saying goodbye," Emma wrote. "Something whispered to me that she had gone to Clyde, but . . . I didn't want to believe that." At the end of July Bonnie came home but "seemed nervous, jumped at the slightest noise, and kept looking out the windows constantly." As Emma later discovered, since leaving home Bonnie had been living with Clyde and Ray Hamilton in a rented cottage in Wichita Falls; there was no job. Bonnie's nerves were jangling over a payroll robbery, which Clyde and Ray executed on July 31.[54]

Once Bonnie joined Clyde as a fugitive, she became an enemy of the state. She and Clyde exited the institutions and community structures that make it possible for historians to know an individual through documentary evidence. Thus, it becomes difficult to tell their story as more than a morality tale or a romantic tragedy. Biographers and relatives solved this problem by constructing twin narratives: there is a sequence of events—the killings, robberies, and shoot-outs—that offer a map of crime between Bonnie's departure from home in June 1932 and the lovers' death in a police ambush on May 23, 1934; and there is the continuing story of their passion, ending when they stood their ground against an unforgiving state.

When Clyde determined that he would die fighting may have been in Huntsville; or it might have been a few days after the payroll heist, when he and Ray crossed into Oklahoma and stopped at a country dance near Atoka. Approached by a sheriff and several deputies, the bandits opened fire, killing a deputy and wounding other officers and bystanders. After a hair-raising escape, in which Clyde stole and wrecked several cars, they made their way back into Texas on country roads. Bonnie joined them in an abandoned farmhouse near

Grand Prairie. "It was not till almost a year later 1933," Emma wrote, "that I saw Bonnie to talk to her about any of these things, and by that time there was no going back for Bonnie either."[55]

In mid-August, the gang decided to leave Texas to visit Bonnie's Aunt Millie in New Mexico. Millie did not know they were wanted and "received them with the open-armed hospitality of the farm." When a local sheriff scrutinized their Texas license plates, they took him hostage and headed home, dumping him outside San Antonio. Continuing on to Houston, they ran into a roadblock: Clyde spun the car around and drove furiously in the other direction as "the laws" opened fire. His fast driving, memory for southwestern back roads, and quick reflexes kept the gang out of the hands of the police in this and many other situations. As Emma recalled, "A thousand miles was nothing unusual for Clyde to cover in a day." He knew every escape route, "not only the main roads, but all the side roads and little country lanes."[56]

The sheriff in charge of the roadblock immediately publicized this confrontation, sending circulars to neighboring counties and requesting information on the gang from the Dallas Bureau of Identification. "TO ALL PEACE OFFICERS IN THE UNITED STATES," it read, describing the two men but not Bonnie, whose Kaufman arrest had never been recorded in Dallas. "[The gang is] EXTREMELY DANGEROUS and every precaution should be taken in arresting them. . . . Wire all information to me collect and please make every effort to arrest these parties and stop their running all over the country shooting officers wherever they go." Attacks on the police were taken seriously in Texas. "Some of our boys had a little fun with that bunch last evening," the sheriff typed in one note to a colleague; "they took two shots at one of our Deputies. We hold warrants for them and sure would like to apperhend [sic] them."[57]

This publicity drove the gang north, away from hostile police departments, to Ray Hamilton's father's house in Michigan, where, still not "news" outside the Southwest, they hid out for a month. In October, Clyde and Ray were charged with another bank robbery and a murder back in Texas; and by the end of October, Bonnie and Clyde were hiding out near their families, while Ray and a fourth gang member, Gene O'Dare, returned to Michigan. There, Ray's flirtation with a café waitress led to a double date at a roller skating rink, where the waitress's other boyfriend, a local cop, arrested him on December 6. Sent back to Texas for trial, Hamilton was sentenced to 263 years in prison and transferred to Huntsville on August 8, 1933.[58]

The winter of 1932 and spring of 1933 were a crucial turning point for Bonnie and Clyde; they went from being local to nationally recognized criminal celebrities as Clyde's victims mounted. In December sixteen-year-old William Daniel "W.D." Jones, a Barrow family friend, joined the gang, and on Christmas

Day Jones and Clyde were charged with the murder of a citizen who had tried to stop them from stealing his car. On January 6, Clyde was charged with another murder, of a deputy sheriff who had attempted to arrest Bonnie, Clyde, and W.D. outside the Hamilton house. Escaping the Texas posse, the gang crossed into Oklahoma and headed to Joplin, Missouri. There they rented an apartment, and in March, paroled from Huntsville, Buck Barrow visited with his wife, Blanche. There, on the afternoon of April 13, they were surrounded by police who had been tipped off by neighbors.

The ambush at Joplin was a disaster all around. In a fierce gun battle, two policemen were killed; and although the gang escaped, Clyde and W.D. were wounded, Buck was once more a fugitive, and Blanche—who had run screaming from the apartment and was found by the gang a few blocks away—was indicted as an accomplice. In less than half an hour, Blanche had gone from being "a good country girl" to a gangster's moll, for which she would eventually serve ten years in prison. Poor Blanche had been reluctant to visit in the first place, Nell remembered, and as she had left home she was "still boo-hooing."[59]

Police combed the apartment for evidence; pictures taken with Bonnie's Kodak were found there, published in the *Joplin Globe* on April 14, and sold to a news syndicate. They illustrated the pleasure Clyde and Bonnie took in their bandit identities: a famous photo of Bonnie chewing a cigar and balancing a pistol on her hip was one of these, as were a number of shots of the gang posing in front of a stolen Ford V-8 with their arsenal of weapons. Bonnie's poses show a particularly keen sense of irony and play: the cigar was a symbol of maleness, as were the guns she sported. In one photo, Clyde holds his hands out helplessly, a pistol dangling from one of them and a silly grin on his face, while a mock serious Bonnie "gets the drop on him" with a shotgun. These performances had unintended consequences, however: wherever they went they were more likely to be recognized.

The photos fetishized guns, but it was the car, and Clyde's skilled use of it, that became the central icon of the rising national fascination with the Barrow gang. Clyde's superhuman driving abilities led to the popular belief that he might show up anywhere, anytime, which in turn led to fatal and near fatal attacks on other automobile tourists. In early May 1934, a West Plains, Missouri, filling station attendant summoned a local posse when two men and a woman bought some gasoline. The vigilantes chased and fired on the car until it skidded off the road, killing the driver.[60]

The car, as technology and as a cultural sign, identified the Barrow gang as modern but also as disorderly.[61] Automobile theft, an act increasingly associated with juvenile delinquents, was Clyde's most frequent felony. He drove hard and on bad roads and needed to steal new cars regularly (usually the powerful, roomy, and anonymous Ford V-8). Automobile theft also made him a federal fugitive. By October 1933 an identification order was distributed to every post office and participating police station, although, in the days before the omnibus crime bill armed bureau agents, there is no evidence in newspaper or Dallas police records that federal agents joined the growing posse of Dallas police officers, prison officials, county deputies, and Texas Rangers who were pursuing the gang.[62]

The automobile that made banditry possible produced a criminal identity that necessarily engaged a semiotics of gender and sexuality. While contemporary advertising shows that during the depression "the family car and its occupants had been chosen to symbolize the best of American life at a time of acute economic, political and social distress," automobile technology also had the potential for undoing its ideal uses, specifically through female "automobility," women's use of cars for their own pleasure rather than family duties.[63] Other sites for moral disarray emerged as well, specifically motor courts and motels. Auto courts

> afforded privacy. The motorist simply paid his fee—usually about one dollar in the twenties—then parked adjacent to the assigned cabin and unloaded his party, an arrangement that appealed not only to tourists but also to couples seeking anonymity for whatever reason. . . . Because the motorist paid in advance, he and his party could depart discreetly without checking out, after a sound night's sleep or a stolen hour on a rented mattress.

One can easily imagine "the motorist" in this scenario as a bandit and his moll, blending in with the other unmarried, anonymous couples. Indeed, the wanted poster circulated on Clyde, Ray, and Bonnie suggested that police "search all tourist camps as hangouts for such people."[64]

The pictures from the Joplin apartment made even auto courts dangerous for the next few weeks. The Barrows were confined to camping out, with Blanche (whose photograph had not been published) making occasional forays into towns to buy food and do laundry. Two other robberies were committed, in Minnesota and Indiana; in the latter, "2 women [were] shot by [a] woman member of the gang during the attempt." After that the gang split up, Blanche and Buck returning to Missouri, while Bonnie and Clyde drove home. Near Wellington, Texas, on June 11 Clyde drove into a ditch; he and W.D. were thrown free, but Bonnie was trapped in a burning car. After Clyde pulled her out, two farmers took them to a nearby house. Suspicious that Clyde refused to call an ambulance, or even a doctor, one of the farmers notified the police when he left briefly to collect some hidden guns. Clyde and the police arrived almost simultaneously. Kidnapping them, he loaded the delirious Bonnie into the farmer's car and drove north to meet Blanche and Buck near Erick, Oklahoma. The gang tied the policemen to a tree and proceeded on to Ft. Smith, Arkansas, where they rented rooms and summoned a doctor. Clyde drove to Dallas and collected Billie Parker, who spent more than a week nursing her cousin back to life. Bonnie was up on crutches by September 1933 but did not walk normally for seven months.[65]

The wreck and the gang's subsequent disappearance were reported in a *New York Times* story that referred to Clyde as a "desperado" and a terrorist. They disappeared into auto courts and campgrounds, surfacing periodically to rob a bank or convenience store and killing another sheriff at a road block. Surrounded in Platte City, Missouri, they escaped after a gun battle in which Blanche was wounded and Buck fatally shot in the head. Resting in a public park in Des Moines, Iowa, they were trapped again when a posse of police, farmers, and National Guardsmen opened fire at dawn. While Buck, who had regained consciousness, exchanged fire with the police, Clyde carried Bonnie into a river and swam downstream; W.D. escaped and hitched to Dallas. Blanche and Buck never saw each other again after their arrest; he died of his wounds on July 29, and she was jailed in Missouri.[66]

Such events underline both the escalating force used against Bonnie and Clyde and police frustration at their elusiveness. Lawmen who encountered the gang had seen their grim determination not to surrender and warned others to use overwhelming force. A Dallas police department circular described male and female gang members as "well armed with automatic pistols" and machine guns. A county circular warned that police should "be very careful in checking [license plate] numbers as they will not hesitate to make their escape and have said they would not be taken alive."[67]

Messages sent between departments, in the absence of any official system of communication, testify to policemen's humiliated rage at the number of colleagues kidnapped, murdered, and wounded by the gang. Federal demands for an end to easy parole met welcome ears in Dallas, where an anonymous officer composed a rhyme for the chief of police:

> For they once had Barrow locked tight in a cell
> And Ross [Superintendent of Prisons] let him out so what the Hell
> Now its up to someone to ketch him agin
> So let that thar Pardon board fetch him in.
> If this was a rule thar ain't no doubt
> They'd be a darn sight carefuller who they let out.

Feelings ran high throughout the Southwest. "Help us catch these dirty crooks," pleaded deputies seeking to avenge their sheriff. The Joplin police, who charged that the gang had "also raped a lady," explained, "[We tried] to see if we can get our rewards changed to 'dead or alive' but we can't get the parties who offered the rewards see like we do. . . . We are ready to go the limit in running them down."[68]

In mid-November, W.D. Jones was arrested in Dallas and, to exonerate himself, eagerly added to his comrades' reputation as ruthless psychopaths. Jones said he had only joined the gang because Clyde had forced him to rob a store at gunpoint. "I didn't want to do it," he told his interrogator. "Clyde raised hell with me because I hadn't helped him hold up the store, and Bonnie laughed at me because I was afraid." During the gun battles in which policemen had been killed, W.D. claimed he was asleep, "out of [his] head from injuries," or "half-drunk," once regaining consciousness "standing in the middle of the road with Buck's [broken] sixteen gauge shotgun in [his] hands." His statement is punctuated with acts he was "forced" to perform: "He made me help him," Jones insisted several times. "Each night," he said, "they handcuffed me to a tree to prevent my making a getaway, as they feared I knew too much and they feared I would escape if I could."[69]

Underneath these evasions and falsehoods are two pieces of information that add to our understanding of these fugitive months and the desperation with which they were lived. The gang may have been selling guns and ammunition to other criminals, and they had a cache of weapons hidden at a relative's house. One crime W.D. did admit to being fully conscious for—although not as a participant—was an armory theft, when Buck and Clyde "brought back so many guns it looked like a gun factory—there were some 46 government automatic pistols, several rifles and two or three cases of ammunition for the rifles." Furthermore, Jones was not "knocked out" for all the crimes he was questioned about, only for those in which a policemen died. This, it seems, was the single crime that bandits believed would guarantee official or unofficial execution for a white criminal in Texas. This might explain why Glen Roy Wright surrendered in Sapulpa: not killing a police officer left the possibility of eventual freedom, or at least a chance that he would live to see his jail cell. He wasn't "yellow," Wright explained, but "life [was] sweet, whether it be spent in jail or at liberty": "In the spot I was in, there probably will be but little difference between jail and the uncertain liberty that was mine."[70] Killing police was a line many bandits chose not to cross; the brief freedom it offered almost ensured death at the hands of other police.

This frontier, already crossed, adds a grim luster to the crime spree that cemented Bonnie and Clyde's reputation as national public enemies. In late January 1934, with a third accomplice, James Mullen, they liberated Ray Hamilton, Joe Palmer, and Henry Methvin and two other convicts from Eastham. As *Time* magazine told the story (titled "Special Delivery") on its new crime page, retrieving hidden guns, the cons broke away from a road gang to a waiting car while Barrow and Mullen covered them with machine guns. "Convicts left behind spotted the handiwork of Clyde Barrow, notorious outlaw-at-large," the reporter wrote, noting that in the getaway car, honking the horn, was "his woman, gun-toting, cigar-smoking Bonnie Parker." Bonnie appeared in the story again as "Clyde Barrow's paramour, the fair cigar-smoking Bonnie ('Suicide Sal') Parker."[71]

This national publication, aimed at a middle-class audience, suggests that the fascination with Bonnie and Clyde had expanded to take up cultural space that the poor rarely occupied. The bandits mentioned in *Time*'s crime section during 1933 and 1934 were almost entirely male, and Bonnie's presence in the gang gave the stories about the Barrow gang a glamorous touch lacking in other news of prison breaks, robberies, and murder. She stood out not because she was a woman but because she committed crimes like a man: shooting guns, driving getaway cars, and enjoying the ultimate symbol of masculine leisure consumption, the cigar, while she coldly murdered others. It is important to emphasize that it was not female criminality itself that was shocking. Rather, it was murder that made Bonnie alarming, partly accounting for descriptions of her that gender her as not fully female. Despite the occasional appearance of female banditry in the interwar period, violent crime was largely a male realm.[72]

Courts and the public tended to view women who killed as desperate rather than vicious: Blanche received only ten years for her complicity in the death of two policemen. However, Bonnie's behavior, and the poems that she wrote about her fugitive life, not only pledged loyalty to Clyde but fashioned her as a transgendered figure, a female bandit. Witnesses began to "see" her as similar to a man, often a savage one. Although Bonnie was never known to wear pants as a number of molls (including Blanche) did, motorists who reported having seen the lovers kill two officers near Grapevine, Texas, on April 1 described her in male attire. "The man and woman, both dressed in riding breeches . . . seized shotguns and opened fire," the Associated Press asserted. Officers placed Bonnie at the scene because of "a cigar stub near the car, the butt bearing the imprint of small teeth."[73]

Responses to Bonnie were also poorly separated in the public mind from images of urban molls, made popular through gangster films, crime fiction, and sensational journalism. Arthur Reeve described female criminal "types" and urban floozies who began as gold diggers and ended as bandits: "Bright Eyes" Margaret Murray, a former New York taxi dancer who drove a getaway car and kept "a weather eye for the cops" while her sweetheart performed stickups; and Celia Cooney, Brooklyn's "Bobbed-Haired Bandit," who robbed banks with her husband, Ed. A moll was a girl who had "forgotten how to blush, whose only tears [were] those of anger and who [was] hard as a keg of nails"; "she lounges around all day in the languid splendor of soft lingerie and when she steps out with her gangster boy-friend at night she carries a reserve gat for him in her jeweled purse."[74] The moll was a female without femininity, a sexual receptor ("her jeweled purse") who hid a murderous penis ("a reserve gat"). Fascination with Bonnie's alleged fetishes for guns and cigars thus fits into broader cultural uncertainties as to the gendering of criminal women.

After the Eastham break, Lee Simmons, the governor of Huntsville prison, employed retired Texas Ranger Frank Hamer to hunt the Barrow gang down. Coordinating the multiple state and county efforts and locating every possible haven for the gang, Hamer put the Parker and Barrow families under close surveillance. Between April 18 and April 30, Dallas police put taps on Emma's, and then Cumie's, telephone, giving us some insight into the state of mind of both families during the final weeks of the manhunt. The two households spoke several times a day; as Nell recalled, "It seemed beyond human endurance that we could go on living through the horrors we were enduring." At great cost to their reputations, she and other family members were brought in for daily interrogations. Such harassment cost Bonnie's cousin Billie her job when her employers came to think she was "too hard-boiled."[75]

The families were also plagued with friends, neighbors, and strangers lurking about the house, hoping to catch sight of the fugitives. Cumie called Nell to say that an acquaintance had called for her "in a good-looking car with a boy." Nell warned her mother not to "tell her anything[;] she is just noseing [sic] around. . . . She is just trying to find out something." Nosing around could have consequences, however. A neighbor of the Hamiltons' was abruptly hauled in for questioning because, as a caller explained to Emma Parker's sister, "He has been talking to Barrows and Hamiltons, fooling around them, I guess they think he knows something."[76]

Interest in the two families' daily affairs was heightened in the final weeks of the manhunt by extensive local newspaper and radio coverage, which the Barrows and the Parkers also used as a source of information about their children. "Did you see that little write-up in the journal yesterday about Clyde and Bonnie?" Billie Parker asked Cumie on April 18. "Yes I saw that[,] wasn't that something," she replied. Later that day, Emma called back when a breaking story about a gun battle was broadcast on the radio. "Call me back after you find out what happened," Cumie replied; the two talked off and on all evening. Newspapers let the families know which friends and enemies had been arrested and bailed out; they also printed anything about the gang they could acquire, authentic or not. A letter to the *Houston Post* signed "Clyde and Bonnie" read, "I notice that the officers have give notice to the turist [sic] to be very careful and stop when they are told to. I also ask them to be very careful who they stop."[77]

Sympathetic allies picked up rumors and passed them on. "Frank" eavesdropped on officers at city hall and called Cumie to report, "The Hi[gh]land Park Police jumped a Ford V-8 sedan with a man and a girl in it and tried to stop it and they turned a machine gun loose on them. Mrs. B. seemed very excited [and] said did they get away? Frank said yes they got away but I thought I would tell you so you could be on the lookout for them." Cumie immediately called Emma to reassure her that Bonnie and Clyde were still alive.[78]

The telephone log contains multiple hang-ups, apologies for wrong numbers, and mysterious exchanges. The two families were aware of the surveillance, and other callers remarked on clicks and noises they heard on the line. One warned, "Don't say much over the phone, you know they are listening to everything you say," and Cumie replied belligerently, "I don't care if they do listen to what I say." On another call, both parties acknowledged an odd connection: "I think that it is someone listening in on [the telephone]," one remarked. Cumie Barrow called Emma at one point for information, and Emma did not reply; she then said, "Call me," and hung up. Perhaps they had telephones in other households that they borrowed when they wished to exchange incriminating information. They also used verbal codes to signal the need for a personal meeting. One call found Cumie in bed; Emma asked Nell's daughter Marie if "a pint would cure her. . . . Mrs. B. said yes she thought it would." Emma replied, "Tell her I'll come over and bring her one." Another signal that the fugitives might appear that night was invoking Bonnie's favorite food, red beans: Cumie called Nell and invited her to share "a big pot of beans and some corn bread."[79]

Clyde's murderous rage toward the end of his career was matched in these final weeks by his family's anger against "the laws" and against the Hamilton clan, whom they suspected of turning state's evidence. Both the Barrows and the Parkers believed that the Hamiltons were using stolen money to bribe the police on Ray's behalf, while their children were hunted down. As one family member complained, "Where are they getting all that money?" Cumie's sister replied, "I don't know but she has been paying $50.00 here and $50.00 there. . . . The officers know they did not get that money honest." In another call, Cumie's sister commented on the battery of attorneys the Hamiltons had hired: "Lawyers don't do that for nothing. . . . I am no damn fool and the officers are not crazy either that is a lot of Bull."[80] The issue of money was a particularly delicate one: members of each family were arrested every day, and it was straining their meager resources to keep everyone bailed out. In addition, police might have been putting pressure on bondsmen not to serve them. As one caller said to another, "The Bonding Co[mpany] was afraid of any Barrow gang [member] and was having trouble," and three attempts to bail out Floyd Hamilton, Ray's brother, had been unsuccessful. When Henry Barrow was arrested on federal charges, several men pulled together to try to post bail: "You know a Federal bond is pretty high," an anxious caller to the Barrow household said.[81]

Cumie Barrow believed a series of mildly contradictory things, which might nevertheless have been true given the character of urban police forces: that the Hamiltons were being paid for information and testimony; that they were simultaneously bribing police and hiring lawyers; that Mary O'Dare, Ray's moll, was "singing" in the hope of getting charges against her dismissed; and that capital indictments pending against Ray and his brother Floyd gave "the laws" a wedge to pressure the Hamiltons for evidence. "I hope they catch Raymond and string him up in front of old lady Hamilton," Cumie snapped on April 21. Later that day, she said she would be "glad" if both Hamilton boys were convicted; and in the evening, told her sister with satisfaction that, despite all those lawyers, the police "told old lady Hamilton she was going to the Pen."[82]

Shortly before his capture, Ray also angered the Barrows by trying to dissociate himself publicly from Clyde. On April 8, a Dallas lawyer received a cash retainer, a hotel registration receipt from New Orleans, and a letter from Hamilton: "I'm sending you one hundred dollars and want this out before the public and proved right away. I'm sending you more money just as soon as I find out that you are doing as I ask. I'm enclosing also my fingerprints on this bill. . . . I want you to let the public and the whole world know that I am not with Clyde Barrow and do not go his speed." Hamilton sent a similar message to Texas governor "Ma" Ferguson, and six days later the letter was released to the newspapers.[83]

The Hamiltons' worst offense, however, was that on April 28 they welcomed Mary O'Dare into their home. Clyde wrote to Ray in jail that he wasn't surprised that Mary was squealing; "she hails from a 'rat' family, and you couldn't expect better from her."[84] Mary became a target for both mothers' rage, along with the now ubiquitous "laws" (or as Cumie now referred to them, "them sons of bitches"). In the conversation they always had first thing in the morning, Emma Parker asked Cumie how she was. As usual, Cumie was "mad as the devil." She had seen "that stool pigeon" walking home with Ray's mother, Mildred:

Mary had a suitcase[.] I guess she is going to stay for awhile. P. said are those people crazy. . . . She will have them all in jail in a week. B. said I don't care if they do get in jail if they don't have any better sense than that. . . . She tried to get the kids caught when she was with them and finally got Raymond caught. . . . [P.] said[,] she made the remark before she left Bonnie and Clyde that she would get them all caught before it was all over. [B.] said[,] yes I know that she will. . . . She had better not show her face around [us] if she wants to live and do well. P. said[,] isn't that so. B. said[,] I know she is going to be coming up here to use my phone. P. said[,] if you let her come in your house I'll never come to see you again. B. said[,] I've got a big iron here if she starts in my house I am going to hit her over the head with it. . . . I am not going to let that dam[n] hussy in my house.[85]

By exchanging opinions about Mary, Emma Parker and Cumie Barrow could also express their own solidarity, with the fugitives and against "the laws," not an insignificant act of resistance, since they knew they were being spied on. Indirectly, they assured each other that neither would "stool" on the other's child. A few weeks later Cumie herself was questioned for almost forty-eight hours; released on Mother's Day, she smugly told reporters outside the jail that she had cooperated except "if it would give away where Clyde was located."[86]

These frenzied weeks in April and May, when arrests occurred daily and Dallas had been virtually closed to Bonnie and Clyde, were also when Bonnie produced her last literary efforts, in an attempt to explain who she and Clyde were and why they had committed their crimes. The first, either an unfinished draft of an essay or preparation for a new poem, was found in a car they abandoned in Kansas. The torn and mangled fragment, missing words and whole sentences, was reprinted in newspapers around the country on April 7. A plea for public sympathy and understanding, it asked audiences to remember that the law did not always tell the truth:

> I am writing the actual . . . and hoping at least part of it . . . consideration. For the few people who have sons or daughters to go astray or be unjustly accused, I can add that the "law" can be mistaken. [To] those who have not had dealings with the "law," except in a friendly or business way, I cannot make you understand how cruel the law can be to a "convict" or a questionably charactered man. Some are guilty but many times a man has been accused and convicted for crimes he has never heard of. . . . In this story, I do not propose . . . anyone. I believe we are innocent. . . . Intend to tell . . . sordid facts . . . guilty of lots . . . and yet there are petty and . . . thieves all over the country. The B—— gang is known for nearly every major crime in four years. That is why this has been written, whomever is favored.[87]

The unfinished phrase beginning "I believe we are innocent . . ." was a tantalizing gap, never to be filled, where romance could blossom for their audience.

Bonnie gave her second and final poem, "The Story of Bonnie and Clyde," to her mother on May 6, when the bandit pair met with their mothers for the last time; it was also found in their car in Arcadia and printed after their death. The importance of public opinion in opposition to the state's truths is an important theme here; in addition, ironic turns on the notion of honor and the elusiveness of true freedom flip the poem's moral perspective so that Bonnie and Clyde are criminals only because these identities have been produced by an unjust state. Although Bonnie did not use words such as "true," "actual," or "real" in the title, the poem is written largely from a third-person perspective that attempts to convey objectivity. From the third verse on, she writes of "they" and "them"; and in the eighth verse, the narrator identifies with her audience, saying that while "we" might be weary and heartbroken, "Our troubles are small / Till we get like Bonnie and Clyde."[88]

In the first verse Bonnie suggests that, despite the news coverage about them, her audience is "still in need / of something to read," and she invites them into the dangerous territory of bandit experience. She asserts that the gang is not arbitrarily murderous, only that they have their own standards of justice: "Their nature is raw / They hate all the law— / The stool pigeons, spotters and rats." The proof of the state's corruption is the person of Clyde Barrow, "once honest and upright and clean" but locked up so many times that he came to believe he would never be free if he did not fight back. This, Bonnie claimed, left them halfway between the "straight" world and the underworld, a nether region where "The road was so dimly lighted; / There were no highway signs to guide." The moral opaqueness that infuses the lives of fugitives presages the opaqueness of death:

> The road gets dimmer and dimmer;
> Sometimes you can hardly see;
>   But it's fight, man to man,
>   And do all you can,
> For they know they can never be free.

This seventh verse slips uncertainly between perspectives, as if any observer could easily find him- or herself in a similar position.

The shouldering of masculine burdens by Bonnie points us to her renunciation of a conventional femininity for honor. At no point is the "Bonnie" of the poem referred to as a woman or, in fact, as female; however, she does not assume a fully male persona either. Rather, the poem's revisioning of femaleness depends on joining with men in a pact that affirms their responsibility for an organic, popular community bound by pride:

> From Irving to the West Dallas viaduct
> Is known as the Great Divide,
>   Where the women are kin,
>   And the men are men,
> And they won't "stool" on Bonnie and Clyde.

The reference to the original Barrow home under the viaduct conveys the tough spirit of the poor, and the willingness to defend freedom against state oppression becomes foundational to a moral community.

Through humor and irony, the poem proposes that no one is immune from state violence and that citizenship is a privilege easily retracted by the government. In the twelfth and fourteenth verses, Bonnie references New Deal rhetoric about inclusion and national rebirth:

> The police haven't got the report yet,
> But Clyde called me up today;
>   He said, "Don't start any fights—
>   We aren't working nights—
> We're joining the NRA.

But, she argues, political reforms have not produced justice:

> If they try to act like citizens
> And rent them a nice little flat,
>   About the third night
>   They're invited to fight
> By a sub-gun's rat-tat-tat.

Characterizing citizenship as merely performative (acting "*like* citizens") permits Bonnie to call for a more independent judgment of their lives than the state is capable of making. In the penultimate verse, she admits "That death is the wages of sin," but it would be a death with many meanings: "To few it'll be grief— / To the law a relief— / But it's death for Bonnie and Clyde."

On May 23, 1934, Frank Hamer and his posse, who had been lying in wait for two days on a dirt road outside Arcadia, Louisiana, saw Henry Methvin's father driving toward them. Flagging him down, they chained him to a tree, out of sight, and jacked the truck up in the hope that Clyde would stop to help the man who had been his host for the past week. Although Attorney General Homer Cummings had announced on April 6 that the Department of Justice was entering the search for the Barrow gang (while transporting a captured policeman across state lines, they had violated the new kidnapping statute), no special agents of the Bureau of Investigation were present. Explaining that he had just sent an omnibus crime bill to Congress, Cummings told reporters, "The activities of Barrow and his associates are an open defiance of the power of law enforcement agencies and illustrate the manifest need of federal assistance in a co-operative effort to suppress this kind of crime."[89] As it happened, all available resources were not sent to Texas that spring but rather to Melvin Purvis, special agent in charge of the Chicago office, who was overwhelmed with kidnapping cases and the hunt for former convict and bank bandit John Dillinger.

However, without federal assistance, Hamer's network of police, sheriffs, deputies, and highway patrolmen had run down every lead, squeezed every informer, and located the fugitives. At about a quarter past nine in the morning, the tan V-8 was spotted. As Clyde recognized the truck and slowed down, he saw the rustle of brush by the side of the road too late. He and Bonnie were caught in a crossfire of bullets: more than 167 rounds were fired, and at least 50 of those lodged in their bodies. As *Time* magazine reported it, after the car ground to a halt "Barrow was found with the door of the car half-open and a sawed-off shotgun in his hand. Bonnie Parker, wearing a red dress, was doubled up with a submachine gun in her lap. There were two other machine guns, another sawed off automatic shotgun, six automatic pistols, a revolver, a saxophone, sheet music, a half-eaten sandwich, a bloody pack of cigarettes, and $507 in cash." Perhaps concerned that the public might look askance at Hamer having not tried to capture the pair, or at least Bonnie, alive, the story quoted him as regretting that circumstances required him to shoot her. "I hated to bust a cap on a woman, especially when she was sitting down, but if it wouldn't have been her it would've been us."[90]

Emma Parker recorded the moment the telephone rang to tell her of her daughter's death: "I remember I was sewing." A reporter for the *Tulsa Daily World* heard Cumie Barrow "cr[y] in anguish, 'And I prayed only last night that I might see him alive again, just once more.'" While the families made arrangements to collect their children's bodies, Arcadia—a town of around five thousand people—swelled to a population of more than twenty thousand sightseers, souvenir hunters, newspaper reporters, and policemen. At the scene, men, women, and children searched for empty shells, and whenever the bodies were left unguarded, onlookers tried to rip away pieces of their clothing and bloodstained parts from the car; several accounts attest to individuals attempting to cut off Clyde's ear and his trigger finger, small children dipping the hems of their clothing in pools of blood, and women ripping out strands of Bonnie's hair. When they were finally removed to a makeshift mortuary at a furniture store, thousands of onlookers filed by the bodies; more than thirty thousand spectators came to view them at their separate funerals a few days later.[91]

Behavior that seems gruesome and outlandish more than sixty years later should be read through bystanders' belief in Bonnie and Clyde's immortality. The urge to view and touch captured or dead bandits became a characteristic of audience response to this form of criminal celebrity, in part because the criminals themselves and their families were powerless to prevent it. When Ray Hamilton was captured in late April a crowd of fifteen hundred "composed of the curious" came to observe him in a Dallas jail, and more than fifteen thousand mourners came to see "Pretty Boy" Floyd in an East Liverpool, Ohio, mortuary in October, with many women bringing small children and babies. By the summer of 1934, any dead bandit drew a crowd: in mid-August, large "crowds of curious" came to a Kansas mortuary to see the corpses of three unknown male bandits.[92] This form of audience play—washing oneself in the blood of the dead, stealing tokens from the body, and elaborate rituals of exhibiting the corpse—was also not specific to bandits as criminalized subjects but was conventional within United States lynching practices; what was rare was that these were white bodies being violated.[93]

At the time of Bonnie and Clyde's death, the Department of Justice was planning to reclaim a national audience fascinated with bandits. The first six provisions of the omnibus crime bill—J. Edgar Hoover's strategy for restoring respectability through the suppression of crime—had been affirmed in Congress that month. This legislative package, which conferred national police powers on the Bureau of Investigation, had emerged, in part, because of Bonnie Parker and Clyde Barrow and the violent acts against the law that had become part of a bandit identity. The new war on crime, or, as it would also be called, the "New Deal for Crime," would evoke the dangers of the psychopathic criminal, recast in a new identity borrowed from Chicago's "Secret Six" crime commission— the public enemy. Violence was central to this new criminal identity, as was the flouting of respectability. If repeal had produced a more sedate urban underworld, by 1934 Bonnie Parker, Clyde Barrow, and others like them had become the object of a popular obsession with criminal violence. That fascination would soon be met on different ground by Hoover, Melvin Purvis, and their gang of government men.

Five

"Another Roosevelt Victory in This War against the Underworld"

Kidnapping, Federal Policing, and the Role of the Public in the War on Crime

I want to reiterate my firm belief that generally the suppression of crime is the obligation of the various states and local political subdivisions . . . [but] the unlawful activities of those who deliberately take advantage of the protection presently afforded them by state lines . . . those classes of criminals who seek to earn their living by threats and violence, moving about from one state to another to avoid detection, require the attention, in my opinion, of the federal government.
— Louis M. Howe to FDR, May 1933

As Herbert Hoover and Franklin Delano Roosevelt campaigned in the spring of 1932, a crime was committed that would shape the New Deal's anticrime agenda. On the evening of March 1, Charles Lindbergh returned to the Hopewell, New Jersey, farm he shared with his wife, Anne, his toddler son, Charles Jr., and several servants. The child had been put to bed earlier; at 10:00, the nurse checked on him. The crib, Anne wrote to her sister-in-law the next day, "was empty and the sides still up." Betty, the nurse, "thought C. had taken him for a joke. I did too, until I saw his face. Evidently they got about one and a half hours start."[1]

Kidnapping was a crime that targeted middle-class as well as wealthy citizens. Between 1932 and 1934, "snatching," aimed at any citizen whose family could be bled for a few thousand dollars, was a new crime firmly associated with the psychopathic criminal. Cases of ordinary people grabbed by bandits made national headlines: an Illinois doctor abducted, robbed, and tied up in a mosquito-ridden swamp; or a North Carolina evangelist kidnapped, robbed, and stripped naked illustrated a national trend of bandit violence against innocent civilians. Both of these cases, side by side on the front page of the *Cairo (Illinois) Evening Citizen,* revealed elaborate details about the humiliations and physical abuse each man endured. The evangelist was "forc[ed] to swallow some kind of tablets" to subdue him and abandoned when the gang understood he had no money. The doctor's hands and feet were bound, "a gag was taped in his mouth and a blindfold taped tightly over his eyes." Witnesses reported that "his wrists were lacerated and bruised."[2]

These abductions, probably carried out by amateurs, would have been of little interest but for a brief rise in celebrity kidnappings like the Lindbergh case. Usually planned in great detail by professional criminals, these snatchings had all the elements of successful melodrama: large ransoms extracted from wealthy families, anguished parents, pitiful victims, and tense negotiations with mysterious villains. Affecting a very few people who wielded a vast amount of political influence, these cases were followed avidly by a national news audience entranced by crime. In reality, major kidnapping cases were so rare in the interwar years that *Modern Criminal Investigation* (1935), a classic police training text, did not mention them at all, despite eighteen detailed sections that describe crime scene techniques for capital felonies. However, a brief epidemic of social register "snatchings" in 1932 and 1933 created a political and cultural atmosphere conducive to the creation of an interventionist federal crime policy.[3]

In addition to criminal ransoms, sensational kidnappings produced legitimate wealth when news organizations and wire services marketed them as a form of mass entertainment. In the few days or weeks of a kidnap drama, radio and newspaper audiences waited breathlessly for fresh details telegraphed in by reporters stationed around the victim's home. Anne Lindbergh complained about such practices, her letters often confirming or denying the latest rumors. When there was no news, "the papers," she explained to her mother-in-law, "especially the tabs [tabloids], bring out wild stories every hour—none of them true, as you know. I am so afraid you get false clues and hopes every hour. They say the New York tabs bring out an extra every night to say the baby is found."[4]

Wild stories sold newspapers, helping print journalists compete with the immediacy conveyed by radio news. Newspaper sales had slumped as broadcasting prospered but, as the *Nation* noted after the first political convention broadcast in 1924 inaugurated the era of "live news," the pleasure of reading and rereading details in a newspaper could not be duplicated:

> The most interesting item in the newspaper is the item that contains your name.
> The next most interesting is the one that relates the incident you saw. You want

to match your eyes against the reporter's—check his accuracy or yours, discover whether you missed a detail, learn the true inwardness of something that puzzled you at the time. . . . The great task confronting the newspaper today is to stimulate the public's interest in news, to arouse a genuine intellectual curiosity as to the world we live in.[5]

Thus, a diverse reading and listening public became a national community by participating in breaking news.

Rendered as news, kidnappings were a form of mass entertainment that compelled a moral reading, a twentieth-century version of what Thomas Laqueur has called the "humanitarian narrative"; kidnapping reports were "imaginative vehicles" through which the public could participate in a national anticrime crusade. These tales of mystery, bondage, and violence produced newly activist citizens, whose moral imagination was incited to specific interests and actions by the suffering of a knowable other.[6] For example, in the months before young Charles's body was found, strangers described their search for clues, reported people who had behaved oddly on March 1, offered advice, and volunteered help in thousands of letters addressed to the Department of Justice.

The Lindbergh baby incited politicians to action as well: President Hoover met with J. Edgar Hoover on March 2, less than a day after the baby's disappearance. The cautious director probably noted that, despite legislation being written at that moment, no federal statute yet permitted the Bureau of Investigation's direct intervention in this matter, but he did agree to coordinate several government agencies embarking on a search that would cross several local, state, and federal jurisdictions. Such a dreadful crime perpetrated against a cultural hero like Lindbergh also moved the president to request protection for his own grandchildren. Director Hoover noted that he had sent a special agent to Pasadena: "Every precaution should be taken to see that no harm comes to these children."[7]

Throughout the 1932 campaign and the first hundred days of Franklin Roosevelt's New Deal, kidnap hysteria dominated national crime news. *Time* magazine suggested that this brutal new crime was indirectly connected to increasing unemployment in the post-Prohibition underworld: "The return of beer has . . . forced the nation's underworld into evolution," one reporter theorized. On May 8, 1933, the *New York Times* reported that Marlene Dietrich, Norma Shearer, and Gloria Swanson had all engaged security services to guard their children and that other Hollywood mothers were arming their chauffeurs and gardeners.[8]

Like bank banditry, kidnapping was a crime that occurred without warning and harmed apparently innocent people. In 1933, there were twenty-seven major kidnappings, with ransoms paid that ranged from forty thousand to one hundred thousand dollars; virtually all these cases were still unsolved the following spring. On June 15, 1933, brewer William Hamm of St. Paul, Minnesota, was bundled into a car in broad daylight; on the evening of July 23, oil baron Charles Urschel was abducted from the porch of his Tulsa home; and that same week, Illinois banker August Luer was snatched. All were successfully ransomed, but real estate broker Frank McClatchey, of Philadelphia's Main Line, was killed resisting kidnappers shortly afterward. That summer, Manhattan lawyer Henry Waters Taft, the brother of the twenty-seventh president, sent his children to Europe because of kidnap threats, and on January 19, 1934, Edward Bremer, son of brewer and Roosevelt crony Adolph Bremer of St. Paul, was snatched and ransomed. In July, *Time* reported a refinement of this crime: high society in Memphis, Kansas City, and Chicago were paying ransoms for the return of beloved pets.[9]

That many of these victims came from socially, and in some cases politically, prominent families undoubtedly contributed to the swift passage of kidnapping legislation that had been debated for at least thirty years. The Urschel kidnapping was the first case to be covered by the new Lindbergh Law, federal kidnapping legislation passed in the spring of 1932 that made transportation of abducted persons or use of the mails in such cases a federal capital offense. Thus, in the first hectic months of the Roosevelt administration, the pursuit of fugitive bandit George "Machine Gun" Kelly was handed over to Hoover's bureau, recently renamed the Division of Investigation to reflect its new status in a revived Department of Justice. In an obvious reference to the legislative interventions and massive infusions of federal dollars that had characterized the president's economic New Deal, rumors flew about a federal anticrime program. The *Washington Mirror* reported on August 1 that Attorney General Homer Cummings had been "authorized to spend as much money as . . . necessary" to quell the crime wave. "We look forward to another Roosevelt victory against the underworld."[10] It came soon: Kelly and his wife, Katherine, were captured on September 26 in Memphis, Tennessee, in a hotel room where the bandit uttered the immortal words, "Don't shoot, G-Men!"

This renaming of special agents in an underworld idiom marked the end of reform and the beginning of the division's ascendancy as the nation's most visible federal police. By choosing Hoover's "Government Men" to prosecute the war on crime, Cummings, like other New Deal bureaucrats, reframed reforms undertaken in previous Republican administrations as New Deal innovations. Articulating a war on crime as part of the New Deal was also a political strategy that framed the expansion of federal police power as ideologically similar to social welfare programs and obscured very recent controversies about state violence. Certainly the political atmosphere in Congress was ripe for a new attempt at federal enforcement. State centralization during Roosevelt's first term was enabled by a panicked and cooperative Congress that, as Paul Conkin has written, "was willing to give Roosevelt an opportunity to work his magic."[11]

Unlike other New Deal innovations, Roosevelt seemed to endorse rather than initiate Justice Department action against crime. In late summer of 1933, Cummings announced to the Daughters of the American Revolution that a legislative package would soon appear in Congress that would end kidnapping and other brutal crimes. "We are now engaged in a war," he announced, "that threatens the safety of our country—a war with the organized forces of crime." Roosevelt's policy statement came much later, in his 1934 State of the Union address, which proposed the enactment of the nation's first omnibus crime bill. The speech highlighted criminal threats to the nation's "security," stock manipulators and speculators, "organized banditry, cold-blooded shooting, lynching and kidnapping"—but not the racketeers that had obsessed earlier anticrime crusaders. "These violations of ethics and these violations of law call on the strong arm of the government for their immediate suppression," the president declared; "they call also on the country for an aroused public opinion." The repeal of Prohibition, he promised, would eliminate the "new forms of crime which [came] from the illegal traffic in liquor."[12]

The war on crime became a tangible, nationalist rallying point for a new interventionist state and a vernacular arena for envisioning a national public committed to the New Deal across party lines. This argument becomes even stronger when we note that the crime of lynching, which represented a deep and racialized split in both parties, was never written into the crime bill, nor did Roosevelt ever endorse such legislation. Rather, during the war on crime, Hoover and Cummings successfully capitalized on preexisting anticrime sentiment among middle-class white voters by projecting a vision of a moral and efficient state that transcended political and cultural differences to unite law-abiding citizens against common dangers. In other words, "the nation," as Daniel Fusfeld explains, "was seen as a larger version of the local community, in which each individual participated in the life of the whole and took responsibility for his or her role." A campaign against bandit crime was thus a crucial political and cultural moment, underlining a New Deal commitment to enlarging federal intervention without fundamentally disturbing the race and class hierarchies that middle-class, white voters imagined when they spoke the word "community."[13]

The Spectacle of Kidnapping

Rewriting kidnapping as a threat to all required significant cultural work; its thrill as mass entertainment simultaneously revealed its characteristics as a class crime. Members of a social, political, or financial elite, a victimized family was not only paying for the safe return of a loved one, but it was "paying" for its status as well, a status originally derived from the stolen labor of the poor. In this scenario, the abducted heir or dependent became a playing piece between two kinds of criminal organizations, the bandit gang and the capitalist family, an innocent victim who served—without consent—as a conduit between the kidnappers and the keepers of undeserved wealth.

Legislators, reformers, and politicians, most often white people of status themselves, responded as a national community of parents to kidnapping cases; calls for federal intervention began early, around 1900, as the crime reached beyond urban slums plagued with petty extortions and into affluent new suburbs. Early efforts to pass local antikidnapping statutes were successful because lawmakers had such clarity about the innocence of the victims; the case of little Eddie Cudahy, ransomed in 1901, prompted ten states and the District of Columbia to pass legislation that year.[14]

The history of such efforts, as well as the strong resemblance of kidnapping dramas to early American captivity narratives, underlines the racial subtext of this crime. In response to the 1907 kidnapping of Horace Marvin Jr., Theodore Roosevelt (a devoted parent) offered federal aid, including the services of his federal special agents. "Save only the crime of assault on women," the president wrote to the Marvin family, invoking yet another form of racialized violence, "there is none so dreadful as that which brought heartbreaking sorrow to your household." Perhaps because men and boys were the victims of choice, Congress was uninspired by the president's passion. However, while federal antikidnapping legislation failed, the Mann Act, criminalizing transportation of women across state lines, known as the "White Slave Act," passed in 1911.[15]

After World War I, the sexualization of white male victims became more pronounced, as psychopathology came to dominate interpretations of criminal behavior. In the summer of 1924, newspaper readers devoured the Chicago slaying of fourteen-year-old Bobby Franks by two wealthy, teenaged geniuses, Richard Loeb and Nathan Leopold Jr. That all three boys were wealthy created a class spectacle; that they were all Jews, a racial one. Dilettante criminals attempting to commit the perfect crime, they were defended by Clarence Darrow in a highly publicized trial. Darrow's insanity defense assumed psychopathic incapacity and was supported by testimony that Leopold and Loeb were either latent or active homosexuals; it won life sentences for them rather than execution. The case helped renew calls for a federal deterrent, and on February 26, 1932, capital kidnapping legislation came before the House Committee on the Judiciary.[16]

Only five days later, the Lindberghs reported their son's disappearance to the New Jersey state police. "Lucky Lindy's" status as a national aviation hero and his late father-in-law's prominence in New Jersey Republican politics infused the crime with political urgency. On March 4, Representative Cochran of Missouri read a speech over the radio, also delivered in Congress, to gather citizen support for the pending bill, which would become known as the Lindbergh Law. Expanding federal jurisdiction would be worth reducing local autonomy, Cochran urged, if only kidnapping could be stopped. Did the public prefer to have "brave officers stopped at State lines because of red tape, professional jealousy?" Or did they "want ferreted out that lowest of all criminals regardless in what State he and his foul companions seek refuge? Of course you do. . . . We must go back to the thought of preservation of the family, the foundation and unit of all government and all civilization."[17] The bill passed on May 19, a week after the dead baby was found.

The Lindbergh case and other celebrity snatchings obscured the different crimes that constituted kidnapping, particularly those for which profit was a secondary motive. Abduction was used by urban racketeers to punish, gain political leverage, or collect debts. In 1930, St. Louis police arrested a gang that "specialized in kidnapping gamblers for ransom." Seven men and one woman had collected more than fifty thousand dollars in three months and were holding a bookmaker for twenty-five thousand. In February 1933, playboy Charles Boetcher II was kidnapped on the streets of Denver and returned a month later, amid rumors of large gambling debts. Boetcher told reporters that no ransom had been paid, but "all obligations were fulfilled." Later that year, John J. "Butch" O'Connell (whose father and uncle were the Democratic bosses of Albany, New York) was ransomed; and Roger Touhy and other members of his North Side Chicago gang were arrested for kidnapping rival racketeer Jake "the Barber" Factor. In Minnesota, accusations that the governor was implicated in a political abduction became part of a recall campaign in 1934. "Floyd B. Olson in the First Kidnapping Murder in 'Gangster Ridden Minnesota,'" asserted a pamphlet printed by the alleged victim's son and sent to the Justice Department by hundreds of concerned Minnesotans.[18]

Obviously, many kidnapping victims could not be portrayed as entirely innocent; thus, the kidnapping of a baby was a cultural and political turning point. "Until in the Lindbergh case they historically overstepped the mark," *Time* magazine noted in July 1933, "the nation's kidnappers had for the most part confined themselves to snatching each other." In early August 1933, Lloyd's of London labeled kidnapping as a class crime when it announced "kidnap insurance," with policy limits of one hundred thousand dollars for adults and fifty thousand for each child, with additional payments for injuries incurred. It was designed specifically for innocent victims. Only "persons of unquestioned reputation" would be allowed to buy the policy, and the names of the policyholders would be kept strictly secret "so that they [would] not be a standing invitation to kidnappers to come get them."[19]

Unlike most kidnappings, the search for the Lindbergh child was a long and anguished one, made worse by a ransom that failed to produce the child. "If we had not done that—and we were urged to do it *immediately*," Anne Lindbergh confided in a letter, "we would have blamed ourselves forever for not doing what works in most cases." As the days dragged on, the case became confused by cranks, false evidence, mysterious intermediaries hinting at underworld contacts (in prison, Al Capone offered help), and newspaper coverage that invited strangers to become famous for a day or so by offering new information. Anne despaired that the search could proceed "until the publicity [died] down." Although the child's body was found, the kidnappers were not, and it was not until September 1934 that Bruno Richard Hauptmann was arrested after spending marked ransom money.[20]

Although the G-men later assisted in gathering evidence for the Hauptmann prosecution, the 1932–33 investigation was a poor debut for Hoover's reforms. On the day after the kidnapping, the director contacted Colonel Norman Schwartzkopf, chief of the New Jersey state police, who had taken charge of the search. "I impressed upon Colonel S. that the Federal government had no police functions in the case," he told the attorney general, "but I wanted him to feel free to call upon the federal agencies for any assistance which they might be able to render. I told him that, in order to avoid confusion and possible duplication of work, you had designated me to act as the coordinating agent for the several Federal investigating agencies." The letter went on to describe procedures that suggest that Hoover was, in reality, positioning himself as a gatekeeper between Schwartzkopf and the federal government.[21]

By this strategy, Hoover hoped to give his own police laboratory privileged access to the evidence generated by the various police agencies that were developing leads in the case. Inevitably, his agents would receive credit if the crime was solved. However, the Department of Justice was careful not to reveal this privileged position to the press, committing little of the bureau's prestige to a difficult case as the weeks of searching turned into months. "You are also advised that the Federal kidnapping statute was passed after the Lindbergh and McPherson incidents," an assistant attorney general replied to one inquiry, "and would not therefore apply to them."[22]

Correspondence on the case suggests that Hoover released information of little value, giving Schwartzkopf access to federal resources that any competent secretary might have coordinated. On May 26, the director forwarded reward notices published in New Jersey to Sanford Bates, director of the Bureau of Prisons, presumably hoping to prod a convict into fingering a former confederate.

Hoover and Schwartzkopf may have communicated more directly by telephone and indirectly through subordinates, but there are no telephone memorandums and little correspondence between them; the surviving evidence suggests that relations between the two quickly broke down. By the fall, Hoover's letters to Schwartzkopf were terse; several times, he transmitted patently useless documents from mentally disturbed people as if they were evidence. Two were signed "Persecuted good woman" and "Woman for righteousness," and a third was transmitted with Hoover's humorless comment, "You will note that the information Mr. Wheeler desires to provide was derived from an alleged vision."[23]

Much of the New York office was assigned to the case, but the absence of memorandums in 1932–33 documenting leads, interviews, and evidence shared with other agencies reflects both Hoover's desire to keep the case to himself and the failure of the investigation. However, the Roosevelt administration's commitment to a war on crime in the summer of 1933 would put the unsolved kidnapping at the top of a federal anticrime agenda, and by the fall of that year, all files and evidence gathered by the government were ordered transferred to the new, consolidated Division of Investigation. Hoover made sure that the shortcomings of other federal investigators were noted in this period. The treasury agent who had been "engaged on this case since shortly after the date of the kidnaping," Hoover complained, had not produced a report in fourteen months. Neither files or a promised summary of evidence appeared until the spring of 1934, and, as Hoover told Homer Cummings, he had to write the report himself.[24]

Because the federal government had no jurisdiction over the case, the new attorney general struggled to justify greater federal authority. As Hoover explained to Assistant Attorney General William Stanley shortly after the inauguration, there was, in his belief, a "basic lack of Federal jurisdiction," but, "I personally feel that one of the few tangible leads in the Lindbergh case lies in the tracing of the sources of this ransom money which from time to time is placed in circulation by the kidnappers." Noting that the New York City police had offered rewards of two to five dollars for each bill, Hoover suggested that the division offer more to bring the evidence directly to the federal crime laboratories. Stanley approved this immediately, and on March 22, the federal reward rose again to top New York's higher bid.[25]

This competition over who would possess the evidence and when was part of a larger competition over which "modern" police force would enhance its reputation by solving the crime. The New Jersey state police had been on the scene first; and although the baby was later believed to have died by accident almost immediately, they were accused by some of not having done enough to find him. As Hoover redoubled the federal efforts in mid-May 1934, special agent in charge of the New York office T. H. Siske warned him that Schwartzkopf planned to go to Cummings to challenge the government's right to see and analyze evidence in New Jersey's possession. Siske also reported that "as a retaliatory measure" division agents had been banned from New Jersey state patrol cars assigned to the investigation.[26]

Hoover exploded on May 22 in a letter to Cummings. Schwartzkopf's petty behavior demonstrated "the obstacles with which the Division [was] confronted in conducting this investigation." New Jersey troopers had fouled their own evidence and were now seeking to take possession of ransom money that the department had acquired. "Colonel S. advises he will be glad to submit a list of the physical evidence in his possession after the case has been solved at which time, it will, of course, be of no particular value," Hoover complained. On June 8, the director sent a detailed letter to Cummings describing the tactics that had been used against him, including a resolution introduced by Schwartzkopf at a national meeting of state police chiefs that condemned the division for "its lack of cooperation in the Lindbergh case." For once, associationalism was used against Hoover: the chief had tried to persuade the New York City police to protest federal intervention at the IACP convention, and Hoover told Cummings that he would hear from both New Jersey senators in the coming week. All of this, Hoover concluded bitterly, was evidence of the "jealous and narrow attitude" harbored by his rivals.[27] Any record of federal progress on the case ceases here and, until Hauptmann's arrest later that summer, is replaced by a voluminous correspondence generated by anxious citizens observing the kidnap melodrama.

It is this flood of letters, which began only days after Charles Lindbergh Jr. disappeared, that so clearly evokes an imaginative world created by citizens who identified with kidnap victims. Many of them hoped to collect rewards offered by police, and some were clearly demented, but most were ordinary citizens who felt some compulsion to connect themselves with the case. A lawyer in Rochester wrote to Cummings to say that his client believed that she had seen the kidnappers and wanted to be deposed. Others sent possible leads: one Chicagoan pointed out that his local pediatric hospital might "possibly provide a hiding place for the kidnapped son of Charles A. Lindbergh."[28]

In 1932, organizations around the country used the kidnapping as an opportunity to remind President Herbert Hoover of their support for federal anticrime measures and urged him to help the Lindberghs at all cost. A Hartford fraternal organization stood "ready and willing to fight to the bitter end for the maintenance and preservation of law, order and human justice." Ironically, other citizens believed that "law" might prevent "justice"—that is, the return of the child—and urged the president to offer immunity to the kidnappers. "You alone can save this baby by making a Radio announcement that you will *positively* give a *full pardon* to all who are connected with the kidnapping [of] our baby Lindy," one wrote, offering to serve the jail time himself: "Society will demand punishment for this crime, and I will gladly supply it."[29]

Ethnic and working-class populations, as well as people of color, were always possible suspects in these letters, making it easy to imagine the writers as white. A number of correspondents assumed that all kidnappings were connected in some way to prewar Black Hand or mafia terrorist organizations. "It is very apparent that the trouble is that element of bad citizen (the Italians) all over our country," one woman wrote. Referring to Al Capone's attempts to find the baby, she pointed out that the heroic Lindbergh's reliance on "a gang leader to act as his mediator [was] truly a disgrace to this country! In order to try and bring about the return of an innocent little child." A New Jersey housewife suggested that Anne Lindbergh's relief work for the Chinese government might have incurred retaliation from the Japanese emperor. "I hope this letter is never made public," she confessed, "as I have a mortal dread of the same consequences to my own son if it should be correct."[30]

A full year before the New Deal and the war on crime, citizens expected the federal government to provide information, listen to their ideas, and respond to their anxieties about the case. In fact, many writers believed that the government was more accessible than celebrities like the Lindberghs. One armchair detective asked for a federal handwriting identification circular, and another (who signed himself "Citizen") urged a policy of deporting felons to a penal colony: "There is no other way to save our country and institutions." A third blamed "the horrors and evils existing all over our fair land" on profanity: "The crime waive [*sic*] in the U.S. would be cut in half in a year if we suppress this stuff," he insisted. A contractor from Ohio was one of many who suggested a plan for rescuing the baby and explained, "A letter to Hopewell or some other points of action in this case would not receive a possible consideration." Voting was a foundational connection between this public and its government. "As a citizen of Pennsylvania," one man wrote, "I demand an end to this reign of gang rule. . . . The people are aroused and demand protection for themselves and their families. They are going to vote accordingly."[31]

The most common letter did not have a political or a policy orientation; it offered to assist in the search, either through supplying arcane evidence or because of an urgent desire to help the Lindberghs. Writers hit hard by the depression saw the crime as an opportunity: Mrs. Velma O'Neill of Jackson, Mississippi, wrote that she was "not presently employed and really in delinquent circumstances"; she explained further, "I have spent lots of time traveling the last six years, and as I am, you might say, homeless, I am free to go where I please. . . . I don't believe it would take me long to furnish all the evidence needed and maybe a confession." Other letters accused the government of incompetence. J. Edgar Hoover passed on to his counterpart at the Secret Service a letter addressed to the president, adding:

> You will note the statement of Mr. Hall to the effect that he had been advised by Mr. Frank Burke, of your Division, that he, Burke, was practically certain of the identity of the kidnappers in the Lindbergh case, and possessed information from which, if he be assigned to the case, he could procure sufficient evidence to bring about the conviction of the guilty parties.

Spite motivated others. One anonymous correspondent told agents to investigate a person "who knows plenty"; and socialite Mrs. Alfred V. DuPont suggested that the Department of Justice look for a couple who left her employ while she was on vacation.[32]

Most of the Lindbergh correspondence reveals that for many citizens spectacular crime had become a passionate interest and a singular connection to the state sphere. One investigator of unknown gender was absorbed in the case. Upon hearing of the baby's death, the correspondent was stricken and then determined to find the killers: "I have never ceased working to accomplish my aims," the person wrote to Homer Cummings in 1934. "I have read articles of nearly every description on the case; attended trials, lectures on crime; and have discussed the Lindbergh kidnapping with people in many walks of life. . . . I have listened to your splendid talks on crime over the Radio; [and have] read the addresses made at Bar associations that I was not able to attend." This consumer of crime had also attended a special Senate hearing on crime in Detroit, wrote regularly to Schwartzkopf, clipped articles on the case, went to talks on crime at the local university, and, after one of them, conferred with Assistant Attorney General Joseph B. Keenan and a United States senator. The desire to participate was surely nurtured by such public forums, which appeared to ask for citizen action against crime: the governor of Oklahoma wrote to Cummings about a constituent who was "a bit 'nutty' over the Lindbergh thing," and forwarded list of suspects she had supplied to him.[33]

This is only a sample of the many thousands of letters received by the federal government during the investigation of the kidnapping and, later, the trial of Bruno Hauptmann. Interestingly, after Hauptmann was convicted and sentenced to die in the electric chair, few citizens wrote in to condemn him; there was instead an upsurge of mail asking that he be spared, with some writers offering to die in his place. What this imaginative world may have demonstrated to J. Edgar Hoover, Homer Cummings, and others at the Department of Justice was that a consolidation of federal police authority could be successfully accomplished through a war on crime because there was a public that already existed, and that could be mobilized, around it. However, the difficulty of conducting prestigious investigations without legislation that gave the Division of Investigation ownership of major felonies like the Lindbergh case was also vividly demonstrated throughout the final year of the Hoover administration and the first months of the New Deal. Even as this legislation was being drawn up in September 1933, Assistant Attorney General William Stanley gave notice to all offices that the hunt for perpetrators of that summer's major abductions was on. "The Department of Justice, at the Direction of the Attorney General," the circular memo read, "is concentrating its forces in a movement to suppress kidnapping and crimes of violence based upon extortion."[34]

A New Deal for Crime

On September 12, 1933, Thomas D. Campbell of Hardin, Montana, opened his morning mail to find a circular letter from the Dedekam Insurance Company of San Francisco. "A good many Americans are carrying *Kidnap Insurance*," the company asserted. "We can insure ransom money at a very low rate of premium." Campbell sent the letter to the Justice Department, with a note deploring the fact that "such a condition exists in the United States whereby our citizens think it advisable to carry insurance against kidnapping." The government, he advised, should regulate this trade, since it was "very apt to stimulate kidnapping and encourage the kidnappers and gangsters."[35]

The circular, with a citizen turning to his government because of it, situates the war on crime at the intersection of New Deal politics and culture. Historians have articulated the campaign against bandit crime as different from other New Deal programs because the state "naturally" moved to repress crime and yet, as many have also noted, the Roosevelt administration did not move to repress all crime: syndicates became more powerful in these years. Similarly, other scholars have shown that particular political moments activate state repression, directing it toward particular subjects. A close look at those who devised the war on crime—Homer Cummings, J. Edgar Hoover, and Louis M. Howe— reveals much about how interventions are conceived in relation to certain felonies and why they are prosecuted.[36]

A war on crime was an opportunity for the new attorney general, Homer Cummings, to reshape a still badly disorganized Department of Justice, using Hoover's reformed bureau as its most public symbol. Although it is difficult to know who originated the idea of the war on crime, it was Cummings who was its primary voice in 1933. Because of repeal, the department he inherited was shrinking: from 1932 to 1936, it would go from a total of 9,103 employees to 7,470, one-fifth to one-eighth the size of the expanding Department of the Treasury.

Its reputation, however, was little changed from the department Mabel Walker Willebrandt had left in 1929. Election year paybacks had "almost wrecked the Department of Justice by loading it to the gunwales with deserving Democrats," one critic wrote. This "terrible crew" was augmented by "Republican holdovers, some of them stretching back to the wild old days when Harry Daugherty was the shake-down artist of the Republican Administration."[37]

This was an opinion shared by those within Roosevelt's inner circle of New Dealers. Public Works Administration chairman Harold Ickes wrote in his diary that he would "put up a stiff fight" against a Cummings proposal to centralize all legal services in the Department of Justice. Giving up his "able, young, straight-thinking lawyers" for Cummings's staff would leave him "helpless," Ickes claimed. "That Department is simply loaded with political appointees and hardly anyone has any respect for the standing and ability of the lawyers over there. Cummings himself is a man of considerable ability, but he is easygoing and apparently has deliberately delivered himself entirely into the hands of the place hunters." Ickes also voiced concerns in a conversation with Felix Frankfurter, who responded, "[The president] thoroughly understands the weakness of the Department. . . . It has some hard-working, earnest lawyers, but no outstanding ones."[38] Cummings reorganized the entire department around the prosecution of felonies, perhaps in order to increase prosecutions that would garner good publicity and enhance its reputation for honesty. Out of fifteen divisions, the Criminal Division emerged from the reorganization as the largest, with thirty-three separate areas of responsibility. No other division had more than twelve subdivisions, and most had fewer than five. What is most vital for understanding Cummings's role in shifting the emphasis toward criminal prosecution, however, is his belief that state interventions on behalf of an orderly society acted in defense of individual liberty. Thus, the development of a strong state had been historically positive, and, as he would write later, "executive law officers had played an important role in the fascinating drama of national life." In lectures delivered at the University of Virginia in 1934, Cummings wove the campaign against crime into a long history of crime and state repression. "Our social order, undoubtedly, is changing, as it has ever changed, but it faces neither collapse or revolution," he argued. Crime, a "perversion" of individual freedom, could be addressed by government expansion; federal policing thus created "conditions in which a finer and more complete personal freedom may exist."[39]

Moreover, as he reflected on the war on crime in 1935, he articulated the non-political administrative state as the only way to enhance the public sphere, since liberty and the public welfare demanded "ever-increasing powers of social control." The "new devices of government" displayed against bandit crime had been demanded by a public that understood that "the relationship between the state, society and individual liberty would have to take on a different character." Some might call this "a new social order," but Cummings saw it as a renewal of tradition, a regeneration of fundamental liberties that required "new agencies to define and secure them."[40]

Cummings's emphasis on order, expertise, and administrative excellence made it unlikely that he would replace Hoover with any of the patronage candidates leading Democrats urged on him. However, despite the director's reappointment on July 29, 1933, it was still not clear that he would survive old enemies and new critics in Washington. Some journalists cited Department of Justice and White House sources for articles that praised Hoover as a "star," the "'Key Man' in Crime War," the "Crime War Chief," and "Uncle Sam's Sherlock Holmes"; others printed rumors that he might yet be replaced. Columnist Drew Pearson asserted on August 19 that FDR's original choice for attorney general, Thomas J. Walsh, had picked a successor before he died (which was likely, given a vendetta between the two that dated from the Palmer years). Pearson's source also claimed that Cummings had also chosen a replacement—but the candidate died. Journalists with more license smelled shifts of power. One gossip writer printed a snide aside about Hoover's rumored effeminacy: the director, wrote Peter Carter, was known by area auctioneers as "Mr. H.," was "an ardent collector of Chinese bronzes and [was] an interested and active bidder at many of Washington's auction sales"; an exchange between *Collier's* and *Washington Herald* columnists also debated the "manliness" of Hoover's stride.[41]

Despite the director's insistence that the bureau was no place for politics, his position was—like all other powerful, government jobs—vulnerable to patronage, and Democratic party regulars continued to suggest publicly that Hoover was a likely candidate for the scrap heap. As late as November, while congressional committees were drawing up the omnibus crime legislation, the *Washington Post* cited a "reliable source" who confirmed that James A. Farley, chairman of the Democratic party, Tammany Hall chief, and postmaster general, had enlisted the aid of "several Southern Senators" to oust Hoover as soon as Farley and Cummings could agree on a replacement. Not surprisingly, New Yorkers led the list; the most serious candidate was former New York City police detective Val O'Farrell.[42]

Thus, while many historians have evaluated the war on crime as a public relations ploy, they have not emphasized enough that Hoover was on the brink of losing his job in the first year of the New Deal. He had gained a temporary reprieve by appealing to his old mentor Harlan Fiske Stone, since 1928 a Supreme Court Justice and a friend of the new president. Hoover had also activated his national constituency: police organizations that he had cultivated since 1924 produced an unrelenting national lobbying campaign throughout 1933.

A third strategy that Hoover pursued was to use his agents to investigate other candidates. O'Farrell, Hoover helpfully informed Cummings following the newspaper rumors, had been linked to organized crime while working as a private detective.[43]

Roosevelt was probably also impressed by the detailed surveillance reports that appeared regularly on his desk, and he understood that this director could be an important source of information during a politically treacherous period. In March 1933, Hoover outlined the history and capabilities of the Bureau of Investigation for the new president. Its work, he wrote, was "three-fold in character: investigation, identification and research." The director emphasized his economies and an improved record of convictions: the bureau employed only 360 special agents in 1932 and maintained a mere twenty-two field offices. Better planning had reduced the cost of travel and per diem expenses. Hoover had cut field expenses by securing office space in federal buildings, a move that also brought the agents into closer contact with other federal employees and emphasized their identity as government workers. FDR soon discovered that Hoover was not as politically naive as he claimed. The block of southern Democrats who had originally opposed Hoover's reappointment mysteriously reversed course in July, despite strenuous opposition from John W. McCormack, the powerful Massachusetts chairman of the House Ways and Means Committee.[44]

Indeed, Hoover's position that his agency represented a set of national interests that transcended party politics was broadly consistent with New Deal liberalism, which viewed the state as "part designer, part umpire, but also part player." *Uniform Crime Reports* and *Fugitives Wanted,* for example, brought different police agencies together in an awareness of a common identity and goal and were a monthly reminder of the state's concern. While promoting a "more orderly keeping of records in local police departments," as Hoover claimed, information that participating departments sent to the bureau helped federal officers maintain "very close contact with all law-enforcement officials and agencies throughout the United States," exchanges that, as Hoover explained to the new president, had created "a national police system in this country."[45]

This latter statement was the kind of exaggeration Hoover's opponents must have exploited with pleasure. By December 1932 the bureau's publications went to only 1,578 departments, which policed less than half of the population. Law enforcement agencies that did not contribute statistics to the bureau did not receive the publications: Tulsa, St. Paul, and Joplin, Missouri, were notable crime-corridor exceptions to the "national police system." Complaints lodged against Hoover in these early months highlighted his tendency to fiddle with the truth for personal gain. "Building publicity around himself for selfish purposes," one wrote, "he has not been hesitant in crediting himself with everything he could. Despite news stories creating [such an] impression, Hoover was not responsible for creating the Identification Division, Wm. J. Burns did that, and as to the wonderful operation of that Division, it operates automatically and a grade school boy can make the count, do the classifying and send back to the police the form telegram." The memo mentioned specific resentment from the Secret Service, the Special Intelligence branch of the Internal Revenue Service, and numerous assistant attorneys general.[46]

Although the war on crime was not Hoover's idea—indeed, it seems unlikely that he would have volunteered for a second try at national enforcement or multiple repetitions of his battle with Schwartzkopf—he may have seized on it as an opportunity to prove his indispensability to the government to which he had given his life. The war on crime probably originated with the president's personal secretary, Louis M. Howe. Indeed, it was Howe who connected Cummings's dramatic announcements of June and July 1933 to the broader moral outlook of the New Deal and the ideals of citizenship it promoted. In an August 1933 radio broadcast, Howe linked state and nation to the crusade against criminals through the symbol of the National Recovery Administration eagle. "A really roused public opinion will amazingly speed up the slow moving wheels of justice," he vowed, "[and] the great organization of the Blue Eagle ... will set an example and will point the way to some kind of an organized movement on the part of our citizens." In this renewed nation, Howe promised, "Juries will convict rather than face public scorn of chicken-heartedness on their part. The wealthy gangster will find that his money will not buy protection."[47]

The architect of Roosevelt's political career, Howe had for some years maintained a passionate interest in the anticrime movement and had promoted it as a political issue. In vain, he angled for a position on George Wickersham's national crime commission and instead had to settle for pushing then Governor Roosevelt to take anticrime stances, including the advocacy of a "Scotland Yard" for New York State. Neither an intellectual nor a reformer, Howe had an uncertain future in the New Deal and may have proposed a war on crime as a way of keeping his place in the inner circle. Brain truster Raymond Moley might also have urged FDR to let Howe publicize the issue: as a participant in several crime commissions and author of their reports, he had urged federal intervention since the 1920s.[48]

By invoking the Blue Eagle for his anticrime campaign, Howe linked his work to a symbol of cross-class cooperation and, as a biographer puts it, to "a people determined to rise from the vortex of disaster."[49] Although there is no evidence that Howe made policy or consulted with Hoover and Cummings, he may have convinced FDR, amid a chaotic legislative agenda, that a war on crime was consistent with New Deal goals. Certainly other people began to believe that the president could be influenced through Howe: in June, 1933, he received a note from Val O' Farrell, proposing a federal law that would make driver's licenses only available on the recommendation of one's local police captain. Cummings's special assistant, Joseph B. Keenan, who would supervise the day-to-day operations of the war on crime, also wrote to suggest that an aroused public could push a president to enact crime legislation: "*Widespread public indignation* following the [Lindbergh] kidnapping . . . resulted in the enactment of a federal statute giving the Federal Government jurisdiction over the crime of kidnapping," Keenan reminded Howe.[50]

By July 27, 1933, Howe had secured FDR's commitment to a federal anticrime effort, and he urged Eleanor Roosevelt to join a civic association of social scientists working on crime and juvenile delinquency. "This fall we are planning a crusade against crime," he advised, "and we may find the association of great value." Two days later (the day Hoover was reappointed), Howe published an article in the *Saturday Evening Post* that drew on established anticrime and police modernization themes. A war on crime would require "a national body of trained crime detectives, with trained crime investigators, and fearless government policemen, unaffected by local politics or local sympathy, always ready to proceed to the scene of any crime and take charge with power, first to identify and then pursue the criminal to the ends of the earth if necessary." The article tread carefully around the Constitution. Such a force would only be mobilized "at the request of the local authorities themselves," Howe promised. About a proposed federal law to limit machine gun sales, he argued that they could not "by any means be construed as a weapon needed by the peaceful citizen to protect his home . . . [but were] obviously for the purpose of crime committing and wholesale murder."[51]

The shape and direction of the war on crime emerged from those in the new administration who had a stake in prosecuting it, the least of whom perhaps was the president. But the question of why bandit gangs became the object of this campaign rather than criminal syndicates suggests that the president did limit its scope, that an anticrime campaign was risky politics. The choice to focus on bandit gangs, ignoring the advice and desires of urban civic reform organizations by not investigating criminal syndicates, exchanged one set of political imperatives for another. A campaign against syndicate crime would have challenged the labor unions and political machines that had engineered the Democratic victory in 1932 (Roosevelt's own Tammany Hall among them) and were then pushing local governments to cooperate in New Deal reforms.[52] In addition, Roosevelt's two closest advisers on crime were Howe and Moley, classic police reform thinkers who believed that modern, professional policemen ought not to be engaging with the vice crimes in which syndicates specialized. Certainly, as his 1934

State of the Union address indicated, FDR also believed that when Prohibition was repealed, syndicates would disappear.

Professional policing, which placed a premium on surveillance and evidence collection, inevitably created unspoken alliances between policemen and criminals. Although historians have charged that Hoover and Cummings were only "preoccupied with the sensational, the spectacular," not unlike New Deal politicians, for information and results bureau agents depended on strategic, long-term connections to the organizations that really ran cities.[53] As the Dillinger and Barker-Karpis gang files demonstrate, bureau agents maintained strings of underworld informants who, for a price, located stolen property and gathered information about federal fugitives. These "snitches" allowed Hoover to increase the reach of the state invisibly and report high statistics of returned property and recovered fugitives without hiring additional agents.

The redefinition of police professionalism around the principles of scientific management, and the extremes to which that was taken in Hoover's new national police, also had an impact on what kind of crime could actually be seen. Bandit crime became visible because of the numbers and types of incidents that were actually reported. However, syndicate crimes were violent and/or parasitical economic enterprises that often insinuated themselves in or masqueraded as legitimate businesses. Thus, syndicate criminals did not produce the incidents that defined criminal activity in the 1930s. When Hoover demonstrated to Congress in January 1934 that there was a crime wave in the United States, he proved his point with figures drawn from the *Uniform Crime Reports* that showed a rise in felonious homicide (murder, manslaughter), rape, robbery, aggravated assault, burglary, larceny, and auto theft.[54]

By the spring of 1934, the surge in kidnappings and the spectacular crimes of the Barrow and Dillinger gangs made passage of the twelve acts of the omnibus crime bill inevitable. By early summer, when Roosevelt signed the legislation, a federal police was articulated as necessary to the survival of the nation. In January 1934, Cummings hosted the National Conference on Crime, which Roosevelt greeted by affirming the importance of federal crime fighting to the New Deal. Lack of coordination between local police made it possible for "bandits [to] have been better equipped and better organized" than the law. "Crime is a symptom of social disorder," the president admonished. "Widespread increase in the capacity to substitute order for disorder is the remedy."[55]

Like Hoover and Cummings, Roosevelt believed that the public played a crucial role in fighting crime and creating moral order, becoming the moral ally of a regulative state rather than the object of regulation itself. In fact, such a public was implicitly produced through the regulative power of other institutions. Crime would be beaten by "marshalling the assets of home, church, community and other social agencies, to work in common purpose with our law enforcement agencies," the president insisted. "I want the backing of every man, every woman and every adolescent child in every State of the United States and in every county of every State for what you and the officers of law and order are trying to accomplish."[56] Indeed, at the Department of Justice plans were being formulated to enroll citizens as participants and as an audience for the war on crime.

Creating a Public

The creation of strategies to publicize government programs, an aspect of state making that had emerged in the United States during World War I, was foundational to the ideology of national revitalization that undergirded the New Deal. Roosevelt's personal relations with the press and his emphasis on direct communication with citizens became a new source of political power that complicated and transformed relationships between the executive, the electorate, and other branches of government. Similar techniques, often understood by historians as far less benign, were employed by J. Edgar Hoover's public relations staff, housed in the Crime Records Division and run by former YMCA publicity director Louis B. Nichols.[57]

The war on crime suggests an important distinction between the institutional uses of publicity and the political goal of shaping a national public. Publicity about the director and his special agents, Richard Gid Powers has argued, ultimately subsumed and shaped their policing duties; the 1930s were, therefore, a formative moment for the crafting of powerful images that by themselves produced agendas for federal policing.[58] However, what Nichols and Henry Suydam (Nichols's counterpart in the attorney general's office) created after 1934 was not just a believable image but a viable audience for that image, a coherent public made from the many citizens who agreed that they were "anticrime." This public was drawn together through flirtations with the unrespectable and given form through symbolic acts that permitted citizens to demonstrate whether they were for or against government. The use of privileged information and detail permitted the Division of Investigation, and Hoover in particular, to act as interlocutors between the public and the fascinating, forbidden world of crime.

More important, the creation of a public for a federal crime war was not specific to Hoover but part of a larger strategy to rebuild the reputation of the Department of Justice during the first New Deal. The emergence of the director himself as a celebrity crime fighter, which coalesced in hundreds of magazine articles published under Hoover's byline after 1934, was another product of Nichols's genius that enhanced federal authority in the public realm. Numerous scholars have credited Hoover with an instinct for the popular that he exploited mercilessly for personal influence. "Hoover usually had a feel for the kind of propaganda that would be effective with most Americans," Robert Sherrill has written, using as evidence the director's keen appreciation for comic strips with heroic narratives, such as *Tarzan, Dick Tracy, Secret Agent X-9,* and *War on Crime.*[59]

A focus on Hoover's instincts obscures the labor of public relations professionals, working under the direction of others, who exploited print and broadcast vehicles to attract audiences initially through fantasy and then retain them with scientific language and the dissemination of facts. The literary materials produced by the Crime Records Division, while apparently centered on the G-man and his investigative techniques, were a thin cover for what really grabbed an audience—details about criminals, criminal methods, and the worlds criminals inhabited. Administrators leaked case files on successful manhunts to favored writers and artists, so that news stories and comic strips authored during this period purported to offer a privileged view of the underworld—as told by the G-men.

Fascination with unrespectable texts such as bandits, their lives and loves, and their violent crimes forced a reader to negotiate a text that was respectable: the G-man, an expert who moved among criminals and could reveal the facts about them that audiences craved. Significantly, after 1934, mass-market popular literature produced through the Crime Records Division featured the underworld in its titles. For example, a detective magazine called *Public Enemy: The Thrilling Exploits of the G-Men,* first published in 1935, by the ordering of its title and subtitle, used popular fascination with criminals to draw an audience for the government. Furthermore, such products (only a small part of the vast, nationalist literary production of the New Deal) offered consumers membership in an imagined community of the lawful, populated by the G-man and his citizen allies. Nichols's publicity machine eventually embraced all forms of consumable culture available to a depression-era audience: movies, prime-time radio shows, comic strips, magazines, and, most important, toys, books, games, clothes, and other items produced for a children's market.[60] Books for adults, like *Farewell, Mr. Gangster!* (1934) and *Ten Thousand Public Enemies* (1935) by journalist Courtney Riley Cooper, opened with a picture of and a signed introduction by Hoover, assuring readers that the details contained within were accurate. As he noted in *Ten Thousand Public Enemies,* Cooper's "knowledge of the inner workings of the Division, his personal acquaintanceship with its wide-flung personnel, his familiarity with the methods, aims and purposes [were] on an equality with the men who actually form[ed] its staff."[61]

As an example of this genre, *Ten Thousand Public Enemies* projects a national body politic made up of individuals who experience crime in similar ways wherever they live. Cooper eradicates the boundaries between criminal and citizen, showing that everyone's "daily lives are intertwined with crime and its perpetrators." As he warns,

> The dreamy-eyed manicurist who files away so enthusiastically at your nails may be thinking only of closing time, when she can hurry to meet the man whose "moll" she can become, arranging his hide-outs, carrying his gun for him, fainting at the scene of a burglary to confuse pursuit. Provided this manicurist works in a shop of heavy patronage, it is almost certain that the very instruments which shape your finger nails have performed the same service for men who have known the cell block and the mess hall of prisons. Your tip after a hotel meal clinks in the same pocket with the gratuity of murderers and kidnappers.[62]

Heterosexual romance and a working girl's fantasies about power are reframed as a dangerously seductive criminal spectacle, more compelling because of its lack of proportion: could a moll hold down a manicurist's job and accomplish all of these criminal acts? Cooper weaves new criminals into a familiar urban reform narrative, the working-class woman who infects respectable society with the moral and physical diseases of the slums.

Significantly, there is a twentieth-century twist to this Victorian morality tale: it is not respectable women but men who are touched by lower-class criminality through the manicurist's file, and men who, through the exchange of money, mingle indiscriminately with other men in the pocket of a (male) service employee. The homoeroticism of these cross-class contacts conveyed for an interwar reading audience, schooled by sexologists, the specter of physical and mental disease embedded in the body politic. However, such narratives were not utterly repulsive, only forbidden. Thus, this literature and other texts about crime provided an imaginative space for the public to mingle with and be stimulated by the underworld without actually touching crime or being touched by it. In fact, in this particular characteristic, sensational crime literature produced under the auspices of the Department of Justice was not markedly different from other genres of New Deal cultural production that relied on the production of a safely distanced "other": oral histories of elderly former slaves; rural photography projects; and James Agee and Walker Evans's *Let Us Now Praise Famous Men*.[63]

These textual spaces, produced under the auspices of the state, were imaginative gathering places for citizens. The literary associationalism of the anticrime public was also complemented in the civic realm by anticrime conferences, rallies, and fingerprinting drives. This last activity permitted citizens to experience personally the techniques of scientific policing and, one might imagine, experience themselves for a moment as occupying a criminal body in the custody of the state. At these festive occasions, often held during community events, citizens were given the opportunity to become part of the law-abiding public, sending a piece of themselves to the Division of Investigation. Thousands volunteered: Boy Scouts, Girl Scouts, Camp Fire Girls, and visitors to the division's Washington headquarters, who could be fingerprinted as part of a tour. Kiwanians, Rotarians, and Masons worked with local police departments to fingerprint their memberships, setting up booths at state and local fairs.[64]

Fingerprinting became so closely associated with the ideals of good citizenship and a crime-free society that Cummings began to advocate the routine collection of fingerprints among people served by New Deal programs, particularly the urban, male youths employed by the Civilian Conservation Corps. Attempts to collect permanent records on these juveniles suggest that working-class audiences may have been less drawn in by the pleasures of the war on crime. Familiar with the consequences of becoming known to the police, CCC workers refused to participate, even at the risk of being expelled from the program. In mid-1935, Harold Ickes recorded a fierce cabinet debate about compulsory finger printing of the enrollees in the CCC camps. "There has been a system of voluntary finger printing, but apparently the great body of the boys in the camps have not submitted . . . of their own free will." Robert Fechner, the administrator of the camps, strongly supported by Cummings and by the secretary of war, asked for a presidential order to force them to comply. "All the rest of us were against it," Ickes wrote later, "and the President was of that opinion too."[65] Although fingerprinting provided a public relations opportunity, it clearly had pitfalls as well, most notably when it activated latent suspicions about the extension of state power.

As these examples show, public relations inevitably brought Hoover and the division into an alliance with the unrespectable: this uneasy coupling between the government and the criminal underworld created audience excitement in a way that the state could never compel by itself. Entrepreneurial journalists like Cooper were a crucial link to this audience. In late 1929 Hoover formed a long-term partnership with *Washington Star* reporter Rex Collier, who scooped other star journalists the following year as "the first newspaperman to be admitted [to and take] you behind the scenes of, this closely guarded sanctum." (Collier was also the author of a G-man comic strip.) In 1933 *New York World-Telegram* crime reporter Lou Weidman debuted the comic strip "Special Agent J-8," while Walter Winchell and Ed Sullivan became allies in radio journalism. These men not only popularized the G-men for a national audience but also made a celebrity out of Hoover. Winchell, for example, boosted his ratings during the 1930s by squiring Hoover and Tolson around New York café society, hinting at their liaisons with starlets at "21," the Stork Club, and El Morocco, or by engineering the director's most interesting public relations coup, his nomination as one of the 1930s "Most Eligible Bachelors."[66]

By articulating him as heterosexually active, Winchell confirmed Hoover's respectability; at the same time, Hoover's alliance with sensational journalism, and Winchell in particular, gave the director glamorous unrespectability. Winchell, in turn, found Hoover a useful ally, because the director was respectable and because he was a source of unique information about underworld personalities that could be "sold" over the radio. Both Winchell and Hoover understood that mass culture was changing notions of citizenship and community at the beginning of the Great Depression, and both understood the nationalist implications of technology. Hoover's publicity techniques, in fact, only copied those invented by Winchell, who seized on new methods of distributing and creating news to launch "a new mass culture of celebrity—centered in New York and Hollywood and Washington, fixated on personalities, promulgated by the media, predicated on publicity, dedicated to the ephemeral and grounded on the principle that notoriety confers power."[67]

Winchell, like Hoover, believed that "success was short-lived; one had to work beyond endurance, beyond exhaustion, to stave off the inevitable descent." As the director had successfully negotiated political scandal and professional disgrace in the aftermath of the Palmer and Teapot Dome years, so did Winchell salvage his own career by making the shift to radio as the depression destroyed the glittering Manhattan nightlife he depended on. He first went on the air at 7:45 on Monday, May 12, 1930, on WABC, initiating what one biographer has called an "intimate relationship with [his] audience . . . the sense of shared culture to which the gossip column had also contributed." Like police work, news-as-entertainment traded in information. In fact, journalists trading in gossip were often accused of unsavory surveillance and blackmail, techniques for wielding power that were central to Hoover's own repertoire (one gossip sheet was forced to close when it was revealed that "investors" preferred supporting the paper to appearing in it).[68]

Hoover was not the first to mine Winchell's popularity, however; Roosevelt was. It may well have been FDR—through Homer Cummings—who suggested the journalist's usefulness to the war on crime. Initially suspicious of the New Deal, Winchell was invited to the White House shortly after the inauguration and dazzled by the president. Winchell's August 1934 radio campaign against Adolf Hitler may have also drawn him to Hoover's attention: shortly thereafter (and not long after other gossip writers had printed allusions to the director's effeminacy), he introduced the director and Tolson to New York night club entrepreneur

Sherman Billingsly, who offered his posh Stork Club as a setting for many of their well-publicized "bachelor antics."[69]

This publicity launched Hoover as a celebrity, but the benefits were not merely personal; rather, such tactics were part of a broader strategy to elevate the reputation of the Department of Justice through the creation of positive news. As Richard G. Conover wrote to Assistant Attorney General William Stanley in June 1934, the department needed to find methods for distinguishing itself in the press, lest it be obscured by general New Deal enthusiasm. "It would intensify the publicity of the Department of Justice if some design, or insignia, were adopted and imprinted on every sheet of paper on which something is typed for publicity purposes," he pointed out. "A design or insignia on each page would . . . exploit the Department with so many more eye-greetings." This strategy would encourage newspapers to feature the Department of Justice regularly, since it would be "a convenience to editors" to be able to identify immediately items generated by it.[70]

Feature articles could be accompanied by a war-on-crime scorecard that registered victories against the underworld. "If a CONSTANT BOX showing achievement were kept up to the date and hour," Conover elaborated,

> every time anything is given to the newspapers relating to the Department's activities, a copy of this constantly checked-up BOX might be given out also.
>
> The theory is that large numbers of people are watching the results of the pursuit of criminals now that more particular responsibility has been placed on the Department. If nothing at all is heard of accomplishments—in the way of numbers—the observer is not satisfied that the Department is active despite its activity.
>
> Perhaps . . . the newspapers will be induced to run it daily like one of their own department strips or features.[71]

Conover, like other public relations experts, blurred the distinction between news and propaganda, creating political publicity that could be slipped into a news format. One 1934 file holds twenty-five different sample editorials prepared for release to influential newspapers about the tax evasion investigation of former secretary of the treasury Andrew Mellon.[72]

The growing importance of the Division of Investigation to the reputation of the Department of Justice during the New Deal can be measured by its increasingly separate public relations operation. Although Hoover's staff had moved into its own building in the fall of 1931, on April 27, 1934, to mark the consolidation of Justice agents in the new Division of Investigation, FDR approved a separate seal, "an eagle balanced for flight on a shield striped in the American design." This symbol, in the words of a Department of Justice spokesman, marked the department's transition from its former status as a poor relation to its current standing as an arm of government.[73]

While many historians have rightly pointed to the ideological intent behind material generated by the Crime Records Division, they have failed to emphasize its context sufficiently. Nichols (and Hoover) were working within a broader departmental emphasis on the creation of news favorable to the interventionist philosophy favored by Cummings and FDR. One circular memo outlined an eight-point method for the preparation and distribution of a weekly syndicated newspaper column that would render as news "the accomplishments of the Division of Investigation, of the Department of Justice." Although the column never materialized, articles written in 1934 titled "Murder Will Out," "Fingerprint Nemesis," and "Prompt Proof of New Laws' Value" illustrated the modern benefits of expanded federal jurisdiction. Possible fears about armed G-men shooting citizens by mistake were addressed in "As Deft with Guns as Desperadoes" and "Scientific Bullet Placement by Special Agents."[74]

Department publicity experts also strategized responses to news and opinions that they did not control. In July 1934, William Stanley asked a staff member to monitor twenty-five influential newspapers that had "evidenced the most bitter opposition to the administration generally and particularly to the Department of Justice." Editorials were to be watched particularly closely, so that responses were produced before they had "gathered momentum and spread a scandal." Staff would also be assigned to investigate quietly the cause of bad press and "apply a remedy quietly." Smaller news organizations could be ignored, since "the less powerful papers [took] their political or editorial cues from the key locality of their section."[75]

Publicists were not confined to news outlets, however, and used specialty publications to reach particular audiences. Such articles helped the citizen-reader to imagine potential participation in the war on crime through first-person narratives and language particular to gender, age, or expertise. A *Popular Science* article, "How Uncle Sam's Detectives Smash Kidnap Gangs" (May 1934), invited a science-oriented reader into a successful organization: "Of twenty-four kidnaping cases recorded since June, 1932," it bragged, "only one remains unsolved!" Which case this referred to was unclear, although it was probably the Hamm kidnapping, since the Lindbergh baby had disappeared in March 1932. The reporter brought his audience into the war room of federal crime control, where "reports were flashing in from twenty-five key cities in the country. They carried isolated bits of information, tips, rumors. They appeared of little consequence, individually. But to the high command of this crack army of law enforcement, they were like pieces of a jig-saw puzzle. They fitted together and made sense; they interlocked and gave clues." Unlike old-fashioned detectives who simply found clues, federal investigators were activist policemen and skilled scientists who *produced* clues from the seemingly random information that littered the world.[76]

The emphasis on the human process of producing clues speaks to an obvious tension between the G-man's identity as part of a scientific and educational elite and the publicist's task of producing cross-class identification with him. Photographs and captions highlighted the familiar, ordinary, and workmanlike qualities of these investigators. For example, two facing pages illustrate various aspects of scientific detection. In one, G-men are *"learning to recognize* the imprints of different shoes" (emphasis added). The second displays a "tool kit" similar to the metal box used by a carpenter or plumber, in which a hammer, screwdriver, pliers, and a magnifying glass make up a montage of intellectual and manual instruments. A third photo shows an early computer, "a long black mechanism through which stream perforated cards." Lest the reader believe that people have simply been reduced to information, the author reminds us, "Each card represents a noted criminal; each perforation an identifying characteristic." And the computer can only do part of the work. The author explains what happens when a kidnapping is reported: "A few minutes later, cards are rushing through the black machine. . . . When this chattering mechanical brain has completed its task, the number of suspects has been narrowed to a handful."[77]

Furthermore, this story promotes the G-man's need for a participatory public. Across the top of one page is a cartoon strip, a narrative medium that concisely conveys ideology and information by inviting readers to identify with the feelings of the characters depicted.[78] The strip tells the story of a kidnapping in six panels: bandits pointing a machine gun at a helpless, frightened couple; two women phoning the G-Men (*"National* 7117"); "a friend of the victim deliver[ing] the ransom"; the victim noting that a plane flew over twice a day; the detectives studying "maps and flying schedules [and] . . . at last learn where the victim is held"; and finally, the victorious G-men bursting in with drawn pistols on a cowering bandit, lying in bed in his underwear.

Lack of information also affects the reading of this comic strip. Because important details are left out (Where was the victim held? How did they find the bandit? Who are these people?), a story about victimization and the return to normality appears to be fully resolved. In the first panel, a male citizen is unmanned by the bandit, and in the last panel the bandit is unmanned by the police in turn; thus, the state remasculinizes the former victim. But, as the panels in between show, the public has participated in its own defense by voluntarily calling in the G-men, by behaving sensibly, and by collecting the information needed to solve the crime. Thus, by the final panel, the G-men do not represent state power but rather a state empowered by an aroused and educated public.

The power of the G-man narrative was such that authors and editors producing popular literature outside bureau controls also worked within a style that strove to create a national public. Melvin Purvis's memoir, *American Agent,* published after he resigned from government service in 1935, originally appeared as a series of articles for *Redbook,* a women's magazine. Introducing himself through masculinized frontier imagery, Purvis produces himself as normal and a ubiquitous, nationalist character. Purvis claims nothing "eventful or extraordinary" about his boyhood. "I did learn to ride a horse at an early age, and I did learn to shoot," he conceded; "but then most of the kids in my group learned these things too." Purvis makes no mention of his family, and within a few pages the "kids" are replaced by a new peer group, the G-men.[79]

Life at the bureau was so absorbing and the call of duty so continual that domestic life is defined by public service: rendering this obsessive, all-male world as normal requires specific cultural work. The agent, Purvis tells us, is "subject to call at any time during the twenty-four hours of a day. . . . So much continuous application to duty has been necessary that to many of us it seemed foolish to go home." Work itself becomes a metaphoric wife; Purvis compares it to "any drive or conquest." Later, he notes that "special agents are not superhumans; their physical strength is ordinarily not more than that of the average citizen; their desires are similar to those of average people—they want to have homes, to rear their children; they need a vacation at least occasionally."[80]

It is interesting that the only mention of domestic space has ungendered children and no wife: the repression of the feminine in *American Agent,* except as a foil for the agent's exploits, is absolute. In fact, the agent proves his coherence as a masculine subject by his discipline over female qualities that rise up to sabotage him at crucial moments: "At the start of a raid, my stomach was invariably as temperamental as an Italian prima donna. It tied itself into a double-hitch or a bow knot and then was swung around on a flying trapeze. I had difficulty swallowing the lump in my throat, and a curious sort of breathless excitement sent the perspiration spouting coldly out of my pores like water from a fire hose." Conquering a treacherous body—a foreign woman within—Purvis projects his emotions outward as weapons. "I had been frightened and probably still was," he writes, "but now I was angry."[81]

The racial borders of the nation also become apparent in this memoir, through African Americans and Native Americans who demonstrate the superiority of the special agent. Inherently untruthful, they endanger the nation by attempting to peddle false information. "War Eagle" tries to pass as an associate of a bank robber but is uncovered by an investigation; as Purvis concluded, "His stupidity had only served to defraud the government of its money, time and energies." The "darkies" in the book are dishonest and spiteful: one black informant delivers false information about white people, and it becomes clear "that the darky's wife had previously cooked for the persons living upstairs [from the accused] and had been discharged, and she and her husband had sought to embarrass the former employer by a raid."[82]

Such images, as Patricia Turner has argued, "communicate the message that whites are superior and civilized while blacks are inferior and savage."[83] *American Agent* contains a complex struggle over whiteness and nationness, materially grounded in the segregationist exclusions of the federal branch, that provides a broader statist context to Hoover's exclusion of black men from investigative roles at the bureau. Bravery, competence, and leadership were qualities necessary to the nation from which black men were institutionally, and ideologically, excluded.[84]

The corporal purity that whiteness demanded in this period was critical to the G-man's tropological function as a nation-space in and of himself; to be criminal was to be racially other and effeminate. While, as Purvis notes, "most of the top-flight hoodlums of the Middle West were 100-per-cent American boys with no foreign background whatsoever," this did not make them white. Criminals wore disguises, rendering their bodies effeminate, imperfect, or foreign. In searching for a gang, Purvis recalled, his agents visited a town where residents remembered having "seen sinister strangers who walked with a limp. Some of the limpers wore glasses, and some of them wore Vandyke beards, and some of them . . . spoke with an accent." Homer Van Meter "was reputed to don a derby hat, pinch-nose spectacles, spats, and to assume the air of a substantial businessman" not unlike a nineteenth-century black imposter, minstrel Zip Coon.[85]

Race and gender—whiteness and masculinity—were affirmed and embodied by Purvis and his brother officers at the bureau; policing these categories was a critical function of policing the nation. It is probably worth noting that we have little understanding of how nonwhite audiences understood the G-man. However, following the work of Ann duCille, we might imagine that the projection of criminals through hated racial stereotypes would provoke contempt for criminals rather than identification with them and that subaltern, anticrime audiences might project imaginative heroic selves through heroic figures, regardless of the fact that they were coded white.[86]

Other, nonstatist ideological systems highlight the use of stereotypes to make crime fantasies to diverse audiences. One of these was homoerotic; Purvis continually describes crime fighting as a dominance fantasy that provokes and reveals the feminine submission of criminals. Under fierce interrogation one kidnapper began "crying hysterically" and was probably "a psychopathic case." Another felon was "a shocking example of the power a gun gives an otherwise weak and enfeebled man." A third "trembled" after his arrest, "relieved that he was not killed." Purvis and a partner had "pounced on him almost like tigers." "[We] reached him almost simultaneously, and the force of the impact of our two bodies had bowled him over."[87]

Here one imagines the occlusion of other important differences through the assertion of masculinist fantasies of physical and psychological power over weaker beings; in products produced for young audiences, this narrative is linked to the freedom and invulnerability associated with an ideal childhood. A 1936 book for boys (and surely read by girls) titled *The G-Man's Son,* by Warren F. Robinson, renders nationalist themes as parables about the state's relationship to family and community. The book stars Stanley Sandborn, the son of a division agent, and his pal John Tallman, both of whom are skilled in photography, sailing, hunting, and tracking. Each lives in a two-parent home, although John's parents never appear, and Stanley's mother is only present at the beginning of the book, serving dinner. Nevertheless, as they solve crimes, their investigations are punctuated by unseen, domestic disciplines: family dinner, regular baths, and an early bedtime.[88]

The story is set in a "typical" town called Burton, alerted to "Dapper Dan" Hogan's escape from federal custody. Like the American public they represent, the citizens of Burton have moral instincts but are unorganized in their response to crime. "Weary pedestrians, homeward bound for supper, became electrified as they stopped to read the bulletin and a staccato fire of exclamations burst from the gathering crowd, expressions ranging from sheer astonishment to hot anger! And in every city, town and hamlet in the land similar scenes were taking place at about the same moment!"[89] Public opinion becomes a weapon in the war on crime, one that can create an anticrime community from spontaneous outrage.

The only fully masculine figure in the story, Agent Sandborn is a cross between a muscular Christian, a soldier, and a banker:

[Sandborn was] a clean-shaven, medium built man in a grey business suit.... He could move with the speed of a panther when aroused and strike with fists like pile drivers or he could set his feet, and with steady hands, pour deadly steel with a machine-gun toward any trapped gangster who wanted to fight it out with the forces of law and decency! A man who . . . had known hardship and physical work, he thought clearly and well in emergencies. A graduate of a New York university with a law degree, he had been a failure at the practice of law. He had been too honest and efficient for the politicians of his home town and they had helped ruin him. Then he had landed a government job and worked his way to a job in the Division of Investigation. Honest, hard-working, clear and clean-thinking, fair, and thorough, he was a typical G-Man, a credit to the country's splendid "crime crusaders!"[90]

Working-class iconography mixes with erudition to produce this allegorical figure. Sandborn is democracy embodied: physically strong and mentally sharp; a classless worker, he is comfortable behind a desk or in the field; he navigates city and country; he seeks justice through action but honors the law.

The alliance between the state and cultural producers did create an aroused public. One unanticipated result of this was that the Department of Justice and the Division of Investigation became tourist attractions. As the attorney general's executive assistant explained to one subordinate in June 1935, "We have been receiving letters and cards asking us to permit visitors to go through the building and be shown its interesting spots."[91]

By August 1935, requests for tours had escalated again, and this time William Stanley asked Conover to begin the project of "establishing a guide service for the Department of Justice building"; he suggested that the Great Hall could be "equipped in some way as a waiting room." One memo to the chief clerk's office suggests that the capacity to control admirers had been sorely tested over the summer: in July high school students had swarmed uncontrollably around the building looking for the heroic G-men. Such visits were positive, Stanley emphasized nervously, but he added, "I have learned that a number of them strayed from the protective folds of their shepherd and roamed at will about the building and the guard force had their hands full for several hours routing them out of private offices and other places in which adolescent youth seems destined to eternally stray."[92]

Having imagined a sympathetic public and encouraged it to imagine them, bureaucrats in the Department of Justice were now in the position of policing their enthusiasm, a problem that would be an increasing preoccupation during the war on crime. The creation of this public was a routine feature of New Deal state making and was integral to the department's enhanced role as a part of that emerging, interventionist state. Although Roosevelt's leadership and his popularity were undoubtedly crucial to the extension of the department's authority, an anticrime public coalesced around particular narratives that permitted the citizen to imagine him- or herself as a participant in national regeneration.

The emergence of kidnapping as a sensational crime that inspired a melodramatic imagination was also crucial to the creation of an activist citizenry. A violation of the homes and bodies of randomly chosen victims, it was tangible evidence of how criminals spawned by Republican Prohibition policies could invade the lives of all Americans. Kidnappers provided the first model for the public enemies who were so vile that, as Homer Cummings promised, they would be incarcerated in the new federal penitentiary at Alcatraz, "so that their evil influences may not be extended to other prisoners." Indeed, the first shipment of federal prisoners to this modern, high-security island prison included Chicago kingpin Al Capone, convicted in 1931 on tax evasion charges, and bandit George "Machine Gun" Kelly, recently convicted for the Urschel kidnapping.[93]

This new public required heroic deeds as well, and it was to this problem that the Division of Investigation turned as the Lindbergh investigation sputtered inconclusively in the spring of 1934. With the omnibus crime bill in committee, Hoover and Cummings committed the bureau's resources to the search for Indiana bank bandit John Dillinger. On March 6, 1934, J. Edgar Hoover dictated a memorandum to Harold Nathan, one of fourteen assistant directors at division headquarters. "Last evening," he began testily,

> I had occasion to call Mr. Purvis at Chicago to inquire of him what steps had been taken in the Chicago Office toward bringing about the apprehension of Dillinger, and much to my surprise the Chicago office had done practically nothing in this matter, notwithstanding the fact that Dillinger is now known to have violated a Federal Statute in that he stole an automobile in Indiana and drove the same into Chicago. . . . This, of course, brings him within the purview of the Dyer Act.

Although the Chicago office should have acted on its own, Hoover noted, Washington had also neglected its duties. "Will you please take immediate steps to see that appropriate instructions are issued to the field offices and that an Identification Order is issued," he ordered.[94]

On May 5, 1934, Roosevelt signed the first six acts of the omnibus crime bill, legislation that permitted federal agents to carry out independent armed investigations across state lines and that made the murder of a government agent a federal felony offense. Earlier that week, the president heard reports that a Chicago movie audience had cheered when Dillinger's handsome face had flashed across the screen and that they had hissed when bureau agent Melvin Purvis promised to track down the elusive bank bandit. Now, at the signing ceremony, Roosevelt lectured that no criminal legislation could be effective "so long as a substantial part of the public looks with tolerance upon known criminals, permits public officers to be corrupted or intimidated by them or applauds efforts to romanticize crime."[95]

Six

"Why Can't the State Forgive Too?"

John Dillinger as Political Actor

Isn't it about time that Uncle Sam put the gangsters on the spot? Why bother to try them for tax violations? Or try them at all for that matter. . . . Just round them up. Declare martial law for 24 hours and shoot them. The public will support the President 100% if he did this.
— Letter from a citizen to Louis M. Howe, August 7, 1933

Vote for JOHN / You All Know Me / for Bank Examiner—Fearless, Courageous, Cunning, Efficient. — Poster with photograph of Dillinger, seen in Green Bay, Wisconsin, October 1934

It was Hoover, not Purvis, who had deferred the Dillinger investigation. On October 14, 1933, Ohio congressman Frank L. Kloeb had contacted the Department of Justice asking for help in hunting John Dillinger and his gang of auto bandits, and on October 25, the governor of Indiana did too. "Uncle Sam has promised aid," the *Evansville Courier* reported, "and for that promise many citizens are devoutly thankful." However, in 1933, Dillinger remained a low priority on the federal agenda: Washington instructed the Chicago SAC to give "any and all possible assistance" but "not to take the initiative."[1]

In part, intervention was delayed while the crime bill was readied; scientific policing would have to be supported by the raw power of guns and swift pursuit across state lines. Like Bonnie Parker and Clyde Barrow, the Dillinger gang was famous for blasting out of dragnets, most recently in Chicago, where a moll had blocked police fire while the bandits shot around her. With the Dillinger case, the moral and legal right to shoot first, and shoot to kill, became crucial to federal crime fighting. The undercover informant, an emblem of state corruption during Prohibition, was also rehabilitated as a weapon against banditry. On March 6, Hoover ordered Purvis to recruit underworld snitches who could be activated "in the event of an emergency arising."[2]

Few at the Department of Justice anticipated that this phase of the war on crime would be prolonged and bloody, and the idea of a war on syndicates had not yet been put aside. At the end of 1933, Joseph Keenan wrote Howe:

> [In the spring] this Department will concentrate its efforts in moving against commercial racketeers. . . . We have already had exhibited the most cordial feeling from the Chiefs of Police of the many cities in our country who recently sent a delegation to the Attorney General. . . . In short, the relationship and conferences with these Chiefs of Police exhibited a general tendency to invite the fullest cooperation with the federal authorities.

The chiefs also presented new ideas for cooperation,"much more drastic in form than expected," which "would greatly broaden the field of federal criminal activities." But the events of early 1934 altered these plans. The Barrow gang's rampage in the southern section of the crime corridor shared headlines with Dillinger's escape in a stolen car from the Crown Point jail, an Indiana facility that also held federal prisoners. In a telephone call on March 6, Hoover expressed "surprise" that Chicago SAC Purvis "had done practically nothing in this matter," and he ordered him to "put forth every effort" to capture the bandit.[3]

Ironically, the Division of Investigation joined the battle against bank robbery at a moment when it was on the decline nationwide, an odd coincidence that made the successful auto bandit appear to be a singular and daring felon. Fewer banks were available to plunder, since many small ones failed or were closed between 1929 and 1933, but those still in business by April 1933 were larger, better defended, and located in towns and cities with professionalized police forces. Newspapers featured these crimes as spectacular events; they also applauded police for killing dangerous fugitives on sight: "The hunt is on," the *Tulsa Daily World* warned, "and many a human mad dog is going to be disposed of in a summary way."[4]

These crimes renewed the call for police reform, a campaign that was given new meaning both by the omnibus crime bill and by ideological contests over the uses and abuses of New Deal social policy. Although local demands for harsh anticrime measures did not translate into a surge of endorsements for a federal police presence, antigovernment sentiment in the crime corridor was mitigated by widespread knowledge that bandits like Dillinger bought protection from the law through syndicate criminals who worked closely with local politicians and police. In addition, economic recovery and anticrime agendas inevitably raised questions about the benefits of an expanding state. In late March, the *Daily World* praised Oklahoma sheriffs for creating cooperative anticrime strategies. "The federal hunt" was a "grim necessity" because other states had failed to do the same. A week later, the paper criticized Oklahoma City politicians for "poor taste" in announcing that they led the nation in public works funds; it also deplored the arming of federal agents.[5]

Because he appeared at a moment when federal policies proposed to embrace the most public functions of state and local government and the power of this new state was untested and often contested, John Dillinger became a critical actor in the cultural politics of the New Deal. Clifford Geertz has suggested, "No matter how peripheral, ephemeral or free-floating the charismatic figure we may be concerned with—the wildest prophet, the most deviant revolutionary—we must begin with the center and the symbols and conceptions that prevail there if we are to understand him and what he means." The hunt for John Dillinger was not only a moment in which the state's capacity to police the nation expanded; it was one in which the New Deal's paradoxical relations to local politics were revealed through the figure of the bandit.[6]

Sensational crime news, generated by the government and by those associated with the Dillinger gang, reflected the broader commercial and political culture of the depression years. Reporters, newsreel makers, and sentimental writers produced audiences for the Dillinger manhunt by exploring bandit crime through familiar, and personal, narratives. Inventing connections between bandits and hinting at links to local politicians and police officials, they renarrativized crime as part of a nationalist exchange between ordinary citizens. Wire service reporters interviewed witnesses to bank robberies, shoot-outs, and escapes, many of whom contributed stories and souvenir pictures so that crime watchers elsewhere could experience these events. A witness in South Dakota snapped a picture of the Dillinger gang and sold it to a news wire, which marketed it nationwide with the caption "Here's a real hold-up in action" (a second sighting of Dillinter was unauthentic, since the bandit had spared a policeman and "failed to live up to the cognomen of 'the killer.' ")[7]

The politics of the New Deal and the unfulfilled promises of previous anticrime campaigns combined to pry the Department of Justice away from detached scientific policing and propel it toward the dangerous territory of confrontation and enforcement. In mid-1933, supervisor Werner Hanni argued against armed pursuit, insisting that its rewards were not worth altering the bureau's character:

> If we stick to the intelligent investigations that the Agents of this Bureau are
> well qualified to pursue . . . it will always be the best and most convincing man-
> ner in which to perform our work. . . . While I have no soft spot in my heart

for any gangsters, or hoodlums, I feel that the only and best way to treat them is by intelligent investigations . . . and not to become excited because of the magnitude of the crime involved.

However, by the Dillinger manhunt in 1934, the new cultural politics of centralized federal policing would replace "cooperation and coordination" with Homer Cummings's famous edict: "Shoot first—then count to ten."[8] In this process, state violence could be constructed against, not a set of social practices or an illegal market that implicated citizen constituencies and class domination, but a psychopathic fugitive who was unique in his viciousness, even among criminals.

Fate and the Bandit's Collision with the State

The Dillinger romance did not glorify individualism; rather, it articulated the individual's tragic and desperate struggle with his own history. When asked about John's refusal to surrender to the federal government, his elderly father answered, "He never told me so, but they laid so many things on him that I guess he rather would have been shot down than arrested again." Like Bonnie Parker, whose poems recalled the social bandit's cry for "a righting of individual wrongs," Dillinger evoked "a traditional world in which men are justly dealt with, not a new and perfect world."[9]

As in many criminal biographies, violence and theft emerge as behaviors learned in John Dillinger's unfortunate youth. Born to John Wilson and Mollie Dillinger of Indianapolis, Indiana, on June 22, 1903, John Sr. was a grocer and property owner, an emotionally remote man who was widowed in 1906. A daughter, sixteen-year-old Audrey, married soon after, leaving the boy in a stereotypically disorganized household: no female influence moderated his masculine impulses, and he was governed by an indecisive father, who alternately beat and bribed him. Truancy, gang violence, petty theft, and sex play prompted a move to rural Mooresville in 1919, in the hope that a different environment (and a new stepmother) would alter John's behavior. However, he refused to attend high school, ran away repeatedly, joined the navy, deserted, and in April 1924 eloped with sixteen-year-old Beryl Ethel Hovious. In September, he was sentenced to ten to twenty years in the Pendleton Reformatory for robbing and beating a town merchant.[10]

Failed parenting and frustrated consumer desire played critical explanatory roles in Dillinger's trajectory from delinquency to criminal violence. As a former friend recounted, John had "attended Sunday School . . . regularly," and his "first trouble arose from the fact that his father did not provide him with sufficient spending money to properly court" a girl, causing "a violent dispute" between them. Dillinger was "forced to commit the crime to realize his ambitions in love." Prison became the place where John forged a homosocial pseudofamily, with future gang members Homer Van Meter, John Hamilton, Harry Pierpont, Charles Makley, and Russell Clark. When his friends were transferred to a high-security prison after an escape attempt, John followed. No Bonnie Parker, Beryl divorced him shortly thereafter.[11]

Like Clyde Barrow, Dillinger returned to crime after parole. Released in May 1933, at the request of his father, two hundred citizens of Mooresville, and the grocer he had robbed, he planned a "crash out" for his friends, a project that required money for bribes, weapons, hideouts, and cars. On July 13, Dillinger and fellow parolee Homer Van Meter robbed a bank in Daleville, Indiana. Witnesses remarked on the young bandit's cheerful manner, his snappy clothes, his good looks, and his graceful vault over a teller's gate. After a second robbery in Lima, John was arrested on September 22 at the Dayton, Ohio, home of Mary Longnaker. Four days later, the moll smuggled money for bribes and guns into the prison, tucking the cash into a banana skin.[12]

Jails were crucial sites for the production of criminal identities; there, convicts reflected on the self and examined the collisions with power that had led to arrest. As Dillinger wrote to his father from the Lima jail, he was "not guilty of half the things" he had been charged with: "I've never harmed anyone. . . . You can't win in this game. . . . I went in a carefree boy and I came out bitter toward everything in general. Of course Dad, most of the blame lies with me for my environment was of the best but if I had gotten off more leniently when I made my first mistake this never would have happened." Like Barrow, Dillinger imagined himself enmeshed in circumstances beyond his control; "mistakes" became fatal opportunities for the state to exert power over him. As Van Meter also explained from prison in 1930, "I was but a boy of nineteen years of age, with all the misguided illusions that one would expect from a wild unthinking youngster and it was inevitable that I should find myself in prison." A man should not be punished forever, he argued, for "the follys of ignorant, unrestrained youth."[13]

Escape and parole violation temporarily reversed these power relations, as the former object of punishment refashioned himself as a fugitive celebrity criminal. Escape drew the public's interest, as jail breaks were marketed by newspapers and radio stations competing for audiences. When Pierpont, Makley, and Clark broke out on October 10, radio station WIND's listeners experienced the crash-out vicariously, as the station scooped its print competitors with continuous interviews of civilian witnesses, prison guards, and police engaged in the search. Reproducing atmosphere and emotions, radio harnessed the power of personal testimony to track the news as it broke. When news flagged, producers invented more: WIND persuaded local police to reenact the gun battle at the prison gates (believing the station had been attacked, state officers rushed over and, furious, arrested the director of the show). On October 12, the fugitives arrived at the tiny Lima jail. During the struggle to free John, one of the bandits shot Sheriff Jess Sarber and beat him to death. In the next two weeks the gang robbed a police arsenal and then hit a bank for seventy-five thousand dollars before laying low in Chicago. Pierpont moved in with Mary Kinder, the sister of a convict, and Dillinger soon met Evelyn "Billie" Frechette, a part Native American woman whose husband was in Leavenworth.[14]

The gun moll played a crucial role in this criminal spectacle. Romance confirmed the bandit's masculinity, refiguring him as the engine of someone else's fate, rather than the victim of his own. As Billie told *True Confessions,* on the night she met Dillinger she only expected "a few bright lights, a glass or two of beer and a chance to dance." Her husband's recent conviction had left her "with a blurred attitude toward life." She entered the dance hall, "groping, trying to find someone in whom [she] could have faith." Suddenly, she felt a powerful gaze: "There was something in those eyes that I will never forget. They were piercing and electric; yet there was an amused, carefree twinkle in them too. They met my eyes and held me hypnotized for an instant." After several dances, "Jack Harris" asked Billie if there was "any chance" they would meet again. "I had waited for such a question from the moment we took the floor," she wrote; "from the moment, in fact, that I saw those eyes advancing toward me across the room. There must be some high order that arranges such things." Dillinger swept Billie into a whirl of expensive urban pleasures, reshaping her identity. Formerly a semiskilled wage laborer and a reservation Native American, Billie acquired wealth, leisure, and status as Dillinger's moll and "Indian sweetheart."[15]

Billie's ethnicity and gender were produced in the story as essential identities, which acted to reveal Dillinger's "true" self as they drove to Florida for Christmas. Having seen guns in the car, Billie "had known for some time that the boy had something up his sleeve." But not being "one to ask questions," Billie waited to be told; "[By then,] I was too happy, too engrossed in the perfection of what I had to question or debate. All I wanted was to follow Dillinger, love him, care for him, please him and know the ecstasy of his love in return." Billie's Native American heritage establishes Dillinger's true nobility: by positioning Billie as an "Indian" conquered by love, the magazine articulates Dillinger as fully white and masculine (and "American") despite his criminality.[16]

"Call it fate," Billie commented sadly about John's subsequent arrest and incarceration. In January, most of the gang went on to Arizona, while Dillinger and Hamilton returned to the Midwest to rob a bank in East Chicago. Hamilton, badly wounded, remained behind while Dillinger joined the gang. On January 23 the hotel where Makley, Clark, and Pierpont were staying caught fire, and a fireman recognized them from mug shots in a detective magazine. Tucson police arrested them on January 25; John and Billie were captured that afternoon. In March, Pierpont, Makley, and Clark were extradited to Ohio for the murder of Jess Sarber; the molls were released; and Dillinger was extradited to Indiana. Highly conscious of his own celebrity, the bandit knew little about the federal agency that had aided the Tucson police. "Dillinger, identified by fingerprints, growled: 'I'll be the laughing stock of the country,'" *Time* reported. "'How did I know that a hick police force would ever suspicion me?'"[17]

While the gang was held in Tucson, citizens were invited to view the prisoners by the sheriff: more than four hundred came in one afternoon. Although the cultural conditions for such spectacles were established during Prohibition, New Deal anticrime initiatives made all fugitives into potential political capital, and local officials exploited them. A similar scene occurred at Crown Point, where politicians posed for photographs with Dillinger; the bandit, about to stand trial for his life, grinned wryly and rested an arm on prosecutor Robert Estill. Only Sheriff Lillian Holley stared grimly into the camera, barely tolerating the media circus.[18]

They would regret these pictures when Dillinger crashed out of Crown Point on March 3. "I first learned of his escape from jail over the radio," Billie wrote. Sitting in a Chicago ice cream parlor, she heard "suddenly, over the air the bell used as a prelude to police calls sounded through the room." A deputy at the jail remembered that "Dillinger pulled this wooden gun from his pocket, exhibiting it to all those locked up and said 'This is how tough your little jail is. I did it all with this little wooden pistol,' knocking on the bars." After robbing two more banks, John sent a picture of himself, with the wooden gun, to an Indianapolis newspaper.[19]

One of these crimes illustrates a dramatic shift in the public meaning of bank robbery as a bandit became famous. Not only was the gang more conscious of producing a spectacle, but citizens consumed it as a historic event. People recognized Dillinger, drew others in an audience, and took souvenir photographs. No one intervened, and an excited crowd grew while the gang cursed, growled, and pushed bystanders around with their weapons; occasionally they fired into the air. Despite "the apparent ruthlessness of the gang," the newspaper reported, "small groups of citizens gathered in the street, others peered from doorways or behind poles or other available shelter to watch the proceedings." A female hostage said they were only acting and "were nice enough."[20]

The Crown Point escape, as well as consumer pleasure in such spectacles, also fueled federal assertions that the crime bill emerging from the House Judiciary Committee was needed to buttress lax local enforcement and citizen apathy. Homer Cummings criticized Indiana authorities in the strongest terms and moved all federal prisoners currently held at Crown Point to other jails. Saying that the publicity circus showed both "a lack of propriety and common sense," Cummings and Hoover implied that Dillinger's captors were paid off.[21]

Hints about corruption were tied to critiques of "the woman sheriff" as conflicts between federal and local officials surfaced in mutual, public accusations. Hoover's contempt for female officers was later echoed by Purvis, who used Holley as an example that "a woman, no matter how strong" could not be a crime fighter; "human nature is one thing and good government is another." *Time* also noted that Dillinger had escaped in the car of "the woman sheriff." However, regional coverage reveals a ruthless female manhunter. One story described her as a mother, blonde, attractive, fond of golf and bridge, an excellent shot, and experienced in armed posse searches. "'If I ever see John Dillinger again,' Holley ground between her teeth," as she strapped on revolvers and stepped into a squad car, "'I'll shoot him dead with my own pistol.'"[22]

A subsequent investigation by the state of Indiana reveals that the federal emphasis on the wooden gun and female incompetence effectively concealed a story of Democratic party patronage and underworld payoffs. The escape originated with Dillinger's lawyer, Louis Piquett, who brought Meyer Bogue, an ex-con and escape artist, to Crown Point. According to Bogue's testimony, "a contact had been made through Hymie Cohen, a lawyer of East Chicago, with Judge Murray. . . . The Judge would see that they gained admission [to the jail]." Cohen, a Republican, and Murray, a Democrat, long-standing political allies, were also co-investors in a real estate deal, and Democratic prosecutor Robert Estill was a client. Cohen also owned a brothel, had attempted to bribe a local prosecutor, and had been indicted in East Chicago as part of a liquor ring that included the mayor, Chief of Police James Reagan (who, by 1934, was Robert Estill's chief investigator), and Detective Sergeant Martin Zarcovitch—who would later claim a federal reward in the Dillinger case.[23]

Like Mabel Walker Willebrandt, Lillian Holley was the only official who *wasn't* "fixed." It is a comment on female isolation within party networks that, apparently, no one tried. Holley "positively refused to admit" Bogue to the jail. Estill did not overrule her, perhaps because he knew he did not have to; at Piquett's request, Judge Murray "signed a written order . . . directing her to admit [them]." Returning to the jail, Piquett told Bogue that the warden, Lewis Baker, had also been "fixed." Although Holley refused the court order, Baker, a Democratic ally of her deceased husband, warned that she might violate Dillinger's legal rights. "After some little argument and persuasive conversation," Holley agreed to the visit only if Bogue and Piquett were searched and supervised by Baker. Baker, a Murray-appointed deputy, and a third man split a thirty-five-hundred-dollar bribe, which included giving Bogue a plan of the jail. After the escape, "approximately each half hour" Piquett received updates from the chief of police in Gary.[24]

Accounts of several escapes highlight the ties between syndicate criminals, police departments, and the Democratic party that complicated, and may have ended, the plan for a federal war on racketeering. Ironically, they also reframed bandit gangs as part of organized crime. Dillinger's flight to Chicago to meet up with Billie and the gang, and from there, to St. Paul, took him though thriving criminal economies that provided shelter, medical care, and protection from the law. Dillinger's new celebrity made him an unattractive client to the Capone organization, however. As an informant explained, after buying some guns the gang left town, fearing that the syndicate "would turn them in, and thereby lessen the 'heat' which might be placed on this particular gang by the Police authorities."[25]

We can speculate that once a bandit gang became too notorious, and thus of little use to the dominant criminal networks in a city, layover deals were rescinded. In St. Paul, on March 30, tipped off by a building manager, a police officer backed up by division agents rapped on an apartment door and asked for "Carl Heller." Billie opened it with the chain on, said her "husband" was not in, and slammed it shut. Climbing out of bed, Dillinger told her to pack a suitcase and "keep her shirt on"; dressing quickly, he slipped on a bulletproof vest, loaded a machine gun, and told her to follow. Agent Rufus Coulter's description of the subsequent confrontation could have been extracted from a pulp novel: "[Dillinger was] standing there against the wall, and as I looked around he used some profane language, and he said, 'You want it. Here it is,' and at that time he started to draw a dark colored automatic pistol."[26] After a fierce gun battle, Billie and John escaped; evidence sent agents to a second hideout where Eddie Green, Dillinger's link to the St. Paul mob, was fatally shot and his moll arrested.

Again, Dillinger's overpowering masculinity and sense of theater are important themes in Agent Coulter's rendition of their encounter. It has a sexual undercurrent, and the escape is projected through the bandit's manly restraint. While witnesses recalled Billie's panic, Dillinger "merely took his time and walked up the alley very casually, always keeping a good look behind him as though covering his retreat." Accounts from Crown Point are similar: he sang "The Last Round-Up," chatted about sex with his "mama," and cautioned the deputy driving the car not to speed. Leaving the hostages, he told them "to be sure to keep their noses clean." Like "Pretty Boy" Floyd, one witness to the St. Paul shoot-out identified him by his attitude: "the cock-sure angle at which his head is set."[27]

While Dillinger, Frechette, and Van Meter hid out with a St. Paul abortionist, division agents combed the two hideouts for evidence and information. The most sobering revelation was the extent of the gang's arsenal, some stolen but most traceable to purchases from a Texas dealer and Capone enforcer Frank Nitti. In Dillinger's apartment were two bulletproof vests, a Thompson submachine gun, a Remington .35 caliber rifle, a .38 Colt Super Automatic converted into a hand-held machine gun, and four boxes of ammunition. A car out front held an automatic rifle and a submachine gun, while Green owned another vest; a single barrel shotgun; an automatic pistol; a submachine gun; ten loaded ammunition clips and drums; and three boxes of automatic shells. Shaken, Hugh Clegg requisitioned more guns for the St. Paul office.[28]

These daring escapes made Dillinger famous, but his celebrity, and the heat that he drew from police and the underworld, reduced his ability to meet his obligations. Found in the apartment, among photographs and news clippings about him, was a letter from the Pierponts reminding Dillinger and his syndicate connections of Harry's upcoming execution: "I think if you will talk this over with the fellows they will realize that Harry has been fair all the way through and wants to continue to be and that they will be willing to help you to help him. It was on their advice and not Harry's that you turned those [banks] over. See what you can do because things are getting hotter for Harry every minute."[29] Was Pierpont playing his last card, the threat to squeal, in the hope that another escape could be engineered? And who were "the fellows" who offered up banks for "turning over"?

The documents do not yield answers to these questions, but they do emphasize the number of criminal enterprises—gun sales, medical care, hideouts, money laundering—that profited from a bandit. Syndicates employed prostitutes, ward heelers, saloon keepers, and wise guys who provided these services. Augusta Salt, a nurse and abortionist who hid Dillinger for three days and dressed a bullet wound, was rewarded with $110, although her normal rate was $5.00 per day. A procurer and her husband acted as purchasing agents; they testified that if the gang needed food and gave them $50.00, they "would not give any change back, whether the amount of groceries purchased would only be $4.00 or $5.00; that on one occasion they were given $2,000 for the purpose of buying a new Dodge automobile, and instead they returned with a stolen Chrysler automobile."[30]

More troubling to the government were the number of seemingly legitimate professionals, like lawyers, who profited from underworld connections. Louis Piquett was paid well by Dillinger for legal (and illegal) services; a pragmatist to the end, he then contemplated turning in his client when capture seemed inevitable. As agents secreted in a moll's house reported, Piquett "had once tried to get Dillinger to surrender for the reward that he, Piquett, would obtain; that he also fixed it so that Dillinger would get a life sentence but if by chance a death sentence was returned against him he had it fixed with the judge who was going to change it to a life sentence." Doing business with criminals and corrupt public officials was always risky: loyalty vanished when the money ran out.[31]

This might explain why the Barrow gang, and to a more limited extent, Dillinger, also relied on networks of family and friends. Although all gang members' families were under heavy federal surveillance, on April 7 and 8 Dillinger came to his father's farm—something that neither the Indiana state police nor the division knew until John Sr. told a reporter two weeks later. "It apparently was common knowledge that the outlaw, with a desperate record as a bank robber, killer and jail breaker, was in town," the *Washington Post* reported, "but the newspapers heard about it before the authorities." The article described a town petition that asked the governor to grant Dillinger amnesty, and it quoted an angry state official, who "could not understand . . . why the good people of the town and the vicinity did not notify the sheriff and some other police agency."[32]

Apparently, many Mooresville residents did not understand the government's concept of justice. One neighbor accused of hiding John's car was uncooperative and sarcastic with agents. Asked if he had let the bandit sleep on the floor, he responded, "Why, I would give him my bed any time." The agent evaluated him as "a very hostile individual of socialistic leanings." "[He] answers all questions . . . by asking why we do not put all the bankers in jail, who stole the people's money; that they must have very little left for John to steal."[33]

Dillinger's ability to draw admirers and sidestep federal surveillance became a national scandal at the end of April when Warner Brothers released a newsreel featuring John Sr. and other Mooresville citizens; reports came from around the nation that audiences had cheered the bandit's photograph and catcalled footage of the G-men. In retaliation, Hoover saturated Mooresville and the area around the Pierponts' Ohio home with agents, who followed family members everywhere, raiding homes that they visited. The Dillingers were threatened with immediate prosecution unless they assisted the government, an order then hastily countermanded by Joseph Keenan. On April 30, Keenan explained to Cummings that Hoover's strong-arm tactics were "highly inadvisable," a public relations disaster. Americans had, he wrote, "a natural sympathy . . . for blood relatives protecting their own."[34]

Hoover secretly persisted, however, turning from Dillinger's voluble elderly father to younger relatives, who were frightened by their new notoriety and who knew John significantly less well. John's youngest brother, Hubert, became an informant, believing that he was protecting his family from further harm. And while John's sister, Audrey, refused to talk to agents, her husband, Norman Hancock, and her son Fred secretly agreed to "turn up Dillinger should he come in there in order to avoid possible charges against the family and also to avoid the possibility of some of them being killed should he be taken at one of these places."

A fourth, unnamed informant was recruited "in the home of Hubert Dillinger who will report to us any activities he learns at any time."[35]

Agents also turned up the heat by squeezing urban informants hard: in mid-April, Billie was picked up by federal agents in a Chicago tavern waiting for a contact. She was clearly the primary target: according to John Hamilton's moll, Pat Cherrington, Dillinger was parked across the street, and in order to arrest Billie G-men had to walk right past him. Outnumbered, he circled the block a few times, and when he learned that she was in custody, "he drove off, 'crying like a baby.'" Added to the loss of his moll was the strong possibility that she had been put on the spot, and if so, that he would be, too. The gang left town in separate cars and met at the Little Bohemia Lodge in Rhinelander, Wisconsin.[36]

Introduced by St. Paul wise guy Pat Reilly, the gang paid Emil Wanatka "well over one thousand dollars" to hide them. The innkeeper and his wife had old syndicate ties, having operated a club in Chicago during Prohibition. They had given up the business after several shootings there; in addition, Wanatka wished "to get away from . . . conditions requiring him to furnish free meals and beer to policemen, etc."[37] Chances are, however, that after repeal he had simply chosen a safer and more profitable way of servicing criminal organizations—helping mobsters ride out the heat in a remote location.

However, Dillinger was too hot; the innkeeper called on federal connections dating from Prohibition, suggesting that he had an earlier career as an informant. "I am in an awful position here," Wanatka wrote a federal prosecutor in Chicago,

> John Dil is here since yesterday. . . . I never squaked [sic] in my life but I don't want to be the fall guy for somebody else. If you come up, come at night and stop to Vosses, Birchwood Lodge. . . . I have all the dope for you there. Come well prepared if you do come. . . .
>
> Don't call up. I'm wached [sic].

Wanatka warned the prosecutor not to trust anyone and ended, "Whatever you do don't put my name into this."[38]

Not lacking in stool pigeons, the division did not have the equipment and coordination to close the net on Dillinger, emphasizing the inevitable weakness of scientific policing against crimes of violence. On Sunday, April 22, Hugh Clegg's men unpacked shotguns and ammunition at the Rhinelander airport; Melvin Purvis and his agents were flying in from Chicago; and two St. Paul agents were driving from the city with gas guns that the pilot had refused to carry. Realizing that they did not have enough cars, Clegg went to the local Ford agency and explained that he was a federal agent who needed to rent vehicles. Initially, the dealer did not want to rent his new cars. "He only had one coupe he could let us have, and he refused to let us have that if we were in any way interested in liquor law violations as he stated that he had to sell his cars to the residents of that section and obviously, he did not want his name connected with rendering aid against liquor law violators." Clegg assured him that they were not revenuers, and the dealer asked if they were after Dillinger. Clegg answered evasively that "it was reasonable to assume that all law enforcement officers were interested in finding Dillinger." The dealer then relented and gave him two more cars.[39]

Thus, a day of haggling and waiting brought the agents to the inn long after dark. The evening supper crowd had arrived, and the lodge's dogs had been left to wander the ground; soon the silence was shattered by wild barking. Guests relaxing in the bar suddenly found themselves choking for air, as the G-men fired tear gas grenades through the windows. Leaving their luggage and their molls, the bandits ran out shooting. As Dillinger, Hamilton, and Van Meter fought their way out of one side of the lodge to their car, agents were caught from behind by a rain of machine gun bullets from Lester Gillis. Gillis ran toward two wounded agents, threw them out of their car, and drove deep into the woods as his three mates escaped to St. Paul.[40]

The Fugitive and the Search for Justice

The *Tulsa Daily World* buried reports about Little Bohemia, devoting its headline to the first six acts of the omnibus crime bill; "Roosevelt Aroused by Dillinger!" the paper announced. Congress was similarly aroused: when the legislation passed three weeks later, members also appropriated twenty-five thousand dollars to reward the "capture of public enemies, dead or alive." Universal Pictures, aroused by Warner Brothers' newsreel scoop, added another five-thousand-dollar bounty. At the signing ceremony on May 18, the president reminded citizens that this was only one part of the New Deal commitment "to curb the evil-doer of whatever class." Linking these new federal police powers to a previous era of reform rhetoric, Roosevelt warned, "Law enforcement and gangster extermination cannot be made completely effective so long as a substantial part of the public looks with tolerance upon known criminals, permits public officers to be corrupted or intimidated by them or applauds efforts to romanticize crime." Cummings also emphasized the state's service to a public that was united in its commitment to the protection of property. "Kidnappers, killers and racketeers are a serious menace to life and property as well as to the supremacy of the law," he announced; the bill was but one part of a "wider program of vigorous and impartial enforcement of the law in all its phases."[41]

By the late spring and summer of 1934, the Division of Investigation had emerged as virtually the only visible player in the war on crime, and no male member of the Dillinger gang was seen alive by the public again. Dillinger himself reentered the public view on July 22 as a bullet-riddled corpse; John Hamilton disappeared, presumed dead, after a chest wound sustained at Little Bohemia; Tommy Carroll was killed on June 7, 1934, by two police officers in Waterloo, Iowa; and Homer Van Meter would be gunned down by St. Paul detectives in early August. Dillinger's disappearance was a particular mystery, since his picture was everywhere. Agents insisted that these images were "very good" and ought to prompt recognition from any citizen.[42]

The seizure by the state of cultural space formerly occupied by Dillinger shifts the terms of analysis for the war on crime by 1934. Here, the bandit becomes an overt political sign, a nationalist site where an expanding state met a receptive, but fractured, body politic. A portion of Dillinger's audience desired his capture, sought to help the G-men, and exhorted the state to show no mercy in delivering him to a just death. Others believed that the New Deal's valorization of the individual was inextricably linked to Dillinger's survival.

Thus, demands on the Roosevelt administration for justice in the Dillinger case were generated from two basic political stances, neither of which were antistatist. One valorized criminal laws and police power as expressions of national will that were necessary to the public good. The other envisioned a "Robin Hood state" that drew its moral vision from the bandit's imagined commitment to the people and promoted national well-being by regulating corruption. As the *Daily World* explained in an article on Dillinger and "Pretty Boy" Floyd's admirers in the region, "Some officers and not a few average citizens consider [Floyd] 'a pretty good fellow who would go right if he had a chance,' claiming that he never shot anyone who wasn't trying to kill him."[43]

Crime enthusiasts, petitioners, and sob sisters produced bandits and molls as key players in a political dialogue between "the state" and "the people" that, in broader terms, also made them sites for debating the future of the nation itself. This focus on the criminal as a site for politics was enhanced by the wave of realistic crime films that were produced immediately before the war on crime. This was a genre particularly conducive to nationalist imaginings, since it positioned violent crime as an American problem and deployed symbols of state violence like World War I and Prohibition to explore crime's ambivalent relationship to national heroic ideals. Through these features, and the several decades of silent crime films that preceded them, audiences not only became conversant with the moral positions articulated by the war on crime but came to feel as though they understood the dilemmas criminals faced. Two of Thomas Edison's first moving pictures, *Tenderloin at Night* (1899) and *How They Do Things on Broadway* (1902), purported to give a privileged view of the urban underworld to their audiences; and Edwin Porter's epic crime film *The Great Train Robbery* (1903) marked a critical turn in production values, in which history was produced as a heroic, nationalist fiction.[44]

In the years immediately preceding the war on crime, studios accused of glamorizing crime for profit latched onto Progressive anticrime agendas, proposing that they too sought to educate and arouse the public. Warner Brothers produced a "social conscience" cycle, including *Little Caesar* (1931), *The Public Enemy* (1931), and *I Am a Fugitive from a Chain Gang* (1932). These films personalized official corruption and the social conditions that produced crime, urging audiences to feel for, and thus learn from, these doomed criminal protagonists. Because these pictures were all released when Prohibition was thoroughly discredited and the psychopathic model dominated criminal diagnosis, producers could use a single body to send equally credible and contradictory messages, as their stars understood. "In every picture so far I've carried a gun," George Raft said in 1931, "and I'm willing to keep it up if that's what they want me to do. It seems to me that the rough characters will always be in demand, on the side of the law, if not against it."[45]

I Am a Fugitive from a Chain Gang, for example, mused on the questions of fate and justice that bandits and their audiences wrote about without pretending to resolve them. Based on Robert Burns's best-selling memoir of a fugitive life, it tells a story of betrayal, harsh punishments and corrupt politicians. Combat veteran "James Allen" returns home to find that he is virtually unemployable, becomes a migrant worker, pawns his army decorations for food, and is falsely accused of a five-dollar robbery. Sentenced to a chain gang, Jim escapes; under the inverted name "Allen James" he finds white-collar success but is betrayed by a woman. Jim negotiates a fine and trusty status, but corrupt officials steal his money and return him to the chain gang. Embittered, he escapes again, disappearing into the underworld and forsaking a respectable future. Although Jim's initial problems result from a failed economy, his tragic end is the result of a state that cannot respond to human needs. Paradoxically, his heroism is only appreciated among criminals: "You got plenty of what it takes, breakin' out of the chain gang," a prostitute muses. "A guy with your nerves got the breaks coming to him."

Allen's lack of ethnicity, in contrast to the immigrant backgrounds of other gangster icons, recalls the nationalist readings bandits like Dillinger inspired. His "Americanness" invites outrage that the state is presiding over the evaporation of historically racial entitlements to property and status. While the film focused on state-level corruption (probably a concession to Hayes office censorship), the best-selling memoir, *I Was a Prisoner on a Georgia Chain Gang!,* explicitly linked the federal government to this miscarriage of justice. In the introduction, Reverend Vincent Burns, the fugitive's brother, reported that his family was watched and followed by the Bureau of Investigation. "It was interesting to know," Burns wrote, "that a federal official was being employed to run down my brother. When we were trying to get him a pardon we were told on many different occasions that his case was purely a state matter and that no federal aid could be given. The U.S. government evidently is willing to lend its aid to help in the destruction of a man but unwilling to aid in the attempt to work out his salvation."[46] Thus, not just any criminal qualified as an appropriate focus for the political struggles of the war on crime; it was the fugitive, a citizen in flight from the state, who generated debates about salvation and justice.

Reformers used Dillinger's fugitive status to demand federal oversight, not just of policing, but of the entire judicial apparatus. Convicted criminals were at large, they argued, because of poor prison security, bribery, lax sentencing, sob sister defenses, and a corrupt pardon system. Thus, otherwise insignificant break-outs from state penitentiaries and local jails in the spring and summer of 1934 became part of the national crime wave, providing opportunities for ambitious local politicians to pin their careers to New Deal crime agendas.[47] A crime-corridor district attorney used the case to demand support for a "three-time loser" law, mandating execution on a third conviction, and a sterilization law, since the children of felons would be "public wards" who "reproduce[d] crime." He also condemned neighboring Oklahoma's high rate of pardons, paroles, and escapes, an echo of Hoover's own beliefs. The above themes argue against a reading of the bandit as a subject produced only by the state or by the popular; nor was he a political person in and of himself; rather, he was a politicized body that invited discussion and evaluation of the New Deal state.[48]

Events like Little Bohemia propelled this body into the public arena in the form of letters from the public that offered praise, criticism, and advice in expressly political terms. Poor citizens suggested that the Dillinger manhunt could become another public works program. "If you can see that my family is supplied with food clothing and shelter," a poor man wrote FDR, "I will get him." To avoid being "put on the spot," he asked that the assignment be kept "a secret between you and I alone." Other writers called for suspension of civil liberties, a military call-up, and temporary federal command of all police forces. The G-men should, as one suggested, join with "each sheriff's force . . . to visit every house in his jurisdiction . . . search every building, . . . patrol the highways for a day and scrutinize and question men traveling out of the zone agreed upon." Many applauded the shoot-on-sight order because, as an Indianapolis resident pointed out, the Dillinger rampage was "the worst crime the state of Indiana has ever suffered" and "the women who were with them even laugh[ed] and joke[ed] about how much fun they . . . had." This man asked FDR to use his "wonderfull [*sic*] power and influence" so that "this bunch of gangsters, women and men, [could] be brought to their justice—death."[49]

A vocal, if smaller, group understood the manhunt as one of many futile and wrong-headed government interventions. A Kentucky woman suggested that Roosevelt ask humorist Will Rogers "to get his rope and 'lasso'" Dillinger. "You have been so successful in [relieving] bad conditions in our country, thought this might be a way out for you on this one." Another asked, "Have you tried poison?" Many pointed out that upper-class criminals went unpunished. "While you are grieving over the 2,000,000 [dollars] that has been wasted in the Dillinger search," one commented bitterly, "dont forget the 10,000,000 old Samuel [Insull] took with him on his world cruise, besides the millions swindled from the widows and orphans before he set sail." Some expressed their scorn by taking the bandit's name. One "Dillinger," who also signed himself "A Citizen," thanked reporters for "big headlines on the front page as I am a glutton for publicity." Another wrote, "Big and brave Federal agents? Sure they are, if you sic 'em on some little fellow that's moonshined a bit of Oklahoma 'cawn.' But when they meet a fellow like [me] they run like a flock of rabbits in the wind!"[50]

Hoover's network of police professional organizations were the staunchest government supporters. But amateur detective clubs ran a close second, the fascination with violent crime having produced a marketable hobby that also operated as a progovernment constituency. The secretary of the Brothers Honorable Secret Service Club of Detroit wrote FDR to offer the services of his membership and suggest that he order every newspaper to print Dillinger's picture on the front page so that "citizens" could capture the bandit. A Nebraska radio club asked for Dillinger wanted posters to distribute "to our network of boy detectives" who had "caught several wanted men, one man three times" (the Boy Radio Detectives stayed tuned and, when notified by the station, combed their neighborhoods for fugitives).[51]

Like the fingerprint campaign organizers, the division saw these groups as prospective political allies. Reporting on the radio club, an agent noted that the station manager expected "to interest the better class of boys in being of assistance to Law Enforcement Agencies and Public Officials, and becoming a high type of citizen." They were "kept well under control," and the club was "not a snooping or nosey organization." Perhaps "these boys would observe and secure valuable information, which the small town officer would never get."[52]

Most letter writers wanted Dillinger to be caught; an initial identification with the state, the New Deal, and the goals of the war on crime moved citizens to contact government figures in the first place. One anonymous informant expressed the spirit of many by signing himself "Pro Bono Publico." Conversely, the writers expressed pervasive contempt for the Dillinger family: one suggested that John Sr. be arrested "so that when his son attempts to free or aid him, your agents can capture him"; another, that "the old rooster" be given the third degree. Much hostility was provoked by the film footage from Mooresville, and many writers wondered why the state did not suppress the newsreel. "Is that the best Will Hays and his board of movie strategy can do in the way of increasing respect for law[?]" one asked. Several worked their own ideas about science into the idea of scientific policing: a woman wrote about "a man that is borned with a second sight," who would be "interested in locating this gang, if his name is kept a secret."[53]

Transformation was another important theme: Dillinger was living as a woman, a nun, a Native American, and an African American. He was in Chicago, one letter asserted, "passing himself off as a Negro." "You no doubt have heard Amos & Andy on the radio, perhaps you have seen them in their characteristic makeup, depicting themselves as negroes & with their acquired dialect seemingly talking like a couple of Southern negroes. Does it not seem possible that Amos & Andy could walk all over the city of Chicago, even into police stations without fear of detection[?]" "Real McCoy" informed Walter Winchell "that John Dillinger attended [the] MacLarin Ross fight, dressed as a woman and John dont make a bad looking gal." Another claimed that he "will be found at the Indian Reservation at Wis[consin] disguised as an Indian woman. Probley [*sic*] with a Baby on his Back. . . . The Indians would hide him as they would consider him Evelyn Frechettes Husband." In August, an anonymous writer reported that "Baby Face" Nelson had also visited family "dressed as a woman."[54]

These charges of whiteness and maleness lurking behind racial and gendered others mark Dillinger and other celebrity bandits as sites of tremendous political struggle. As a white person imitating blackness, a real person imitating a radio character, and a white husband disguised as a brown wife, he was ambiguously gendered and racially indeterminate, simultaneously powerful and powerless. Furthermore, to save himself from the greater power of the state he assumed subject positions of less political and social influence than he would normally occupy, forsaking the privileges of race and gender to which he was entitled.

One writer explored the range of Dillinger's cultural power by placing him above mere politics. Mrs. Eulalia Callendar believed the bandit was an angel come to earth, whose destruction would be calamitous to the nation. A sob sister, Mrs. Callendar was a prodigious and delusional correspondent who wrote rambling letters to the Dillinger family, Hoover, Louis Piquett, Louis M. Howe, Walter Winchell, FDR, and Governor McNutt, among others, outlining the divine plan at work: "I mean—*can't* you see—you *can* see can't you there *is some* substantial power protecting & helping John Dillinger?! *Some* divine power I feel *sure*—I guess God has *other* plans for J.D. besides the 'chair.' I guess God *can send down* just *one* angel *more* powerful than *all* the *police*." Reprimanding

Winchell for taking the government's side, Mrs. Callendar advised that she knew "truths" about "Johnny D." and "Bonnie" that should bring these manhunts to a halt. Praying day and night, she had "tried so hard to help the kid 'go straight'" but she could not accomplish this alone. "And if God forgives a man," she demanded, "why can't the State forgive too? Be merciful and forget. This is supposed to be a Christian nation, isn't it? . . . If shoot they must they might do well to shoot first some of our own Blessed Beautiful Bankers!!!"[55]

Unlike most correspondents, Mrs. Callendar actually connected with the object of her devotion and became a minor celebrity. In response to one missive, Piquett invited her to visit him, remarking on the "very tender feeling reading between the lines of your short message" and "the trend of your beautiful heart." Promising to deliver her letters to Dillinger, he assured her that the bandit was "devoting the balance of his life in this world to God," that he was "a great student of the bible." Piquett then forwarded the correspondence to Hoover. Heartened, Mrs. Callendar released to *Time* a letter from Audrey Hancock assuring her, "John is alive. We heard from John. . . . We don't know where he is hiding. . . . We have so much mail for him. . . . I don't believe he would surrender."[56]

Although the frequency and tone of her letters might suggest that Mrs. Callendar was harmlessly deranged, her success in establishing a connection to the Dillinger camp and a manic confidence in her capacity to do violence through prayer resulted in a summer visit from the G-men. As it turned out, she was also obsessed with Pierpont, Makley, and Clark, who were appealing death sentences from the Ohio State Penitentiary. In a letter to the warden, she promised that if they were not released, her prayers would cause the prison to collapse and the prison's staff to drop dead. She also appealed to sixty Episcopalian bishops ("about fifty of whom did not reply," the investigating agent reported). The division closed the case, deciding that she was a lunatic "with an exaggerated sympathy for criminals."[57]

Dillinger sympathizers were most frequently not identifiable lunatics, however; many argued that banks were themselves criminal and could not therefore be the victims of crime. The petition from Mooresville asked Governor McNutt to pardon Dillinger, alluding to the pardon that had permitted Frank James to surrender with honor. It concluded, "Many of the financial institutions of the state have just as criminally robbed our citizens without any effort being made to punish the perpetrators. . . . [The] new deal can manifest itself in no better way than to remove from the execution of the law the vindictive spirit of the barbaric past." Demanding that the governor of Ohio withdraw the bounty on "an Indiana Man," an anonymous writer warned, "People over here do not want him found or hunted down. . . . If he got a little money from the banks it was not as much as they have stole from the people." A self-proclaimed childhood friend advised that a just resolution to the case would be to offer Dillinger the prestige and security he had earned—a government job.[58]

During the period of Dillinger's disappearance, his audience fantasized about who he really was and who they might be in relation to him. Because of this, women associated with Dillinger also received fan letters, from people who fantasized about the bandit code and their own commitment to the fugitive. "Good Girls, Dont talk," wrote a sob sister who promised the molls captured at Little Bohemia that if they needed help, she would "go the limit—and then some." A man wrote to Billie that he loved her because of her loyalty: "You are a genuine heroine concerning love, towards a regular he man." Another wrote from Australia to tell her she had "many friends throughout the world."[59] Such letters explore the imaginative possibilities that emerged for a New Deal audience as the spectacular defeat of fugitives the government had promised failed to materialize, a period of cultural play that nevertheless resonated with the political themes of an uncertain moment of state expansion.

Producing John Dillinger

The government's failure to capture Dillinger in the spring of 1934 caused agents to be dispatched from every division office to run down the most remote tips and recruit new informants. As Hoover assured the public that arrests were "in sight," agents' confidential reports showed that the bandits slipped in and out of surveillance networks at will. In May, Hoover reprimanded Purvis severely, citing "too many instances" in which surveillances had not been properly conducted. "I cannot continue to tolerate action of investigators that permits leads to remain uncovered, or at least improperly covered." His frustration increased when the molls who had been in custody vanished, shortly after a federal judge sentenced them to probation. Without consulting Hoover the judge believed that "the men the defendants were with prior to their arrest [would] attempt to contact them" and could then be arrested. When Hoover's men lost the molls, the division was publicly ridiculed. "It was the Judge's place to have put these three women in the penitentiary," Hoover fumed defensively, "but in view of some peculiar mental quirk, he apparently decided to put them on probation."[60]

Hoover's political skills were never more crucial. In addition to conflicts within the Department of Justice, Indiana authorities had to be mollified constantly. As Harold Nathan explained to Hoover in mid-May, "Governor McNutt's chief desire is to have a member of the State Police present when Dillinger is captured." Nathan had told him "that whenever possible [the division] would call upon the State troopers," through the director of Public Safety rather than state police chief Matthew Leach, whose dislike of the G-men was well known. Passage of the crime bill had shifted the balance of power toward Hoover, however, and he could well afford a symbolic deference that barely masked his unwillingness to cooperate with others in the search. Now, many at the division felt free to say that local police were poorly trained and ill disciplined. As Tamm wrote to Hoover, incorporating local officers might result in "innocent persons being shot in the mistaken belief they are Dillinger." Clegg agreed, adding that police alerts should be limited, since officers could get "shot while making an investigation."[61]

But where was Dillinger? A memorandum to Cummings on May 16 expressed Hoover's thin confidence that Dillinger was playing "a lone wolf game" and that the case would soon be "brought to a successful consummation." A wire service report cited Purvis's opinion that Dillinger was dead, a story that was "an absolute fabrication and concoction," Purvis hastily assured his superiors later in the day. In mid-June, however, agents did begin the search for John Hamilton's grave. Jean Crompton, recaptured after Tommy Carroll's death, confirmed that Hamilton was "either seriously injured, paralyzed or dead"; and an informant also reported that he had been fatally wounded at a roadblock.[62]

Because he disappears from the official record at this point, it is difficult to piece together the eight remaining weeks of Dillinger's life, but it is probable that he went underground in Chicago and East Chicago, territory controlled by the Capone syndicate and two famously corrupt police departments. An informant reported "that Dillinger actually paid protection to the Chicago Police Department" through a saloon owner. Despite his celebrity, Dillinger was not that easily recognized, nor were underworld connections likely to turn him in while his money lasted. Moll Marie Conforti remembered Dillinger bragging "that he had been attending night clubs and other public places and as 'hot' as he was, nobody had recognized him."[63]

Dillinger probably did not assume the disguises that his audience imagined; however, he fooled his nephew once by dressing and grooming himself as a laborer, suggesting that Dillinger could protect himself by abandoning the appearance of celebrity. Fred Hancock later told agents that he arrived one day that summer "dressed in overalls, wearing glasses, no coat, wearing a sleeveless jacket." "He was unshaven, and . . . I did not recognize him at the time. . . . When I looked at him more closely I realized that it was John." John left money in small amounts among family members and left again, eluding federal agents parked outside. Police and agents also failed to recognize him when he was not disguised. A moll reported that one of the bandit's favorite games was to pull up to a traffic cop and ask if Dillinger had been spotted. Policemen, she said, were notorious for engaging in prolonged conversations with gang members without identifying them. After a traffic accident, Hamilton and his moll were taken to a local police station; Hamilton opened his coat as they went through the door, showing her his guns. He warned, "Pat, I may have to blast my way out of here," but they left unrecognized an hour later (Cherrington's reply had been: "Go to it, big boy.")[64]

These stories reveal another kind of technique for disguise: bandits were not recognizable when they looked and behaved like "normal" people. Cherrington recounted that one day

> Van Meter and Dillinger purchased new clothes and called on the president of a bank in a rather small town; that they identified themselves as being officials of the NRA from Washington, they having with them some forged credentials bearing the forged signature of a Washington official; ... they advised the bank president that they were calling on all the banks throughout the state in a survey, and that they were very much interested in how the various codes were operating.

Having received a tour of several local banks, lunch, and dinner with the local bankers' association, they returned and robbed the first bank two weeks later. Subsequently, Van Meter toured the police station in another town "representing himself as a writer for *True Story* magazine"; he and Dillinger went back "and relieved them of all their ammunition and rifles."[65]

Catching Dillinger became a question of chance for the G-men: a poorly concocted cover story, a betrayal, a photograph seen in a detective magazine, or the eventual decision of a syndicate that Dillinger was worth more dead than alive. It was the last that proved decisive. The confrontation in front of the Biograph Theater, commonly understood to have been orchestrated by "the woman in red," Romanian procurer and prostitute Anna Sage, did not occur because Sage suddenly recognized Dillinger as her friend's new lover and did her duty, as the newspapers reported. Rather, Sage was probably an intermediary who satisfied three potentially contradictory interests: the division's desire to capture the bandit in a way that gave them the most public credit; the anxiety of Chicago politicians and police factions that their connections with the underworld would be exposed; and the Capone syndicate's need to halt the constant federal raids, particularly on houses of prostitution, which interfered with business.

As Evelyn Frechette wrote, call it fate. But fate was also helped along by a recklessness that characterizes anecdotes about Dillinger, an insistence on personal display that marked his adult criminal career. Hubris made him, and others, more vulnerable: his belief that he could live openly in Chicago precipitated a break with his former allies, limiting his access to information, money, and weapons. An associate remembered that Dillinger was "ejected from the gang" by Van Meter shortly before because he was "running around with too many women and that he talked too much. . . . A great failing of Dillinger was too many women and too much talking."[66]

Dillinger's celebrity status ended his usefulness as a criminal worker and made him a liability to too many syndicate interests. On July 6, a United Press reporter escorted to Melvin Purvis's office a Chicago police officer who "stated that he had been approached by members of the Capone outfit who had informed him that the Government's activities with reference to the Dillinger investigation [were] hampering their activities . . . and that they intended to furnish [him] with information . . . in order that he might be eliminated." Did someone in the Chicago police department desire a cooperative relationship with the division, hoping that his links with organized crime would not be exposed? Cooperation benefited both sides: after all, in St. Paul, detectives put Homer Van Meter on the spot and took full credit for it themselves. As a moll mused later, "Maybe it was a good thing for Brown and the rest of the St. Paul police dept. that he wasn't taken alive. If he talked it would have been just too bad for them."[67]

The federal reward gave Dillinger cash value at a moment in which he was becoming an irritant to, rather than a producer for, the syndicates. While the federal heat forced bandits to go underground and spend their money, it also kept them from working and paying protection. In this context, the reward money became a final way of squeezing a profit out of Dillinger for anyone willing to take on the dirty business of producing him. Louis Piquett had seen it as a viable option, and so did others. As an informant reported, the officer who enlisted Sage, East Chicago police detective Martin Zarcovitch, "had known where Dillinger was for sixty days. . . . In collusion with the two women, he had put Dillinger on the spot, [and] did so for the apparent purpose of obtaining possession of Dillinger's wealth—money and securities."[68] Whether this wealth existed or not, Zarcovitch did successfully claim reward money and possibly a portion of Sage's five thousand dollars as well.

Not scientific policing but a more capable local network of politicians, police, mobsters, and criminal workers produced Dillinger at the Biograph Theater on Sunday, July 22. Did some ironic hand choose the movie as well? That evening the bandit, Polly Hamilton, and Sage attended *Manhattan Melodrama,* a gangster picture starring Clark Gable, in which the handsome star is executed at the end of the picture. As the show let out, the crowd surged onto the sidewalk, the urban landscape hiding the special agents and Chicago detectives poised for a signal from Purvis that the bandit had exited the theater. When Purvis saw Sage in her red dress, he waited for them to separate from the other pedestrians and lit a match, the signal that his G-men should shoot first—and then count to ten.

From the moment his body hit the ground, Dillinger's death became a working narrative that provided new opportunities and dilemmas, a process that began immediately through the quick thinking of a local businessman. In December 1934, the Reliance Dental Manufacturing Company offered Hoover a copy of the "Death Mask of John Dillinger, showing every feature of this notorious character even to the scars and blemishes where he underwent the face lifting. The marks of the bricks upon which he fell and the bullet wound are shown completely." Hoover added the artifact "to the exhibit maintained . . . in the New Department of Justice Building" (where it remains a feature of the FBI tour today).[69]

Dillinger's family also became intermediaries for the interpretation and reproduction of his life. Reporters rushed out to the Mooresville farm, where John Sr. received them, hoping that John had enough money on him to pay for a funeral. "If he didn't it will be an awful burden but I'll do the best I can." Quotes like this portrayed the Dillingers as a poor family, despite the fact that they were property owners. *Time*'s report featured a rustic picture of John Sr. as a confused hillbilly farmer, making explicit connections between Dillinger and Clyde Barrow, whose pious and uneducated relatives had been featured only a few months before: "Barefoot, clad in overalls, he stood in the doorway, tears streaming down his cheeks. "Is it really true?" he asked, bewildered. "Are you sure there is no mistake? I have prayed and prayed it would not happen."[70] Poverty, of course, implied that John's family had not benefited from his crimes. Bandits' relatives often used reporters in this way to pronounce their respectability, in their communities and before the law. As these carefully orchestrated interviews and the newsreel appearance would suggest, they were shrewd about representing themselves to the public.

"Crowds packed the Lyric Theater in Indianapolis," one publication reported in September, "as the [Dillinger] family shared memories of their late relative." A vaudeville contract was signed almost immediately after John's death, committing the Dillinger and Hancock families to five months of performances through New Year's Eve. They were so popular that by the first week in August their agent "was in Chicago endeavoring to obtain bookings for them." Around this time, division agents seeking to interview Fred Hancock received a "courteous" response that he would be happy to answer questions at 1:45, "after his first appearance at the Lyric Theater."[71]

The vaudeville performance was also an interrogation, in which the audience asked questions and family members revealed bits of information about John. Admission was twenty-five cents until 6:00 P.M. and forty cents in the evening. Here, John Sr.'s image as a poor farmer deflected charges that the family was exploiting the bandit's death for personal profit, reinforcing his identity as a local man. "I had an offer to appear in New York for five hundred dollars a week," he told the audience: "I was used to being at work dressed in overalls and they do not have any green farms around New York City. I had a telegram which offered ten thousand dollars for John's body, another offer of one half the receipts and then on Friday two gentlemen came from St. Paul, Minnesota and wanted to take the body up and take it around on exhibition and I said you have not got enough money to have me do this." The audience applauded loudly. When asked why he was now appearing, Dillinger replied, "Well, I had quite a little expense and did not have the money to meet it . . . and I thought I would come to get what money I could for my expenses."[72]

Since the government had kept the agreement with Hubert and Fred, the expenses were probably fictitious. Others still struggling with prosecutions and appeals did have expenses, however, and the Dillinger family contributed to the creation of a market for authentic revelations primarily generated by and for women. The division monitored these efforts closely, since some public enemies were still at large. On August 14, the *Los Angeles Herald Express* reported that Harry Pierpont's mother, Lena, had tried to sell his story to Paramount Studios. In a letter, she had offered "pictors" and memories from "befor[e] the prison walk out." Later she also sold ghost-written memoirs that presented "evidence" of her son's innocence. In one, she wrote of a secret visit from Dillinger in which he confirmed that Harry was home with her "eating supper, when the sheriff was slain" by (the now deceased) Homer Van Meter.[73]

The Pierpont family was desperate for money at this point, and Mary Kinder signed a contract to perform at the Chicago World's Fair. Harry upbraided her, as did her brother-in-law, who called her "a publicity seeker." Having already pawned her jewelry, Mary responded that she only wanted to finance the appeal. "Honey, I don't want you to think I am talking too much," she wrote. "I never said anything that would hurt anyone or told our sacred memories, but I thought it was a chance to make some money and I took it. Now honey, I have talked it over with [your lawyer] and she said it was alright. I gave her half of what I got to go ahead with your case. . . . Money seems our only chance now." Soon, however, Mary hoped for a real show business career. "Now about the fair," she wrote:

> Honey I have [an] agreement with a man in Chicago who is to pay my expenses and buy me a few evening gowns and give me 25% of what we make. It is to be in the "Streets of Paris" and that is like a night club and other girls are there and I am just to talk a few minutes and sell these articles I wrote. That was where Sally Rand was last year. It may give me a start honey so please don't feel hurt or bad about it. I know your code and darling I will always try to live up to it.

Mary lasted for only two performances. As she wrote dolefully several weeks later, "The Fair officials came and stopped me for a week to investigate and see just who I was."[74]

Detective magazines saw the potential for "sacred memories" before Dillinger's death: *True Detective* and *True Romance* bought the story of Billie and John's love affair (which was remarkably consistent with her court testimony and may have been partially drawn from it) and finally published it under her byline in September 1934. At the end of August, the *Boston Record* purchased the newspaper rights to Billie's life story and began negotiations with the Bureau of Prisons for interviews. The Department of Justice made such deals difficult to carry out, however. When the *Chicago Journal-American* proposed that it pay "as much as $1,000 to [Evelyn Frechette] for information leading to the apprehension of Dillinger," it was refused. "This sounds like a publicity stunt," Hoover advised Purvis; "we cannot be a party to any such stunt."[75]

Although bandit families used publicity with varying degrees of sophistication, they watched the bottom line as well; the lack of shrewdness shown by Emil Wanatka, who sold the use of his name to *Startling Detective Adventures* for only $12.50, was rare. The widow of one bandit, who sent an unpublished memoir of her life as a moll to the division in February 1935, was also "the source of the recent copyrighted stories published in a Chicago newspaper." In giving this glimpse of the underworld, she wrote, "I fully realize that I take my life in my hands." But she had promised her husband that she would tell his "true" story, and the book was "offered . . . as a recital of plain facts by one who knows." Tamm believed that she had sent the book to Hoover first hoping he would endorse it as part of the war on crime.[76]

Not everyone enjoyed or profited from publicity, however. When reporters interviewed Pierpont, Makley, and Clark at the Ohio State Penitentiary before their scheduled execution on July 9, 1934, Makley charged that "it was the newspapers that got them into the fix they are now in, by publication of wild stories and down-right lies." Others were embarrassed by the loss of privacy. "I have been bothered by quite a lot of different men coming to the door a couple of weeks ago wanting my picture," a moll's mother wrote. "They . . . finally confessed they wanted it for a magazine but I told them he would never see enough money for my picture. It was the detective magazine I think."[77]

These postmortem narratives are important because the twin themes of romance and fate that had earlier explained the careers of Bonnie Parker, Clyde Barrow, and John Dillinger now produced the bandit and his moll as people whose extraordinary choices resembled ordinary human dilemmas. *Startling Detective*'s account of Tommy Carroll quoted a friend's claim that he "was spotted for a bullet the day he was born, although he never believed himself he would get it. He had one great failing and that was his love for the spotlight and his desire to show off." The story described the usual history of youthful delinquencies and jail time. In 1925, he met "a girl who was 'different'":

> Their marriage was ill-starred from the beginning. Nine years later, she was to sob her story of their mating to Federal agents in St. Paul, as she fought the claims of a younger woman. . . .
>
>   "We were just kids," she told Federal men and police. "But we were in love. I knew he was a fugitive, but I loved him.
>
>   "It was only a short time after we were married until they put Tommy in the county jail in St. Louis and tried to pin a robbery charge on him."

The wife watched her husband make bad decisions despite her love, and "still her loyalty was so great that she could not bring herself to desert him." However, a federal arrest doomed them: "But from here on, Fate was to swirl him upward in a dizzy tornado of crime that, perhaps, has never before been rivalled in bloodiness and sensation, and certainly has never before been approached in its spectacular twists and unexpected turns." Through the weather metaphor, fate performs a distinctly different function in this narrative, urging the reader to identify with this bandit couple as ordinary lovers trapped by the crime wave itself.[78]

If "true" bandit stories could ultimately offer no hope of personal salvation, the magazines themselves did. The articles were surrounded by advertisements for publications, products, and self-improvement programs. Evelyn Frechette's *True Confessions* tale, "My Love Life with Dillinger," was enclosed by ads for Dr. Walters's Reducing Garments, and Dr. McCaskey's Prescription Tablets, which promised swift weight loss so that "overweight" did not "rob you of popularity." Others commanded readers to "Pick Your Job!" and "Learn at Home to Make Good Money in Radio"; one for *Screenplay* asked, "Do You Want to Get into the Movies?" Many spoke to the fascination with crime that had brought readers to the magazine in the first place, offering "professional" fingerprint kits and home study courses to become "an Expert Criminologist and Court Expert— With crime increasing there is constant demand for the expert criminologist. He succeeds where ordinary detectives fail."

Claiming to be staunchly anticrime, these magazines depended for their success on producing criminal lives as romantic tragedies and then letting readers return to the safety of their own lives. The editor of one police journal misunderstood the point entirely when he complained that it was "almost impossible to understand . . . the nauseating display of mushy sentimentality" evoked by bandits. Sentimentality permitted readers to believe that they knew bandits and their molls, an illusion that writers knew could be dissipated by realism. A *True Detective* writer asked for access to division files so that his story would be "somewhat true." He was refused because he would not agree to submit the final draft to division fact checkers. "Mr. Herous," T. D. Quinn explained, "did not want any objectionable matter taken out of it."[79]

The mania for consuming crime presented obvious challenges to the division's ideas about what story should be told and when. Hoover permitted no special radio broadcasts or newsreels at the Biograph, and numerous requests for information about Melvin Purvis and the task force were refused. When news services appealed to Henry Suydam, Homer Cummings's special assistant for press relations, Hoover released some information to the Associated Press under protest. While he was "always agreeable to any policy which the Department feels should be followed . . . details concerning the lives and activities of the individual investigators of this division should not be made public."[80]

Other authors have noted that Hoover abhorred publicity he could not control; more precisely, he resisted the incorporation of G-men into narrative forms that centered on heroic bandits. The Dillinger publicity had been a "mistake," Hoover told Suydam, and no agent should ever be singled out "as the man responsible for the death or capture of a notorious desperado"; "no one employee of this Division can ever be responsible for the successful termination of any one case. . . . Through cooperative efforts a case is broken." By producing the story as an institutional one, Hoover successfully submerged the traditional detective narrative in the modern statist romance of scientific policing; he also depersonalized the bandit, producing him as a bureaucratic case.[81]

Hoover saw the production of the division in public discourse as a primary field of professional activity that gave fixed meanings to crime and to the state that policed it. On the day after Dillinger's death, Hoover expressed his "extreme displeasure" about the handling of press releases. "There is no more important matter, in my estimation, than this under your supervision at the present time," he lectured Ed Tamm. Another memo emphasized the importance of accurate captions on photographs and "no delay in the issuance of appropriate press releases in Division cases." Typically, Tamm suggested firing everyone. Hoover, although agreeing that this was "entirely proper," urged him to take more time in "proper training and supervision" for the new staff. "No doubt there are many things confusing to them," he cautioned. "I do not want them to become 'rattled' or panic-stricken in their work." However, when Louis Piquett was arrested, there was an unseemly hour and a half of silence because press releases had not yet been duplicated. "I have previously complained about the improper preparation of material for press releases, but with very little improvement," Hoover wrote.[82]

Hoover's concern about control led him to avoid negative publicity, even if it meant abandoning prosecutions. Although the division denied it, Melvin Purvis received hate mail and death threats after Dillinger's death, much of which impugned his masculinity and criticized the state's use of a woman informant. "Dear Melville," one sneered; "such a nice Sunday school name." Another charged, "That was a cowardly way to kill a 'man.'" In this context, making an example of the Dillinger family, as Texas authorities had done with the Barrows and the Parkers, could produce popular emotions that division publicists could not promise to contain. Hoover might have been discouraged by his failure to prosecute Louis Piquett or to obtain more than minimum sentences against any of the molls. He also had an institutional interest in keeping his deal with Dillinger's relatives a secret, since he had been ordered to leave them alone. In November, Hoover advised William Stanley, "[Because] of the length of time which has elapsed since the death of John Dillinger, I am inclined to the view that no action should be taken with respect to the relatives."[83]

The Department of Justice did pursue harboring cases against people who had provided Dillinger with services. These prosecutions, such as the trial of Dr. Clayton May and nurse Augusta Salt, who treated Dillinger after the St. Paul shoot-out, served two purposes. They aired the government's case against fugitives, since most bandits were killed, not tried; and they demonstrated appropriate public attitudes toward crime in a public forum. As an agent reminded a middle-class man who said he could not testify in the Frechette trial, "as a citizen he [had] a certain duty to perform in assisting in law enforcement regardless of his personal feelings in the matter."[84]

Hoover did not recommend a harboring case for prosecution without studying the individual's status in the community and the possible political consequences; despite evidence against a number of politicians and policemen in these documents, only service providers and molls were pursued by the courts. In the case of a physician who treated Dillinger, Sam Cowley advised that the doctor had "some prestige" in the local political underworld but none among St. Paul's better classes and would thus be a good subject for prosecution. A Texas dealer who had sold guns to the Dillinger gang was similarly vulnerable. "It is my honest belief," the San Antonio SAC wrote,

> that if each and every individual known to give aid and comfort in any manner to any of these gangsters is dragged out into the open, where the citizens of the town can look him over and know what he is doing, it will tend to close up some avenues of refuge and supplies. . . . The so-called respectable citizens throughout the country who have been surreptitiously rendering aid to these gangsters will not know when they will be next to be advertised among their home-town people.[85]

Such rhetoric demonstrates the perfect melding of the old, Progressive state that produced the ideology of scientific policing and the new interventionist state that implemented it. If citizens could see corruption, they would wish to take action against it; they would also be able to envision the might of such a state aimed against them.

The death of Dillinger was a triumph for the war on crime and for the New Deal; warm congratulations passed between the White House, the attorney general, the Chicago office, and the director. Hoover's relief and gratitude was expressed to Purvis in an unusually intimate letter. "Dear Melvin," he wrote,

> I wanted to write and repeat to you my expressions of pleasure and commendation which I tried to convey to you last night. The shooting and killing of John Dillinger by the Agents of your office under your admirable direction and planning are but another indication of your ability and capacity as a leader and an executive.... I did want you to know that my appreciation of the success with which your efforts have met in this case is lasting and makes me most proud of you.

Hoover's emotional tone reveals his fondness for Purvis but also how much institutional prestige had been wagered on a successful outcome to this manhunt. As Hoover concluded, "I was glad that the Division could 'get' Dillinger and 'get' him itself."[86]

The division's unwillingness to parade Purvis before the public did not prevent celebrity. After his resignation in 1935, the G-man parlayed his reputation as "the man who got Dillinger" into a number of semilucrative commercial projects. In the immediate aftermath of the Biograph incident, hundreds of fans sought to establish or reestablish a connection with him, a phenomenon that partly caused the end of his career. Although his success would propel Hoover and the division on to greater prestige, the seductive and inescapable publicity, probably urged along by envy among an increasingly close and ambitious cadre of Washington administrators, ended Purvis's friendship with Hoover.

Fan mail also suggests that while victory in the Dillinger case had contributed to the professional reputation of federal policing, the masculinized model of enforcement also had a matinee audience. Purvis's public was almost exclusively female; thus his memoirs were first published as a *Redbook* serial. Women wrote to offer themselves, or single friends and relatives, as candidates for marriage. "I like to see your pitcha in the paper," one stranger teased. Another wrote that she thought Purvis was "the greatest man in Chicago." "Will you send your picture to the undersigned 'Miss'?" Many of these letters were from female acquaintances; a friend noted that she and her unmarried sister were visiting Washington that summer and would love to see him; and a second woman who "knew [him] 'when'" invited Purvis to spend the summer with her. "I think if I had been in your shoes when Dillinger looked you in the eye, I would have dissolved and merged with the night air," she gushed. "Polly" reminded him of their past: "We really did have some good times—don't you think?" Even married women wrote to Purvis with romance in mind; one "with a couple of kids" confessed wistfully that she could not "forget the hours and times" they spent together. "I wonder if you ever have time for reminiscing?"[87]

If the Dillinger case was a public relations triumph, it also left too many questions about the future of state intervention unanswered, in particular, whether scientific policing could successfully track a fugitive and whether the government could intervene to prevent or reduce crime. It also revived difficult questions about the connections between syndicate crime and the local political structures that underwrote New Deal reforms. Although the war on racketeers was seen as a next possible step for federal crime intervention, this idea was dropped during the Dillinger manhunt and did not resurface until the Republican postwar period.

Seven

"A Central Bureau at Washington"

The Barker-Karpis Gang, Surveillance, and the Victory of Federal Policing

May I say that I believe that the majority of your fellow countrymen prefer MORE OF DEPARTMENT OF JUSTICE HOOVER AND LESS OF CONGRESSIONAL HOOEY. —R. Erskine Kerr, Lake Charles, Louisiana, July 17, 1936

[We] synthesized Ma Barker down to having the one son instead of four. . . . Then we went back and said, "We'd like to do Ma Barker and have the gangster with a mother complex and play it against Freudian implications that she's driving him to do these things, and he's driving himself to self-destruction. Play it like a Greek tragedy." They said, "Fellas . . . ?" We said, "Believe us it will work." —Ben Roberts and Ivan Goff, authors of *White Heat* (Warner Brothers, 1949)

A week after John Dillinger's death, the *Tulsa Tribune* reported on the federal government's renewed determination to eradicate bandit crime. A photo of Hoover was ringed by drawings of identical G-men pointing pistols, submachine guns, and rifles outward at an unseen enemy. "In a sedate brick building on Vermont Avenue a short, compactly muscular man sits at a desk," it began:

> In a crisp voice he speaks into one after another of a battery of telephones.
> A few miles away machine gun bullets spatter on a target, shattering the somnolent peace of the Maryland countryside—sounding a warning to "Baby Face" Nelson and other killers of his ilk.

The G-men had guns and cars "such as the gangsters use," but the writer criticized Congress for not funding armored cars and airplanes. The state's greatest resource, vigilant citizens, was also highlighted in a follow-up piece that noted the many Dillinger tips G-men had fielded. "We couldn't afford to overlook a single one," Hoover said.[1]

The pleasure in "getting" Dillinger was short lived, giving way to political struggles over the future of federal enforcement. By September 4, Hoover had initiated discussions about "the desirability of changing the name of the Division of Investigation to the Federal Bureau of Investigation," a title that would distinguish the G-men as an elite among federal police. However, publicity about Anna Sage's informant status in the fall of 1934 tainted Hoover's claim to professionalism. Sam Cowley's first memo as Purvis's replacement on the fugitive task force addressed this problem. Demanding reward money, police who claimed to have "put Dillinger on the spot" threatened to expose a number of informers. Cowley proposed to strike first, telling reporters that "no police officer with any experience or intelligence would disclose the name of any informant," adding, "But if he [does,] he is a 'dirty rat.'" Hoover agreed but questioned the dignity of the phrase "dirty rat," substituting, "if he had proper conception of the duties and responsibilities of his office."[2]

From another direction, reformers who believed that sensational pursuits obscured the need for community-based interventions pushed at the Department of Justice to promote crime prevention. In particular, a coalition of lawyers at the American Bar Association imagined a New Deal for crime cut in the model of the National Recovery Administration: a statist agenda that enforced reform, changed behavior, and dissolved when the crisis was past. This assumed, of course, a belief that a crime wave (like a bad economic cycle) had specific causes and could be corrected, a notion Hoover did not share. The director believed that crime, like political sedition, was perennially dangerous because it was committed by defective people. In *Persons in Hiding* (1941), Hoover drew on a pathogenic model to describe crime as "a dread disease, like cancer, or tuberculosis, or bubonic plague"; scientific policing provided the "necessary antiseptic conditions" that protected innocent citizens.[3] Not insignificantly, the narrative of *Persons in Hiding* also revolves around the Barker-Karpis gang, a family that reproduced crime and criminals so rapidly that it had to be exterminated.

That Hoover's belief in pursuit and punishment increasingly distanced him from social reformers was not surprising; but increasingly, it set him at odds with police reformers as well. Throughout 1935, the ideals of professional policing, as articulated by Woods and Vollmer, gave way to enforcement strategies shaped by the politics of centralized repression. Municipal corruption had to be taken for granted, and cooperation was really a one-way street in which federal experts extracted what information they could from local police but circumvented them whenever possible. When Hoover sent Cowley to monitor arrests in the Barker-

Karpis manhunt, he confided that the local SAC would not "dominate the Cleveland Police." "I want it handled in our own way." The emergence of individual heroes among the corps of agents was to be suppressed as well in the interests of public awe for the state. After Cowley, Agent Neal Hollis, and bandit Lester Gillis died in a shoot-out in November 1934, Hoover told Hugh Clegg "that he should state that both . . . fired, and as a result [Gillis] was killed."[4]

The first national crime conference sponsored by the Department of Justice met in December 1934 to promote a centralization agenda, revealing in the process the fragility of the anticrime coalition assembled before the New Deal. Hoover, the keynote speaker, praised the "banding together" of police forces. "We face desperate men and equally desperate women," he announced, "who have respect only for a power greater than theirs . . . an intricate system of fraternization among lawbreakers . . . a brotherhood and sisterhood, the scope of which has become nationwide." As a police journal reported, however, Hoover ignored local officials' growing hostility toward federal intervention. The police chief of "a large eastern metropolis" groused during the speech, "Are the 'Feds' going to cite their record again, further glorify the Department of Justice, and adjourn?" And when former secretary of state Henry Stimson blamed Chicago's crime rate on urban corruption, Illinois politicians shouted back from the convention floor.[5]

The war on crime highlighted the inherent conflict between New Deal commitments to local revitalization and its actual path toward enhanced state power. Perhaps because of this, Homer Cummings enrolled Justin Miller, most recently dean of Duke University's school of law and a leading member of the American Bar Association (ABA), as a special assistant in July 1934 to placate an increasingly restless group of reformers troubled by Department of Justice policies. One of the first projects on Miller's desk was the conference. The second was to kill an ABA proposal that the division be reorganized into ten, more efficient regional bureaus, each with its own director. Predictably, Hoover had responded with a nasty, four-page, single-spaced memo that threatened, in turn, to alienate prestigious supporters. Miller used his influence and contacts to bury the proposal and placate both sides. The national interest, he instructed Arthur Freund, chair of the Criminal Division, required that the ABA mollify Hoover with a letter "assuring him that the matter is not one which has yet gone beyond your committee, and that our desire is not to embarrass the Federal Government or the International Association of Chiefs of Police by any proposals which we make but rather to cooperate with them in arriving at mutual understandings in *preventing* irritation and thus in ultimately achieving more effective law enforcement." At Miller's request, Judge Oscar Hallam of St. Paul also wrote against decentralization, "a needless duplication of effort and expense." "[It is] as easy to get prompt information from a central bureau at Washington with present means of communication as it is to get the same information from a bureau one hundred miles away," Hallam scolded Freund.[6]

Progressives like Miller did not understand that the time to shape policy at the Department of Justice to a social reform agenda had passed. While the ABA hoped to broaden the war on crime to include social work, its acquiescence to enforcement effectively precluded the reform models many cherished. Politically powerful jurists pushed for prevention agendas that addressed the origins of violent crime, persisting in the belief that federal repression did not preclude federal support for grassroots interventions. As the chief justice of the Minnesota Supreme Court wrote to Hoover in December 1934, "Behind the study of every crime commission . . . is the question also of the cause of crime such as juvenile delinquency, unemployment, mental and physical deficiencies, and again the question of the public attitude concerning crime."[7]

It was symbolic of Hoover's victory over reformers that the surveillance methods that Harlan Stone had banned in 1924 were rearticulated during the war on crime as necessary to felony enforcement and complementary to scientific techniques. Informants had been crucial to the capture of John Dillinger; underworld "squawkers" were supplemented by family, molls, and embittered former gang members who broke down when faced with long federal prison terms. These informants grew in importance in the fall of 1934. As Hoover well knew, his political influence over liberals like Arthur Freund depended on continuous arrests and prosecutions. When Homer Van Meter was killed on August 23 by detectives who had been trailing him for "approximately two weeks," Hoover knew he was in a race with local police to capture other federal public enemies. On October 9, Cowley went to St. Louis because, as Ed Tamm reported to Hoover, local police would "have [had] Floyd bumped off and Richetti too." "[Cowley] would rather get them first than have them bumped off before we get to them," Tamm explained.[8]

The division's capture of the Barker-Karpis gang was not just a necessarily prestigious end to the war on crime, solving two final kidnapping cases. It also provided narrative opportunities to demonstrate the inevitable, unchangeable criminal consequences of heredity and environment, short-circuiting the attempts of the ABA, Justin Miller, and others to channel federal resources into decentralized, community crime prevention programs. If John Dillinger is the best-remembered bandit of the war on crime, the Barker-Karpis gang was the quintessential criminal family: four brothers and a surrogate son who yielded unusual power and influence to a woman. Alvin Karpis and the Barker sons—Herman, Lloyd, Fred, and Arthur—were the gunmen and strategists for the gang, but this group of public enemies was held together and given continuity over ten years by their mother. Called Kate, or "Mother" by gang members but most commonly known as "Ma" Barker, by the summer of 1934 she was in her early sixties and, as Hoover described her, "a monument to the evils of parental indulgence."[9]

The Discovery of the Barker-Karpis Gang

As Eddie Green lay dying in a St. Paul hospital on March 25, 1934, his thirty-six-year-old moll, Bessie, was quizzed in relays by federal agents. She was a promising source, Clegg reported, "of above average intelligence for the kind of person she [was]." She was just yielding to her interrogators when several unsolved kidnappings were raised. She responded that it was "generally believed in the Twin Cities that Mr. Bremer was kidnapped by the Barker-Karpis gang." Stunned agents saw her identify Alvin Karpis, as well as "the two Barker boys with the woman they called Mother, and known to her as Kate Barker," who had patronized her nightclub "on several occasions in the late Fall of 1932."[10]

Gangs were often made up of kin and fictive kin relationships, but the Barkers were a true family enterprise. "Mother" was Arizona Clark, married to George Barker in 1895 in Aurora, a small mining town in the Missouri Ozarks that declined as an industrial center around 1900. George attempted to remain there as a farmer, but the family soon moved to Carthage, seven miles northeast of Joplin. Inexorably, the Barkers entered a class of white southern workers in transition from precarious rural independence to wage labor. By World War I, they had lived in several industrial cities, often partially supporting themselves by farming, and ended up in Tulsa. The move to a metropolis marked two important changes. "Arrie" Barker changed her name to the less countrified "Kate," and in 1927 she divorced George, who returned to Joplin.[11]

If George had been drawn to Tulsa by big-city wages, his sons enjoyed urban opportunities to avoid labor. The booming underworld of Tulsa, a center for the Southwest's thriving oil industry, offered work for the four eldest boys in several notorious gangs. After multiple arrests and convictions, by 1922 Arthur ("Doc") was sentenced to life for murdering a bank guard, and Lloyd was serving a twenty-five-year stretch at Leavenworth for mail robbery. Kate lobbied the state parole board on her sons' behalf and tried to keep their spirits up. Lloyd's letters to his mother, later reproduced in a tabloid newspaper, exude affection for "Darling Mother," acknowledging frequent cards, gifts, and food baskets. "I sure hope my little pal is alright and enjoying good health. . . . Love and kisses to my little pal. XXXXX as ever, Lloyd."[12]

Letters like this were later used by the division as evidence that Kate cultivated unnatural relations with her sons, that she "dominated their every move," manipulated them into a life of crime, and became "the 'brains' of the gang."

However, the three middle children had no criminal record and had left Tulsa by 1934. Crime created bitter divisions in the family: after Fred and Kate were killed in 1935, George would not attend their funeral. "They chose their path years ago and I chose mine," he told reporters. It is not surprising that the law-abiding siblings disappeared; as Kate became the central psychopathic symbol of the war on crime, her children were often described by Hoover as "murderous satellites" and "spawn of hell."[13]

Unlike other famous bandits, Kate never wrote or spoke publicly, and no relative attempted to correct this portrait of deranged motherhood. Accounts of these early years rely primarily on interviews with George and on inventions produced by the Crime Records Division that portray her as a parent for whom crime was a religion. One account of her early years placed Kate in a group of "zealots" who evangelized pedestrians while confederates picked their pockets. An article jointly written with Hoover quoted George's memory that Kate took the boys "to Sunday school every Sunday" but encouraged them in their delinquencies. Whenever he tried to "straighten them up she'd just fly into [him]." George elaborated that "when they were good boys," he encouraged "clean pursuits" like hunting, but their jealous mother prevented it.[14]

The Barker divorce may have been triggered by conflict over harboring a fugitive son. In January 1927, Herman, the eldest, was arrested in Joplin and extradited to Arkansas on a bank robbery charge. He escaped in March, went to his girlfriend's house in Muskogee, and disappeared for more than five months. In August, he surfaced in Cheyenne, Wyoming, cashing travelers' checks stolen from a Kansas bank. The bank teller notified a deputy sheriff, who was later found shot dead on the highway, his gun in its holster. On August 29, police caught up with Herman and two other bandits, and Herman shot himself when capture seemed inevitable.[15] Whether Herman committed suicide or was executed with his own gun, this incident seems also to confirm other evidence that a bandit could not hope to survive the murder of a law officer.

The dead brother would be replaced, however. Born to working-class parents in Montreal, Canada, on August 10, 1907, Alvin Karpis was the only son of four children. As a child, he lived in Topeka, Kansas, and Chicago and worked briefly as a baker before becoming a full-time criminal. Significantly, Karpis repudiated the psychopathic model by resisting environmental or hereditary explanations of criminality that might have made him an object of public sympathy. He claimed to have chosen crime as a profession, saying that he had "no regrets for anything" and had never "see[n] anything wrong about robbing a bank or kidnapping a person, or killing anybody who interferes during the performance of the crime." First sentenced as an adult in 1926, Alvin used the Kansas prison system, in the words of one superintendent, as "a trade school" for crime. Classified as a "hard case," he was sent to a maximum security penitentiary where he met Fred Barker.[16]

"My very first meeting with Freddie was an unforgettable event," Karpis wrote in 1972. Barker was a politically powerful prisoner, with guards on his payroll. As Karpis described it, "He arranged a transfer for me to his cell, and when I arrived, I was impressed, to say the least, with his writing table and bookshelf and his stock of canned sardines, jams, and crackers. . . . Freddie used to set up lunches in the yard . . . that featured treats like canned chicken, fresh bread, and pies and pastries." After their release in 1931, Barker and Karpis collaborated on a series of bank and payroll robberies in the crime corridor and in December killed a sheriff in Missouri. A wanted poster listed a one-hundred-dollar reward for "Old Lady Arrie Barker" as an accomplice.[17]

Karpis always denied that Ma had anything to do with the gang's work, telling federal agents that although she was aware of what they did, "at no time did she aid in the planning of the crimes or have prior knowledge of them." In his autobiography, this was modified further. "She was just an old-fashioned homebody from the Ozarks," he wrote. "Her spare time was spent working jigsaw puzzles and listening to the radio—the way any mother would whose family had grown up. Ma was superstitious, gullible, simple, cantankerous and, well, generally law-abiding." Indeed, if Kate Barker had been "the brains" of the gang, it should have shown up in the investigative file, and it does not—despite the many other accomplices identified by informants.[18] But Kate's status as a homemaker did not make her peripheral to gang activities, and she did profit from the boys' crimes. She was supported by their criminal earnings, and her home was used as a meeting place and message drop. Her age and apparent respectability permitted the gang to hide out "disguised" as a family. As "Mrs. Hunter" and "Mrs. Anderson" she rented houses, paid bills, shopped, and did household errands. Age made Kate more socially invisible than a moll; it also gave her authority over the younger women when weeks of hiding out produced boredom, frayed tempers, and bouts of drunkenness among them. The molls who spoke of her to agents disliked her, which later enhanced her image as a grasping mother. Even Karpis admitted, "Whenever Freddie or I got serious about a girl, we'd move out of Ma's place and keep [her] in another hotel or apartment."[19]

When St. Paul racketeer Jack Peiffer arranged for the Barker gang to reside in the Twin Cities in the spring of 1933, the gang had to come to terms with tightly disciplined criminal syndicates. A layover deal had costs as well as benefits, which a gang had to judge shrewdly. The Barkers had tried Chicago first, where a Capone "Big Shot" tried to hire Karpis as a strong-arm man; when he refused, he was told "that if he knew what was good for his health he would do [it]." Karpis was firm, since he "did not consider himself a hoodlum." A hoodlum was, as an interrogator reported, "a person who kills for money and he has never done that. He [was] a thief, [and] may have secured money dishonestly and . . . he may have killed somebody. . . . If he had killed somebody it was not for money." Peiffer, however, arranged protection in return for a political contribution of several thousand dollars. As an informant explained, "badly wanted fugitives were comparatively safe in St. Paul from police interference as long as they had the proper connections," but these connections could only be maintained through a sense of mutual obligation. Peiffer initially offered them a piece of the slot machine racket, but Fred agreed with Karpis that "there was too much work connected with the operation of slot machines." But bank robbery, the gang's specialty, had became difficult and dangerous. In April 1933, through Peiffer, Fred accepted a contract from an anonymous St. Paul power broker to kidnap thirty-eight-year-old brewery heir William Hamm.[20]

At 12:45 on June 15, when Hamm left work, a man loitering nearby extended a hand and asked, "You are Mr. Hamm, aren't you?" Hamm replied that he was. Suddenly, his arm was in the firm grip of a bandit, while a second man pushed him into a car. "I was shoved down on the floor," Hamm remembered, "and a white sack was put over my head and shoulders." The kidnapping made national headlines for the four days before Hamm was ransomed for one hundred thousand dollars. Throughout, it was a cordial experience: the brewer complained about being on the floor of the car, and they pulled him up on the seat; he received plenty of food and a bed to sleep in. The gang also reported on his investments every evening. "We had quite a lot of conversation," Hamm remembered. "We discussed beer, repeal, Roosevelt's policies, advertising. . . . We were trying to kill time and be decent to one another."[21]

Although Hamm remained calm, his relatives could not. This case offers a vivid example of the trauma kidnappers deliberately induced in a family. Contacts were watched, abused over the telephone, and threatened with violence. The pace of negotiations was quick, often conducted at odd hours of the night, and elaborate directions and rituals were devised to keep the victim's family responsive to ransom demands. In the Hamm case, a brewery executive was told to prepare the ransom in small bills; the male caller finished by shouting, "God Damn you, see that they're not marked!" The executive shouted back, and "the party at the other end of the line said 'Now shut up and listen to what I have to say. . . . Follow the instructions you will receive over the phone tomorrow night at five o'clock, and if you tell a soul about this it will be just too bad for Hamm and you.'. . . Then he just hung up." The family called St. Paul chief of police Tom Dahill—who then notified the chief of detectives and head of the special kidnapping squad, Tom Brown. That evening, the kidnappers warned them again not to call the police because "we'll get Hamm and you too"; they said that they knew that the line was tapped and that the money should be thrown out of a moving car on an empty stretch of highway.[22]

Chief Dahill notified the division immediately, but the G-men's work had to be kept secret initially because the St. Paul police had "published in the newspapers their intention to withdraw fully from the case until such time as Hamm [was] released." Intimidating them by their seemingly complete knowledge of the negotiators' movements, the kidnappers sent another ransom note, which warned, "You brought the coppers into this now you get rid of the ———." What the division did not know was that Brown was on Jack Peiffer's payroll; a gang member later confessed that Brown kept them "advised of the developments at the Police Department during the time the victim was being held." This, among kidnappers, was "money well spent," as it made the crime as easy as "getting money from home."[23]

The scale of Chief Brown's corruption was impressive, giving a sense of what was at stake from federal intervention in one crime-corridor city. While each participant received seventy-eight hundred dollars, Peiffer took ten thousand, and Tom Brown was paid a staggering twenty-five thousand. As the division began to unravel the plot in 1934, this political corruption was further complicated by a prominent family's links to graft and racketeering. Hamm was not a random victim. As Karpis admitted, the kidnapping "was political and had something to do with the Police Department and the County Officials of Ramsey County in which St. Paul is located." The Hamm brewery's corruption was also extensive: Hamm had sold beer through Peiffer during Prohibition, and through the local syndicate, he had helped a college friend open a speakeasy. The kidnappers' contact at the brewery also had a criminal past: before being hired by Hamm, he had been "the collector for the Police Department at St. Paul."[24]

Division agents were frustrated by Hamm's vagueness, and he may have deliberately misled them in a botched investigation that resulted in the false indictment of Chicago's Touhy gang. As an agent grumbled, he now understood "why [the crime] is called 'kidnapping.'" Hamm refused to appear at the August 12 indictment, and, as a Milwaukee private investigator pointed out in disgust, none of the kidnappers matched descriptions Hamm had initially given. "If Mr. Cummings or our good President intend to operate a Scotland Yard," he wrote, "for God's sake, whatever you do employ real experienced detectives, men who know the criminal world and can go out and solve crimes. Why, this Touhy affair is the laughing stock of the underworld."[25]

As the Barker gang rested comfortably at a resort north of St. Paul, the government went to trial with holes in the case that the defense exploited fully. No one around the site of the kidnapping identified any member of the Touhy gang, and there was "nothing uncovered to definitely establish that the Subjects, or cars involved in the kidnapping, were in [the] vicinity when [the] act occurred." Although several witnesses placed the gang in Minneapolis that day and one claimed to have seen them near where Hamm was released, the car used in the crime was not found, nor did Ed Touhy's summer cabin "fit [the] description of [the] hideout where Hamm was held." Hamm was an irritable witness, and Werner Hanni, special agent in charge in Minneapolis, believed that he was lying. The division's first informant in the case was placed among Hamm's new bodyguards, "a reliable person" who would "possibly obtain information which would become of value in this case." Lost in the division's intense focus on the Touhys was a report in which a gas station attendant identified Alvin Karpis as the man he had served on the highway where the ransom was delivered, and witness reports that also placed the Barker family in St. Paul on the day of the kidnapping.[26]

The Touhy gang was, quite properly, acquitted on December 8, 1933. This was a turning point for the division, when the values of scientific policing, rigorously applied, had failed to supply the information agents, prosecutors, and juries needed. As Hanni wrote, such information required more traditional attitudes toward evidence: "We should cast away our gloves and deal with suspects, witnesses, as well as victims, in a more determined and absolute manner. We should waive our gentlemanly manners and whenever found convenient should apply the 'speaking tube' to any one of them hesitating, dodging or concealing his, or her, position of responsibility in connection with the case."[27] Bureaucratic order and the meticulous assembling of physical evidence did not necessarily make a good case: juries wanted the "truths" only humans told.

As if mocking the division's failure, six weeks after the Touhy acquittal a second St. Paul businessman was kidnapped and ransomed. On January 19, 1934, Edward Bremer, heir to another brewing fortune, dropped his daughter off at school and drove to his office. As he halted at a stop sign, a car pulled in front. Volney Davis and Arthur "Doc" Barker jumped out, wrestled Bremer from his car, and knocked him unconscious; the bandits then drove him to the same hideout that was used for the Hamm kidnapping. Adolph Bremer, Edward's father, an influential local Democrat, was a friend of Franklin Roosevelt's who had mustered the St. Paul business community behind the national ticket in 1932. While *Time* reported that Adolph had "pleaded frantically with Federal and State authorities to keep out of the case," it is likely that a well-placed call to the president kept the G-men away until Edward was returned.[28]

Whereas the reason for the Hamm kidnapping is not immediately apparent in the investigative file, this second case—the ransom of another brewing heir— suggests a realignment of political and economic interests between syndicate criminals and upper-class businessmen in St. Paul, with the Barker-Karpis gang serving as an informal underworld police force. In the spring of 1934, Prohibition was ending, and urban criminals needed to adapt once again to a changing marketplace. Conversely, legal beer seemed to free the Hamm and Bremer breweries from dependence on, and sharing profits with, local syndicates. Adolph's insistence on dealing with the kidnappers personally suggests that he knew the reason for Edward's confinement; the son may also have gone behind his father's back to try to make a settlement on his own. "I have done my part and kept my word 100% as I said I would," the brewer wrote to the kidnappers. "Now, boys, I am counting on your honor. Be sports and do the square thing and turn Ed loose immediately and tell him to come first to my home. ADOLPH." Edward was released with enough cash to make his way home by bus, train, and cab. Reporters camped on the lawn heard "a piteous tale of beatings, confinement and fright" before Edward broke down and went to bed.[29]

There is ample evidence to show that in the Twin Cities, the police force itself was often indistinguishable from a criminal gang. As Cummings told Louis M. Howe and the president in February, "From a criminal standpoint, Minneapolis is one of the worst spots with which we have to deal." A memo marked "Personal and Confidential" (heavily censored in its archival form) reveals that around this time ten prominent citizens (none of whom was a member of the Hamm or Bremer families) contributed ten thousand dollars each "to be used for conducting an undercover investigation of the Police Department in St. Paul." These upper-class vigilantes hired an undercover agent and installed telephone taps at headquarters, hoping to find enough information to indict chief of detectives Tom Brown but accomplishing little other than inconveniencing corrupt cops. Brown, for example, simply stopped using police telephones during this period.[30]

Because law enforcement, politicians, and criminal syndicates were so interwoven in urban areas, bandits could purchase powerful protection that was difficult for outsiders to penetrate. Hoover's solution, as it had been during the Palmer years, was to recruit insiders, exchanging regular rewards for information. Although the division's reliance on sophisticated laboratory techniques would continue to grow over the next decades, during the final two years of the war on crime, informants—captured and embittered gang members, as well as syndicate entrepreneurs—would become the primary route for expanding the state's capacity to enforce the new interstate crime laws. While the division continued to encourage tips from the public, throughout 1934, agents would expand networks of snitches, competing with local police to get the information first and providing local officers with incentives to circumvent their own commanders and report directly to federal agents. In the summer of that year, these methods produced John Dillinger, and by the following January, they would also produce the real kidnappers in the Hamm and Bremer cases.

The End of Reform and the
Victory of the Enforcement Model

The questions informants raise about the nature of the state's anticrime policies lead back to the differences, and contradictions, between New Deal centralized policing and the reform models of the 1920s. During the war on crime, these differences were obscured to some extent by Hoover's employment of a language of family and community that seemed to address issues similar to those raised by Arthur Woods and August Vollmer. This is precisely why kidnapping, despite its low incidence in comparison with other violent crimes, and the apparent brutality of kidnappers, became crucial evidence for subsequent historical accounts of the rebirth of federal policing. The nationalist cultural work that such histories performed is more than obvious. For example, *Persons in Hiding*, published as the FBI prepared for a counterespionage role in World War II, framed the inevitability of such interventions, and the futility of local crime prevention initiatives, in terms of the government's elimination of a deviant family of kidnappers, the Barker-Karpis gang.

That family's fugitive status came to an end in early 1935, in an attack on criminal domesticity that became an enduring legend of federal enforcement. On January 8, Doc Barker and two other gang members were captured in Chicago, probably as a result of underworld tips. While Doc remained silent, another suspect told agents that Ma and Fred were living near Ocala, Florida. Keeping the Chicago arrests a secret, E. J. Connelley mustered a task force, and at 6:00 A.M. on January 16, ringed by a dozen armed agents, he approached the house.[31]

As a reporter described it, Connelley asked the fugitives to surrender, but "machine gun fire was the answer." All neighbors but two had been evacuated. "It was like war," one woman told reporters afterward:

> I was suddenly awakened by guns firing. I got out of bed and as I stood up some bullets came through the closed door between my bedroom and my dining room and hit the face of the door above my head. . . .
>
> My daughter was in bed. I broke open the back window of our room and told her we had to get out. About that time some more bullets came smacking through the dining room window and hit the wall.

As they fled their house, agents, assuming they were molls, shouted at them to surrender and then fired at them.

Miraculously, no bystander was hit during the attack; for almost six hours, agents fired tear gas bombs and fifteen hundred rounds of ammunition into the house, while a crowd of more than two hundred reporters and onlookers picnicked behind the lines. At noon, return fire ceased, and agents forced a black cook who had worked for the Barkers into the hideout. Fred was dead, eleven machine gun bullets in his shoulder and three in his head; Ma, one bullet in her skull, was slumped over a machine gun.[32]

Although John Dillinger could never be fully recuperated as a cultural worker for the state, the Barkers could, a process that began at Hoover's January 17 press conference. Describing the Barker-Karpis gang as "the brainiest and most desperate of all," he enhanced the government's victory by emphasizing the obviously superior abilities and intelligence of federal police. Ma was "the brains of the gang," and Hoover explained the puzzle of her missing criminal record by asserting that she was "so clever she had never been arrested." Mother Barker was also revealed as a death dealer: Hoover claimed she had opened the door and shouted to Fred, "Let 'em have it!" Federal agents had used force reluctantly. "Bullets came from all windows of the house," Hoover told reporters, "indicating that 'Ma' and her son ran up and down stairs with machine guns in their hands."[33]

The Kate Barker who was produced as a murder-mad female referenced broader cultural themes about family, social disorder, and the benefits of centralized government. Hoover's particular animus toward female enemies of the state—Emma Goldman, Kate Barker, and Ethel Rosenberg—has been noted, and it expressed historically specific beliefs about the relationship between domesticity, parental authority, and good citizenship. Anxiety about the collapse of families has been a persistent theme throughout the twentieth century; paradoxically, while New Deal initiatives sought to rebuild the economic basis for family security, they also inspired fears that a strong state would undermine the domestic authority that produced disciplined citizens. As a radio evangelist announced shortly after the shoot-out, civic order depended on traditional institutions: "I name you!" he shouted. "The Home, The School, The Church, Organized Womanhood— As Soldiers in the Army of the Right."[34]

Representing corrupt maternity, Kate Barker became a cultural symbol who explained the production of public enemies in terms of the failure of these traditional institutions. Family worked as a metalanguage at this political moment, masking the state's aggressive role in shaping new social and institutional relations, the real power of the state's growing enforcement apparatus, and opposition from reformers within the Department of Justice. Ma Barker's appearance in a major kidnapping ring was, of course, fortuitous. However, the general prominence of gun molls in bandit gangs gave Hoover and other police professionals a familiar set of gendered symbols through which new crimes could be expressed as particularly dangerous to the natural order that a healthy body politic required.[35]

As Robert McIlvaine has highlighted in an edited collection of letters between citizens and the government, the New Deal made the links between fragile domesticity and state power explicit. One representative letter made a direct link to the war on crime, articulating banditry as the product of frustrated masculine impulses. "We have plenty of John Dillingers, pretty boy Floyds, Jessie James roaming all over our land today wanting jobs," one man wrote, "desiring to marry and settle down and live a comfortable life and cannot get hold of enough money to buy a marriage license." Another male writer, seeking to halt a foreclosure, linked his own imperiled future to the nation's: "if I can save [my house]," he wrote, "I will be able to raise my family to be *good useful citizens.*"[36]

The historiography of these years emphasizes a crisis of paternal authority, but mothers, as nationally syndicated columnist Dorothy Dix revealed daily, were also under siege. A woman whose teenager ran with a "wild" crowd wrote in despair, "When . . . I remonstrate with her she tells me to shut up. It is her business and she will do as she pleases. Oh, Miss Dix, I don't believe you know this generation of young people as they are and the impudence and disrespect they show their parents!" Another reported that her eighteen-year-old unmarried daughter "says I have no right to dictate to her, that she is old enough to do what she likes. . . . Shall I allow her to 'sass' me with impunity?" Even the character of marriage was changing. Mothers complained about the women their sons pursued, who preferred play to homemaking. Fears about the consequences of these shifts in authority reflected real changes that took place in the interwar years, both in the forms of family life and in the emergence of critiques that revealed the increased isolation of mothers and wives within the home. In this pre–*Feminine Mystique* era, women wrote to "Miss Dix" about the relentless drudgery of housework. There was nothing, one complained, "in marriage to keep a woman GLAD. . . . With a woman it is the everlasting grind of work, with house and children, day in and day out." Another wrote about her stingy husband, saying she was "never well-dressed."[37]

These anxieties were reflected in widely read work by scholars and criminologists, who predicted dire results for households in which fathers were unemployed or absent. Sheldon and Eleanor Glueck explicitly linked female criminality to weak "family attachments" and "indifferen[ce] to the major responsibilities of marriage, family and children."[38] Hoover's revelations about the Barker family drew on similar pathological explanations. Even their loyalty to each other was evidence of their criminal deviance, proof of fanaticism and a deformed family. Through their deficiencies—an emasculated father, a dominant mother, and criminal sons—they became an important site for rearticulating a set of patri-archal values that New Deal social interventions explicitly reinforced.[39] Most important, the Barkers invaded apparently respectable families, stealing children and selling them back to their parents.

In the Barkers, the unrespectable and the criminal were indistinguishable, and publicity about Ma and her sons contributed to a reinterpretation of other bandits' families as well. The Dillinger vaudeville act disappears from the public record in January 1935; and in March of that year, when the Parker and Barrow families were prosecuted under federal harboring statutes, they were savaged in the national press. In "Roots Up," *Time* lodged responsibility for Clyde and Bonnie's crimes with their parents: "Such rank weeds . . . sprang from roots deeply embedded in the darkest social soil. Loudly has the Department of Justice proclaimed its purpose not only to cut down the weeds but also to dig up their roots. Therefore last week a Federal grand jury in Dallas, Texas convicted 15 grubby persons who had nourished and protected bandits Barrow and Parker." Sentenced to between one month and two years were Bonnie's mother and sister; Clyde's mother, sister, brother, brother-in-law, and two sisters-in-law; and twelve friends. Five family members who had previously pleaded guilty were not there. Cumie Barrow's appeal to maternal privilege—"He was my boy. I loved him"—was coldly rebuffed: "Thirty days," the judge replied.[40]

News stories deployed the language of family to figure the domestic sphere as both attacked by criminals and, in its weakened form, producing crime. In "The Epic of the G-Men," journalist Harold Finley positioned kidnapping as a crime that "struck at the heart of America." The resulting panic had not been "hysteria misplaced," he argued. "Kidnapping had become a crime against the United States." Mrs. Walter Ferguson, a columnist for a Denver paper, asked parents to "lend an ear" to Hoover's warnings about child rearing. A true war on crime would address private and public, since good parenting, a prosperous economy, a moral society, and "our political systems" were interdependent:

> It takes leisure and concentration to be a good parent.
>
> Moreover, boys and girls who observe the shenanigans we employ in business, the law and politics are not likely to have a good opinion of their elders who tell them how to behave and at the same time set such strange examples.
>
> In a manner of speaking, the decadence of family life may be laid at the door of a commercialism which has run the home out of business.

As she warned, it was "easier, according to statistics, to bring up criminals in America than it has ever been before."[41]

The arguments are slightly different, but in each, the family is at risk. Finley's anticrime stance is articulated around a male defense of the parental sphere, while

Ferguson warns that inadequate parenting (specifically, mothering) has public consequences. Both were responding to a speech Hoover had made that used Kate Barker as an example of a mother who was "as guilty as [her criminal] sons." Federal vigilance was necessary, the director insisted, until parents restored "the American viewpoint toward better parental discipline and a greater sense of law abidance, beginning in the home." All crime began "in some American home in which the father and mother made a terrible mess of their most important job. Back of almost every criminal stands a parent who failed." What is crucial to the nationalist cultural work of this paradigm is its argument that bad parents, not bad social conditions, produce crime, a premise that reveals traditional social reform agendas as outdated and ineffectual. It also makes representing the family as a secure social location impossible: bad ones undermined good ones, and only the state could ensure domestic security. "When the Lindbergh baby was kidnapped," one husband wrote after Bruno Richard Hauptmann was arrested in that case, "many a mother . . . held her child close to her night after night for months, in constant fear. As a result of your good work, the fear of parents has been allayed."[42]

What is instructive is that, although the progressive reform model of the 1920s produced federal centralization, centralization rested on an enforcement philosophy that displaced the principles of social critique and corrective intervention that had originally produced the idea of the modern policeman. Federal intervention was framed as an armed defense of the good families who were foundational to the national body politic—and a campaign to exterminate the products of bad families. This was a radical reformulation of the reform model: the policeman no longer created community by example, centering and stabilizing otherwise disorganized individuals. Rather, assuming the psychopathological origins of crime, he repressed lawbreakers in the name of well-organized, innocent families.

Conflict between Hoover and special assistant Justin Miller between late 1934 and early 1936 demonstrates that the decentralized community work that reformers believed in was incompatible with the strong state that they had imagined would stamp out the national crime wave. Throughout Prohibition and into the New Deal years, Miller and colleagues at the ABA had promoted the systemic social critiques that undergirded an activist, reform vision. This view articulated all individuals as basically good and criminals as produced by environment and circumstance. As a Milwaukee attorney wrote in a letter copied to Miller in 1931, a twelve-year-old boy who had been sentenced to life for shooting a sheriff could not be understood as criminal in his essence: "I know nothing about the breeding, bringing-up or environment of this boy, but, regardless of what it was, it seems to me that when a twelve year old boy can be incarcerated for life, no matter under what circumstances, something needs correction in this great country of ours." Like many professional organizations, the ABA sought to promote such views through persuasion and education. As Miller wrote to president Guy Thompson later that year,

> Of course, your suggestions of "the way to really accomplish something is to determine upon a particular line of work and follow it through systematically and comprehensively, doing the necessary research work and then bringing the results of the labors properly to the attention of the public, public officials, bar associations and special groups that are interested and that will be of assistance in making effective the work that has been done" checks exactly with my conception of the way in which the work must be done.

As part of this work, he coordinated "around a dozen" lectures on the crime problem for NBC radio.[43]

Although Miller's emphasis on prevention was philosophically opposed to Hoover's project of centralized enforcement, they did share a common distrust of virtually all forms of political activity. In 1932, Miller noted that the anticrime discussions that absorbed ABA committees were "frightfully unknown to that small group of politicians who seem[ed] to be interested in securing the presidency [of the ABA] for their members and distributing the financial pie." Guy Thompson, a section chair, sympathized with Miller's frustration. In a letter, he detailed the different lobbying efforts he had engaged in on behalf of the association's anticrime program. Prestigious corporate attorneys had backed him fully, but the criminal lawyers secretly worked against it, fearing that the profits they made from underworld figures would be reduced.[44]

This similarity was also a source of difference. Perhaps because of its association with other New Deal programs, Miller saw centralized enforcement as an inevitably politicized solution. Initially, he may not have even understood the institutional permanence of Hoover's project. He believed that the war on crime was, like many early New Deal programs, an experiment and a pet project of Raymond Moley's that FDR had agreed to in exchange for his work on the campaign. Ironically, Moley's refusal of a cabinet post, or any other political appointment, may have given federal anticrime intervention credibility in Miller's eyes and persuaded him to accept an appointment to the attorney general's office in the summer of 1934. A year earlier, he had urged ABA colleagues to become involved in the anticrime movement, since they "might produce results which could not come from a politically-controlled body."[45]

Miller was one of the few to voice concerns about the damage federal anticrime rhetoric could do to the process of producing lasting, community-based solutions to the crime problem. Keenly aware of the power of rhetoric to turn untested ideas into law, at the height of the 1933 kidnapping hysteria, he urged moderation among colleagues who lined up behind the attorney general's proposal for a federal crime war. One friend sent a speech that urged parole reform, a machine gun ban, and liberal federal intervention: "The crime condition of this country, particularly among the young, for the past decade has been worse than the fifth of the century prior thereto," it opened. Miller urged reason and perspective; the young were no "worse than the young people of the present century prior to the last decade." Rather, he argued,

> Our world is much more complicated, much more difficult, that family control, that normal employment of young people, that community controls, and other social controls have broken down, largely as a result of the inefficiency of those of us who are responsible for the present situation. . . . The stimulation that has come from the motion pictures, the highways, and a generally speeded-up life has put these youngsters into a crisis which none of us were forced to go through.

Miller understood crime as responsive to structural solutions that addressed social issues, not to repression. The atmosphere of crisis, he suggested, might be less due to an increase in crime than to a failure of coordination among the many bureaucracies working separately for social justice. A proper war on crime would also scrutinize lawyers, particularly those "specializing in the defense of criminals, and who are in fact *racketeers*."[46]

When Justin Miller joined the attorney general's office, he brought reform credentials to a Justice Department that had already abandoned social policy solutions. This was undoubtedly a move by Homer Cummings to tie federal policing, however precariously, to the professional, elite, Republican constituencies Miller represented. The national crime conference, while ostensibly an opportunity to address a range of issues, was planned by a committee that was heavily weighted with bureaucrats committed to an enforcement model, Hoover among them, and who shaped the conference to that agenda. Including Miller, half of the twelve committee members were drawn from Cummings's staff, and eight represented enforcement interests. Only one—Grace Poole, president of the General Federation of Women's Clubs and the only woman—was a social reformer. As a result, only seven governors attended the conference, and each session was packed with federal employees (seventy-four U.S. attorneys and sixty-nine marshals registered). Like other war on crime events, publicity was heavy. During a week of meetings, Washington newspapers alone ran more than 1,500 column inches of news stories and editorials, 269 photographs, and 112 cartoons. In Cummings's view, the conference was a great success.[47]

Futile as these efforts seem to be in retrospect, Miller continued to promote reform on the Advisory Committee. He planned a committee to study "the use of finger prints for non-criminal purposes . . . the establishment of credit, identification of lost persons, etc."; and in January 1935, he explored "the ways and means of establishing a national scientific and educational center in Washington, DC, for the better training of carefully selected personnel in the broad field of criminal law administration and the treatment of crime and criminals." Neither proposal matured, although Miller did establish the new Division of Legal Information on a reform model that could easily be turned to the purposes of centralization. It aided cities and states in drafting legislation; communicated with legislators and citizenship organizations; responded to requests for information from the general public; prepared bibliographies; and promoted committee members for service on anticrime commissions.[48]

Gradually, Miller began to oppose new interventions, arguing that state power was most legitimate when it relied on persuasion. "Why not tax crime pictures on the same theory as is applied to the taxation of tobacco and liquor?" he suggested to the attorney general in early 1935. "If this were done it might have the effect, incidentally, of limiting the production thereof." Miller also created alliances with others at Justice who opposed the sensationalism of federal anticrime policy. One of these was Sanford Bates, who, throughout 1935, fought Hoover's determination to create a "penal colony" for the most notorious federal prisoners—a project that materialized in 1936 on Alcatraz Island, California. Bates stalled and asked Cummings for "a careful study . . . of the experience in this line of other countries." Perhaps believing that such a study would fall to Miller's committee, Bates enlisted his support. Miller advised Cummings that Bates opposed "the 'Rat Island' idea." "In my opinion it has some possibilities, although I realize that a group of outlaws on an island by themselves might easily create an embarrassing situation."[49]

As the records of Justin Miller's office show, crime prevention and community interventions were the roads not taken in a political struggle to define the character of federal policing. The social reform initiatives promoted by Miller and others were buried, in part because the spectacular successes of the war on crime proved the case made by centralization advocates like Cummings and Hoover. Shortly after the national conference, Hoover circulated a draft program titled *Federal Aid of State Criminal Law Enforcement,* which Miller opposed vehemently. Although there is no written record of Hoover's response, it must have been scathing, since Miller, when detailing his objections in a memo to Cummings, reminded him, "The records of the department should contain a letter I wrote at the time of the change of administrations, urging that Mr. Hoover be retained in his present position." Contradicting everything Miller thought the New Deal stood for, Hoover's program contained no federal grants of money to states, and it included virtually no training or support for local police. The report, Miller complained, "would make us the laughing stock of the country," particularly since Cummings had promised state and local officials that the division would spread the gospel of scientific policing through training programs.

"Of course," Miller continued, "if all we have in mind is a 'Lady Bountiful' attitude toward the States, and a desire to work with them on a basis of extending favors when we please, then, perhaps, preservation of the status quo is desirable." He again advocated comprehensive community training programs for social workers, teachers, and juvenile officers. "I have never heard Mr. Hoover reveal much acquaintance or understanding [of prevention and rehabilitation]," he wrote bitterly, "and I have heard him on several occasions reveal an intolerance and ignorance which cannot but provoke resentment and antagonism from those who are concerned with those phases of the problem."[50]

Only a few weeks after the death of Ma and Fred Barker, this exchange and its outcome mark a decisive victory for the enforcement model, underlining the gang's significance in Hoover's political victory over the interests represented by Justin Miller. Concessions to the reform model were predictably small in 1935; courses given at the newly renamed Federal Bureau of Investigation were made available to all police officers within a year of this exchange. Clearly, the war on crime's major accomplishment was not the repression of crime but the repression of alternative anticrime programs that failed to promote state centralization. Although the Department of Justice continued to maintain relationships with social service organizations, Hoover virtually broke off his relations with Miller's committee in the spring of 1935, after which the files that should contain a continuing record of the FBI's connection to social reformers are only filled with the director's fan mail, political cartoons about the G-men, and fading news clippings.[51]

Centralized Enforcement and the Return of Informants

If the Hamm and Bremer cases were reopened in 1934 by Bessie Green's admission that she knew the names of the kidnappers—and a great deal more—they were closed two years later when Alvin Karpis refused to speak about any gang member not already dead or in custody. The last member of the Barker-Karpis gang to be captured, Karpis was peacefully arrested in New Orleans on May 1, 1936. Hoover and Tolson were present and flew with the prisoner to St. Paul for a quick indictment; in July, Karpis plead guilty to the Hamm kidnapping and was sentenced to life. During eight weeks of interrogation, he revealed much about the Hamm case but refused to divulge other names. As Tamm reported, "Karpis is not lying about anything and if he does not care to comment upon a particular question will state that he will not answer that question. . . . Karpis repeatedly states that he will not 'snitch' on anyone who has ever befriended him." This made him unusual by 1936, when the "underworld code" Karpis adhered to had largely dissolved in relation to bandits. New federal harboring laws provided for heavy penalties for those who did not cooperate with the government, and support networks of molls, doctors, landlords, and family members had already been prosecuted.[52]

The government's success in these prosecutions meant that few who were arrested in the summer and fall of 1934 failed to trade whatever information they had in the hope of a favorable court decision or the possibility of parole. The G-men had also, as Werner Hanni had recommended, "taken off the gloves." Arrests followed by harsh interrogations, moving prisoners around to evade habeas corpus proceedings, threats against family members, and false assertions that others had already talked were among the repertoire of unscientific devices that were used to extract information and evidence. As Hugh Clegg suggested in late June 1934, moll Opal Long "might be induced to adopt a more helpful attitude towards the Government" if she was held indefinitely. Charges would not even be discussed with her until she "demonstrated a proper attitude."[53]

Whereas the division's growing networks of underworld informants were motivated primarily by profit, for family and gang members, squealing was a response to dire circumstances. Since Bessie Green's lover had been killed, her affiliation to the gang had dwindled, and she was focused on beginning a new life away from crime. Green also had a teenage son who was, an agent noted, "rather an imposing lever to hold over her head." Initially, people often talked just enough to protect loved ones, a naive compromise that was frequently only an initial step toward full cooperation. When agents learned that Lester Gillis was with bank robber Paul Chase, Chase's moll asserted that she would "protect Chase in any way possible" but promised to "put [Gillis] on the spot" if she was released. As the interrogator "seemed quite enthused about her sincerity and felt that she would cooperate," she became an informant, leading agents to her lover as well. Pat Reilly, in a different calculus, agreed to inform on only the least powerful men in his network. "No inducements in the world" could get him to testify against the criminals and politicians who ran St. Paul, but he "advised that as soon as he [was] released he [would] make every effort to put Alvin Karpis 'on the spot.'"[54]

A special agent's regular information network was made up of entrepreneurs and volunteers, many of whom hoped to establish long and profitable relationships with the Department of Justice. Some were reminders of an ugly past: one man who had volunteered for the bureau's Red squad during the war was just "a bug with a detective complex," an agent reported. The best informants were criminals. A man who claimed to know Dillinger received fifteen dollars, but his contact recommended "that his services be terminated" if he did not produce within two weeks. If the informant turned out to be reliable, he had a good government job. One St. Paul snitch was paid fifty dollars a week, about half a G-man's starting salary, and supplied with a car. The war on crime drew in a number of these experts, such as Glenn A. Noel, a convicted criminal, who was recommended by the Denver office in October 1934. He had informed professionally since 1916, specializing in "working his way into Italian mobs." Although he did not speak Italian, his "actions and dress [were] such as to enable him to gain entrance to roadhouses and gambling establishments without arousing suspicion," his contact explained. "He is also well-versed in hoodlum vernacular." Another skilled female informant "had served as the finger woman in the arrest of a notorious bank robber" in Detroit.[55]

Unlike captive gang members, professional informants were unpredictable and evasive, since squawking was but one of the many ways they made a living. Ironically, to remain undercover they also needed to behave like normal criminals, so that when the federal heat was on (and the government's need for information was correspondingly greater), they left town. As Clegg reported from St. Paul after the shoot-out with Dillinger, information was scarce because "the gangsters and mobsters of the underworld . . . scuttled out, had their telephones disconnected and . . . moved." "Everyone is on the hideout, knowing that they would be brought in for questioning." Informants also bartered information in several markets. One sought out a reporter, represented himself as a G-man, and offered to sell "the Dillinger story" for three thousand dollars. Others held out on agents for more money. One, an exasperated Purvis reported in May 1934, was "awaiting passage of the Reward Bill before divulging his information." Hoover quickly removed this impediment. "Tell him we will pay well now," Hoover scribbled on this memo, "& there is no need waiting for the passage of the bill."[56]

Ironically, the division found itself fighting crime by employing criminals; if the campaign against racketeers imagined by Joe Keenan had not already been compromised by the demands of national politics, then its fate was surely sealed as the division daily became more dependent on local wise guys for its spectacular arrests. Since they were not above selling out anyone, anywhere, snitches retained some leverage in their relations with the state. For example, the St. Paul office came to believe that it was a federal informant who had fingered Homer Van Meter for the St. Paul police. "There is a possibility that after we sponsored him for a considerable time," Tamm explained, "he went in there and sold his wares to somebody else."[57]

One outcome of the division's surveillance strategy was that gang members soon became suspicious and fearful of each other. Nervous that other molls had noticed her long sessions with federal agents (and unaware that they were singing too), Pat Cherrington tried to transfer out of her West Virginia prison, claiming that she wanted to "console" Billie Frechette. Soon, any amount of time in custody was cause for suspicion. As Marie Conforti told agents, after Little Bohemia, Homer Van Meter "said he was going to kill her" after Lester Gillis accused her of snitching, "but she denied having been running around with any Federal Agent. She said Van Meter was apparently satisfied with this story," but Gillis broke contact with both of them.[58]

Agents knew they were creating conflict in gang networks through such tactics. One moll upbraided an associate over accusations she had snitched: "Why should I have guys threaten to kill me and tell me I've got pretty teeth and they'd like to knock out a few?" she snapped. Bandits' families became surveillance targets in similar ways; although they yielded little real information, coming home or confiding in relatives became dangerous for gang members. Like the Barrows, Alvin Karpis's family resisted surveillance vigorously, employing unusual techniques. On a prison visit to Dolores Delaney, Alvin's moll, they brought Dolores's and Alvin's toddler son. Agents hoped to record the conversation, but as they admitted, "Difficulty was encountered in recording the conversation because of the noise created by the child. . . . And after it had ceased crying it bounced a ball around and opened and shut drawers in file cabinets in this room. Thereafter it played a harmonica more or less steadily." When an agent invited Alvin's father to bring the child into the next room, the women began to talk in voices too low to be overheard.[59]

As the Dillinger case demonstrated, however, fear of the government could also lead individual family members to cooperate secretly for what they believed was the good of the group. Some also harbored bitterness against those who they believed had abandoned or led astray a son or daughter. Others, like Bonnie Parker's aunt, were simply horrified by their criminal relatives. As one bandit's sister and brother-in-law told an agent, "They would rather see [him] killed or captured than to have him running about the country the way he is at the present time." Helen Delaney, whose daughters had all become molls, agreed to inform but worried about alienating them. As an agent pointed out, letters to Dolores from her mother "indicating that she would not approve of her daughter doing anything that might result in the capture of Karpis, may have been written to assure her daughter that she was not furnishing any information." Neighbors and friends were also enlisted, but agents could not force them to continue if they had no criminal involvement in the case. "Undoubtedly, if he possessed intestinal stamina enough to ask more questions," an exasperated agent wrote about a neighbor who feared exposure, "additional information would be forthcoming but he has indicated considerable fear. . . . It will be necessary to have him go along in his own way with the hope that information will be dropped by one of these persons."[60]

The Pierpont family was particularly embittered against Harry's former pals, as appeals failed to lift his death sentence and help was not forthcoming from the gang. As the date for Harry's electrocution approached, his mother believed that "Dillinger ha[d] not given her sufficient funds to file an appeal in the Ohio Supreme Court"; that Harry was innocent of murder, and Dillinger knew it; and that Indiana was determined to execute her son because of Dillinger's celebrity. Fred Pierpont said he would also try to help the division find another gang member who had "failed" Harry. Hoover suggested in late 1934 that the family be offered a "sum of money" for everything they knew. Indiana authorities complained to FDR, and Louis M. Howe admonished William Stanley, who, in turn, upbraided Hoover. "I stated to Mr. Stanley," Hoover noted blandly, "that I thought the matter could be satisfactorily 'cleaned up,' that for a few dollars we could get the whole story from the Pierponts." The deal rapidly turned into a federal headache as agents discovered that the family, bankrupted by Harry's defense, had nothing to tell. Worse, Lena Pierpont was hospitalized as a result of an automobile accident and pressured the division to pay her a disability benefit.[61]

Molls revealed information when they were most vulnerable, physically run down from a fugitive life, and grief-stricken over a dead or imprisoned lover. One told an agent that she was glad to have been alone when she heard of her boyfriend's death because she would have gotten "the whole business out of her system"; however, since she had recovered, "she would keep on telling the same kind of lies she has told thus far." Many also felt that a lover's death cut their gang ties, and they quickly allied themselves with another powerful man, the interrogator. Oblique conversations hinted at what was desired by the government and what the prisoner expected in return. Once imprisoned, Bessie Green was called into the warden's office, where an agent told her that a moll would be placed in her cottage. He "suggested" that she "be kind to [her] and sort of look out for her while she was there." Bessie mentioned that she was due to come up for parole in five months, and, while "she did not like to 'poke' in other people's affairs," she would nevertheless, "if she could win Jean's confidence."[62]

Getting a moll to talk required the right combination of pressure and persuasion, harsh questioning interrupted by a kinder interrogator who appeared to have the prisoner's best interests at heart. For example, Bessie's last resistance was eliminated by talk of new raids. One agent "told her there was going to be blood shed in those places; maybe some of their men would be killed, maybe some of her friends would be killed." Subsequently, another proposed that if she talked "perhaps arrangements could be made to avoid that bloodshed." Pat Cherrington "assumed an attitude of silence" in prison and said "that when she entered the prison she forgot everything." Asked if she would talk in exchange for her ex-husband's early pardon, she initially refused, but when the offer was repeated, she said that if she saw the offer "in black and white, she might be willing to 'get everything off of her chest.'"[63]

Few molls held out against third-degree tactics, and they often complained that the G-men were no more professional in this regard than beat cops. Billie Frechette's interrogation took place over the course of four sleepless days, during which she was denied meals and a lawyer and questioned in relays. Agents asserted her complicity in Dillinger's crimes, "telling me or wanting me to admit and I didn't say anything. I said, 'If you know, why ask me?' He said, 'You might as well come on and tell us. We know everything anyway.'" In such an interrogation, different agents not only varied the intensity and character of the questioning but, as Billie's trial showed, no single agent could testify that sleep or food had been withheld, and the exhausted prisoner was unlikely to remember the precise details of her confinement.[64]

These confinements were a physical ordeal, but for tough molls like Evelyn Frechette and Bessie Green, it was emotional abuse that produced what agents wanted. Interrogators handled molls roughly, threatening worse violence. While one agent admitted to lifting Billie's chin, she remembered that "he hit it up, instead of lifting it up. . . . I remember one fellow coming over there and saying, 'Well, maybe Evelyn wouldn't like these lights,' and he [shone] them right in my face." Nevertheless, she held out until after the trial. Her resistance finally crumbled in prison "when the point was stressed to her that Dillinger and the other members of the gang were known to be associated with a great many other girls and that evidently she had been completely forgotten about."[65]

The failure of the Helen Gillis interrogation highlights the importance of emotional and physical isolation to division techniques and, conversely, the ways that molls could turn the tables on the state by generating publicity. Gillis was only twenty-one when captured and a mother of two. She was from a working-class Chicago family, with no criminal record prior to her federal arrests. She was quiet and "unqualifiedly loyal to her husband. Although she professed love for her two small children, she admitted that her love for her husband was greater, and consequently she desired to travel with him, notwithstanding his murderous activities, rather than remain with her children." Helen was arrested in November 1934, days after Lester was killed. Despite her husband's death, Helen refused to talk. As Hoover wrote angrily,

> [She had] some crazy ideas of loyalty to these fellows. . . . She won't identify them for us, [and] while she will get to the point of telling everything she won't "come through." . . .
> I instructed Mr. Connelley to "work on her" constantly and not let her get any sleep. . . . I stressed the point that she should be made to talk.

Six days after Helen's arrest, Hoover finally announced that she was in custody, but she was "held incommunicado as long as possible." He told Clegg to "go ahead with the plan of bringing someone there as her lawyer, and any other pretext which might get information from her." Helen, however, obtained her own lawyer, who negotiated probation in a plea bargain. As the U.S. attorney apologized, "it rapidly became evident that she, her sympathizers and the Press, would succeed in picturing the case as a vengeful prosecution of an unfortunate wife and mother." Joe Keenan had predicted that such a trial might provoke antigovernment sentiment; worse, a newspaper had published a picture of her children, planned to post bail and publish her story, and announced it would fight for her release.[66]

Given the centrality of science and skill to New Deal anticrime publicity, it is not surprising that the G-men's growing reliance on informants was hidden. In the Dillinger case, Purvis paid Anna Sage and her confederates "in cash so that there would be no photographs of checks floating around." Local police were also part of this secret information network, receiving funds earmarked as reward money that were both payment for past cooperation and incentives for the future. The SAC in Los Angeles recommended that two police officers be given five hundred dollars each, "as this would clearly show these officers that we not only make promises of rewards, but that whenever possible, the police who do work with us wholeheartedly do get part of the reward which they might be entitled to." This "would be one of the best investments the Division could make to stimulate active interest in police officers in this district to give information directly to this Division" (presumably bypassing their own commanders).[67]

Reporters covering the war on crime, tipped off by contacts on local police forces, pushed G-men to reveal their informants; this heightened colorful publicity at the expense of the division's reputation as a professional police force. The Chicago office initially stalled when rumors of a "woman in red" surfaced in relation to the Dillinger ambush, realizing that excessive publicity not only tarnished its scientific image but damaged the division's integrity in underworld circles as well. However, Anna Sage soon came forward with her own story, in part to publicize her deportation case and pressure the Department of Justice to intervene in it. Sage's long, and unsuccessful, court battle focused attention on the spectacle of female informants as the war on crime peaked in 1935; ironically, it also diverted attention from the division's far more effective underworld networks. Blasting Hoover's men as a secret police similar to those existing in Italy, Germany, and the Soviet Union, a Wisconsin judge denounced the government at a meeting of the state bar. "Just why the power of the government in apprehending Dillinger was obliged to resort to the bribery of a scarlet woman," he argued, "is not exactly clear, nor is it complimentary to the state."

A political columnist agreed. "The case of the Lady in Red," he observed, "merely demonstrates what a good many people already knew before all the nonsense about John Edgar Hoover's super-men was disseminated—that is, that the most reliable agent in crime detection is and always has been the stool pigeon."[68]

The undercover agent was once more at the center of federal enforcement, but the character of the state's police power had changed dramatically since the stool pigeon first came before the public through critiques of Prohibition. Now, the informant was part of a sophisticated professional surveillance apparatus, linked to and destined to dominate almost every police department in the nation. The informant also worked on behalf of the public, not against it. Most important, the New Deal bureaucracy had made an important move toward making policing and surveillance central to the notion of good government. If social reformers had championed government as the protector of family and community, Hoover had, by the end of the campaign against the Barker-Karpis gang, triangulated that relationship: now family, community, and the state were united against crime.

Conclusion

War Ends, Drugs Win.   —Headline, *Nation,* January 6, 1997

The legacy of the transformation of federal policing during the New Deal has been a continuing war on crime, one that is fully integrated into daily political and civic life in the United States. On February 9, 1936, Walter Winchell went on the air to urge citizens to lobby for an increased budget for the new Federal Bureau of Investigation. "Attention, Mr. and Mrs. America," he began in a clipped, urgent tone;

> your Department of Justice and mine, has requested Congress to increase its appropriations $800,000. This will allow Attorney General Homer Cummings to give John Edgar Hoover an extra 114 men. They are needed, ladies and gentlemen, as one-half of the 15,000 cases pending right now are not receiving attention. The G-Men last year spent $4,600,000, but they saved in recovered property, $38,000,000—$38,000,000—in other words, for each dollar spent, $8 was returned to tax payers or to the Government. The G-Men have solved every one of the 62 kidnapping cases. They have cut bank robberies in half. They secured 95 per cent convictions in all cases—a notable record and achievement and a thing to encourage.

Hoover's budget was approved, as it would be every year until his death in 1972. By May 1936, the FBI had thirty-seven offices and more than 650 agents; by 1940, almost 900 agents. World War II, as the previous global conflict had done, caused a massive recruitment of agents and almost tripled the FBI's prewar strength.[1]

In the years after the war on crime was brought to a successful conclusion, the expansion of federal policing was explicitly linked to the need for national vigilance against an ever present criminal population. When the Senate made cuts in the House-approved budget in 1936, Hoover warned that kidnappings would return if the money was not restored. As *Time* reported, budget theater required a series of arrests, "an intensive blood-and-thunder show," of rounding up felons, which generated bigger headlines than "the big gangster hunt of 1934." The funds were replaced. As one southern Democratic explained, "I would not revive by any act or vote of mine one hope in the bosom of a gangster by withholding the means that are necessary to pursue him to the gates of Hell."[2]

Roosevelt himself may have intervened in this struggle over the future role and function of this new federal police force. In August 1936, Hoover went to the White House to discuss the needs of the executive branch and possibilities for expanding the FBI's activities. In Hoover's notes from the meeting, he recorded FDR's concern that there was no government agency tracking communist and fascist movements; Hoover suggested that legally, the State Department could request that the FBI provide such a service. In Hoover's words, and with his emphasis, the president "stated that he is reluctant to have a formal request come through the State Department because of the many leaks therein, but that what he would do would be to put a *handwritten memorandum of his own in his safe in the White House, stating that he had instructed the Secretary of State to request this information* to be obtained by the Department of Justice." By 1938, this led to huge budget increases for counterespionage activities, triple the amount awarded to Military Intelligence or Naval Intelligence.[3] Hoover had come full circle: the campaign against bandits had led back to a new war on political dissent.

The end of the war on crime was not as spectacular as the budget battles. In August 1935, a body—fingerprints, face, and tattoos rotted away by lime—was exhumed on a lonely country road outside Chicago. An informant identified it as the missing John Hamilton. Jack Peiffer, sentenced to thirty years in Leavenworth on July 31, died a gruesome death from strychnine poisoning in his cell that afternoon. It was Alvin Karpis, however, who provided the cultural closure to this episode in the history of policing in the United States. After his arrest in May 1936, he responded to many of the agents' questions by saying, "No comment." When asked why,

he advised that he had read in numerous newspapers that when Mr. Hoover
was interviewed he often stated he had no comment to make, but that the newspapers usually wrote about a column anyway, that in view of this . . . he
thought he might as well start saying "No comment" also. In this connection
he mentioned the fact that the "No comment" answer was the only thing
which he and Mr. Hoover had in common, as it [was] well known that they
[were] on opposite sides of the fence in all other regards.[4]

Karpis's ironic identification with Hoover displayed a shrewd awareness of the
role he played in the director's rise to national leadership and that they shared
a mutual public.

Even the division's failures were wrapped up in this final year of the war on
crime, although not without dissent from the journalists who were not on
Hoover's team. As a wire story explained disingenuously, the government's case
against the Touhy gang was not utterly unfounded, since "there were three sets
of 'twins' in the Barker-Karpis and Roger Touhy gangs. Three men in one of the
mobs so resembled three members of the other that for months agents pursued
blind alley clues seeking to connect suspects with the kidnappings." But, as a
disgusted syndicated columnist responded a week later, instead of pursuing urban
mobsters and corporate criminals like Samuel Insull, "Diamond Dick Hoover,
the eye that never sleeps, examines a goosefeather with a magnifying glass and
is off on a trail of deduction and adventure which culminates in a machine-gun
battle which rubs out a 65 year old woman in a Florida village." The Department
of Justice's record "in shelling a lot of bare-foot hillbillies and sending the sur-
vivors to prison is good feature matter for the papers," but it was compiled at the
expense of catching real criminals.[5]

Although the federal government has never put an end to crime, it has per-
sistently expanded its capacity to police the nation through the identification of
public enemies and the creation of new crimes: German, and most prominently
Japanese, "enemies" during World War II; radical lefts, real and imagined; drug
dealers; and, in the 1990s, right-wing constitutionalist and militia movements. Like
the bandits of the 1930s, none of these so-called criminals are invented out of air,
nor are they particularly easy to police. However, the creation of enforcement
agendas against them are purposeful and political acts that inevitably expand state
power over noncriminal citizens as well.

Furthermore, this initial war on crime generated a gendered language and
set of domestic symbols that are identified with national enforcement efforts
to this day and lend a cultural urgency to federal enforcement agendas that
other forms of interventionist activity cannot produce. Wartime and postwar

anxieties about juvenile delinquency were often framed by fears about working mothers and absent fathers; cold war anticommunism was also expressed in the language of dissipated or corrupt families and sexualities. *My Son John* (1952) and the prosecution of Julius and Ethel Rosenberg are only two cases in which corrupt homes, and specifically mothers, rallied "normal" families on the side of the state. Beyond the FBI, statist interventions like President George Bush's war on drugs and even the Great Society's war on poverty have deployed such language to criminalize the poor and justify enhanced state intervention.[6]

Hoover's greatest contribution to modern policing and the criminalization of individuals, and perhaps to twentieth-century political culture, was his worship of data and information, and it is noteworthy that these techniques have taken on new meanings at the state and municipal level since his death in 1972. Fingerprinting, DNA, and other forms of identifying information are foundational to any investigation and prosecution: television audiences who believed that football star O. J. Simpson murdered his wife in 1994 did so because they believed in the absolute truths contained in scientific data presented by the prosecution. As the anticommunist campaigns of the McCarthy and civil rights years demonstrated, for the state to have information automatically criminalized the citizen, a logic that has reached its crudest form in Los Angeles chief of police Darryl Gates's Operation Hammer during the 1980s. One of the precipitating conditions of the 1992 Los Angeles uprising was the creation, by the LAPD, of "a rap sheet on virtually every young black male in the city" through the use of regular roundups and dragnets. Thus, currently, "data are not simply being kept on people arrested, but rather people are being detained solely in order to generate new data."[7]

Perhaps the most decisive shift made during the war on crime was the permanent suppression of community-based federal social reform initiatives in favor of enforcement philosophies that criminalize, pursue, and punish in the name of justice. Between 1933 and 1936, policing agendas invented and proposed at the local level became the dominant form of federal crime intervention in the United States, resulting in the multiplicity of armed federal enforcement agencies that exist today. Ironically, not only did the omnibus crime bill create a more flexible and potent federal police, but it set a precedent for other post–New Deal judicial expansions into state and municipal criminal and civil codes that burdened local officers with new, and proliferating, enforcement problems such as narcotics and immigration restriction.

Hoover's success in capturing the public enemies of the 1930s returned him to the business of political surveillance as the world careened toward war in

1936–37. Anticipating new public enemies—communists, fascists, and the infiltration of spies into the Japanese-American community—the president and his congressional allies sent forward legislation for a renamed Federal Bureau of Investigation that nearly doubled the roster of agents and added new staff to type and sort raw surveillance data.[8] The battles between sophisticated "Government Men" and psychopathic others have become a familiar narrative for the increasingly complex encounters between state and citizen throughout the twentieth century. It is no accident that yet another Hollywood remake of the Parker-Barrow story, Arthur Penn's *Bonnie and Clyde* (1967), became a huge hit at the precise moment that the antiwar, antiracist, and gay rights movements were erupting into violent demonstrations against state power, nor that the sophisticated weaponry and police strength mustered against the Branch Davidian compound in 1994 (not dissimilar to the scene at Ocala fifty years earlier) was justified because of allegations that children inside the compound were being abused.

The war on crime pushes historians of the New Deal to consider the crucial importance of enforcement to other statist agendas of the period. Economic order rested on social order, and the Division of Investigation was empowered both to rally a "moral" citizenry behind the government and to prove that this new Democratic administration, unlike previous Republican ones, had the will to enforce its own laws. This focus on the war on crime shifts attention away from the emergence of a welfare apparatus, the other most prominent political legacy of this period, and toward questions of state capacity and power. Although Roosevelt employed a language of public participation in other New Deal programs, the anticrime campaign did actually enroll citizens and local bureaucracies outside the bureau as active supporters of the state.

Subsequently, the extension of the state's capacity to police through voluntarist citizen action had important implications for the enforcement of patriotic nationalism during the World War II and cold war decades. Throughout the war on crime, citizens responded to Hoover's call for action and participated directly and indirectly in law enforcement. Testimony to the broad appeal of the campaign was the range of letters Hoover received, from the poorest citizens to the most wealthy. In June 1936 John D. Rockefeller Jr., a powerful Republican and opponent of the New Deal, wrote to commend the director for putting a stop to kidnapping, "this particularly heinous type of crime." The country "would feel safer because a man of your courage, determination and high technical training is at the head of the Federal Bureau of Investigation." By publicizing protection of property, Hoover cemented a population of adults, not to New Deal liberalism, but to the state; and by aiming so much of his publicity at the young,

Hoover created a constituency that would come of age in support of statist anti-radical agendas in the conservative postwar years.[9]

Why state managers emphasize certain crimes as particularly worthy of federal resources is an important historical question with implications for contemporary public policy. For the first years of the depression, bank robbery and kidnapping were categories of property crime that appealed to a range of audiences. In bank robbery, Hoover focused on a felony that mostly affected poor and middle-class citizens who feared for their savings; and in kidnapping, a crime that identified anxiety among elites that their fortunes and families were threatened by rising numbers of poor Americans on the dole. Elite citizens like John D. Rockefeller responded warmly to the bureau's developing a rhetoric and structure that allowed more direct rule of disorderly behavior—despite the fact that he opposed similar developments in other spheres of state activity.

The war on crime also benefited those outside the FBI. Because it produced tangible and quantifiable results, a war against property crime appealed to a range of policymakers, members of the executive branch—and Roosevelt himself—primary among them. Federal judges and Justice Department prosecutors also enhanced their reputations through the crime war. Federal judge Matthew M. Joyce, who sentenced Alvin Karpis, Charles J. Fitzgerald, and Jack Peiffer in the Hamm case, felt that the G-men were not only more professional, but they made his work easier, since strong federal cases forced more guilty pleas. As two agents assigned to Joyce as a bodyguard reported, "the work of the Bureau had been a revelation to him; that they could take a set of facts and make deductions which, by the evidence they obtained to support them, were incontrovertible."[10]

Responses were more mixed outside the federal bureaucracy, reflecting a continuing tension between the state and the community-level politicians and party apparatuses it relies on. Judges tied to state and local constituencies viewed the growth of federal judicial power with a jaundiced eye. That they voiced their criticism of increased federal authority through the G-men is compelling evidence that these federal agents had become a national symbol of state power during the New Deal. As one judge remarked in 1935, local officers did most of the legwork in solving kidnappings, but Hoover took all the credit; and a Wisconsin judge accused the bureau of being a "secret police."[11]

Yet, such opposition had limited effects, in part because of the forms of political centralization, characteristic of the twentieth-century United States, that the New Deal state enhanced. Hoover and the FBI prospered throughout the next three decades, pioneering models of federal enforcement that would be duplicated in new agencies invented to capture new public enemies: the Bureau of Alcohol, Tobacco, and Firearms (ATF), the Drug Enforcement Agency (DEA), and the special agents of the Immigration and Naturalization Service (INS). Goals that were common to the nation at large were a cornerstone of New Deal state making, and the war on crime was one of the most visible symbols of that. Hoover always claimed a mandate from, and service to, a public that went beyond the victims of any individual crime. By targeting bandits as the nation's most dangerous criminals, Hoover articulated them as a symbolic counterpoint to an invasive but beneficial state that was "guarding the crossroads" of American life.

Notes

Archival Sources

Library of Congress, Manuscript Division, Washington, D.C.:
  Records of the Association Against the Prohibition Amendment (RAAPA),
    (1923–1940)
  Papers of Harlan Fiske Stone (HFSP)
  Papers of Thomas James Walsh (TJWP)
  Papers of Mabel Walker Willebrandt (MWWP)

Federal Bureau of Investigation, Washington, DC:
  Barker–Karpis gang, 7-77
  John Dillinger, 62-29777
  J. Edgar Hoover, Official File, 67-561
  Bonnie Parker and Clyde Barrow, 52-5645
  Melvin Purvis, 80-84 and 67-7489
  Edward A. Tamm, 67-15585
  Clyde Tolson, 67-9524
  Walter Winchell, 62-3165
  Lindbergh Kidnapping, 62-43010

Minnesota Historical Society, St. Paul:
  Records of the United States District Court, St. Paul.
  Ramsey County, District Court, Criminal Case Files, 1930–1936

National Archives, Washington, D.C.:
  Records of the Department of Justice, RG 60
    Records of the Attorney General's Advisory Committee on Crime, 1934–1938
    Records of the special assistant to the attorney general, 1923–1940, including
      the Justin Miller Papers (JMP)
    Classified Subject Files: Kidnapping (Kidnapping Files–NA)
    J. Edgar Hoover Scrapbooks (JEH–SB)

Dallas Municipal Archives, Office of the City Secretary, Dallas (DMARC):
Barrow Gang File
Police Department Records (PDR)

Franklin Delano Roosevelt Presidential Library, Hyde Park, New York (FDRL):
Crime (OF 117)
Department of Justice (OF10a–10b)
Department of the Treasury, Narcotics Bureau (OF21x)
Louis M. Howe Personal Papers, 1933–1936 (LMH)
Presidential Secretary's File (PSF)

Texas and Dallas History Collection, J. Erik Jonsson Central Library, Dallas:
Arrest and jail logs for the City of Dallas
Log book of Dallas City Police Department Wiretaps on the Barrow and Parker
household telephones

Introduction

1. See Alan Brinkley, "The New Deal and Southern Politics," in *The New Deal and the South,* ed. James C. Cobb and Michael V. Namorato (Jackson: University Press of Mississippi, 1984), and "The New Deal and the Idea of the State," in *The Rise and Fall of the New Deal Order, 1930–1980,* ed. Steve Fraser and Gary Gerstle (Princeton: Princeton University Press, 1989); Paul Conkin, *The New Deal* (New York: Thomas Y. Crowell, 1967); Linda Gordon, *Pitied but Not Entitled: Single Mothers and the History of Welfare* (Cambridge: Harvard University Press, 1994); Alice Kessler-Harris, "Designing Women and Old Fools: The Construction of the Social Security Amendments of 1939," in *U.S. History as Women's History: New Feminist Essays,* ed. Linda Kerber, Alice Kessler-Harris, and Kathryn Kish Sklar (Chapel Hill: University of North Carolina, 1995), 87–106; William E. Leuchtenberg, *Franklin D. Roosevelt and the New Deal, 1932–1940* (New York: Harper and Row, 1963); James Patterson, *The New Deal and the States: Federalism in Transition* (Princeton: Princeton University Press, 1969) and *Congressional Conservatism and the New Deal: The Growth of the Conservative Coalition in Congress, 1933–1939* (Lexington: University of Kentucky Press, 1967); Albert U. Romasco, *The Politics of Recovery: Roosevelt's New Deal* (New York: Oxford University Press, 1983); Theda Skocpol and Kenneth Finegold, "State Capacity and Economic Intervention in the New Deal," *Political Science Quarterly* 94 (Summer 1982): 255–278, and "State, Party, and Industry: From Business Recovery to the Wagner Act in America's New Deal," in *Statemaking and Social Movements: Essays in History and Theory,* ed. Charles Bright and Susan Harding (Ann Arbor: University of Michigan Press, 1984); and Susan Ware, *Beyond Suffrage: Women in the New Deal* (Cambridge: Harvard University Press, 1981), and *Partner and I: Molly Dewson, Feminism, and New Deal Politics* (New Haven: Yale University Press, 1987).

2. Don Whitehead, *The FBI Story: A Report to the People* (New York: Random House, 1956), unpaginated forword.

3. See David J. Garrow, *Bearing the Cross: Martin Luther King and the Southern Christian Leadership Conference* (New York: William Morrow and Co., 1986); Curt Gentry, *J. Edgar Hoover: The Man and His Secrets* (New York: Norton, 1991); Richard Gid Powers, *Secrecy and Power: The Life of J. Edgar Hoover* (New York: Free Press, 1987); Richard Polenberg, *Fighting Faiths: The Abrams Case, the Supreme Court, and Free Speech* (New

York: Viking Penguin, 1987); Kenneth O'Reilly, *Hoover and the Un-Americans: The FBI, HUAC, and the Red Menace* (Philadelphia: Temple University Press, 1983); Natalie Robins, *Alien Ink: The FBI's War on Freedom of Expression* (New Brunswick, N.J.: Rutgers University Press, 1992); Anthony Summers, *Official and Confidential: The Secret Life of J. Edgar Hoover* (New York: G. P. Putnam's Sons, 1993); Athan Theoharis, ed. *From the Secret Files of J. Edgar Hoover* (Chicago: Ivan R. Dee, 1991); Pat Watters and Stephen Gillers, eds., *Investigating the FBI* (Garden City, N.Y.: Doubleday & Co., 1973); and Sanford Ungar, *FBI* (Boston: Little, Brown, 1975).

4. See Joan Hoff-Wilson, *Herbert Hoover: Forgotten Progressive* (Boston: Little Brown, 1975); Albert U. Romasco, *The Poverty of Abundance: Hoover, the Nation, and the Depression* (New York: Oxford University Press, 1975) and "Herbert Hoover's Policies for Dealing with the Great Depression: The End of the Old Order or the Beginning of the New?" in *The Hoover Presidency: A Reappraisal,* ed. Martin L. Fausold and George T. Mazuzan (Albany: State University of New York Press, 1974), 69–86; for an analysis of economic continuities, see Thomas Ferguson, "Industrial Conflict and the Coming of the New Deal: The Triumph of Multinational Liberalism in America," in Fraser and Gerstle, *Rise and Fall of the New Deal Order,* 3–31, and Theda Skocpol, *Protecting Soldiers and Mothers: The Political Origins of Social Policy in the United States* (Cambridge: Harvard University Press, Belknap Press, 1992).

5. Feminist scholars have created a sound foundation for engagements between cultural and political history; see Joan Wallach Scott, *Gender and the Politics of History* (New York: Columbia University Press, 1988); Claudia Koonz, *Mothers in the Fatherland: Women, the Family, and Nazi Politics* (New York: St. Martin's Press, 1987); Carroll Smith-Rosenberg, "Dis-Covering the Subject of the 'Great Constitutional Discussion,' 1786–1789," *Journal of American History* 79 (December 1992): 841–873; and Judith Walkowitz, *Prostitution and Victorian Society: Women, Class, and the State* (New York: Cambridge University Press, 1980); see also Tomas Almaguer, *Racial Fault Lines: The Historical Origins of White Supremacy in California* (Berkeley and Los Angeles: University of California Press, 1994).

6. For resistance to strong state philosophies, see Lynn Dumenil, "'The Insatiable Maw of Bureaucracy': Antistatism and Education Reform in the 1920s," *Journal of American History* 77 (September 1990): 499–524; and for the complexity of interwar criminal justice reform politics, see Estelle B. Freedman, *Maternal Justice: Miriam Van Waters and the Female Reform Tradition* (Chicago: University of Chicago Press, 1996).

7. See Richard Gid Powers, *G-Men: Hoover's FBI in Popular Culture* (Carbondale, Ill.: Southern Illinois University Press, 1983), and David E. Ruth, *Inventing the Public Enemy: The Gangster in American Culture, 1918–1934* (Chicago: University of Chicago Press, 1996).

8. Altina Waller has shown how criminal events that have become mythologized can be reclaimed as a historical explanation for large, material transformations: see *Feud: Hatfields, McCoys, and Social Change in Appalachia, 1860–1900* (Chapel Hill: University of North Carolina Press, 1988).

9. Kenneth O'Reilly, "A New Deal for the FBI: The Roosevelt Administration, Crime Control, and National Security," *Journal of American History* 69 (December 1982): 638–658.

10. Alvin Karpis, with Bill Trent, *The Alvin Karpis Story* (New York: Coward, McCann, & Geoghegan, 1971), 15.

11. Eric Hobsbawm, *Bandits* (New York: Pantheon, 1982) and *Primitive Rebels* (New York: Norton, 1959); for a comparative study based on the Hobsbawm model, see John McQuilton's study of the nineteenth-century Australian outback, *The Kelly Outbreak* (Queensland: University Press, 1979). For a well-researched narrative treatment of the bandits in this study, see John Toland, *The Dillinger Days* (New York: Random House, 1963).

12. For bandit and outlaw histories in the United States, see Richard White's work on the James-Younger and Doolin-Dalton gangs in "Outlaw Gangs of the Middle Border: American Social Bandits," *Western Historical Quarterly* 12 (October 1981): 387–408; Richard E. Meyer, "The Outlaw: A Distinctive American Folktype," *Journal of the Folklore Institute* (1980): 94–124; Roger Allan Hall, "Frontier Dramatizations: The James Gang," *Theatre Survey* 21 (November 1980): 117–128; and Edward Magdol, "Against the Gentry: An Inquiry into a Southern Lower-Class Community and Culture," *Journal of Social History* (Spring 1973): 259–283.

13. Warren I. Sussman, "The Culture of the Thirties," in *Culture as History: The Transformation of American Society in the Twentieth Century* (New York: Pantheon, 1984), 150–183; for the intersection between mass culture and "the collective dreams and desires" of depression-era audiences, see Rita Barnard, " 'When You Wish upon a Star': Fantasy, Experience, and Mass Culture in Nathanael West," *American Literature* 65 (June 1994): 325–351.

14. "The Story of Bonnie and Clyde," in Emma Parker and Nell Barrow Cowan, *The True Story of Bonnie and Clyde* (New York: New American Library, 1968), 167.

15. Lizabeth Cohen, *Making A New Deal: Industrial Workers in Chicago, 1919–1939* (Cambridge: Cambridge University Press, 1990), 101, 157.

16. Ruth E. Dickens, Enfield, N.C., to Melvin Purvis, 7/24/34, contained in Purvis to JEH, 8/13/34, FBI 67-7489-280x.

17. Approaches to reading documents and other texts generated by the state are addressed in Theoharis, *Secret Files of J. Edgar Hoover*, 1–11, 295; Robins, *Alien Ink;* Michel Foucault, *Discipline and Punish: The Birth of the Prison* (New York: Vintage Books, 1979), particularly 32–69; and Marc Bloch, *The Historian's Craft* (New York: Vintage, 1953).

18. Fred Cook, "Organized Crime: The Strange Reluctance," in Pat Watters and Stephen Gillers, eds., *Investigating the FBI* (New York: Doubleday, Doran & Co., 1972), 141; 145; 161–163.

19. Renate Siebert, among others, has argued that the Mafia excludes women "by definition"; see *Secrets of Life and Death: Women and the Mafia*, trans. Liz Heron (New York: Verso, 1996), 7; for the role of bandit women in gangs, see Claire B. Potter, " 'I'll Go the Limit and Then Some': Gun Molls, Desire, and Danger in the 1930's," *Feminist Studies* 21 (Fall 1994). For methods of reading racialized and gendered subjects in the twentieth-century United States, see Michel Foucault, *The History of Sexuality: An Introduction* (New York: Vintage Books, 1990); Evelyn Brooks Higgenbotham, "African-American Women's History and the Metalanguage of Race," *Signs* 17 (Winter 1992): 353–375; Toni Morrison, *Playing in the Dark: Whiteness and the Literary Imagination* (New York: Random House, 1992); Gail Bederman, *Manliness and Civilization: A Cultural History of Gender and Race in the United States, 1880–1917* (Chicago: University of Chicago Press, 1995).

20. This study also responds to calls for a political history that embraces the complexity

of power in the postindustrial United States; see William E. Leuchtenberg, "The Pertinence of Political History: Reflections on the Significance of the State in America," *Journal of American History* 73 (December 1986): 585–600.

One   "Crude Methods of Enforcement"

1. See Burl Noggle, *Teapot Dome: Oil and Politics in the 1920s* (New York: Norton, 1962).
2. Mabel Walker Willebrandt (hereafter cited as "MWW") to David and Myrtle Eaton Willebrandt (hereafter cited as "DW" and "MEW"), 4/20/24, MWW Correspondence, 1924, MWWP. Willebrandt maintained an almost daily correspondence with her parents that, among other things, provides a running commentary on Washington politics from her appointment in 1922 to her resignation in 1929.
3. The Wilson presidency and state expansion during World War I is generally acknowledged as the moment when Progressive ideologies became institutionalized in the United States government: see David Kennedy, *Over Here: The First World War and American Society* (New York: Oxford University Press, 1980); Robert H. Wiebe, *The Search for Order, 1877–1920* (New York: Hill and Wang, 1967); William E. Leuchtenberg, "The Impact of War on the American Political Economy," in *The Impact of World War I*, ed. Arthur S. Link (New York: Harper and Row, 1969), 57–70; Arthur S. Link and William Leary, eds., *The Progressive Era and the Great War* (New York: Appleton-Century-Crofts, 1969); and Ellis Hawley, *The Great War and the Search for a Modern Order*, 2d ed. (New York: St. Martin's Press, 1979).
4. Michael Woodiwiss has argued that federal prohibitions intended to enforce moral positions in the twentieth century have always created crime, undermined civil liberties, and legitimized government lawlessness. Although both political corruption and criminal organizations predated the Volstead Act, "Prohibition immediately made the problem of crime and corruption in the United States considerably worse"; see *Crime, Crusades, and Corruption: Prohibitions in the United States, 1900–1987* (New Jersey: Barnes & Noble Books, 1988), 1–22. For the role Prohibition played in the creation of organized crime syndicates, see Humbert S. Nelli, "American Syndicate Crime: A Legacy of Prohibition," in *Law, Alcohol, and Order: Perspectives on National Prohibition*, ed. David Kyvig (Westport, Conn.: Greenwood Press, 1985), 123–138.
5. Lawson Stone to Harlan Fiske Stone, 4/3/24, Lawson Stone correspondence, container 1, HFSP.
6. This sentiment was expressed as early as 1915 by Benjamin Parke DeWitt in his reform manifesto, *The Progressive Movement: A Non-Partisan, Comprehensive Discussion of Current Tendencies in American Politics*. In the introduction to this volume, DeWitt noted "the insistence by the best men in all political parties that special, minority, and corrupt influence in government—national, state and city—be removed" and that "the structure of our machinery of government . . . be so changed and modified that it will be more difficult for the few, and easier for the many, to control"; as quoted in introduction to Arthur Mann, ed., *The Progressive Era: Liberal Renaissance or Liberal Failure?* (New York: Holt, Rinehart, and Winston, 1963), 2. John Higham has also argued that by the late Progressive Era, reformers had shifted their concerns about political corruption from fraudulent voting among the foreign-born to the stranglehold that political bosses had on government; see Higham, *Strangers in the Land* (New York: Atheneum Press, 1963).

7. MWW to Mrs. J. D. Smith, WCTU/Washington, 3/23/25, MWW Correspondence (General), 1923–1957, MWWP, container 4; MWW to DW and MEW, 5/23/24, MWW Correspondence, MWWP, container 2.

8. Robert T. Small, *Washington Star,* 12/29/24.

9. For bigotry and progressive reform, see Kathleen M. Blee, *Women of the Klan: Racism and Gender in the 1920s* (Berkeley and Los Angeles: University of California Press, 1991); Steven Skowronek, *Building a New American State: The Expansion of National Administrative Capacities, 1877–1920* (Cambridge: Cambridge University Press, 1982), 12.

10. For relations between the state and its client groups in the 1920s, see Alan Dawley, *Struggles for Justice: Social Responsibility and the Liberal State* (Cambridge: Harvard University Press, 1991), 3–4, and introduction to John L. Shover, ed., *Politics of the 1920s* (Waltham, Mass.: Ginn-Blaisdell, 1970).

11. This is not to say that the question of whether the federal government could or should intervene in local and state affairs was resolved in other spheres in the 1920s: both Theda Skocpol and an influential work by James Patterson argue that, for a variety of reasons, pre–New Deal reformers were most innovative and effective when they enlarged government functions at the state level; see Skocpol, *Protecting Soldiers and Mothers: The Political Origins of Social Policy in the United States* (Cambridge: Harvard University Pres, Belknap Press, 1992), and James Patterson, *The New Deal and the States* (Princeton: Princeton University Press, 1926); see also John L. Shover's introduction to Shover, *Politics of the 1920s,* ix–xiii.

12. Dewey excerpt is from Joseph Ratner, ed. *Intelligence in the Modern World: John Dewey's Philosophy* (New York: Modern Library, 1939), 380.

13. On national Prohibition, see Paul E. Isaac, *Prohibition and Politics: Turbulent Decades in Tennessee, 1885–1920* (Knoxville: University of Tennessee Press, 1965), particularly chap. 14. Other local studies that come to similar conclusions are Norman H. Clark, *The Dry Years: Prohibition and Social Change in Washington* (1965; Seattle: University of Washington Press, 1988); Robert Smith Bader, *Prohibition in Kansas: A History* (Lawrence: University Press of Kansas, 1986); and Jimmie Lewis Franklin, *Born Sober: Prohibition in Oklahoma, 1907–1959* (Norman: University of Oklahoma Press, 1971). An excellent history of Prohibition politics that appeared at the time of repeal is Charles Merz, *The Dry Decade* (Seattle: University of Washington Press, 1931). For other secondary accounts, see Sean Dennis Cashman, *Prohibition: The Lie of the Land* (New York: Free Press, 1981), and David E. Kyvig, *Repealing National Prohibition* (Chicago: University of Chicago Press, 1979). For overviews of Prohibition, see John J. Ruinbarger, *Profits, Power, and Prohibition: Alcohol Reform and the Industrializing of America, 1800–1930* (Albany: State University of New York Press, 1989), and Jack S. Blocker Jr., *Retreat from Reform: The Prohibition Movement in the United States* (Westport, Conn.: Greenwood Press, 1976).

14. Roy Haynes, *Prohibition Inside Out* (Garden City, N.Y.: Doubleday, Page & Co., 1923), xi.

15. Merz, *Dry Decade,* 68.

16. Ibid., 69–70.

17. Ibid., 70.

18. Dorothy Brown, *Setting a Course: American Women in the 1920s* (Boston: Twayne Publishers, 1987); Estelle Freedman, "The New Woman: Changing Views of Women in

the 1920s," *Journal of American History* 61 (September 1974): 372–393; Susan Zeiger, "Finding a Cure for War: Women's Politics and the Peace Movement in the 1920's," *Journal of Social History* 23 (Fall 1990): 69–86.

19. See Estelle B. Freedman, *Maternal Justice: Miriam Van Waters and the Female Reform Tradition* (Chicago: University of Chicago Press, 1996), and Susan Ware, *Partner and I* (New Haven: Yale University Press, 1990) and *Beyond Suffrage: Women in the New Deal* (Cambridge: Harvard University Press, 1981). Like many of these women, Willebrandt may have lived with a close female companion toward the end of her life; a condolence letter to her adopted daughter Dorothy asks her "to remember us to your mother's friend, Laura, and give her our love too": Hannah Sparks to Dorothy van Dyke, 4/8/63, Condolences, MWWP, container 1. No "Laura" appears anywhere else in the collection.

20. MWW to David Walker (father), 11/29/24, 1924 correspondence, MWWP, container 2.

21. See Linda Gordon, "Social Insurance and Public Assistance: The Influence of Gender in Welfare Thought in the United States, 1890–1935," *American Historical Review* 97 (February 1992): 19–54, and "Black and White Visions of Welfare: Women's Welfare Activism, 1890–1945," *Journal of American History* 78 (September 1991): 559–590.

22. Margaret Ann Smith (secretary) to Myrtle Eaton Walker (MWW's mother), 10/11/22, DW and Myrtle Walker General Correspondence, 1922–1945, MWWP, container 2; MWW to DW and MEW, 3/22/22, MWW Correspondence, Parents, 1922, MWWP, container 2.

23. Entries for 12/7/22 and 5/16/23; diary of MWW, MWWP, container 3. Willebrandt kept a diary only sporadically throughout her life but wrote in it regularly in this period, as if she were guarding against some future investigation of her section's activities.

24. *New York Times,* 2/29/20; 12/30/20; 5/19/21.

25. Haynes, *Prohibition Inside Out,* 63; 30–35; 156.

26. *Official Records of the National Commission on Law Observance and Enforcement: Report on the Enforcement of the Prohibition Laws of the United States* (Washington, D.C.: GPO, 1931), 5:477 (hereafter cited as *NCLOE*). Similar conclusions were drawn by a study outside government, but with strong influence in policy-making circles, *The Bureau of Prohibition: Service Monographs of the United States Government, No. 57* (Washington, D.C.: Brookings Institution, 1929).

27. *NCLOE,* 1:14–15.

28. MWW to DW and MEW, 6/19/23, MWW Correspondence, 1923, MWWP, container 2.

29. MWW to DW, 9/2/23, MWW Correspondence, 1923, MWWP, container 2.

30. Franklin, *Born Sober,* 37; *NCLOE,* 4:51–52.

31. "Detection and Prosecution of Crime," Statement of J. E. Hoover, Director, Bureau of Identification, Department of Justice to the House Appropriations Committee, *Congressional Record,* December 16, 1926, 52; *NCLOE,* 5:931.

32. Rayman L. Solomon, "Regulating the Regulators: Prohibition Enforcement in the Seventh Circuit," in Kyvig, *Law, Alcohol, and Order,* 81–96.

33. *NCLOE,* 1:205–206; see also 171.

34. Ibid., 5:818; 1:212.

35. See U.S. Treasury Department [Bureau of Prohibition], *State Cooperation: Federal and State Responsibility under the Concurrent Power* (Washington, D.C.: GPO,

1930), 7. Here we see a good example of federal goals in direct conflict with local law-and-order strategies. Containing vice to poor and working-class districts was a more common practice than trying to eliminate it; see John C. Schneider, "Public Order and the Geography of a City: Crime, Violence, and the Police, 1845–1875," *Journal of Urban History* 5 (February 1978): 183–208. Hans von Hentig has noted that in rural communities, order was maintained by the sheriff's legal powers and by a cooperative citizenry; furthermore, since a sheriff was given his authority by the community, he was more likely to take the side of a constituent than a stranger; see *The Criminal and His Victim: Studies in the Sociobiology of Crime* (New Haven: Yale University Press, 1948; New York: Schocken Books ed., 1979), 233. Bertram Wyatt-Brown has also argued that "in rural and unsophisticated American (not just Southern) communities, the officers of the law saw themselves as mediators between the populace and the institution they represented." See *Honor and Violence in the Old South* (New York: Oxford University Press, 1986), 190.

36. Comparisons with cities in other parts of the country with similar populations also show that new federal felony codes did not create larger police forces. Mount Vernon, New York, employed 2 police per thousand; Pasadena, California, 1.3; and Brockton, Massachusetts, and Dearborn, Michigan, led with 2.3. See Bureau of Investigation, *Uniform Crime Reports,* vol. 1, no. 1, August 1930 (Washington, D.C.: GPO, 1930), table IV-C, p. 33.

37. *NCLOE,* 1:156.

38. Ibid., 1:172.

39. Wayne B. Wheeler to Thomas J. Walsh, 2/16/21, box 303, Legislation File 1913–1933, TJWP.

40. Fred B. Smith, ed. *Law vs. Lawlessness: Addresses Delivered at the Citizenship Conference,* Washington, D.C., October 13, 14, 15, 1923 (New York: Fleming H. Revell Co., 1924), 6. This pamphlet is a complete account of the first meeting of this organization. MWW wrote to her parents about Smith, "I think he's one of the finest men in the East. He is on the Council of Federated Churches and has given up his entire time to mobilize religious sentiment in favor of law observance"; see MWW to DW and MEW, 2/10/24, MWW correspondence, 1924, MWWP, container 2.

41. George Gordon to Thomas J. Walsh, 5/26/26, box 303, Legislation File 1913–1933, TJWP.

42. J. C. Burnham has argued that the Great Depression signaled a sudden shift in public opinion about Prohibition. Two established repeal arguments had immediate relevance, that legalized liquor would provide badly needed tax revenue and that class conflict made society fragile; "New Perspectives on the Prohibition 'Experiment' of the 1920s," *Journal of Social History* 6 (Spring 1973): 67. For a sample of the popular debate, see Irving Fisher, *The "Noble Experiment"* (New York: Alcohol Information Committee, 1930), and Fabian Franklin, *The ABC of Prohibition* (New York: Harcourt, Brace and Co., 1927).

43. "Property owners ban violators"; "Realty aid curbs liquor traffic"; "Civic leaders promote enforcement"; and "Citizens perform public service." Other sections urged citizens to use their votes to retire "lax public officials" and to report crimes directly to federal agents, not to local police; U.S. Treasury Department [Bureau of Prohibition], *Public Cooperation in Prohibition Law Enforcement* (Washington, D.C.: GPO, 1930), 25–54; U.S. Treasury Department [Bureau of Prohibition], *State Cooperation,* 8.

44. "An Overseas War Veteran" to Thomas J. Walsh, 1926, box 305, Correspondence, TJWP; L.E.H. Smith to MWW, 6/30/25, 1925 correspondence, MWWP, container 3.

45. Ella A. Boole to MWW, 2/1/27, MWW Correspondence (general), 1923–1957, MWWP, container 4. Boole continued to fight for temperance after MWW's resignation; see Ella A. Boole, *Give Prohibition a Chance* (Evanston, Ill.: National WCTU Publishing House, 1929). MWW, "First Impressions," speech given in May 1928 (audience unknown); Speeches and Writings, MWWP, container 4.

46. See David M. Chalmers, *Hooded Americanism: The First Century of the Ku Klux Klan, 1865 to the Present* (New York: Doubleday and Co., 1965), and Paul L. Murphy, "Sources and Nature of Intolerance in the 1920s," *Journal of American History* 51 (June 1964): 60–76. Indiana was at least one area where the Klan was immersed in politics; see Blee, *Women of the Klan;* Leonard J. Moore, *Citizen Klansmen: The Ku Klux Klan in Indiana, 1921–1928* (Chapel Hill: University of North Carolina Press, 1991); and M. William Lutholtz, *Grand Dragon: D. C. Stephenson and the Ku Klux Klan in Indiana* (West Lafayette, Ind.: Purdue University Press, 1991).

47. MWW to DW and MEW (undated), 1928 correspondence, MWWP, container 3.

48. Figures are drawn from fatality reports in A. W. Woodcock, *Special Report on the Enforcement of the Eighteenth Amendment Relative to the Prohibition of Intoxicating Liquors, Prepared for the Commission,* nos. 3 and 4 in letters of transmittal, vol. 1 of *NCLOE.*

49. Martin L. Fausold and George T. Mazuzan, introduction to *The Hoover Presidency: A Reappraisal* (Albany: State University of New York Press, 1974), 6; also in Fausold and Mazuzan, Donald R. McCoy, "To the White House: Herbert Hoover, August 1927–1929," 37–38; see also Martin L. Fausold, *The Presidency of Herbert C. Hoover* (Lawrence: University Press of Kansas, 1985), 29–62.

50. David B. Burner, "Before the Crash: Hoover's First Eight Months in the Presidency," in Fausold and Mazuzan, *Hoover Presidency,* 55.

51. Burnham, "New Perspectives on the Prohibition 'Experiment,'" 67.

52. U.S. Congress, House of Representatives, *Hearings before the Judiciary, House of Representatives, Seventy-first Congress, Second Session on H.J. Res. 11, 38, 99, 114, 219, and 246* (February 12, 13, 19, 20, 26, 27, March 4, 1930), pt. 1 (Washington, D.C.: GPO, 1930), 17. For a similar account, see Brand Whitlock, *The Little Green Shutter* (New York: D. Appleton and Co., 1931).

53. As historian Eric Monkonnen has theorized, "The answer to the question of what causes crime follows simply once the crime has been defined. The State causes crime"; see *Police in Urban America* (Cambridge: Cambridge University Press, 1981), 18.

54. U.S. Congress, House of Representatives, *Hearings,* pt. 2, 705.

55. Linda Gordon, *Pitied but Not Entitled: Single Mothers and the History of Welfare, 1890–1935* (New York: Free Press, 1994); U.S. Congress, House of Representatives, *Hearings,* pt. 2, 703–705; for the use of sexual images in political discourse, see Joan W. Scott, "'L'Ouvriere! Mot impie, sordide . . .,'" in *Gender and the Politics of History* (New York: Columbia University Press, 1988), 139–166, and Jeffrey Weeks, *Against Nature: Essays on History, Sexuality, and Identity* (London: Rivers Oram Press, 1991).

56. See Report to the Directors, Members, and Friends of the AAPA, submitted by the Executive Committee of the Board of Directors for the Year 1928, RAAPA, box 1; pamphlet file, 1920–1933, box 1, RAAPA.

57. Isabel Leighton, "A Charming Aristocrat," *Smart Set,* 3/30/29, AAPA clipping file (box 6).
58. U.S. Congress, House of Representative, *Hearings,* pt. 1, 441.
59. See Gail Bederman, *Manliness and Civilization: A Cultural History of Gender and Race in the United States, 1880–1917* (Chicago: University of Chicago Press, 1995); Jacqueline Dowd Hall, *Revolt against Chivalry: Jesse Daniel Ames and the Women's Campaign against Lynching* (New York: Columbia University Press, 1974); Nell Painter, "'Social Equality,' Labor, Miscegenation, and Power," in *The Evolution of Southern Culture,* ed. Numan V. Bartley (Athens: University of Georgia Press, 1988), 47–67; and Jane Sherron De Hart, "Gender on the Right: Meanings behind the Existential Scream," *Gender and History* 3 (Autumn 1991): 246–267.
60. For largely thwarted attempts at federal intervention in the race/caste system of the Deep South in the pre–civil rights era, see Pete Daniel, *The Shadow of Slavery: Peonage in the South, 1901–1969,* rev. ed. (Urbana: University of Illinois Press, 1990).
61. For a short description of Wickersham's activities during this period, see Richard Polenberg, *Fighting Faiths: The Abrams Case, the Supreme Court, and Free Speech* (New York: Viking Penguin, 1987), 113.
62. *NCLOE,* 1:14.
63. Ibid., 1:16, 18.
64. Ibid.
65. Ibid., 1:16–17.
66. House of Representatives, *Summary Report of the National Commission on Law Observance and Enforcement,* House Document no. 722 (Washington, D.C.: GPO, 1931), 54–55, 43.
67. Barry Karl argues that in the 1920s "vivid recollections of wartime government intervention served as both a warning and a temptation" to businessmen and local administrators in all sections of the country; see Karl, *The Uneasy State: The United States from 1915–1945* (Chicago: University of Chicago Press, 1983), 52–54. Richard Bensel emphasizes "the consistent hostility of the agrarian periphery to the creation and expansion of a permanent central state bureaucracy" over the last century. He also notes that in states where racial hierarchies were enacted in law "proposals to expand the civilian bureaucracy were scrupulously reviewed with reference to their impact on segregation"; *Sectionalism and American Political Development, 1880–1980* (Madison: University of Wisconsin Press, 1984), 56–59. For resistance to and suspicion of centralized state control of local affairs in Missouri, see David Thelan, *Paths of Resistance: Tradition and Dignity in Industrializing Missouri* (New York: Oxford University Press, 1986), 205–211.
68. *NCLOE,* 1:53, 79.
69. See James R. Mock and Cedric Larson, *Words That Won the War: The Story of the Committee on Public Information, 1917–1919* (Princeton: Princeton University Press, 1939), and Stephen Vaughn, *Holding Fast the Inner Lines: Democracy, Nationalism, and the Committee on Public Information* (Chapel Hill: University of North Carolina Press, 1979).
70. *NCLOE,* 5:488.
71. Ibid., 1:44–46.
72. James J. Britt (Chief Counsel, Bureau of Prohibition), *NCLOE: View as to the Improve-*

ment of Prohibition Enforcement, #5 in the letter of transmittal (Washington, D.C.: GPO, 1931), 108–111.

73. Hoover quote in Richard Gid Powers, *Secrecy and Power: The Life of J. Edgar Hoover* (New York: Free Press, 1987), 183–185; Louis Ruppel to Louis M. Howe, November 27, 1933, OF 21x, Department of the Treasury-Narcotics Bureau, box 19, FDRL.

Two   "Trained and Intelligent Men of Good Character"

1. Melvin Purvis, *American Agent* (Garden City, N.Y.: Doubleday, Doran & Co., 1936), 22–24. For Purvis's application to the bureau and supporting documents, see FBI 67-7489-1 and FBI 67-7489-4.

2. Fred J. Cook, *The FBI Nobody Knows* (New York: Macmillan, 1964), 147.

3. William W. Turner, "The Inside Story: An Agent's Dilemmas," in *Investigating the FBI,* ed. Pat Watters and Stephen Gillers (Garden City, N.Y.: Doubleday & Company), 84–110, 86. See also William C. Sullivan, *The Bureau: My Thirty Years in Hoover's FBI* (New York: Norton, 1979), and Mark W. Felt, *The FBI: Pyramid from the Inside* (New York: Putnam, 1979).

4. Steven Skowronek, *Building a New American State: The Expansion of National Administrative Capacities* (Cambridge: Cambridge University press, 1982), 209.

5. Ibid., viii, 4, 16.

6. For the making of a professional managerial class, see Richard Ohmann, *Selling Culture: Magazines, Markets, and Class at the Turn of the Century* (New York: Verso, 1996), 118–174; William J. Burns, Director, to J. Edgar Hoover (hereafter cited as "JEH"), 5/22/22, FBI 67-561-0.

7. JEH to Allard H. Gasque, 12/22/26, FBI 67-7489-3.

8. Hoover adopted modern and professional practices that municipal police forces had used to stabilize their labor forces several decades earlier: regular paychecks, pensions, relief for widows and orphans, standard working hours, regular days off, and paid holidays. These strategies also mimicked 1920s welfare capitalism, which sought to bind the worker to the company through financial and social inducements. For police reform, see Haia Shpayer-Makov, "The Making of a Police Labour Force," *Journal of Social History* 24 (Fall 1990): 109–134. For welfare capitalism, see Edward D. Jones, *The Administration of Industrial Enterprises* (1016; New York: Longmans, Green & Co., 1925), 499–519; Martha May, "Bread before Roses: American Workingmen, Labor Unions, and the Family Wage," in *Women Work and Protest: A Century of U.S. Women's Labor History,* ed. Ruth Milkman (Boston: Routledge & Kegan Paul, 1985), 1–21; and Lizabeth Cohen, *Making a New Deal* (Cambridge: Cambridge University Press, 1990), 159–211.

9. Eric Monkkonen, *Police in Urban America, 1860–1920* (Cambridge: Cambridge University Press, 1981), 4; Gerda Ray, "From Cossack to Trooper: Manliness, Police Reform, and the State," *Journal of Social History* 18 (Spring 1985): 565–586. Lizabeth Cohen has emphasized the dual nature of cultural technologies, in that they can both reinforce a sense of individual or local identity and create broader arenas of shared identity; Cohen, *Making a New Deal,* 99–158; for the creation of common vernaculars and their role in the emergence of national identities, see Benedict Anderson, *Imagined Communities: Reflections on the Origins and Spread of Nationalism* (London: Verso, 1991).

10. William Keller has usefully noted that this kind of strategy demonstrates a bureau "animated by state interests"; see *J. Edgar Hoover and the Liberals: The Rise and Fall of a Domestic Intelligence State* (Princeton: Princeton University Press, 1989), 5; see also Peter Hay, "Property, Authority, and the Criminal Law," in *Albion's Fatal Tree: Crime and Society in Eighteenth-Century England,* ed. Peter Linebaugh (New York: Pantheon, 1975), 17–64.

11. *Dearborn Independent,* 1/24/25. Harry Daugherty, Harding's attorney general, was committed to the open, or nonunion, shop: see T. H. Watkins, *The Great Depression: America in the 1930's* (New York: Little, Brown, 1993), 45. For the use of private detectives and police as strikebreakers, see Frank Donner, *Protectors of Privilege: Red Squads and Police Repression in Urban America* (Berkeley and Los Angeles: University of California Press, 1990), 2; Sidney L. Harring, *Policing a Class Society: The Experiences of American Cities, 1865–1915* (New Brunswick, N.J.: Rutgers University Press, 1983); and Frank Morn, *"The Eye That Never Sleeps": A History of the Pinkerton National Detective Agency* (Bloomington: Indiana University Press, 1982).

12. *Washington Star,* 12/29/24; *Pittsburgh Graphic,* 1/15/25.

13. Richard Gid Powers, *Secrecy and Power: The Life of J. Edgar Hoover* (New York: Free Press, 1987), 36–55; Athan Theoharis and John Stuart Cox, *The Boss: J. Edgar Hoover and the Great American Inquisition* (Philadelphia: Temple University Press, 1988), 35–70; Anthony Summers, *Official and Confidential: The Secret Life of J. Edgar Hoover* (New York: G. P. Putnam's Sons, 1993), 26–30, 35–40.

14. See Warren Sussmen, "Culture and Civilization: The Nineteen-Twenties" and "Culture Heroes: Ford, Barton, Ruth," in *Culture as History: The Transformation of American Society in the Twentieth Century* (New York: Pantheon, 1984), 99–149.

15. Spokane Press, 1/9/25.

16. Don Whitehead, *The FBI Story: A Report to the People* (New York: Random House, 1956), 67.

17. Clipping from a magazine biography, source unknown, JEH-SB, box 2, 1925–32. For the redefinition of policing as middle-class work after the police strikes of 1919, see Donner, *Protectors of Privilege,* 13–59. For the interdependence of political machines and urban police forces, see Robert M. Fogelson, *Big City Police* (Cambridge: Harvard University Press, 1977). Philip J. Ethington argues that models of good government emerged several decades earlier, in relation to controlling political violence: see Ethington, "Vigilantes and the Police: The Creation of a Professional Police Bureaucracy in San Francisco, 1847–1900," *Journal of Social History* 20 (Winter 1987): 197–227.

18. Eric Monkonnen, *Police in Urban America, 1860–1920* (Cambridge: Cambridge University Press, 1981), 53; Sanford Unger, *FBI* (Boston: Little, Brown, 1975), 54; J. Edgar Hoover, "The Work of the Bureau of Investigation," *American Journal of Police Societies* 2, no. 2 (March–April 1931): 101–107. The crimes were bankruptcy, antitrust, the National Motor Vehicle Theft Act, National Banking and Federal Reserve Acts, Mann Act, interstate theft statutes, civil rights violations, laws governing crime on the high seas, fraud against the government and impersonation of a government official, peonage, theft/embezzlement/illegal possession of government property statutes, violation of election laws, bribery of government officials, espionage, crimes committed in Indian territory, intimidation of wit-

nesses, pardon/parole/probation violations, perjury, escaped federal prisoners, neutrality violations, and the Corrupt Practices Act. Powers has noted that the bureau's poor reputation "made firing agents in itself a reform"; by 1930, Hoover employed 579 agents (half of the staff in 1920) and had reduced 53 field offices to 22; Powers, *Secrecy and Power,* 151.

19. Keller, *J. Edgar Hoover and the Liberals,* 26 n. 67; Theoharis and Cox, *Boss,* 105.
20. Skowronek, *Building a New American State,* 202–203; United States Civil Service Commission, *Annual Report of the United States Civil Service,* 35th Report (Washington, D.C.: GPO, 1918), xxvii.
21. Gene H. Carte and Elaine Carte, *Police Reform in the United States: The Era of August Vollmer, 1905–1932* (Berkeley and Los Angeles: University of California Press, 1975); also August Vollmer and Alfred E. Parker, *Crime and the State Police* (Berkeley and Los Angeles: University of California Press, 1935) and *The Police and Modern Society* (Berkeley and Los Angeles: University of California Press, 1936).
22. Unknown newspaper, Altoona, Pennsylvania, 7/8/25, JEH-SB, box 2; *Washington Star,* 5/10/25.
23. *National Spectator,* 1/9/26; Frederick Jackson Turner, "The Significance of the Frontier in American History," in *The Early Writings of Frederick Jackson Turner,* ed. Everett B. Edwards (Madison: University of Wisconsin Press), 185–229; Richard Slotkin, *Gunfighter Nation: The Myth of the Frontier in Twentieth Century America* (New York: Atheneum Press, 1992), 16; *Washington Star,* 9/21/26.
24. Quoted in Powers, *Secrecy and Power,* 150.
25. Resolution adopted by the IACP at the annual convention, Atlanta, Georgia, June 6, 1929, FBI 67-561.
26. Joseph A. Gerk, St. Louis Metropolitan Police Department, to JEH, December 28, 1929, FBI 67-561-36; H. Norman Schwartzkopf to JEH, September 17, 1929, FBI 67-561-31.
27. For a broader view of the New Deal's history in the adoption and rejection of Progressive ideas, see Otis Graham, *The Old Progressives and the New Deal* (New York: Oxford University Press, 1967).
28. A. R. Baker to JEH, March 29, 1930, FBI 67-561-[number illegible].
29. David Williams, "The Bureau of Investigation and Its Critics, 1919–1921: The Origins of Federal Political Surveillance," *Journal of American History* 68 (December 1981): 560–579.
30. MWW to JEH, February 26, 1925, FBI 67-561-7; Stanley H. Ford, Colonel, General Staff, to JEH, May 10, 1929, FBI 67-561-19.J; JEH to John B. Dingell, March 20, 1933, FBI 67-061-A-1115. The last series of numbers on this document suggests that this may have been one of a great many letters that were sent to supporters after the inauguration.
31. Charles Bright has argued that the administrative state that marks the early twentieth century was not a complete break with Skowronek's "state of courts and parties": see "The United States during the Nineteenth Century," in *Statemaking and Social Movements: Essays in History and Theory,* ed. Bright Harding and Susan Harding (Ann Arbor: University of Michigan Press, 1984), 121–158.
32. *Washington Post,* 12/22/29; Purvis, *American Agent,* 26; Unger, *FBI,* 442–458.
33. Donner, *Protectors of Privilege,* 3; George Chauncey, "Christian Brotherhood or Sexual Perversion? Homosexual Identities and the Construction of Sexual Boundaries in

the World War I Era," in *Hidden from History: Reclaiming the Gay and Lesbian Past,*
ed. Martin Duberman, Chauncey Vicinus, and Martha Vicinus (New York: New
American Library, 1989), 294–317.

34. Chicago Police Department newsletter, September 1930.
35. U.S. Congress, House of Representatives, *Hearings,* pt. 1, 17–18, 23.
36. Ellis Hawley, *The Great War and the Search for a Modern Order,* 2d ed. (New York:
St. Martin's Press, 1979); memorandum by S. J. Tracy, September 19, 1935, FBI 67-
561-66.
37. Harring, *Policing a Class Society,* 17, 225.
38. *Pittsburgh Graphic,* 1/15/25.
39. MWW to DW and MEW, (undated) 1926, 1926 correspondence, MWWP, container
3; Frederick S. Calhoun, *The Lawmen: United States Marshals and Their Deputies,
1789–1989* (New York: Penguin Books, 1989), 232–235.
40. Unknown newspaper, Altoona, Pennsylvania, 7/8/25, JEH-SB, box 2, 1925–1932.
41. Vern Countryman, "The History of the FBI: Democracy's Development of a Secret
Police," in Watters and Gillers, *Investigating the FBI,* 33–63.
42. Richard Gid Powers, "One G-Man's Family: Popular Entertainment Formulas and
J. Edgar Hoover's FBI," *American Quarterly* 30 (Fall 1978): 471–492.
43. W. C. Durant, ed., *Law Observance: Shall the People of the United States Uphold the Constitution?* (New York: Durant Award Office, 1929), 22. Durant distributed this volume
widely; the volume I worked from had been donated by him to the Wesleyan University
library.
44. James Patterson, *The New Deal and the States: Federalism in Transition* (Princeton:
Princeton University Press, 1969).
45. Arthur Woods, *Policeman and Public* (New Haven: Yale University Press, 1919), 13.
46. For the translation of gender ideology into political practice, see Kathryn Kish Sklar,
"Two Political Cultures in the Progressive Era: The National Consumers' League and
the American Association for Labor Legislation," in *U.S. History as Women's History,*
ed. Linda Kerber, Alice Kessler-Harris, and Kathryn Kish Sklar (Chapel Hill: University
of North Carolina Press, 1995).
47. Woods, *Policeman and Public,* 96–98, 156–161.
48. Carte and Carte, *Police Reform in the United States,* 24–25; 84–85; Kevin Starr,
Material Dreams: Southern California through the 1920's (New York: Oxford University Pres, 1990), 171–172; Vollmer quotes are from his contribution to Illinois Association for Criminal Justice, *Illinois Crime Survey* (Chicago: Blakely Printing Co.,
1929), 357–60.
49. Illinois Association for Criminal Justice, *Illinois Crime Survey,* 339–341.
50. Bruce Smith, *The State Police: Organization and Administration* (1925; Montclair, N.J.:
Patterson Smith Publishing, 1969), 138–141.
51. Carte and Carte, *Police Reform in the United States,* 13–14; JEH to Burns, April 25, 1924,
FBI 67-561-[number illegible], J. Edgar Hoover Official File, sec. 1; Woods, *Policeman
and Public,* 168; Harring, *Policing a Class Society,* 3–8, 13–14.
52. Eugene J. Watts, "Police Response to Crime and Disorder in Twentieth-Century
St. Louis," *Journal of American History* (September 1983): 340–358.
53. Larry K. Hartsfeld, *The American Response to Professional Crime, 1870–1917* (Westport, Conn.: Greenwood Press, 1985), 5–7; see George Chauncey's description of the
expansion of "gay" spaces during Prohibition in *Gay New York: Gender, Urban Cul-*

ture, and the Gay Male World, 1890–1940 (New York: Basic Books, 1994), 302–329; Whitehead, *The FBI Story,* 85.

54. George C. Henderson, *Keys to Crookdom* (New York: D. Apppleton & Century, 1924), 358–359.

55. Ronald L. Trekell, *History of the Tulsa Police Department, 1882–1990* (Tulsa: Tulsa Police Department, 1990), 21–29, 40–64, 107.

56. The bureau, like any good fraternal organization, rewarded faithful wives but only in the instance of their husbands' death. The director claimed over the years that he attempted to provide support for needy widows by finding them a position in the bureau's stenographic and clerical corps, and in 1935 he went to Congress to ask for an appropriation to increase pensions for the families of agents killed in action. See Richard Milne, "Boss of G-Men Tells How Gangsters Are Made," *Boston Sunday Post,* 6/23/35, and *Washington Herald,* 7/8/35.

57. C. W. Stein to JEH, 3/31/36, FBI 7-77-462.

58. Phillippa Levine, "'Walking the Streets in a Way No Decent Woman Should': Women Police in World War I," *Journal of Modern History* 66 (March 1994): 34–78; see also Susan Erlich Martin, *Breaking and Entering: Police Women on Patrol* (Berkeley and Los Angeles: University of California Press, 1980), and Chloe Owings, *Women Police: The Status of the Women Police Movement* (Montclair, N.J.: Patterson Smith, 1969).

59. *Denver Post,* 5/3/35.

60. *Washington Post,* 8/9/35.

61. *Washington Herald,* 9/2/33; *New York Press,* October 1933, JEH-SB, box 3.

62. Purvis to JEH, 2/15/28, FBI 7489-40; Egan to JEH, 2/15/28, FBI 67-72-177; Connelley to JEH, 8/16/30, FBI 67-7489-107; Cullen to JEH, 3/28/31, FBI 67-14000-73; JEH to Purvis, 9/19/30, FBI 67-7489-115; Cullen to JEH, 8/10/31, FBI 67-286-210.

63. JEH to Agent (name censored), 5/26/30, FBI 67-11225-31.

64. Keller, *J. Edgar Hoover and the Liberals,* 25; Schilder to JEH, 3/31/30, FBI 67-7489-181; Joseph L. Schott, *No Left Turns* (New York: Praeger Books, 1975), 115.

65. *Washington Brevities,* 10/8/32, JEH-SB, 1925–32; *Washington Post,* 1/2/33.

66. *Boston American,* 4/7/20; *Boston Post,* 4/14/20.

67. Clyde A. Tolson to JEH, Memorandum, 7/1/31, FBI 67-9524-140.

68. Purvis, *American Agent,* 22–24; J. M. Keith to JEH, Report of Interview with Applicant E. A. Tamm, Butte, Montana, for appointment as special agent, 8/19/30, FBI 67-75585-2.

69. JEH to Appointment Clerk, 1/24/27, FBI 67-7489-16; Omar W. Barber to JEH, 1/18/27, FBI 67-7489-8; report by C. D. White, 2/7/28, FBI 67-9524-15; J. M. Keith to JEH, 8/19/1930, FBI 67-75585-2.

70. Report by C. D. White, "Applicant for position as special agent," 2/7/28, FBI 67-9524-15.

71. Omar W. Barber to JEH, 1/18/27, FBI 67-7489-8; J. M. Keith to JEH, Report of Interview with Applicant E. A. Tamm, FBI 67-75585-2; D. O. Smith to JEH, Memorandum for the Director, 9/20/30, FBI 67-15585-13.

72. See E. A. Tamm to JEH, 10/14/30, FBI 67-15585-16, and JEH to Tamm, 11/17/30, 67-15585-18.

73. J. M. Keith to JEH, 12/11/30, FBI 67-15585-2; Tamm to JEH, 3/30/31, FBI 67-15585-30; Tamm to JEH, 10/31/32, FBI 67-15585-66; Tamm to JEH, 6/30/31, FBI 67-15585-35.

74. JEH, Memorandum for Personnel Files (New York City Office), 4/16/32, FBI 67-72-471.
75. E. J. Connelley to JEH, 12/14/33, FBI 67-15585-80; Tamm to JEH, 12/20/33, FBI 67-15585-81; JEH to Tamm, 2/23/34, FBI 67-15585-89.
76. Perry Watzman to JEH, Re. Special Agent M. H. Purvis Jr., 11/7/27, FBI 67-7489-38.
77. Report of Inspector Egan, 11/2/27, FBI 67-825-49; Purvis to JEH, 8/24/27, FBI 67-7489-33; Egan to JEH, 2/15/28, FBI 67-72-177; Purvis to JEH, Memorandum, 2/8/29, FBI 67-8225-22; and Purvis to JEH, Memorandum, 2/14/29, FBI 67-8225-23; Harold Nathan to JEH, 3/19/29, FBI 67-7489-63; and Purvis to JEH, Memorandum, 3/23/29, attachment to FBI 67-7489-64.
78. JEH to Purvis, 5/9/29, FBI 67-7489-73; L. C. Schilder to JEH, 6/21/29, FBI 67-380-126; Schilder to JEH, 10/15/29, FBI 67-7489-84; Efficiency Rating Sheet submitted by Schilder, 6/30/29, FBI 67-7489, attachment to 67-7489-101.
79. Nathan to JEH, Memorandum, 6/17/30, FBI 67-6099-61; E. J. Connelley to JEH, 6/19/30, FBI 67-11225-31.
80. T. F. Cullen to JEH, Memorandum for the Director, 3/28/31, FBI 67-14000-73; Cullen to JEH, Inspection, Washington Field Office, 8/10/31, FBI 67-286-210; JEH to Purvis, 8/18/31, FBI 67; note from Hoover is appended to V. W. Hughes to JEH, 8/15/31, FBI 67-7489-168; see also Purvis to JEH, Memorandum, 9/9/31, FBI 67-7489-172.
81. JEH to Purvis, 2/27/32, FBI 67-7489-192; H. H. Clegg to JEH, contained in "Inspection—Chicago Office," 3/15/32, FBI-67-7489-193.
82. JEH to Purvis, 8/29/33, FBI 67-7489-226; Purvis to JEH, 7/18/33, FBI 67-7489-222.
83. Drew Pearson, "The Daily Washington Merry-Go-Round," 8/19/33, JEH-SB, box 3.
84. *Akron Beacon-Journal,* 7/24/33.

Three   "People No Longer Respect Respectability"

1. For moral panics, see Jeffrey Weeks, "Inverts, Perverts, and Mary-Annes: Male Prostitution and the Regulation of Homosexuality in England in the Nineteenth and Twentieth Centuries," in *Against Nature: Essays on History, Sexuality, and Identity* (London: Rivers Oram Press, 1991), 46–67; Gayle Rubin has made a similar analysis in "Thinking Sex: Notes for a Radical Theory of the Politics of Sexuality," in *The Lesbian and Gay Studies Reader,* ed. Henry Abelove, Michele Aina Barale, and David M. Halperin (New York: Routledge, 1993), 62–90. For the adoption of working-class pleasures by middle-class youth, see Paula Fass, *The Damned and the Beautiful: American Youth in the 1920s* (New York: Oxford University Press, 1977).
2. Historians are divided as to whether crime asserts itself in "real" patterns that provide material evidence of social transformation or whether those transformations themselves produce rituals, disciplines, technologies, and cultural practices that constitute the realm of the criminal. See Roger Lane, *Violent Death in the City: Suicide, Accident, and Murder in Nineteenth Century Philadelphia* (Cambridge: Cambridge University Press, 1979) and *Policing the City: Boston, 1822–1885* (Cambridge: Harvard University Press, 1967). Historians who argue that criminal statistics are best understood as ethnographic evidence are Natalie Zemon Davis, "The Rites of Violence," in *Society and Culture in Early Modern France: Eight Essays* (Palo Alto, Calif.: Stanford Uni-

versity Press, 1979), and Anton Blok, *Infamy* (New York: Oxford University Press, 1989) and *The Mafia of a Sicilian Village, 1860–1960: A Study of Violent Peasant Entrepreneurs* (New York: Harper and Row, 1975). Critical realms of analysis that trouble materiality and lead us to look to look to culture as the primary arena for the construction of criminal identities are state transformation, race, class, gender, and sexuality: see Stuart Hall et al., *Policing the Crisis: Mugging, the State, and Law and Order* (New York: Holmes and Meier, 1978); Judith Walkowitz, *Prostitution and Victorian Society: Women, Class, and the State* (New York: Cambridge University Press, 1980); Alan Berube, *Coming Out under Fire* (New York: Free Press, 1990); and Michel Foucault, *Discipline and Punish* (New York: Pantheon, 1979). My argument that culture and material evidence are interdependent realms finds resonance in Peter Spierenberg in "Faces of Violence: Homicide Trends and Cultural Meanings, Amsterdam, 1431–1816," *Journal of Social History* 18 (Summer 1994): 701–716.

3. Robert and Helen Lynd, *Middletown: A Study in American Culture* (New York: Harcourt, Brace and Co., 1929), 498.

4. William R. Leach, *Land of Desire: Merchants, Power, and the Rise of a New American Culture* (New York: Vintage Books, 1994), 3–4; Warren I. Sussman, *Culture as History: The Transformation of American Society in the Twentieth Century* (New York: Pantheon, 1984), 99–104; Neal Gabler, *Winchell: Gossip, Power, and the New Celebrity* (New York: Knopf, 1994), 184–185.

5. Cornelius Vanderbilt Jr., "How Al Capone Would Run This Country," *Liberty,* October 17, 1931; see also Fred D. Pasley, *Al Capone: The Biography of a Self-Made Man* (Binghamton, N.Y.: Ives, Washburn, 1930); for a biography of Capone, see John Kobler, *Capone: The Life and World of Al Capone* (1971; New York: Collier Books, 1982).

6. Fred Allen, *Only Yesterday: An Informal History of the 1920's* (New York: Harper and Row, 1964), 223–224.

7. John Fiske, *Understanding Popular Culture* (New York: Routledge, 1989), 103–127; Arthur B. Reeve, *The Golden Age of Crime* (New York: Mohawk Press, 1931), 10–11, 187. T. H. Watkins has argued that the stock market crash created a "permanent distrust of the 'financial community'" in the United States and that "the virtues of thrift and responsibility to which white, middle-class America had given its heart was shattered"; see *The Great Depression: America in the 1930's* (New York: Little, Brown, 1993), 14. See also David E. Ruth, *Inventing the Public Enemy: The Gangster in American Culture, 1918–1934* (Chicago: University of Chicago Press, 1986).

8. U.S. Congress, House of Representatives, *Hearings before the Judiciary Committee, House of Representatives,* February 12–March 4, 1930, pt. 1 (Washington, D.C.: GPO, 1930), 78–79.

9. Paul G. Cressey, *The Taxi-Dance Hall: A Sociological Study in Commercialized Recreation and City Life* (1932; New York: AMS Press, 1971), 289–290. See also Paul Boyer, *The Urban Masses and Moral Order in America, 1820–1920* (Cambridge: Harvard University Press, 1978); Kathy Peiss, *Cheap Amusements: Working Women and Leisure in Turn-of-the-Century New York* (Philadelphia: Temple University Press, 1986); and George Chauncey, *Gay New York: Gender, Urban Culture, and the Gay Male World, 1890–1940* (New York: Basic Books, 1994); and Mary Murphy, "Bootlegging Mothers and Drinking Daughters," *American Quarterly* 46 (June 1994): 174–194.

10. Sinclair Lewis, *Babbitt* (1922; New York: Signet Classic Edition, 1950), 267; Kenneth Anger, *Hollywood Babylon* (New York: Bell Publishing Co., 1975); Gabler, *Winchell,* 77–81.

11. Reeve, *Golden Age of Crime,* 139.

12. Hazel V. Carby, "Policing the Black Woman's Body in an Urban Context," *Critical Inquiry* 19 (Summer 1992): 738–755; Fass, *Damned and the Beautiful;* for the creation of subcultural styles, see Dick Hebdige, *Subculture: The Meaning of Style* (New York: Routledge, 1979).

13. John Modell, *Into One's Own: From Youth to Adulthood in the United States, 1920–1975* (Berkeley and Los Angeles: University of California Press, 1989), 129.

14. *State of Minnesota v. Florence Hoffmann,* case #13480; *v. Robert Coleman (William Brisbane),* case #13525; *v. Thelma Sherry,* case #13774; *v. Fred Marsh,* case # 14035; see Ramsey County, District Court, Criminal Case Files, 1930–1936, microfilm roll 1, 1930, St. Paul Historical Society, St. Paul, Minn. For the origins of the kleptomania defense, see Elaine Abelson, *When Ladies Go A'Thieving: Middle-Class Shoplifters in the Victorian Department Store* (New York: Oxford University Press, 1989).

15. As Michel Foucault has argued, the desire to observe, classify, and produce knowledge about disorderly and rebellious bodies has been characteristic of the rise of the modern state; production of criminal subjects is a critical lens on the evolution of state power; see *Discipline and Punish,* 195–230, and David Rothman, *Conscience and Convenience: The Asylum and Its Alternatives in Progressive America* (Boston: Little, Brown, 1980).

16. Carl Murchison, *Criminal Intelligence* (Worcester, Mass.: Clark University Press, 1926), 7, 32–57, 289–91.

17. Estelle B. Freedman, "Uncontrolled Desire: The Response to the Sexual Psychopath, 1920–1960," *Journal of American History* 74 (June 1987): 83–106.

18. John Ellis, *Social History of the Machine Gun* (Baltimore: Johns Hopkins University Press, 1975).

19. George C. Henderson, *Keys to Crookdom* (New York: D. Appleton & Century, 1924), 29, 103.

20. Ibid., 107–108.

21. Ibid., 390.

22. Several chapters of Reeve's *The Golden Age of Crime* use "thrill" as both a cause and an effect of violent crime: the young commit crimes "for thrills," and audiences experience thrill when they read about murderous exploits; see 222–232 and 259–272.

23. Athan Theoharis and John Stuart Cox, *The Boss: J. Edgar Hoover and the Great American Inquisition* (Philadelphia: Temple University Press, 1988), 121.

24. For a good overview of the midwestern, southern, and southwestern farm economy and the cultural changes brought on by drought, see Watkins, *Great Depression;* Donald Worster, *Dust Bowl: The Southern Plains in the 1930's* (New York: Oxford University Press, 1979); Pete Daniel, *Standing at the Crossroads: Southern Life in the Twentieth Century* (New York: Hill and Wang, 1986); Robert S. McElvaine, *The Great Depression: America, 1929–1941* (New York: Times Books, 1984). The average farm wage fell from a high of $65.40 a month in 1920 to $48.25 in 1923, rose a few dollars over the next six years, plummeted to $38.38 in 1931, and dropped to $25.67 in 1933; see Bureau of the Census, *Historical Statistics, 1789–1945* (Washington, D.C.: GPO, 1949), 25. A good contemporary account of the state of small businessmen and

skilled workers in Oklahoma's northeastern coal mining counties and the changes in their communities by the early 1930s is Frederick Lynne Ryan, *The Rehabilitation of Oklahoma Coal Mining Communities* (Norman: University of Oklahoma Press, 1935). For population figures, see table 14, "Composition of the rural population, Farm and Non-Farm, by Counties, 1930," Bureau of the Census, *Fifteenth Census of the United States: 1930,* vol. 1, *Population* (Washington, D.C.: GPO, 1930).

25. See Donald H. Grubbs, *Cry from the Cotton: The Southern Tenant Farmers Union and the New Deal* (Chapel Hill: University of North Carolina Press, 1971); C. Vann Woodward, *The Origins of the New South* (Baton Rouge: University of Louisiana Press, 1951), 235–263, 369–395; Jack Temple Kirby, *Rural Worlds Lost: The American South, 1920–1960,* (Baton Rouge: Louisiana State University Press, 1987) 147–152; Edward Ayers, *The Promise of the New South: Life after Reconstruction* (New York: Oxford University Press, 1992); Jacqueline Jones, *The Dispossessed: America's Underclasses from the Civil War to the Present* (New York: Basic Books, 1992); David Thelan, *Paths of Resistance: Tradition and Dignity in Industrializing Missouri* (New York: Oxford University Press, 1986); John Shover, "The Farmer's Holiday Association Strike, August 1932," in *Riot, Rout, and Tumult: Readings in American Social and Political Violence,* ed. Roger Lane and John J. Turner Jr. (Westport, Conn.: Greenwood Press, 1978), 280–292.

26. *Tulsa Daily World,* 7/10/30; 7/12/30.

27. Ibid., 7/10/30.

28. Ibid.

29. The belief that mothers were particularly responsible for male and female delinquency was widespread: see Barbara Meil Hobson, *Uneasy Virtue: The Politics of Prostitution and the American Reform Tradition* (New York: Basic Books, 1987), 184–199.

30. *Tulsa Daily World,* 7/10/30.

31. Murchison, *Criminal Intelligence,* 261.

32. I chose the *Daily World* because Tulsa is the largest metropolis in the northeast corner of the state and is at the center of the tristate area. Following a method suggested by Charles Tilly, I used a survey technique to create data in the absence of available police records for the period. Going through each roll of microfilm for the year 1930, I photocopied every story that mentioned an armed robbery, bank job, or stickup, taking care not to duplicate reports on any crime. The primary disadvantage of this method of assembling data is that it is undoubtedly incomplete: banks may have wished to suppress reports of a robbery to conceal their vulnerability, and newspapers may have only printed the most violent reports. In addition, bandits who were not caught were probably counted more than once in some of my categories, such as gender and race, and not at all in others—age, for example. As I have noted, police and court data are incomplete in different ways. I have been pleased to see, however, that the conclusions I came to are generally confirmed by the other sources I have used for this study.

33. *New York Times,* 7/1/20; 12/4/20. See also reports on the American Bankers Convention and other associations in editions of 10/4/22; 9/5/24; 12/11/25; and 11/16/28.

34. In my average figure, I have excluded the ten jobs that netted less than $100, and one spectacularly successful heist of $142,000, which six bandits accomplished outside this region at the Bank of Willnar in Minnesota. If I were to estimate the error on

either of these figures, I would argue that the bank heist losses are too low: banks might not have wanted to undermine the confidence of depositors and shareholders by publishing their actual losses. Victims of stickup artists might have inflated their losses, however, in the hope of recovering more money from insurance companies or a captured bandit.

35. Bureau of the Census, *Historical Statistics, 1789–1945*, 25; *Tulsa Daily World*, 7/26/30.
36. Charles Hamilton, ed., *Men of the Underworld: The Professional Criminal's Own Story* (New York: Macmillan, 1952), 150.
37. Interrogation of Charles Fitzgerald, 4/11/36, in report by J. H. Hanson, FBI 7-77-505.
38. U.S. Department of Commerce, Bureau of Foreign and Domestic Commerce, *Statistical Abstract of the United States, 1930* (Washington, D.C.: GPO, 1930), 74; Bureau of the Census, *Statistical Abstract of the United States, 1938* (Washington, D.C.: GPO, 1939), 76; Missouri Association for Criminal Justice, *The Missouri Crime Survey* (New York: Macmillan, 1926), 4.
39. *Official Records of the National Commission on Law Observance and Enforcement: Enforcement of the Prohibition Laws of the United States*, vol. 1 (Washington, D.C.: GPO, 1931), 422–423.
40. *New York Times*, 11/7/30; 7/21/28.
41. Ibid., 4/7/27; 11/29/30; 7/6/25; 9/24/25.
42. Illinois Association for Criminal Justice, *The Illinois Crime Survey* (Chicago: Illinois Association for Criminal Justice, 1929), 342. For an overview of American vigilantism, see Richard Maxwell Brown, "The American Vigilante Tradition," in Lane and Turner, *Riot, Rout, and Tumult*, 80–111. Anticrime vigilance committees must be contextualized by a literature on Klan activity in the area of the crime corridor; in southern Indiana and southern Illinois in particular, Klans organized themselves around antivice vigilance and occasional bloody wars against bootleggers; see David Chalmers, *Hooded Americanism: The First Century of the Ku Klux Klan, 1865 to the Present* (New York: Doubleday, 1965), and Kathleen M. Blee, *Women of the Klan: Racism and Gender in the 1920s* (Berkeley and Los Angeles: University of California Press, 1991).
43. Carl Degler, *Place over Time: The Continuity of Southern Distinctiveness* (Baton Rouge: Louisiana State University Press, 1977), 24–25; *Tulsa Daily World*, 2/13/30; 2/17/30; *Tulsa Daily World*, 7/3/30, 7.
44. *Uniform Crime Reports* (Washington, D.C.: GPO, 1930–1936); *Tulsa Daily World*, 2/27/30. Feminist historians have shown that community consent to domestic violence had its limits, and bringing punishments into the public arena was one of them; see Linda Gordon, *Heroes of Their Own Lives: The Politics and History of Family Violence* (New York: Viking, 1988), 256, and Ellen Ross, "Fierce Questions and Taunts: Married Life in Working Class London," *Feminist Studies* 8 (Fall 1982): 575–602.
45. Gordon, *Heroes of Their Own Lives*, 213; Bertram Wyatt-Brown, *Honor and Violence in the Old South* (New York: Oxford University Press, 1988), 25–39; *Tulsa Daily World*, 1/3/30.
46. Sheldon Hackney, "Southern Violence," *American Historical Review* 74 (February 1969): 90–125, and Nancy Tomes, "A Torrent of Abuse: Crimes of Violence between Working Class Men and Women in London, 1840–1875," *Journal of Social History* 10 (Spring 1978): 45–67.
47. *Tulsa Daily World*, 8/28/30; 8/14/30.
48. Ibid., 11/13/30.

49. Ibid., 9/21/30; 9/18/30.
50. Ibid., 10/15/30; 9/19/30.
51. Ibid., 11/9/30; 2/12/30.
52. Ibid., 7/30/30.

Four   "It's Death for Bonnie and Clyde"

1. Jan I. Fortune, ed., *The True Story of Bonnie and Clyde, As Told By Bonnie's Mother and Clyde's Sister, Mrs. Emma Parker and Mrs. Nell Barrow Cowan* (New York: New American Library, 1968), 80–88 (hereafter cited as "Parker and Cowan, *True Story*").
2. Ibid., 82–84.
3. See Claire Bond Potter, "'I'll Go the Limit and Then Some': Gun Molls, Desire, and Danger in the 1930s," *Feminist Studies* 21 (Spring 1995): 41–65; Parker and Cowan, *True Story,* 175, 91.
4. *Time,* 6/4/34; Parker and Cowan, *True Story,* 24.
5. *Tulsa Daily World,* 5/31/34; 6/2/34.
6. Jacqueline Jones, *The Dispossessed: America's Underclasses from the Civil War to the Present* (New York: Basic Books, 1992), 78.
7. Sheldon Glueck and Eleanor Glueck, *One Thousand Juvenile Delinquents: Their Treatment by Court and Clinic: Harvard Law School Survey of Crime in Boston* (Cambridge: Harvard University Press, 1934), 74–80, 105.
8. Lawrence Levine, "American Culture and the Great Depression," in *The Unpredictable Past: Explorations in American Cultural History* (New York: Oxford University Press, 1993), 222–223.
9. Claude S. Fisher, "Changes in Leisure Activities, 1890–1940," *Journal of Social History* 28 (Spring 1994): 453–475; for the relationship of narrative forms to nationalism, see Benedict Anderson, *Imagined Communities: Reflections on the Origin and Spread of Nationalism* (New York: Verso, 1983).
10. James Inciardi, Alan A. Block, and Lyle A. Hallowell, *Historical Approaches to Crime: Research Strategies and Issues* (Beverly Hills: Sage Publications, 1977), 48.
11. By "masculinist," I am suggesting that many of these ideologies and political movements cited below were articulated around male rights to property and liberty, as they related to the protection of women and children; see Michael Kammen, *Spheres of Liberty: Changing Perceptions of Liberty in American Culture* (Ithaca, N.Y.: Cornell University Press, 1986), 9, 20–23, 115–172. Donald Grubbs, *Cry from the Cotton: The Southern Tenant Farmers' Union and the New Deal* (Chapel Hill: University of North Carolina, 1971).
12. Richard Maxwell Brown, *No Duty to Retreat: Violence and Values in American History and Society* (New York: Oxford University Press, 1991), 6–26.
13. The following articles discussing the relationship of folklore and historical method were featured in the *American Historical Review* 97 (December 1992): Lawrence W. Levine, "The Folklore of Industrial Society: Popular Culture and Its Audiences"; Robin D. G. Kelley, "Notes on Deconstructing 'The Folk'"; Natalie Zemon Davis, "Toward Mixtures and Margins"; T. J. Jackson Lears, "Making Fun of Popular Culture," 1372–1419.
14. Marion Goldman's distinction between "intentional" and "unintentional" sources, a borrowing from Marc Bloch, has been useful to sorting out this evidence; her concept

of the "fundamental interdependence and similarity between the 'normal' and the 'deviant' in American society" has also been foundational to understanding the ways bandits reflected alternative understandings of community order. See Marion Goldman, *Gold Diggers and Silver Miners: Prostitution and Social Life on the Comstock Lode* (Ann Arbor: University of Michigan Press, 1981), 8–9.

15. John Treherne, *The Strange History of Bonnie and Clyde* (New York: Stein and Day, 1984), 23–25; Parker and Cowan, *True Story,* 33, 44.

16. Parker and Cowan, *True Story,* 44, 49; Treherne, *Strange History of Bonnie and Clyde,* 27.

17. Parker and Cowan, *True Story,* 51–6.

18. Ibid., 24–25.

19. Ibid., 26–28.

20. Ibid., 29; Miriam deFord, *The Real Bonnie and Clyde* (New York: Ace Books, 1967), 12.

21. Treherne, *Strange History of Bonnie and Clyde,* 37–49; Fort Worth Police Department Identification Report #4316, Barrow gang file, DMARC.

22. Figures compiled from the arrest and jail log records for the city of Dallas, Texas and Dallas History Collection. The numbers for the specific charges against people and property are even higher than they should be for African Americans; at least a quarter of each are charges against black men and women for "assault to murder," a charge that, in the South, indicated disrespect to, but not actual violence against, a white person.

23. W. M. Thompson, Chief of the Bureau of Records and Identification, to Mr. D. E. Walsh, Bureau of Identification, Police Department, Dallas, Tex., 5/17/32, Barrow gang file, DMARC.

24. Division of Investigation, Washington, D.C., identification order no. 1211, in "Photocopies—Paper Documents; Bonnie and Clyde"; Police Department Records, Office of the City Secretary, Dallas, Tex. (hereafter referred to as PDR).

25. Parker and Cowan, *True Story,* 37, 42, 58.

26. Quoted in ibid., 60–62; for the changing character of romance, see Pamela Haag, "In Search of the 'Real Thing': Ideologies of Love, Modern Romance, and Women's Sexual Subjectivity in the United States, 1920–1940," in *American Sexual Politics: Sex, Gender, and Race since the Civil War,* ed. John C. Fout and Maura Shaw Tautillo (Chicago: University of Chicago Press, 1993), 161–192.

27. Parker and Cowan, *True Story,* 62–63, 69.

28. Jones, *Dispossessed,* 149; Alex Lichtenstein, *Twice the Work of Free Labor: The Political Economy of Convict Labor in the New South* (New York: Verso, 1996); Edward L. Ayers, *Vengeance and Justice: Crime and Punishment in the Nineteenth Century American South* (New York: Oxford University Press, 1984); Treherne, *Strange History of Bonnie and Clyde,* 59–60, 78.

29. David Rothman, *Conscience and Convenience: The Asylum and Its Alternatives in Progressive America* (Boston: Little, Brown, 1981), 139–141; Treherne, *Strange History of Bonnie and Clyde,* 60; Parker and Cowan, *True Story,* 78.

30. Parker and Cowan, *True Story,* 79–81.

31. Christopher Finch, *Highways to Heaven: The AUTObiography of America* (New York: HarperCollins, 1992), 80–85; Commonwealth of Pennsylvania, *Biennial Report of the Pennsylvania State Police for the Fiscal Years of 1927–1928* (Harrisburg: 1928), 8; Illi-

nois Association for Criminal Justice, *The Illinois Crime Survey* (Chicago: Blakely Publishing Co., 1929), 337.

32. James N. Gregory, *American Exodus* (New York: Oxford University Press, 1989); Richard White, "Outlaw Gangs of the Middle Border: American Social Bandits," *Western Historical Quarterly* 12 (October 1981); O. S. Barton, *Three Years with Quantrill: A True Story, Told by His Scout, John McCorkle* (New York: Buffalo-Head Press, 1966).

33. E. P. Thompson, *Whigs and Hunters: The Origins of the Black Act* (New York: Pantheon, 1975); E. J. Hobsbawm and Georges Rude, *Captain Swing* (1968; New York: Norton, 1975); David Thelan, *Paths of Resistance: Tradition and Dignity in Industrializing Missouri* (New York: Oxford University Press, 1986); Richard Maxwell Brown, *No Duty to Retreat: Violence and Values in American History and Society* (New York: Oxford University Press, 1991); Eric J. Hobsbawm, *Bandits!* pp. 33–38, and 159; Eric Monkonnen, *Policing in Urban America* (Cambridge: Cambridge University Press, 1981), 16–29; Charles Tilly, "War Making and State Making as Organized Crime," in *Bringing the State Back In,* ed. Peter Evans, Dietrich Rueschemeyer, and Theda Skocpol (Cambridge: Harvard University Press, 1985), 169–181.

34. Criminal organizations, as Florike Egmond points out, "cannot be studied separately from the social structure and customs of the groups involved—as if crime were a totally discrete section of their existence, or as if illegal activities could only be understood by classifying them as abnormal behavior." Modern states also need criminals to cultivate the norms of citizenship: they are "taken to do and be everything a respectable citizen did and was not"; see *Underworlds: Organized Crime in the Netherlands, 1650–1800* (Cambridge, England: Polity Press, 1993), 4–5, 17–20, 184–195.

35. Humbert S. Nelli, *The Business of Crime: Italians and Syndicate Crime in the United States* (New York: Oxford University Press, 1976), xi, 139, 168; Albert Fried, *The Rise and Fall of the Jewish Gangster in America* (New York: Holt, Rinehart and Winston, 1980), 108–109; D. R. Cressey for the President's Commission on Law Enforcement and Administration of Justice, *The Structure and Function of Criminal Syndicates* (Washington, D.C.: GPO, 1967); Immanuel Wallerstein, *Historical Capitalism* (New York: Verso, 1983), 76, 15.

36. Mark H. Haller, "Organized Crime in Urban Society: Chicago in the Twentieth Century," *Journal of Social History* 6 (Fall 1972): 211–234.

37. Jenna Joselit, *Our Gang: Jewish Crime in New York, 1900–1940* (New York: Hill and Wang, 1983); Nelli, *Business of Crime,* 219–253.

38. Clarence D. McKean to JEH, 1/10/27, FBI 26-9961-28.

39. White, "Outlaw Gangs," 397; Susan Berman, *Easy Street:The Story of a Mob Family* (New York: Dial Press, 1981), 114; Karpis confession, report by McKee to JEH, 5/8/36, FBI 7-77-697; James Henry Audett, *Rap Sheet: My Life Story* (New York: William Sloane, 1954), 91, 99.

40. *Tulsa Daily World,* 3/4/34.

41. Ibid.

42. Alvin Karpis with Bill Trent, *The Alvin Karpis Story* (New York: Coward, McCann, and Geoghegan, 1971), 124–125.

43. *Pittsburgh Sun-Telegraph,* 10/23/34; Parker and Cowan, *True Story,* 27.

44. *Tulsa Daily World,* 3/16/34. Cal Winslow has drawn similar conclusions for eighteenth-

century British smugglers: see "Sussex Smugglers," in Albion's *Fatal Tree: Crime and Society in Eighteenth-Century England,* ed. Peter Linebaugh (New York: Pantheon, 1975), 119–166.

45. *Tulsa Daily World,* 3/16/34.
46. Ibid., 3/17/34; 3/16/34.
47. Audett, *Rap Sheet,* 157–159.
48. Ibid., 140; Larry K. Hartsfeld, *The American Response to Professional Crime, 1870–1917* (Westport, Conn.: Greenwood Press, 1985), 6–7.
49. *Tulsa Daily World,* 3/20/34.
50. George C. Henderson, *Keys to Crookdom* (New York: D. Appleton and Co., 1924), vii, 85–89.
51. *Tulsa Daily World,* 3/13/34; 4/9/34.
52. Inciardi, Block, and Hallowell, *Historical Approaches to Crime* (Beverly Hills: Sage Publications, 1977), 12. This volume preceded major developments in cultural history; therefore, its call for "accuracy" and "scientific method" (see 55) is somewhat dated. The authors' insistence that the historians of crime should separate legend from documentation is not dated, however, nor are speculations about how new arenas of popular culture created legends and myths about frontier outlaws to serve contemporary ends; see 55–89.
53. Parker and Cowan, *True Story,* 89.
54. Ibid., 90.
55. Ibid., 91.
56. Ibid., 95–98.
57. J. C. Willis, sheriff, Wharton County, Tex., to Chief of Detectives, Bureau of Identification, Police Department, Dallas, Tex., 8/19/32; D. E. Walsh, Superintendent, Bureau of Identification, Police Department, Dallas, Tex., to C. J. Koehe, deputy sheriff, Wharton County, Tex., 8/22/33; general circular from J. C. Willis, sheriff, Wharton County, Tex., Barrow gang file, DMARC.
58. Treherne, *Strange History of Bonnie and Clyde,* 103.
59. Parker and Cowan, *True Story,* 111–112.
60. *Tulsa Daily World,* 5/4/34.
61. James J. Flink, "The Ultimate Status Symbol: The Custom Coachbuilt Car in the Interwar Period," in *The Car and the City: The Automobile, the Built Environment, and Daily Urban Life,* ed. Martin Wachs and Margaret Crawford (Ann Arbor: University of Michigan Press, 1979), 154–166.
62. Federal Identification Order no. 1211, October 1933; there is also an undated memo to Detective Doug Walsh, Dallas Police Department, that mentions an interview of Jim Muckleroy, Cumie Barrow's brother-in-law, by a bureau agent. This suggests that the indecipherable file on the gang at the FBI consists of a series of these interviews: see Barrow gang file, DMARC.
63. Virginia Scharf, *Taking the Wheel: Women and the Coming of the Motor Age* (New York: Free Press, 1991), 164; Michael Berger, "The Car's Impact on the American Family," in Wachs and Crawford, *Car and the City,* 57–74.
64. Finch, *Highways to Heaven,* 93–94; John D'Emilio and Estelle Freedman, *The History of Sexuality in America* (New York: Vintage, 1987), 279–283; general circular issued by J. C. Willis, sheriff, Wharton County, Tex., 8/30/32.

65. "Wanted Report," 5/8/33, Lucerne, Indiana Police Department, to Bureau of Identi-fication, Dallas, Tex., in Barrow gang file, DMARC; Parker and Cowan, *True Story,* 123–129.

66. *New York Times,* June 12, 1933; Parker and Cowan, *True Story,* 133–139.

67. Bulletin no. 279, Dallas Police Department, 5/1/33; J. C. Willis, sheriff, Wharton County, Tex., general circular, 8/30/32, Barrow gang file, DMARC.

68. Anonymous poem to chief of police, Barrow gang file; sheriff's department, Tulia, Texas to Dallas Police Department, 1/24/33, reward circular enclosed; Ed Patley, Chief of Detectives, Joplin, Mo., to Chief of Police, Dallas (circulated to all jurisdictions with warrants out for the Barrows), Barrow gang file, DMARC.

69. Voluntary statement of W. D. Jones to Dallas Police Department, 11/18/33; voluntary statement of W. D. Jones to Winter R. King, assistant district attorney, Dallas, Tex., Barrow gang file, DMARC.

70. Voluntary statement of W. D. Jones to Dallas Police Department, 11/18/33; *Tulsa Daily World,* 3/16/34.

71. *Time,* 1/29/34.

72. Julia Kirk Blackwelder, *Women and the Depression: Caste and Culture in San Antonio, 1929–1939* (College Station: Texas A&M University Press, 1984), 157. J. M. Beattie, in an article that compares the criminality of rural and urban women in eighteenth-century England, suggests that the characteristics of city life that permitted women to exist independently of a domestic sphere also resulted in higher rates of female violent crime: see Beattie, "The Criminality of Women in Eighteenth Century Eng-land," *Journal of Social History* 9 (Summer 1975): 80–117.

73. Blackwelder, *Women and the Depression,* 165; *Tulsa Daily World,* 4/2/34.

74. Arthur B. Reeve, *The Golden Age of Crime* (New York: Mohawk Press, 1931), 141–150.

75. Parker and Cowan, *True Story,* 164; log book of Dallas City Police Department wire-taps on the Barrow and Parker household telephones, 4/18, 6, Texas History Collection (hereafter cited as "log book").

76. Log book, 4/18, 7–8; 4/21, 20.

77. Ibid., 4/18, 7, 12; *Tulsa Daily World,* 4/13/34.

78. Ibid., 4/26, 45–46.

79. Ibid., 4/23, 27; 4/24, 29; 4/18, 12; 4/20, 16, 4/26, 42.

80. Ibid., 4/20, 17.

81. Ibid., 4/20, 16; 4/20, 17; 4/21, 18.

82. Ibid., 4/21, 18; 4/21, 22; 4/23, 25.

83. Raymond Hamilton to A. S. Baskett, 4/8/34, folder #3, Raymond and Floyd Hamilton, RG 91-019-DPD, box 11, DMARC; *Tulsa Daily World,* 4/14/34.

84. Clyde Barrow to Raymond Hamilton, 4/27/34, reprinted in Ted Hinton, as told to Larry Grove, *Ambush: The Real Story of Bonnie and Clyde* (Austin: Shoal Creek Publishers, 1979), 152–154.

85. Log book, 4/26, 43; 4/28, 56–57.

86. *Tulsa Daily World,* 5/13/34.

87. Published in ibid., 4/7/34. An interview with Henry Barrow, owner of a filling station and Clyde's father, reported that Clyde was working on his life story and planned to have it published. The writing in this fragment was identified as Bonnie's and prob-ably is, since Clyde's handwriting was labored and his style awkward.

88. Parker and Cowan, *True Story,* 167–169. The following quotes are all taken from this edition of the poem.
89. *Tulsa Daily World,* 4/7/34.
90. *Time,* 6/4/34.
91. Parker and Cowan, *True Story,* 170; *Tulsa Daily World,* 5/24/34; *Austin Daily Dispatch,* 5/24/34; Hinton, *Ambush,* 182–190; Treherne, *Strange History of Bonnie and Clyde,* 205–212.
92. *Tulsa Daily World,* 4/26/34; *New York Daily News,* 10/24/34; *Tulsa Daily World,* 8/11/34.
93. For similar fetishizing of the criminal body, see Peter Linebaugh, "The Tyburn Riot against the Surgeons," in Linebaugh, *Albion's Fatal Tree,* 65–118.

Five   "Another Roosevelt Victory in This War against the Underworld"

1. Anne Morrow Lindbergh, *Hour of Gold, Hour of Lead: Diaries and Letters, 1929–1932* (New York: Harcourt Brace Jovanovich, 1973), 226–227; for accounts of the Lindbergh case, see Joyce Milton, *Loss of Eden: A Biography of Charles and Ann Morrow Lindbergh* (New York: HarperCollins, 1993), and Jim Fisher, *The Lindbergh Case* (New Brunswick, N.J.: Rutgers University Press, 1987).
2. *Cairo Evening Citizen,* 8/18/34.
3. Harry Soderman and John J. O'Connell, *Modern Criminal Investigation* (New York: Funk and Wagnalls, 1935); Ernest Kahler Alix, *Ransom Kidnapping in America, 1874–1974: The Creation of a Capital Crime* (Carbondale: Southern Illinois University Press, 1978), x, 4–10, 123.
4. Lindbergh, *Hour of Gold,* 233.
5. *Nation,* 8/27/24; *Nation,* 12/24/24.
6. Thomas W. Laqueur, "Bodies, Details, and the Humanitarian Narrative," in *The New Cultural History,* ed. Lynn Hunt (Berkeley and Los Angeles: University of California Press, 1989), 176–204.
7. Richard Gid Powers, *Secrecy and Power: The Life of J. Edgar Hoover* (New York: Free Press, 1987), 175; JEH to Attorney General, 3/2/32, folder 31, box 15187, Kidnapping, Department of Justice Central Files, Classified Subject Files, Record Group 60, National Archives (hereafter cited as Kidnapping Files—NA).
8. *Time,* 7/24/33; *New York Times,* 5/8/33.
9. *Time,* 7/31/33; 3/12/34.
10. *Washington Mirror,* 8/1/33.
11. Paul Conkin, *The New Deal* (New York: Thomas Y. Crowell, 1967), 30; see also James T. Patterson, *Congressional Conservatism and the New Deal: The Growth of the Conservative Coalition in Congress, 1933–1939* (Lexington: University of Kentucky Press, 1967); Otis Graham, *An Encore for Reform: The Old Progressives and the New Deal* (New York: Oxford University Press, 1967).
12. Powers, *Secrecy and Power,* 184; Athan Theoharis and John Stuart Cox, *The Boss: J. Edgar Hoover and the Great American Inquisition* (Philadelphia: Temple University Press, 1988), 122; Frank Freidel, *Franklin D. Roosevelt: Launching the New Deal* (Boston: Little, Brown, 1973), 60–82; Annual Message to Congress, 1/3/34, contained in Samuel I. Rosenman, ed., *Published Papers of Franklin Delano Roosevelt,* 4 vols. (New York: Random House, 1938), vol. 2, doc. 1, pp. 12–13. See also vol. 4, doc.

74, pp. 248–249, for June 10, 1935, FDR to Homer Cummings (hereafter "HSC"), "The Department of Justice Is Requested to Investigate Prior Paroled Kidnapping Suspects," for a later example of Roosevelt giving his official stamp to a Justice Department initiative.

13. For the rise of a new middle class and its relationship to state making, see Robert H. Wiebe, *The Search for Order: 1877–1920* (New York: Hill and Wang, 1967); for the failure of lynching legislation, see Harvard Sitkoff, *A New Deal for Blacks, the Emergence of Civil Rights as a National Issue: The Depression Decade* (New York: Oxford University Press, 1978), 268–297. For an analysis of the New Deal that links the war on crime to other forms of federalism that addressed community problems, see William E. Leuchtenberg, *Franklin D. Roosevelt and the New Deal* (New York: Harper and Row, 1963), particularly 334–335; Daniel R. Fusfeld, "The New Deal and the Corporate State," in *Franklin D. Roosevelt: The Man, the Myth, the Era,* ed. Herbert D. Rosenbaum and Elizabeth Bartelme (New York: Greenwood Press, 1987), 137–152.

14. Alix, *Ransom Kidnapping in America,* 19–20.

15. Ibid., 26. For captivity narratives, see John Demos, *The Unredeemed Captive: A Family Story from Early America* (New York: Vintage, 1994); and for the enduring nationalist uses of captivity narratives, see Ann duCille, "The Unbearable Darkness of Being: 'Fresh' Thoughts on Race, Sex, and the Simpsons," in *Birth of a Nation'hood: Gaze, Script, and Spectacle in the O. J. Simpson Case,* ed. Toni Morrison and Claudia Brodsky Lacour (New York: Pantheon, 1997), 293–338.

16. Alix, *Ransom Kidnapping in America,* 38–67.

17. U.S. Congress, House of Representatives, *Record of the 75th Congress* (March 4, 1932), 5585–5586.

18. *Tulsa Daily World,* 2/33/30; *Time,* 3/13/33; *Time,* 7/31/33, 13; Harold Birkeland, "Floyd B. Olson in the First Kidnapping Murder in 'Gangster Ridden Minnesota,'" privately printed pamphlet (Minneapolis, 1934), box 3427 (enclosures), Kidnapping Files—NA. A fictional account of the O'Connell kidnapping, as well as its context in New York machine politics and racketeering, is William Kennedy, *Billy Phelan's Greatest Game* (New York: Viking, 1978).

19. *Time,* 7/24/33; *New York Times,* 8/5/33.

20. Lindbergh, *Hour of Gold,* 240; Theoharis and Cox, *Boss,* 129, 137, 279.

21. JEH, Memorandum for the Attorney General, 3/2/32, folder 31, box 15187, Kidnapping Files—NA.

22. Nugent Dodds, assistant attorney general, to Rachel C. Hazeltine, 9/9/32, folder 11, box 15187, Kidnapping Files—NA.

23. JEH to Sanford Bates, Director, Bureau of Prisons, 5/26/32, folder 9, box 15187; JEH to Col. Norman Schwarzkopf, Superintendent N.J. State Police, 11/7/32 and 10/20/32, folder 14, box 15185, Kidnapping—NA.

24. Guy T. Helvering, Commissioner of Internal Revenue to HSC, 10/11/33, folder 12; JEH to HSC, 11/8/33, box 15187; JEH to HSC, March 21, 1934, box 15187, folder 11, Kidnaping Files—NA.

25. JEH to William Stanley, 3/5/34; 3/10/34; JEH to T. H. Sisk, NYC office, 3/22/34, folder 11, box 15187, Kidnapping Files—NA.

26. T. H. Siske to JEH, 5/16/34, folder 14, box 15187, Kidnapping Files—NA.

27. JEH to HSC, 5/22/34, folder 14, box 15187; JEH to HSC, 6/8/34, folder 14, box 15187, Kidnapping Files—NA.

28. William MacFarlane (Rochester) to HSC, 10/27/33, box 15185; JEH to SAC New York City, 3/14/32, folder 30, box 15191, Kidnapping Files—NA.
29. Edward E. Aspinall, Grand Keeper of Records and Seal, Knights of Pythias (Hartford) to Herbert Hoover, 5/16/32, box 15186; William A. Taylor (Detroit) to "Dear Beloved President" (3/6/32). For immunity sentiment, see also F. G. Farr, telegram to Herbert Hoover, 3/5/32, and lawyer Raymond Synestveldt (Philadelphia) to Hoover, 3/5/32: see all of box 15185, Kidnapping Files—NA, for letters to Herbert Hoover about the Lindbergh baby and the ongoing investigation.
30. Mrs. Rhea Stieldon (Kansas City, Mo.) to Herbert Hoover, 3/6/32; Mrs. Florence J. Muth (Irvington, N.J.) to Herbert Hoover 3/8/32, box 15185, Kidnapping Files—NA.
31. William Doak to AG, 6/21/32; Earle Stafford, "Citizen," to JEH, 3/5/32; H. L. Grace, lawyer (Gilmer, Tex.), to Herbert Hoover 3/4/32; J. H. Schmitt (contractor, Canton, Ohio) to AG W. D. Mitchell, 3/5/32; Harold May (Philadelphia) to Herbert Hoover, 6/20/32, folder 10, box 15185, Kidnapping Files—NA.
32. Mrs Velma O'Neill (Jackson, Miss.) to Department of Justice, 8/3/32, folder 12; JEH to W. H. Moran, Chief, Secret Service Division, Treasury Department, 11/1/33, folder 10; anonymous note rec'd. 8/3/32 at Justice, folder 12; Mrs Alfred V. DuPont to Department of Justice, 7/12/34, folder 11, box 15185, Kidnapping Files—NA.
33. Unknown to HSC, 10/8/34; William H.Murray, governor of Oklahoma, to HSC, 9/1/34; folder 15, box 15188.
34. William Stanley, assistant to the attorney general, Department of Justice Circular No. 2466, 9/13/33, box 3427, Kidnapping Files—NA.
35. Circular letter from Barry O'Neill, Dedekam Insurance (San Francisco) to Thomas D. Campbell (Campbell Farming Corp., Hardin, Mont.), 9/12/33; Thomas Campbell to the Department of Justice, 9/16/33, subject file B, box 15191, Kidnapping Files—NA.
36. For another illuminating example of a war on crime in the United States, see Jimmie L. Reeves and Richard Campbell, *Cracked Coverage: Television News, the Anti-Cocaine Crusade, and the Reagan Legacy* (Durham, N.C.: Duke University Press, 1994).
37. Powers, *Secrecy and Power,* 201; United States Civil Service, *Annual Report of the United States Civil Service, 1932–1935* (Washington, D.C.: GPO, 1932–1936); "Unofficial Observer," in *The New Dealers* (New York: Literary Digest, 1934), 262–263.
38. Harold L. Ickes, *The Secret Diary: The First Thousand Days, 1933–1936* (New York: Simon and Schuster, 1953), entry for December 11, 1934, 241–243; entry for December 13, 1934, 247.
39. HSC, Order No. 2507, December 30, 1933, folder 1, box 1, General Records of the Department of Justice Records of the Special Assistant to the Attorney General, 1923–1940; Miscellaneous Records, 1924–1939 (Entry 130), RG 60, National Archives, Washington, D.C. (hereafter cited as GRDC); Homer Cummings and Carl McFarland, *Federal Justice: Chapters in the History of Justice and the Federal Executive* (New York: Macmillan, 1937), vi; Cummings, *Liberty under Law and Administration* (New York: Charles Scribner, 1934), 4, 17–20.
40. Cummings, *Liberty under Law,* 45, 85, 104–107.
41. *Kansas City Star,* 8/9/33, *Newsweek,* 8/12/33; *Philadelphia Public Ledger,* 8/14/33; Drew Pearson, "The Daily Washington Merry-Go-Round," 8/19/33, JEH-SB, box 3; "Peter Carter Says," *Washington Herald,* 8/3/33. For Walsh's dislike of JEH, see

Theoharis and Cox, *Boss,* 111; the *Collier's–Herald* exchange is raised in Powers, *Secrecy and Power,* 185. The political columnist for the *Akron Beacon-Journal* commented that if Hoover's job "sticks to him, wise guessers lose," 7/24/33; and the *Philadelphia Record* reported A. V. Dalrymple, a former head of the Bureau of Prohibition, as one candidate for Hoover's job, 7/24/34.

42. *Washington Post,* 11/5/33; for Val O'Farrell, see Theoharis and Cox, *Boss,* 114–116.

43. A typical communication was sent by the Tennessee and Mississippi Peace Officers Associations, including a motion passed at their annual meeting that expressed their "unanimous desire that the administration of the United States Bureau of Investigation be continued under the supervision of the honorable J. Edgar Hoover." S. R. Coleman, president, Tennessee and Mississippi Peace Officers Association, Inc., to Hon. Sam D. McReynolds, U.S. Congress, 4/27/33, FBI-67-561-[number illegible] (p. 208 of Hoover's personal file); Theoharis and Cox, *Boss,* 114.

44. John T. Elliff, "The Scope and Basis of FBI Data Collection," and discussion by Arthur Schlesinger Jr. in Pat Watters and Stephen Gillers, eds., *Investigating the FBI* (New York: Doubleday, 1973), 256, 293. JEH to FDR, 3/17/33, OF 10b, box 10, Justice Department, FBI, 1933-1934, FDRL. Among those who weighed in heavily among their southern colleagues were J. J. McSwain of South Carolina, chairman of the House Military Affairs Committee, and Russell Elzey of Mississippi, chairman of the House Labor Committee; see McSwain to FDR, 7/25/33, and Elzey to FDR, 8/18/33, OF 10b, box 10, Justice Department, FBI, 1933-1945, FDRL. Earlier, Congressman McCormack claimed to have heard "disquieting rumors" that he had already discussed with the attorney general, and requested an audience with the president to communicate them; see McCormack to FDR, 7/7/33, OF 10b, box 10, Justice Department, FBI, 1933-1945, FDRL.

45. David K. Adams, "The New Deal and the Vital Center," in Rosenbaum and Bartelme, *Franklin D. Roosevelt,* 1003–1118; Richard Adelstein, "'The Nation as an Economic Unit': Keynes, Roosevelt, and the Managerial Ideal," *Journal of American History* 78 (June 1991): 160–187; JEH to FDR, 3/17/33, OF 10b, box 10, Justice Department, FBI, 1933–1934, FDRL.

46. Bureau of Investigation, *Uniform Crime Reports, 1932* (Washington, D.C.: GPO, 1932); author unknown, "Memorandum Re. Article in Wash-Herald, Sunday April 7, 1933. On J. Edgar Hoover," OF 10b, Justice Department, box 10, FBI, 1933–1934, FDRL.

47. Louis M. Howe script delivered on the RCA Victor Radio Hour, 8/6/33, LMH Personal Papers, 1933–1936, container 107.

48. Alfred B. Rollins, *Roosevelt and Howe* (New York: Knopf, 1962), 271, 367–369. Kenneth Davis suggests that Howe believed a new inner circle had increasingly excluded him from the nomination on; see Davis, *FDR: The New York Years, 1928–1933* (New York: Random House, 1979), 307–328.

49. Rollins, *Roosevelt and Howe,* 385.

50. Val O'Farrell, New York City, to Louis M. Howe (hereafter cited as LMH), 6/19/33; Joseph B. Keenan to LMH, 7/19/33, "Crime," LMH, box 72, FDRL.

51. LMH to Eleanor Roosevelt, 7/27/33, "Crime," box 72, LMH, FDRL; "Uncle Sam Starts after Crime," carbon of article prepared for the *Saturday Evening Post,* published 7/29/33; "Crime," box 72, LMH, FDRL.

52. For a good analysis of the coalition that produced the Roosevelt victory in 1932, see Arthur M. Schlesinger Jr., *The Age of Roosevelt: The Crisis of the Old Order* (New

York: Knopf, 1957). Bonnie Fox Schwartz also suggests that the Hoover administration's unwillingness to address the unemployment crisis made Roosevelt an overwhelming choice for unions and political machines; see Schwartz, *The Civil Works
Administration, 1933–1934: The Business of Emergency Employment in the New Deal*
(Princeton: Princeton University Press, 1984), 14–22. For Roosevelt's interaction
with individual political machines, see A. Cash Koeniger, "Roosevelt and the Byrd
Organization of Virginia," *Journal of American History* 69 (March 1982): 876–896;
also Raymond L. Koch, "Politics and Relief in Minneapolis during the 1930's,"
Minnesota History 49 (Winter 1968): 153–170; and Lyle W. Dorsett, "Kansas City
and the New Deal," in *The New Deal: State and Local Levels*, ed. John Braeman,
Robert Bremner, and David Brody, vol. 2 (Columbus: Ohio State University Press,
1975), 407–419.

53. Fred Cook, *The FBI Nobody Knows* (New York: Macmillan, 1964), 220.

54. See Hoover testimony before the House Judiciary Committee, 1/3/34–1/22/34, on
behalf of H.R. 6363; H.R. 6661; H.R. 6683; and H.R. 6913-6922 (the omnibus crime bill);
categories of crime I am drawing on are listed in *Uniform Crime Reports, 1930–1936*
(Washington, D.C.: GPO, 1930–1936.)

55. Rosenman, *Public Papers of Franklin Delano Roosevelt*, doc. no. 193, "Address to the
Conference on Crime Called by the Attorney General of the United States, December 10, 1934," 3:495.

56. Ibid.

57. For FDR and the press, see Betty Houchin Winfield, *FDR and the News Media*
(Urbana: University of Illinois Press, 1990); Graham J. White, *FDR and the Press*
(Chicago: University of Chicago Press, 1979). See also Richard Gid Powers, "One
G-Man's Family: Popular Entertainment Formulas and J. Edgar Hoover's FBI,"
American Quarterly 30 (Fall 1978): 471–492.

58. Richard Gid Powers, *G-Men: Hoover's FBI in Popular Culture* (Carbondale: Southern
Illinois University Press, 1983), 95.

59. Robert Sherrill, "The Selling of the FBI," in Watters and Gillers, *Investigating the FBI*,
3–32.

60. Powers, "One G-Man's Family," 471; for the New Deal, see David Peeler, *Hope Among
Us Yet: Social Criticism and Social Solace in Depression America* (Athens: University
of Georgia Press, 1987).

61. Courtney Riley Cooper, *Ten Thousand Public Enemies* (Boston: Little, Brown, 1935),
ix.

62. Ibid., 3–4.

63. Powers, *G-Men*, 74.

64. Ickes, *Secret Diary*, 2/6/35, 547.

65. Rex Collier, "Uncle Sam's Scientists Turn Detective in War against Organized Crime
in America," *Washington Sunday Star*, 9/14/30; Walter Winchell "On Broadway,"
JEH-SB, 9/29/35, box 14; *New York Daily News*, 1/1/30.

66. Neal Gabler, *Winchell: Gossip, Power, and the Culture of Celebrity* (New York: Knopf,
1994), xiii, 155, 172.

67. Ibid., 107–111, 122, 183.

68. Ibid., 192–202.

69. Richard G. Conover to William Stanley Jr., June 12, 1934, "Suggestion no. 2: Publicity," folder 2, box 1, GRDC.

70. Richard G. Conover to William Stanley Jr., June 12, 1934, "Suggestion no. 3: Publicity," folder 2, box 1, GRDC.

71. Short editorials ordered by Mr. Wm. Stanley in 1934 respecting Andrew Mellon, undated, folder 2, box 1, GRDC.

72. "Progression and Expansion of the Attorney Generalship: Contrasts in Status through 149 years" (1938), 25–9, folder 1, box 1, GRDC.

73. Publicity Suggestion Respecting Outstanding Weekly Accomplishment Reported by the Division of Investigation (1934), folder 2, box 1, GRDC.

74. Instructions from William Stanley on monitoring press coverage to Miss Berard, 7/18/34, Envelope labeled "Miss Berard's Task," box 1, GRDC.

75. Edwin Teale, "How Uncle Sam's Detectives Smash Kidnap Gangs," *Popular Science* (May 1934): 15–18.

76. Ibid.

77. Ariel Dorfman and Armand Mattelart, *How to Read Donald Duck: Imperialist Ideology in the Disney Comic* (New York: IG Editions, 1991).

78. Powers, *Secrecy and Power,* 222–226; Melvin Purvis, *American Agent* (Garden City, N.Y.: Doubleday, Doran & Co., 1936), 22–24.

79. Purvis, *American Agent,* 26, 62.

80. Ibid., 247, 154.

81. Purvis, *American Agent,* 29–33, 53–54, 220.

82. Toni Morrison, *Playing in the Dark: Whiteness and the Literary Imagination* (Cambridge: Harvard University Press, 1992).

83. Patricia A. Turner, *Ceramic Uncles and Celluloid Mammies: Black Images and Their Influence on Culture* (New York: Anchor Books, 1994), 65–66. For an influential study that addresses similar constructions of whiteness in nineteenth-century popular culture, see Eric Lott, *Love and Theft* (New York: Oxford University Press, 1993).

84. Mark Ellis, "J. Edgar Hoover and the 'Red Summer' of 1919," *Journal of American Studies* 28, no. 1 (1994): 39–59.

85. Purvis, *American Agent,* 94, 103, 150.

86. Ann duCille, "Toy Theory: Black Barbie and the Deep Play of Difference," in *Skin Trade* (Cambridge: Harvard University Press, 1996), 8–59.

87. Purvis, *American Agent,* 110–111, 163, 172–173.

88. Warren F. Robinson, *The G-Man's Son* (Chicago: Goldsmith Publishing Co., 1936), 13–14. Published by the Goldsmith Publishing Company of Chicago, it was part of a series that starred heroic boys and young men faced with challenging situations. To give an idea of the range of this literature, other titles included *Herb Kent, West Point Cadet, Sky Detectives,* and *Young Franklin Roosevelt.* See also Stephanie Coontz, *The Way We Never Were: American Families and the Nostalgia Trap* (New York: Basic Books, 1992), 59–60. The domestic contrast with other contemporary teenage detectives is striking. Nancy Drew and the Hardy Boys, for example, lived in one-parent families with a widowed father and a kindly housekeeper: mothers represented a threat to self-reliance and adventure. The Nancy Drew books, authored by Carolyn Keene, made their debut in 1927; the Hardy Boys series, written by Frank Dixon, was begun in 1929.

89. Robinson, *G-Man's Son,* 17–18, 13.

90. Ibid., 20–21.

91. Carusi, exec. asst. to AG, to Donaldson, 6/25/35, pamphlet folder, box 1, GRDC.

92. William Stanley to Conover, 8/6/35; Lord to H. G. Donaldson, Chief Clerk (undated; probably July 1935), pamphlet folder, box 1, GRDC.
93. *Time,* 10/23/33; *Washington Herald,* 10/15/33.
94. JEH to Mr. Nathan, Memorandum, 3/6/34, FBI 67-26-287.
95. *Washington Herald,* 5/1/34; FDR press release of 5/18/34, PSF, Justice Department, box 76, #308.

Six "Why Can't the State Forgive Too?"

1. Smith to Hughes, 10/14/33, FBI 62-29777-2. The charges against the gang were murder, jail delivery, and bank robbery. Four days later, Hoover received a second request from Howard G. Robinson, assistant superintendent of the Ohio state police; see Robinson to JEH, 10/18/33, FBI 62-29777-4. For newspaper report, see *Evansville (Indiana) Courier,* 10/25/33. For the first division briefing by the Indiana state police, see E. J. Connelley to JEH, 10/28/33, FBI 62-29777-9.
2. John Toland, *The Dillinger Days* (New York: Random House, 1963), 133–154; JEH to Purvis, 3/6/34/, FBI 62-29777-93NRI; record of telephone conversation between Purvis and S. P. Cowley, 3/6/34, FBI 62-29777-101. Useful studies of FBI surveillance and data collection include John T. Ellieff, "The Scope and Basis of FBI Data Collection," in Pat Watters and Stephen Gillers, eds. *Investigating the FBI* (Garden City, N.Y.: Doubleday & Company, 1973), 255–296, and Frank Donner, "Political Informers," in Watters and Gillers, *Investigating the FBI,* 338–368.
3. Joseph B. Keenan to LMH, 11/3/33, Justice Department files, 9–12, 1933, box 1, OF 10, FDRL; memorandum to Nathan from JEH, 3/6/34, FBI 67-26-287.
4. *Tulsa Daily World,* 3/5/34; 3/6/34.
5. Ibid., 3/24/34; 4/3/34.
6. Clifford Geertz, "Centers, Kings, and Charisma: The Symbolics of Power," in *Local Knowledge: Further Essays in Interpretive Anthropology* (New York: Basic Books, 1983), 143; see also Carroll Smith-Rosenberg, "Davy Crockett as Trickster: Pornography, Liminality, and Symbolic Inversion in Victorian America," in *Disorderly Conduct: Visions of Gender in Victorian America* (New York: Oxford University Press, 1985), 111–143.
7. One newspaper headline featuring pictures of Parker, Barrow, and Dillinger was headlined "Deadly Competition for the Limelight"; see *Tulsa Daily World,* 4/14/34; also 3/10/34.
8. Werner Hanni to JEH, 7/31/33, FBI 7-77-102; *Tulsa Daily World,* 5/5/34.
9. *Nashville Tennessean,* 7/24/34; Eric J. Hobsbawm, *Primitive Rebels: Studies in Archaic Forms of Social Movement in the Nineteenth and Twentieth Centuries* (New York: Norton, 1959), 5. Sean McCann, "'A Roughneck Reaching for Higher Things': The Vagaries of Pulp Populism," *Radical History Review* 22 (Spring 1995): 4–34.
10. Toland, *Dillinger Days,* 5–12. Toland's material in this volume is largely based on oral interviews of Dillinger's contemporaries, witnesses to his crimes, family, and others.
11. Report by L. E. Kingman, 4/11/34, FBI 62-29777-794; Toland, *Dillinger Days,* 22, 23.
12. Toland, *Dillinger Days,* 3–4, 34. Dillinger's release was fairly standard in a time when boards granted parole on the basis of testimonials collected from friends, physicians, lawyers, and clergymen, as well as neighborhood petitions; see David J. Rothman, *Conscience and Convenience: The Asylum and Its Alternatives in Progressive America*

(Boston: Little, Brown, 1980), 164; Toland, *Dillinger Days,* 71–72; Clegg to JEH, 4/13/34, FBI 62-29777-560.

13. Toland, *Dillinger Days,* 126–127; Homer Van Meter to C. C. Spears, Bureau of Investigation (Chicago office), 4/23/30, contained in S. P. Cowley to Director, 9/10/34, FBI 62-29777-3842. Their self-analyses are strongly marked by the public and scholarly debates about crime that this study has outlined; see also Rothman, *Conscience and Convenience,* 383–388.

14. Toland, *Dillinger Days,* 108, 114–119, 128–136; report by F. T. Mullen, 10/22/33, FBI 62-29777-115.

15. Evelyn Frechette, "My Love Life with Dillinger," *True Confessions* (September 1934): 13–14. For the use of Native American images in United States popular culture, see Robert Berkhofer Jr., *The White Man's Indian: Images of the American Indian from Columbus to the Present* (New York: Vintage, 1979).

16. *True Confessions* (September 1934): 15.

17. Ibid., 46; Toland, *Dillinger Days,* 174–178; *Time,* 2/3/34.

18. *Time,* 4/2/34; Toland, *Dillinger Days,* 190, 206–209.

19. F. T. Mullen, FBI 62-29777-115, 62-29777-134; *New York Times,* 3/4/34; 3/14/34.

20. *Tulsa Daily World,* 3/7/34.

21. Ibid., 3/9/34.

22. Melvin Purvis, *American Agent* (New York: Doubleday, 1936), 216; *Time,* May 7, 1934; *Tulsa Daily World,* 3/4/34.

23. J. Edward Barce [special investigator for Governor Paul V. McNutt of Indiana], Confidential Report Concerning the Crown Point Jail Break, in S. P. Cowley to JEH, 11/9/34, FBI 62-29777-4428.

24. Ibid.

25. Interviews after the Michigan City break revealed that police forces in southern Indiana and eastern Illinois had also been paid to help the gang; E. J. Connelley to JEH, 10/28/33, FBI 62-29777-9; report by T. F. Mullen, 7/9/34, FBI 62-29777-115; report by D. L. Nicholson, 5/11/34, FBI 62-29777-1356.

26. Testimony of Harold H. Reinecke, special agent, in United States District Court, District of Minnesota, Third Division, May 15, 1934, *U.S. v. May et al.,* p. 137; testimony of Rufus C. Coulter, special agent, in *U.S. v. May et al.,* p. 179.

27. Testimony of George J. Schroth, in *U.S. v. May et al.,* pp. 95, 99; report by T. F. Mullen, 7/9/34, FBI 62-29777-115.

28. Report by V. W. Peterson, 5/17/34, FBI 62-29777-1478; report to JEH by D. L. Nicholson, 4/9/34, FBI 62-29777-466; H. H. Clegg to JEH, 4/11/34, FBI 62-29777-513.

29. Undated letter found in St. Paul Dillinger hideout (March 1934), attached to telephone memorandum from Rorer 3/31/34, FBI 62-29777-380.

30. Testimony of Augusta Salt, in *U.S. v. May et al.,* pp. 571, 576; report by V. W. Peterson, 5/17/34, FBI 62-29777-1478.

31. Memorandum for S. P. Cowley by M. Chaffetz, containing "the gist of a conversation between Louis Piquett and Ann Patzke," 11/19/95, FBI 62-29777-4488.

32. *Washington Post,* 4/20/34.

33. Report by E. J. Connelley, 5/25/34, FBI 62-29777-1657.

34. *Time,* 4/26/34; Keenen to Stanley, 4/30/34, FBI 62-29777-1572.

35. JEH to Cowley, 4/24/34, FBI-62-29777-774; E. G. Peterson to JEH, 4/26/34, FBI 62-29777-801.

36. Statement of Patricia Cherrington, in report by D. L. Nicholson, 7/16/34, FBI 62-29777-2696; Toland, *Dillinger Days,* 262.
37. Reports by V. W. Peterson, 6/14/34, FBI 62-29777-2041, and 5/3/34, FBI 62-29777-1291.
38. Text of note from Emil Wanatka to L. E. Fisher contained in report filed by V. W. Peterson, 5/3/34, FBI 62-29777-1291.
39. Report by H. H. Clegg to JEH, 6/2/34, 62-29777-9101; H. H. Clegg to JEH, 4/25/34, FBI 62-29777-910.
40. *Time,* 5/4/34.
41. *Tulsa Daily World,* 4/24/34; *Time,* 5/13/34; White House Press Release, 5/18/34, Justice Department file (#308), box 76 (1933–37), PSF, FDRL.
42. Testimony of Thomas Dodd, special agent, in *U.S. v. May et al.,* p. 292.
43. *Tulsa Daily World,* 3/5/34.
44. Robert Sklar, *Movie-Made America: A Cultural History of American Movies* (New York: Vintage, 1975; updated version, 1994); Nick Roddick, *A New Deal in Film Entertainment: Warner Brothers in the 1930's* (London: British Film Institute, 1983).
45. Sklar, *Movie-Made America,* 91, 175; Roddick, *New Deal in Film Entertainment,* 6; *New York Times,* 1/1/33.
46. Introduction to Robert E. Burns, *I Am a Fugitive from a Georgia Chain Gang* (New York: Grosset & Dunlap, 1932), 33–334.
47. Rothman, *Conscience and Convenience,* 157–3201. In the Southwest, claims of corruption and inefficiency were substantiated by daily newspaper reports of escapes by petty criminals and dangerous felons alike, who took advantage of part-time staff and elderly facilities. In 1934, two female bandits, Evelyn Barton, seventeen, and Ardell Hampton, sixteen, picked the lock of their Denton, Texas, jail cell with a hairpin, also releasing ten male prisoners. Raymond Hamilton crashed out three times between 1934 and 1935, once from a death-row cell, before he was finally executed. The collaboration of prison officials in such escapes was always likely. Hamilton claimed that the death of two guards at Eastham had been accidental; he had actually bought his way out, and the violence had been staged to protect officials (the wooden gun may have played a similar role at Crown Point). One former con, pardoned for squealing on an escape plot, boasted that if bribery did not work, a convict could "become a trusty and just walk away." For escapes see, *Tulsa Daily World,* 3/3/34; 8/1/34; 4/26/34; 8/12/34. For bribery and corruption, see statement of Mrs. Walter Marsh (formerly Mrs. Gus Winkler) detailing uses of gang money in O. C. Dewey to JEH, 5/20/36, FBI 7-77-805; also statement made by Alvin Karpis to the St. Paul Pioneer Press, 8/8/36.
48. *Time,* 1/8/34 and 1/29/34; *Tulsa Daily World,* 3/3/34; Clarence D. McKean to JEH, 1/10/27, FBI 26-9961-28. By legal pardons alone, 2,214 convicted felons were released in Oklahoma between 1931 and 1934; *Tulsa Daily World,* 6/22/34. Following S. Paige Baty, we might call Dillinger a "representative character": as Baty has argued, "The representative character is a cultural figure through whom the character of political life is articulated"; see *American Monroe: The Making of a Body Politic* (Berkeley and Los Angeles: University of California Press, 1995).
49. For the unemployed, see Harold Rissmiller, Reading, Pa., to FDR, 5/15/34, FBI 62-29777-1332. For explicit political links, see Ralph M. Edwards, Plainfield, N.J., to FDR, 4/10/34, FBI 62-29777-632; F. Nejim, Hope, Ark., to JEH, 4/24/34, FBI-62-29777-823; John F. Druar, St. Paul, Minn., to Department of Justice, 4/23/34, FBI 62-

29777-1071; telegram from Jack Abernathy, Newark, N.J., to FDR, 4/24/1934, FBI 62-29777-1112; Frank M. Beall, Baltimore, to HSC, 5/3/34, FBI 62-29777-1221; Milburn Wallace and Charles Caldwell, Chicago, 4/27/34, FBI 62-29777-1322. People also wrote to private detective agencies with Dillinger tips: see L. G. Thery, Greenfield, Okla., to Burns Detective agency, 4/12/34, FBI 62-29777-873. For mass involvement, see Jesse T. Kennedy to FDR, 11/22/33, FBI 62-29777-41. This writer may have been a frequent correspondent, as he begins his letter by telling the president he has "shown the proper spirit in welcoming adverse criticism and suggestions from the rank and file—may I impose on you again?" See also C. S. Landis, Wilmington, Del., to FDR, 4/25/34, FBI 62-29777-1113. Mrs. Frances Leyanna to HSC, 3/21/34, FBI 62-29777-303. One writer, probably a child, suggested that Dillinger be lured into an ambush where a trip wire would set off a series of machine guns (Paul Thompson, Ashland, Ohio, to JEH, 4/25/34, FBI 62-29777). For support of the shoot-on-sight policy, see A. Jasper Jenkins, New York, to JEH and Keenan, May 1934, FBI-62-29777-1017. Hoyet M. Lowe to FDR, 1/29/34, FBI 62-29777-74.

50. Betty DeWeese, Latonia, Ky., to FDR, 5/12/34, FBI 62-29777-1602; C. R. Vaughn, Visalia, Calif., to JEH, 5/7/34, FBI 62-29777-1193; anonymous to bureau, May 1934, FBI 62-29777-1017; unknown author, Indianapolis, to Associated Press, 4/13/34, FBI 62-29777-575; unknown author to HSC, 4/21/34, 62-29777-747.

51. See the following letters from the IACP and other police organizations: Charles A. Wheeler (president, IACP) to JEH, 4/6/34, BI 62-29777-418; Lawrence Benson to JEH, 5/1/34, and Benson to *Chicago Evening American,* 5/1/34, FBI-62-29777-1582; Edward J. Michel to JEH, 4/24/34, FBI 62-29777-750; William A. Braun, Manitowoc, Wis., to Purvis, 4/25/34, FBI 62-29777-944. See also William Bishop to FDR, 3/29/34, FBI 62-29777-311; and A. C. Thomas to JEH, 4/11/34, FBI 62-29777-503. A number of citizens seemed to have made writing to Hoover a hobby in and of itself: a good example of this is Robert N. Carson, Iowa City, Iowa, to JEH, 4/28/34, FBI 62-29777-1012.

52. Memorandum by E. E. Conroy, SAC Norfolk, Va., 5/10/34, FBI 62-29777-1339.

53. Anonymous to Division of Investigation, 5/6/34, FBI 62-29777-1260; Hubert S. Austin, North Plainfield, N.J., to JEH, 4/24/34, FBI 62-29777-748; C. H. McCulloh to JEH, New York, 4/25/34, FBI 62-29777-802; Mrs. Francis Leyanna, Cadillac, Mich., FBI 62-29777-813. See also Harry S. Krasny, Milwaukee, to JEH, 4/25/34, FBI 62-29777-829; and John X. Hart, Toledo, to HSC, 5/9/34, FBI 62-29777-1471. Ronald Crawford, District of Columbia, to HSC, April 1934, FBI 62-29777-872. Many letters argued that Dillinger enjoyed his notoriety, and commercial publicity should be censored: see Francis E. Thompson, Passaic, N.J., to JEH, 4/26/34, FBI 62-29777-1070; Mrs. Luna Berry, Wichita Falls, Kans., to FDR, 5/25/34, FBI 62-29777-1326.

54. Mary L. Woodruff, Genolden, Pa., 4/26/34, 62-29777-1151; anonymous to Walter Winchell, attached to B. K. Sackett to SAC New York, 6/6/34, FBI 62-29777-1951NR14; T. J. McHale to Department of Justice, 5/8/34, FBI 62-29777-1276; Mary Coholan, Chicago, to Division, 5/5/34, FBI 62-29777-1241; C. F. Hill to U.S. attorney general, 8/27/34, FBI 62-29777-3687.

55. Mrs. Eulalia Callendar to JEH, transmitted by Louis Piquett in a letter of 4/24/34, FBI 62-29777-913; Mrs. Eulalia Callendar to Walter Winchell, 5/20/34, contained in F. X. Fay to JEH, 6/7/34, FBI 62-29777-1967.

56. Louis M. Piquett to Eulalia Callendar, 3/7/34, FBI 62-29777-880; *Time,* 7/2/34.

57. H. D. Bray to JEH, 7/8/34, FBI 62-29777-1967.

58. Toland, *Dillinger Days,* 258–3259; anonymous to Governor George White, Ohio, postmarked 5/12/34; and "A Friend" to Joseph Keenan, received 5/14/34, FBI 62-29777-1433; R. L. Heines, Savannah, to FDR, 3/4/34, FBI 62-29777-198.
59. Anonymous to Evelyn Frechette, 5/27/34, FBI 62-29777-1664; J. Leslie Stone to Frechette, postmarked 12/3/34, FBI 62-29777-5135.
60. *Tulsa Daily World,* 4/24; JEH to Purvis, 5/29/34, FBI 62-29777-1832; Patrick T. Stone to William A. McGrath, 5/25/34, copied in report by V. W. Peterson, 6/14/34, FBI 62-29777-2041; JEH to Ed Tamm, 6/25/34, FBI 62-29777-2202.
61. Memorandum by JEH, recording a telephone conversation with Harold Nathan, 5/4/34, FBI 62-29777-1176; E. A. Tamm to JEH, 6/13/34, FBI 62-29777-2072.
62. JEH to HSC, 5/16/34, FBI 62-2977-1689; Purvis telegram to JEH, contained in JEH to HSC, 5/31/34, FBI 62-29777-1997; *Minneapolis Tribune,* 7/11/34; E. A. Tamm to JEH, reporting telephone conversation with Clegg, 6/14/34, FBI 62-29777-2006; telegram to JEH and Clegg from Cowley, 6/16/34, FBI 62-29777-2028.
63. Report by V. W. Peterson, Chicago, 9/27/34, FBI 62-29777-4051; statement by Marie Conforti, contained in Cowley to JEH, 8/29/34, FBI 62-29777-3702.
64. Report by E. J. Connelley, 8/7/34, FBI 62-29777-3274; statement of Patricia Cherrington, in report by D. L. Nicholson, 7/16/34, FBI 62-29777-2696.
65. Statement of Patricia Cherrington, in report by D. L. Nicholson, 7/16/34, FBI 62-29777-2696.
66. Report by V. W. Peterson, Chicago, 9/27/34, FBI 62-29777-4051.
67. Purvis to JEH, 7/6/34, FBI 62-29777-2525; Opal Milligan to Pat Reilly, January 1935, in report by E. J. Connelley, 1/19/35, FBI 62-29777-5405.
68. JEH to E. A. Tamm, recording conversation with Cowley, 7/27/34, FBI 62-29777-2966.
69. Harold N. May to JEH, 12/21/34, FBI 62-29777-5031; JEH to Harold May, 12/29/34, FBI 62-29777-5030.
70. *Nashville Tennessean,* 7/24/34; *Time,* 7/30/34.
71. *Nationalist* (September 1934), JEH-SB, box 5, report by E. J. Connelley, 8/7/34, FBI 62-29777-3274; report by E. J. Connelley, 8/7/34, FBI 62-29777-3274.
72. E. J. Connelley to JEH, 7/29/34, FBI 62-29777-2979.
73. J.E.P. Dunn, SAC Los Angles, to SAC, Indianapolis, 8/16/34, FBI 62-29777-3473; *Ohio State Journal,* 9/24/34.
74. Report by E. J. Connelley, 8/7/34, FBI 62-29777-3274; Mary Kinder to Harry Pierpont, undated (August 1934), contained in report by M. B. Klein, 8/21/34, FBI 62-29777-3536; "Mrs. Harry Pierpont" (Mary Kinder) to Harry Pierpont, 8/17/34, contained in E. J. Connelley to SAC Chicago, 8/17/34, FBI 62-29777-3652; Mary Kinder to Harry Pierpont, 8/27/34, contained in report from SAC Chicago to SAC Cincinnati, 9/7/34, FBI 62-29777-[number illegible] (section 64).
75. T. D. Quinn to Clyde Tolson, 8/30/34, FBI 62-29777-3693; S. P. Cowley to JEH, 5/3/34, FBI 62-29777-1099.
76. D. M. Ladd to JEH, 7/13/34, FBI 62-29777-2655; E. A. Tamm to JEH, 2/12/35, FBI 62-29777-5325; unpublished manuscript by Mrs. Gus Winkler, FBI 62-29777-5325.
77. Report by Klein, 7/12/34, FBI 62-29777-2604; "Mother" to Jean Crompton (undated—July/August 1934), FBI 62-29777-3121.
78. *Startling Detective* (September 1934).
79. Al Dunlap, editorial, *The Detective* (May 1934); T. D. Quinn to JEH, 5/16/35, FBI 62-29777-6066.

80. E. A. Tamm to JEH, recording a telephone conversation with S. P. Cowley, 7/22/34, FBI 62-29777-2817; JEH to Henry Suydam, 12/3/34, FBI 67-7489-646; T. D. Quinn to JEH, 10/27/34, FBI 80-84-4; memorandum of a telephone conversation between JEH and Mr. Connor, *Chicago News,* 10/26/34, FBI 80-84-4.

81. JEH to Henry Suydam, 12/3/34, FBI 67-7489-646.

82. JEH to Tamm, 7/25/34, FBI 67-15585-101; memorandum for Tolson, Quinn, Tamm, and Lester from JEH, 9/5/34, 67-15585-104; JEH to Tamm, 11/3/34, FBI 67-15585-120; JEH to Tolson, 9/1/34, FBI 62-29777-3757.

83. Laboratory Report #1557, 8/8/34, FBI 62-29777-3280; memorandum for the director by T. D. Quinn, 8/15/34, FBI 62-29777-3457; JEH to William Stanley, 11/7/34, FBI 62-29777-4451.

84. Report by D. L. Nicholson, 5/11/34, FBI 62-29777-1356.

85. S. P. Cowley to JEH, 4/24/34, FBI 62-29777-1010; Gus T. Jones, SAC San Antonio to JEH, 5/2/34, FBI 62-29777-1130.

86. JEH to Melvin Purvis, 7/23/34, FBI 67-7489-270.

87. Letters are drawn from unnumbered entries in FBI 67-7489, sec. 2.

Seven   "A Central Bureau at Washington"

1. *Tulsa Tribune,* 7/30/34; 7/31/34.

2. Memorandum for Tamm, recording a telephone conversation with Sam Cowley, 9/5/34, FBI 62-29777-3828.

3. J. Edgar Hoover, *Persons in Hiding* (Boston: Little, Brown, 1941), 312.

4. JEH to William Stanley, 9/4/34, FBI 62-29777-3768; memorandum to Tamm, recording a telephone conversation with Cowley, 9/7/34, FBI 62-29777-3851; memorandum by JEH, recording a telephone conversation with Clegg, 11/28/34, FBI 62-29777-4683.

5. Francis J. O'Connor, "The Nation Looks at Crime," *Police 13–13* (January 1935): 5–8.

6. JEH to Arthur Freund, 7/28/34, box 1, JMP; Justin Miller to Arthur J. Freund, chair of a committee of the Section of Criminal Law of ABA, ABA Meeting, Milwaukee, box 1, JMP; Judge Oscar Hallam, St. Paul, to Arthur Freund, St. Louis, 8/2/34, ABA Meeting, box 1, JMP.

7. Will Shafroth to JM, 8/19/34, ABA Meeting, Milwaukee, August 28, 29, 30, 31, box 1, JMP; John P. Devaney, Chief Justice of the Minnesota Supreme Court, to Will Shafroth, 8/7/34, ABA Meeting, Milwaukee, August 28, 29, 30, 31, box 1, JMP; Shafroth to JEH, 12/24/34, FBI 7-77-337.

8. Report by R. T. Noonan, 6/18/36, Werner Hanni, to JEH, 8/24/34, FBI 62-29777-3595; 7-77-880, Tamm to JEH, 10/9/34, FBI 62-29777-4139.

9. Hoover, *Persons in Hiding,* 9.

10. Report by H. H. Clegg, 3/25/34, FBI 62-29777-1711; statement from Bessie Skinner (a.k.a. Beth Green, Bessie Green), contained in H. H. Clegg to JEH, 4/13/34, FBI 62-29777-568.

11. George Barker gave 1895 as the year of his marriage, but a federal investigation of Herman Barker lists his birth as 1891: see *Washington Journal Post,* 3/13/36, and report by F. G. Grimes, 6/23/27, FBI 26-9961-51. For premarital relations among southern mountain folk, see Altina Waller, *Feud: Hatfields, McCoys, and Social Change in Appalachia, 1860–1900* (Chapel Hill: University of North Carolina Press, 1988), 69;

for southern Missouri, see Charles Ravensway, ed., *The WPA Guide to 1930's Missouri* (Lansing: University of Kansas Press, 1986; originally published by the Missouri State Highway Patrol, 1941), 434. Neosho's economic base was in berry farming, and the town's main employer was a federal fish hatchery, while Webb City boasted diversified agricultural, gravel manufacture, road building, two textile factories, and mining; see Ravensway, *WPA Guide,* 436–437, 421, 422. The exact date that the Barkers' marriage dissolved is unclear, but an April 1927 bureau report on Herman Barker lists them as sharing a Tulsa address; see report by J. V. Murphy, 5/9/27, FBI 26-9961-49.

12. Reprinted in the *Chicago American,* 3/9/35, JEH-SB, box 9. If these letters are genuine, then at least one member of the Barker family cooperated with the press, since they are photographic reproductions. Lloyd Barker was killed in Denver on April 15, 1949, by his estranged wife, Jennie. At the time he was working as the assistant manager of a small bar and grill. We can assume that Lloyd was prone to high levels of domestic violence, since Jennie shot him with both barrels of a shotgun as he was attempting to unlock the door of their home, telling the police later that "she feared her husband would kill her and her children": see *Tulsa Tribune,* 3/22/49, and SAC Denver to JEH, 5/12/49, FBI 62-89785-2.

13. Don Whitehead, *The FBI Story: A Report to the People* (New York: Random House, 1956), 335; identification order no. 1219, March 23, 1934, reproduced in Courtney Riley Cooper, *Ten Thousand Public Enemies* (Boston: Little, Brown, 1935), 211; United Press wire service report, 1/17/35, JEH-SB, box 8; *Tulsa Tribune,* 3/22/49; Hoover, *Persons in Hiding,* 9.

14. *Kansas City Star,* 3/29/36; *American Magazine* (April 1936); Philip Wylie, *Generation of Vipers* (New York: Rinehart, 1955).

15. Report by Charles Jenkins, 2/2/27, FBI 26-9961-31; report by J. D. Glass, 4/18/27, FBI 26-9961-41; report by T. G. Melvin, 4/25/27, FBI 26-9961-50; report by William S. McKinley, 5/7/27, FBI 26-9961-48; report by J. V. Murphy, 5/9/27, FBI 26-9941-49; report by L. J. Barkhausen, 8/10/27, FBI 26-9961-70; report by L. C. Duke, 9/2/27, FBI 26-9961-75.

16. Report of Karpis confession by S. K. McKee, 7/28/36, FBI 7-77-990; Alvin Karpis, *The Alvin Karpis Story* (New York: Coward, McCann, 1972), 26-29; J. R. Perkins, "At the Prison Gate," *Rotarian* (July 1930); report from C. W. Stein, 1/28/36, FBI 7-77-365x.

17. Karpis, *Alvin Karpis Story,* 40–343, 56; identification order issued by Mrs C. R. Kelly, sheriff of West Plains, Mo., issued 1/12/32, FBI 32-16384-1.

18. Report by S. K. McKee, 5/8/36, FBI 7-77-697; Karpis, *Alvin Karpis Story,* 63, 80-82, 91; *St. Paul Pioneer Press,* 4/22/36.

19. Report by D. P. Sullivan, 3/3/36, FBI 7-77-401; A. Rosen to Director, 4/3/36, FBI 7-77-469x; report by J. H. Hansen, 4/11/36, FBI 7-77-505; *St. Paul Dispatch,* 4/22/36; statement of Isabelle Born, in S. K. McKee to JEH, 4/27/36, FBI-7-77-647; Karpis, *Alvin Karpis Story,* 90.

20. Statement of Alvin Karpis in report by S. K. McKee, 5/8/36, FBI 7-77-697; A. Rosen to JEH, 4/3/36, FBI 7-77-469x; K. R. McIntyre to JEH, 5/26/36, FBI 7-77-769; report by McKee, 7/28/36, FBI 7-77-990; Karpis, *Alvin Karpis Story,* 18.

21. Werner Hanni to JEH, 6/17/33, FBI 7-77-1; interview of William Hamm Jr. contained in report by Hanni, 6/26/33, FBI 7-77-20.

22. Report by Werner Hanni, 6/26/33, FBI 7-77-20.

23. Werner Hanni to JEH, 6/17/33, 7-77-1; report by Frank Gordon, 6/29/33, FBI 7-77-30; statement of Bryan Bolton, 1/27/36, FBI 7-77-365x.

24. C. W. Stein to JEH, 6/13/36, 7-77-853; report by McKee, 4/27/36, FBI 7-77-647; statement of Bryan Bolton, 1/27/36, FBI 7-77-365x.

25. Clegg to JEH, 5/8/34, FBI 7-77-317; B. J. Husting to Melvin Purvis, 7/28/33, 7-77-NR; *Time,* 7/24/33; 8/28/33; Purvis to Husting, 7/29/33, 7-77-NR; report by J. D. Smith, 8/5/33, FBI 7-77-93; *Time,* 8/7/33; R. P. Cunningham to Keenan, 7/26/33, FBI 7-77-94; Hanni to JEH, 7/31/33, FBI 7-77-102.

26. Report by R. L. Nalls, 8/18/33, FBI 7-77-129; Hanni to JEH, 9/7/33, 7-77-157; report by O. G. Hall, 10/20/33, 7-77-179.

27. Hanni to JEH, 12/8/33, FBI 7-77-259.

28. Karpis, *Alvin Karpis Story,* 166; *Time,* 1/29/34.

29. See statement of Gladys Sawyer in K. R. McIntyre to JEH, 5/26/36, FBI 7-77-769; *Time,* 2/19/34; A. Rosen to JEH, 4/3/36, FBI 7-77-469x; see statement of Robert Steinhardt in C. W. Stein to JEH, 6/12/36, 7-77-824x; Karpis, *Alvin Karpis Story,* 166–168; *Time,* 2/19/34.

30. JEH to HSC to LMH, 3/20/34, with appended *St. Paul News* article of 3/8/34, Justice Department Files 1–4/1934, box 2, OF 10, FDRL; HSC to FDR, Justice Department Files, 7–10, 1934; HSC to McIntyre, 2/3/34, Justice Department Files, 1–4, 1934; C. W. Stein to JEH, 6/12/36, FBI 7-77-824x.

31. Toland, *Dillinger Days,* 338–3339.

32. Associated Press wire service in *New York Times,* 1/17/35.

33. *Pittsburgh Press,* 1/17/35. There are several versions of this story. In another, Ma "eye[ed] the agent for a brief, brisk moment," then yelled upstairs, "What're you waiting for, Fred?" See *Chicago American,* 3/9/35.

34. Text of Dr. Charles Fleischer's broadcast over NBC Basic Blue Network, from New York, Saturday, 2/17/35, at 5:15 EST, JEH-SB, box 8.

35. I am drawing on Evelyn Brooks Higgenbotham's argument in "African American Women's History and the Metalanguage of Race," *Signs* (Winter 1992): 251–274.

36. D.B.P. (male), Nashville, Tenn., to ER, 8/15/36; A. G. (male) to FERA, 12/12/34, Robert S. McIlvaine, *Down and Out in the Great Depression: Letters from the Forgotten Man* (Chapel Hill: University of North Carolina Press, 1983), 60, 194.

37. *Tulsa Daily World,* 5/20/30; 12/28/29; 3/6/30; for the changing geography of middle-class life and female isolation, see Kenneth Jackson, *The Crabgrass Frontier: The Suburbanization of the United States* (New York: Oxford University Press, 1985); *Tulsa Daily World,* 8/7/30; 2/25/30.

38. See Robert S. Lynd and Helen Merrell Lynd, *Middletown in Transition: A Study in Cultural Conflicts* (New York: Harcourt Brace Jovanovich, 1937); Sheldon Glueck and Eleanor T. Glueck, *Five Hundred Delinquent Women* (New York: Knopf, 1934), 105.

39. Alice Kessler-Harris, "Designing Women and Old Fools: The Construction of the Social Security Amendments of 1939," in *U.S. History as Women's History: New Feminist Essays,* ed. Linda Kerber, Alice Kessler-Harris, and Kathryn Kish Sklar (Chapel Hill: University of North Carolina Press, 1995), 87–106.

40. *Time,* 3/11/35.

41. *Los Angeles Times,* 5/19/36, 5/20/36; *Denver Rocky Mountain News,* 5/22/36.

42. *Atlantic City Daily World,* 5/16/36; Walter Parker to JEH, 6/25/36, FBI 62-43010-731.

43. Douglas Mangan, Milwaukee attorney, to Guy Thompson, 10/30/31, passed on to JM; JM to Thompson, 11/30/31; JM to Louis S. Cohane, Esq., 11/17/32, ABA correspondence, box 1, JMP.

44. JM to Andrew D. Christian, Esq., 2/26/32; Guy A. Thompson, President ABA, to JM 2/26/32, ABA correspondence, box 1, JMP.

45. JM to Mrs. Olive G. Ricker, 11/17/32, ABA correspondence, box 1, JMP; JM to Clarence Martin, 7/29/33, ABA correspondence, box 1, JMP.

46. Justin Miller, Dean, Duke Law School, to Clarence E. Martin, Esq., President of the ABA, 8/10/33, American Bar Association Correspondence, Records of the Special Executive Assistant to the Attorney General, 1923–1940, box 1, JMP.

47. VSH(?) to Suydam, 1/5/35; Envelope—"Conference on Crime," HSC to FDR, 2/1/35, box 2, GRDC.

48. Memorandum on the Advisory Committee meeting of 1/4/35 and HSC to Scott M. Loftin et al., 1/14/35; General Correspondence, Advisory Committee folder, 1934–37, memorandum for the AG from JM, 1/5/37, Attorney General—Memoranda Folder; box 1, Records Relating to Special Investigations and Survey, Records of the Attorney General's Advisory Committee on Crime, 1934–1938.

49. Memorandum to the Attorney General from JM, 1/28/35, memorandum for the AG from Sanford Bates, Bureau of Prisons, 12/10/35, memorandum for the AG from JM, 11/19/35; Attorney General—Memoranda folder, box 1, Records Relating to Special Investigations and Survey, Records of the Attorney General's Advisory Committee on Crime, 1934–1938.

50. Memorandum for the AG from JM, 2/16/35, memorandum for AG from JM, 12/6/35; Attorney General—Memoranda folder, box 1, Records Relating to Special Investigations and Survey, Records of the Attorney General's Advisory Committee on Crime, 1934–1938.

51. JM to Herman Koppleman, Rep. CT, 6/22/35, J. Edgar Hoover folder, box 3, Records Relating to Special Investigations and Survey; for relations with social service organizations, see "Welfare" folders, box 5, Records of the Attorney General's Advisory Committee on Crime, 1934–1938.

52. Tamm to JEH, 5/4/36, FBI 7-77-670; report by S. K. McKee, 5/8/36, FBI 7-77-697.

53. H. H. Clegg to JEH, 6/23/34, FBI 62-29777-2162.

54. Erik G. Peterson to JEH, 4/6/34, FBI 62-29777-341; E. A. Tamm to JEH, 10/10/34, FBI 62-29777-4172; A. Rosen to JEH, 4/3/36, FBI 7-77-469x.

55. Report by E. J. Connelley, 8/7/34, FBI 62-29777-3274; Werner Hanni to JEH, 6/25/34, FBI 62-29777-2206; S. P. Cowley to JEH, 4/30/34, FBI 62-29777-1119; Jay C. Newman to JEH, 10/15/34, FBI 62-29777-4286; S. P. Cowley to JEH, 4/8/34, FBI 62-29777-468.

56. S. P. Cowley to JEH, 4/8/34, FBI 62-29777-468; telegram from Purvis to JEH, 4/18/34, FBI 62-29777-666; W.H.D. Lester to JEH, recording telephone conversation with Purvis, 5/14/34, FBI 62-29777-1430.

57. E. A. Tamm to JEH, 8/24/34, FBI 62-29777-3630 and 8/26/34, FBI 62-29777-3636; see also JEH to Melvin Purvis, 11/7/34, FBI 67-7489-302.

58. Report by J. J. Waters, 8/13/34, FBI 62-29777-3332; report by V. W. Peterson, Chicago, 9/27/34, FBI 62-29777-4051.

59. Opal Milligan to Pat Reilly, January 1935, in report by E. J. Connelley, 1/19/35, FBI 62-29777-5405; R. H. Reinecke, 6/23/36, FBI 7-77-880.

60. W. Larson, SAC Detroit, to JEH, 5/8/34, FBI 62-29777-1272; report by J. E. Brennan, 2/15/36/ FBI 7-77-423; Larson to SAC Chicago, 6/18/34, FBI 62-29777-2069; T. E. Kidd, Postmaster, Leipsig, Ohio, to SAC Detroit, 4/12/34, FBI 62-29777-666NR4.

61. Tamm to JEH, 7/5/34, FBI 62-29777-2515; report by W. R. Lorry, 7/30/35, FBI 62-29777-6304; JEH to Tamm, record of a telephone conversation with Cowley, 11/1/34, FBI 62-29777-4339; record of a telephone conversation with Stanley, 11/1/34, FBI 62-29777-4340; E. J. Connelley to SAC Detroit, 12/20/34, FBI 62-29777-4913.

62. Report by V. W. Peterson, 6/23/34, FBI 62-29777-2211; report by Lee F. Malone, 6/20/34, FBI 62-29777-2101; Bessie Green to Hugh Clegg, undated, enclosed in H. H. Clegg to JEH, 6/4/34, FBI 62-29777-1800.

63. Sam Cowley to JEH, 4/19/34, FBI 62-29777-1584; interview with Pat Cherrington by A. A. Muzzey, 5/22/35, FBI 62-29777-6093; H. H. Clegg to JEH, 6/23/34, FBI 62-29777-2162.

64. Testimony of Evelyn Frechette, in *U.S. v. May et al.,* pp. 599–610.

65. Testimony of Harold H. Reinecke, special agent, pp. 142–149, 160, 165, and testimony of Evelyn Frechette, pp. 599–610, in *U.S. v. May et al.;* William Larson to H. H. Clegg, 6/27/34, FBI 62-29777-2267.

66. Report by V. W. Peterson, 12/14/34, FBI 62-29777-4866; JEH to Tamm, record of a telephone conversation with Connelley, 11/30/34, FBI 62-29777-4566; JEH to Tamm, recording telephone conversation with Ladd, 12/1/34, FBI 62-29777-4570; Tamm to JEH, recording a conversation with Clegg, 12/4/34, FBI 62-29777-4687; H. H. McPike to HSC, 12/23/35, FBI 62-29777-6604.

67. Memorandum of telephone conversation with Purvis by JEH, 7/28/34, FBI 62-29777-2935; E. P. Guinane to JEH, 12/20/34, FBI 62-29777-5055; Nathan to JEH, 12/26/34, FBI 62-29777-5056.

68. Manuscript by Jack DeWitt, *American Detective* magazine, checked by Hoover on August 6, 1934, FBI 62-29777-3265; *Des Moines Register,* 6/30/35; *Denver News,* 6/31/35.

Conclusion

1. Excerpt from Walter Winchell's broadcast on NBC-WJZ, 2/9/36, FBI 62-3165-31; Richard Gid Powers, *Secrecy and Power: The Life of J. Edgar Hoover* (New York: Free Press, 1987), 218.

2. *Time,* 4/27/36; 5/4/36.

3. See Confidential Memos, FBI Director J. Edgar Hoover, August 24, 25, 1936; Strictly Confidential Memo, FBI Director J. Edgar Hoover to FBI Assistant Director Edward Tamm, September 10, 1936; and Confidential Memo, FBI Director J. Edgar Hoover, November 7, 1938; reprinted in Athan Theoharis, ed. *From the Secret Files of J. Edgar Hoover* (Chicago: Ivan R. Dee, 1991), 181-183.

4. Report by E. J. Connelley, 9/9/35, FBI 62-29777-1381; report by S. K. McKee, 8/1/36, FBI 7-77-1005; confession of Alvin Karpis in report by S. K. McKee, 5/6/36, FBI-7-77-697.

5. *Pittsburgh Press,* 7/20/35; *Buffalo Times,* 7/26/35.

6. John Gilbert, *A Cycle of Outrage: America's Reaction to the Juvenile Delinquent in the 1950s* (New York: Oxford University Press, 1986); Marjorie Garber and Rebecca L. Walkowitz, eds., *Secret Agents: The Rosenberg Case, McCarthyism,*

and Fifties America (New York: Routledge, 1995); Elaine Tyler May, *Homeward Bound: American Families in the Cold War Era* (New York: Basic Books, 1988).

7. Andrew Ross, "If the Genes Fit, How Do You Acquit? O.J. and Science," in *Birth of a Nation'hood: Gaze, Script, and Spectacle in the O. J. Simpson Case,* ed. Toni Morrison and Claudia Brodsky Lacour (New York: Pantheon, 1997), 241–272; "Uprising and Repression in L.A.: An Interview with Mike Davis by the *Covert Action* Information Bulletin," in *Reading Rodney King, Reading Urban Uprising,* ed. Robert Gooding-Williams (New York: Routledge, 1993), 147–148.

8. Athan Theoharis and John Stuart Cox, *The Boss: J. Edgar Hoover and the Great American Inquisition* (Philadelphia: Temple University Press, 1988), 130.

9. John D. Rockefeller Jr. to JEH, 6/1/36; Robert Sherrill, "The Selling of the FBI," in Pat Watters and Stephen Gillers, eds., *Investigating the FBI* (New York: Doubleday, 1973), 3–32.

10. C. W. Stein to JEH, 8/5/36, FBI 7-77-1032.

11. *Police Reporter* (October 1935); *Des Moines Register,* 6/30/35.

Index

Allen, Frederick Lewis, 58–59
American Bar Association (ABA),
170–172, 184–185. *See also* Arthur
Freund; Justin Miller
anticrime movement, 2, 58–59, 125,
127, 140, 171; kidnapping statutes
and, 111, 115; mass culture and,
151–153, 164; Eleanor Roosevelt
and, 123; Henry Stimson and, 171.
See also National Conference on
Crime; National Crime Commission
Association Against the Prohibition
Amendment, 21–22, 24–25

bandits, 59–60, 123, 126, 179, 193, 202;
community tolerance for, 87–90, 94,
148; definition and significance of,
4–5, 63–68, 84–85, 151, 153,
161–164, 181; harboring of, 88–89,
146, 158, 166, 183, 189; organization
of, 85–86; self-fashioning, 93–96,
142, 144, 148, 159; techniques of, 62,
73, 147
bank robbery, 139, 142, 144, 175–176,
201; and crime wave, 67–73
Barker, Arizona Clark "Ma" (Kate

Barker), 65, 173–175, 180–181;
marriage to George Barker,
173–174; representations of, 169,
183–184
Barker gang: Arthur "Doc," 172–173,
178, 180; Fred, 172–176, 180–181;
Herman, 65, 172, 174; Lloyd "Red,"
65, 172–173; Charles "Big Fitz"
Fitzgerald, 68, 201. *See also* Alvin
Karpis
Barrow, Clyde, 74–105, 138, 161, 163,
183
Barrow, Cumie, 76–77, 83, 98–101,
104, 183
Barrow, Henry, 80, 99–100
Barrow gang: Blanche Barrow, 83, 93,
95, 97; Buck Barrrow, 80–81, 83, 93,
95–96; Raymond Hamilton, 82–83,
91–92, 94, 96, 99–100, 104; W. D.
Jones, 92–94; Mary O'Dare,
100–101
Bremer, Adolph, 109, 178–179
Bremer, Edward, 109, 173, 178–179
Brown, Richard M., 78
Bureau of Investigation. *See* Federal
Bureau of Investigation

Walsh, Thomas J., 19, 120
war on crime, 110, 122–123, 182, 194,
 196–202; conditions for, 107–108,
 114, 117–118; and the New Deal,
 128, 130–131, 150, 171; opposition
 to, 185–188; political corruption
 and, 144–146
Watzman, Perry, 52–53
Weidman, Lou, 128
Wickersham, George, 22. *See also*
 National Crime Commission

Willebrandt, Mabel Walker, 10–11,
 15–25, 30, 38–41; and Ella Boole,
 19–20. *See also* Bureau of
 Prohibition; Department of Justice;
 prohibition
Wilson, Woodrow, 13
Winchell, Walter, 128–129, 155, 196
Women's Christian Temperance
 Union, 11, 19–21, 23, 25
Woods, Arthur, 42–43, 170, 180
Wright, Glen Roy, 88

About the Author

Claire Bond Potter is an associate professor at Wesleyan University, where she teaches in the history department and the American studies program. A historian of twentieth-century politics and culture, she is currently at work on a study of segregation, nationalism, and the emergence of new historical texts during the Progressive Era. She lives in Middletown, Connecticut, and New York City.

CPSIA information can be obtained at www.ICGtesting.com
Printed in the USA
LVOW08s1505081013

356005LV00002B/466/P